Edward Barton Segel

THE UNRELENTING STRUGGLE

The Right Honourable Winston S. Churchill, C.H., M.P.

THE UNRELENTING STRUGGLE

War Speeches by the

RIGHT HON. WINSTON S. CHURCHILL, C.H., M.P.

Compiled by

CHARLES EADE

With five half-tone plates

CASSELL AND COMPANY LTD.

LONDON, TORONTO, MELBOURNE, AND SYDNEY

Registered at the G.P.O., Melbourne, for transmission
through the post as a book.

First Edition - - 1942.

Wholly set up and printed in Australia by Wilke and Co. Pty. Ltd.,
19-47 Jeffcott Street, Melbourne.

CONTENTS

CONTENTS

INTRODUCTION

M R. WINSTON CHURCHILL'S speeches from November 12, 1940, to December 30, 1941, have been collected together in this book. They form a history of the war during some of its most momentous phases, and carry the story of the unrelenting struggle from the death of Neville Chamberlain, Mr. Churchill's predecessor, to the Prime Minister's visit to the United States and Canada. Major Randolph Churchill, M.P., who collected his father's speeches into book form in "Arms and the Covenant" and "Into Battle," is now on active service in the Middle East, and in his absence I have compiled the present volume.

On the day that Neville Chamberlain passed from the scene, in the sixty-second week of the war, Germany stood triumphant in Europe. Her armies held the Continent from Norway to the borders of Spain, from Poland to the Atlantic. Only Britain still stood as "a strong and resolute foe." The Germans' attempt to smash this country and its people by mass air raids had been beaten back, but up to that day more than 14,000 civilians had been killed and 20,000 seriously wounded. Invasion was a menace, possibly to be faced at any hour. A rapidly-expanding Army and 1,700,000 Home Guards were ready to meet it.

The U-Boat War against all ships sailing to these islands was growing again in its intensity and was being bitterly fought. Fifty destroyers received from the United States in exchange for naval bases in the Western Hemisphere were then rapidly coming into service. Britain, despite grievous losses, still had nearly as much merchant shipping tonnage as she had at the outbreak of the War.

Across the Atlantic Franklin Delano Roosevelt had three days earlier been elected President of the United States for the third time. British hopes of American aid rose as trans-Atlantic industry was steadily becoming geared for war production.

In Africa an Italian Army stood on the eastern frontier of Libya, a constant threat to Egypt and the Suez Canal, but on the borders of Greece and Albania their troops had been shamed and flung back by the Greeks. In the Balkans German infiltration was going on steadily. Bulgaria, Hungary and Rumania were independent only in name, but the direct Nazi threat to Yugoslavia and Greece was still to develop.

This then was the state of the War when Neville Chamberlain died and when Winston Spencer Churchill, who had succeeded him as Prime Minister six months before, rose in the House of Commons to pay tribute to his memory. This speech begins the second volume of Mr. Churchill's war speeches.

CHARLES EADE

THE UNRELENTING STRUGGLE

TRIBUTE TO NEVILLE CHAMBERLAIN

SPEECH DELIVERED TO THE HOUSE OF COMMONS
NOVEMBER 12, 1940

November 9. Mr. Neville Chamberlain died at his country home
in Hampshire, aged 71.

November 10. R.A.F. Raids extended from Danzig to the Bay of
Biscay.

November 11. Aircraft of the Fleet Air Arm attacked the Italian
Fleet at Taranto, reducing Italy's battleship strength
by half. Hurricane Squadrons shot down thirteen
Italian bombers and twelve German bombers which
were raiding convoys on the South East coast of
England.

November 12. Molotov, Russian Prime Minister, had interview with
Hitler and Ribbentrop in Berlin.

[*November 12, 1940.*

SINCE we last met the House has suffered a very grievous loss
in the death of one of its most distinguished Members, and of
a statesman and public servant who, during the best part of three
memorable years, was first Minister of the Crown.

The fierce and bitter controversies which hung around him in
recent times were hushed by the news of his illness and are silenced
by his death. In paying a tribute of respect and of regard to an
eminent man who has been taken from us, no one is obliged to alter
the opinions which he has formed or expressed upon issues which
have become a part of history ; but at the Lychgate we may all
pass our own conduct and our own judgments under a searching
review. It is not given to human beings, happily for them, for
otherwise life would be intolerable, to forsee or to predict to any
large extent the unfolding course of events. In one phase men
seem to have been right, in another they seem to have been wrong.

1

Then again, a few years later, when the perspective of time has lengthened, all stands in a different setting. There is a new proportion. There is another scale of values. History with its flickering lamp stumbles along the trail of the past, trying to reconstruct its scenes, to revive its echoes, and kindle with pale gleams the passion of former days. What is the worth of all this ? The only guide to a man is his conscience ; the only shield to his memory is the rectitude and sincerity of his actions. It is very imprudent to walk through life without this shield, because we are so often mocked by the failure of our hopes and the upsetting of our calculations; but with this shield, however the fates may play, we march always in the ranks of honour.

It fell to Neville Chamberlain in one of the supreme crises of the world to be contradicted by events, to be disappointed in his hopes, and to be deceived and cheated by a wicked man. But what were these hopes in which he was disappointed ? What were these wishes in which he was frustrated ? What was that faith that was abused ? They were surely among the most noble and benevolent instincts of the human heart—the love of peace, the toil for peace, the strife for peace, the pursuit of peace, even at great peril, and certainly to the utter disdain of popularity or clamour. Whatever else history may or may not say about these terrible, tremendous years, we can be sure that Neville Chamberlain acted with perfect sincerity according to his lights and strove to the utmost of his capacity and authority, which were powerful, to save the world from the awful, devastating struggle in which we are now engaged. This alone will stand him in good stead as far as what is called the verdict of history is concerned.

But it is also a help to our country and to our whole Empire, and to our decent faithful way of living that, however long the struggle may last, or however dark may be the clouds which overhang our path, no future generation of English-speaking folks—for that is the tribunal to which we appeal—will doubt that, even at a great cost to ourselves in technical preparation, we were guiltless of the bloodshed, terror and misery which have engulfed so many lands and peoples, and yet seek new victims still. Herr Hitler protests with frantic words and gestures that he has only desired peace. What do these ravings and outpourings count before the silence of Neville Chamberlain's tomb ? Long, hard, and hazardous years lie before us, but at least we entered upon them united and with clean hearts.

I do not propose to give an appreciation of Neville Chamberlain's life and character, but there were certain qualities always

2

admired in these Islands which he possessed in an altogether exceptional degree. He had a physical and moral toughness of fibre which enabled him all through his varied career to endure misfortune and disappointment without being unduly discouraged or wearied. He had a precision of mind and an aptitude for business which raised him far above the ordinary levels of our generation. He had a firmness of spirit which was not often elated by success, seldom downcast by failure, and never swayed by panic. When, contrary to all his hopes, beliefs and exertions, the war came upon him, and when, as he himself said, all that he had worked for was shattered, there was no man more resolved to pursue the unsought quarrel to the death. The same qualities which made him one of the last to enter the war, made him one of the last who would quit it before the full victory of a righteous cause was won.

I had a singular experience of passing in a day from being one of his most prominent opponents and critics to being one of his principal lieutenants, and on another day of passing from serving under him to become the head of a Government of which, with perfect loyalty, he was content to be a member. Such relationships are unusual in our public life. I have before told the House how on the morrow of the Debate which in the early days of May challenged his position, he declared to me and a few other friends that only a National Government could face the storm about to break upon us, and that if he were an obstacle to the formation of such a Government, he would instantly retire. Thereafter, he acted with that singleness of purpose and simplicity of conduct which at all times, and especially in great times, ought to be the ideal of us all.

When he returned to duty a few weeks after a most severe operation, the bombardment of London and of the seat of Government had begun. I was a witness during that fortnight of his fortitude under the most grievous and painful bodily afflictions, and I can testify that, although physically only the wreck of a man, his nerve was unshaken and his remarkable mental faculties unimpaired.

After he left the Government he refused all honours. He would die like his father, plain Mr. Chamberlain. I sought permission of the King, however, to have him supplied with the Cabinet papers, and until a few days of his death he followed our affairs with keenness, interest and tenacity. He met the approach of death with a steady eye. If he grieved at all, it was that he could not be a spectator of our victory ; but I think he died with the comfort of knowing that his country had, at least, turned the corner.

3

At this time our thoughts must pass to the gracious and charming lady who shared his days of triumph and adversity with a courage and quality the equal of his own. He was, like his father and his brother Austen before him, a famous Member of the House of Commons, and we here assembled this morning, Members of all parties, without a single exception, feel that we do ourselves and our country honour in saluting the memory of one whom Disraeli would have called an "English worthy."

THE ATTACK ON THE ITALIAN FLEET AT TARANTO

A STATEMENT TO THE HOUSE OF COMMONS
NOVEMBER 13, 1940

November 13. Revealed that, when aircraft of the Fleet Air Arm attacked the Italian Fleet at Taranto on November 11, the two battleships were partly sunk and another severely damaged; two cruisers were put out of action and two auxiliaries were left with their sterns under water.

[November 13, 1940.

I HAVE some news for the House. It is good news. The Royal Navy has struck a crippling blow at the Italian fleet. The total strength of the Italian battle fleet was six battleships, two of them of the "Littorio" class, which have just been put into service and are, of course, among the most powerful vessels in the world, and four of the recently reconstructed "Cavour" class. This fleet was, to be sure, considerably more powerful on paper than our Mediterranean Fleet, but it had consistently refused to accept battle. On the night of the 11th-12th November, when the main units of the Italian fleet were lying behind their shore defences in their naval base at Taranto, our aircraft of the Fleet Air Arm attacked them in their stronghold. Reports of our airmen have been confirmed by photographic reconnaissance. It is now established that one battleship of the "Littorio" class was badly down by the bows and that her forecastle is under water and she has a heavy list to starboard. One battleship of the "Cavour" class has been beached, and her stern, up to and including the after-turret, is under water. This ship is also heavily listed to starboard. It has not yet been possible to establish the fact with certainty, but it appears that a second battleship of the "Cavour" class has also been severely damaged and beached. In the inner harbour of Taranto two Italian cruisers are listed to starboard and are surrounded with oil fuel, and two fleet auxiliaries are lying with their sterns under water. The Italian communiquê of 12th November, in admitting that one

5

warship had been severely damaged, claimed that six of our aircraft had been shot down and three more probably. In fact, only two of our aircraft are missing, and it is noted that the enemy claimed that part of the crews had been taken prisoner.

I felt it my duty to bring this glorious episode to the immediate notice of the House. As the result of a determined and highly successful attack, which reflects the greatest honour on the Fleet Air Arm, only three Italian battleships now remain effective. This result, while it affects decisively the balance of naval power in the Mediterranean, also carries with it reactions upon the naval situation in every quarter of the globe. The spirit of the Royal Navy, as shown in this daring attack, is also exemplified in the forlorn and heroic action which has been fought by the captain, officers and ship's company of the *Jervis Bay* in giving battle against overwhelming odds in order to protect the merchant convoy which they were escorting, and thus securing the escape of by far the greater part of that convoy.

The Mediterranean Fleet has also continued to harass the Italian communications with their armies in Libya. On the night of 9th-10th November a bombardment was carried out at Sidi Barrani, and, though the fire was returned by shore batteries, our ships sustained no damage and no casualties. Moreover, one of our submarines attacked a convoy of two Italian supply ships escorted by destroyers, with the result that one heavily-laden ship of 3,000 tons sank and a second ship was certainly damaged and probably sunk. I feel sure that the House will regard these results as highly satisfactory, and as reflecting the greatest credit upon the Admiralty and upon Admiral Cunningham, Commander-in-Chief in the Mediterranean, and, above all, on our pilots of the Fleet Air Arm, who, like their brothers in the Royal Air Force, continue to render the country services of the highest order.

6

PARLIAMENT IN WARTIME

A SPEECH TO THE HOUSE OF COMMONS AT THE
OPENING OF A NEW SESSION
NOVEMBER 21, 1940

---

*November 14. Great all-night air raid on Coventry, 250 people
being killed and 800 injured.
R.A.F. raided Berlin.
Molotov returned to Moscow.*
*November 15. Seven hospitals and five convents hit in severe raid
on London.*
*November 20. The King opened a new session of Parliament and
said: "I am confident that victory is assured."*

[*November 21, 1940.*

EVEN in times of the bitterest political controversy and party
strife it has always been customary for all parties to listen
with appreciation to the speeches of the Mover and the Seconder
of the Address, and even when sometimes the circumstances have
not entirely sustained the compliments which were paid, those
compliments have not been denied. But to-day I am sure that all
the compliments which were paid were not only sincere but were
well deserved. We were very glad indeed to hear my hon. and
gallant Friend the Member for North St. Pancras (Squadron-
Leader Grant-Ferris) and I think it is gratifying to the House that
one of our fighter-pilots who has taken part in severe actions, and
will be engaged again, should be able to take his place here to-day
and discharge his Parliamentary duties. I entirely agree with
what has been said about the desirability of Members of Parliament
serving not only in the military forces but in all other forms of
warfare, and discharging their Parliamentary duties at the same
time or in alternation. No doubt difficulties arise, but I think they
are well covered, and that the good sense of the House and of hon.
Members will enable these dual and occasionally conflicting
functions to be discharged.

In bygone days the House of Commons not only struggled for
political power, but it did conduct a very great part of the business
and activities of the country. Hon. Members led troops and

squadrons of the Fleet and performed all kinds of functions of Government at the same time as they conducted their work here. Some of the things that they did would not entirely commend themselves to our present higher standards of decorum, but, none the less, that this House should be a House of active, living personalities, engaged to the hilt in the national struggle, each according to the full strength that he has to give, each according to the aptitudes which he possesses, is, I think, one of the sources of the strength of the Parliamentary institution, and will carry forward into the future the traditions that are our heritage and the precedents that have come down to us from the past. I thought the House was absolutely right in the cordial welcome which it gave to these speeches, and we hope that we shall hear both hon. Members again on matters which they are particularly qualified to speak upon.

I do not feel that this is a moment when it would be very convenient to make a statement on the war in the Mediterranean theatre—the two wars going on there, in both of which we have the very greatest interest. There is the defence of Egypt and the Canal, against greatly superior numbers of the enemy, which six months ago, at all events, looked rather a difficult affair, a doubtful affair, but which at the present time gives us a measure of confidence that we shall be able, as I said, to give a good account of ourselves when the invasion forces fall upon us—if they do fall upon us. And then there is the valiant, sudden uprising of the Greek nation, who, although taken by surprise and struck a felon's blow, have already almost entirely purged their soil of the conscript invaders, who were launched upon them in an enterprise which cannot be described as other than pure unmitigated brigandage. We have both those theatres to consider, and I can only say that we shall do our best. I feel that deeds, not words, are what are expected from us, and I certainly hope that we shall be able to give from our resources, which are always heavily strained, a helpful measure of assistance to the Greeks, and that we shall be able to discharge our responsibilities to Egypt in defending its soil and in guarding the vital artery of the Suez Canal.

The War Damage (Compensation) Bill is a Bill of great complexity and difficulty, but every effort will be made to bring it before Parliament at the earliest moment and it will be a measure of amplitude and scope which will deal effectively with the damage which falls, now here and now there, upon individuals throughout the country. It will give effect to the feeling that there must be equality of risk and equality of treatment in respect of the damage done by the fire of the enemy. In other ways, many

8

people have suffered material loss by the conditions of the war, but this measure deals with damage done by the fire of the enemy, and must be confined to that. Otherwise we should get into difficulties which would be beyond our powers to unravel. I feel that, if one man's home is smashed, that should be no special misfortune to him alone, and that all whose homes are not broken up should stand in with him as long as the need may last; and even if all the homes of the country be levelled, then we shall still be found standing together to build them up again after the fighting is over.

In present circumstances our efforts must be concentrated upon those matters or measures which are vitally connected with the effective prosecution of the war at home and abroad. So far as opportunities for Debates are concerned, the House must have noticed how many general Debates we have had, and I see no reason why that process should not continue in the new Session. We are, in fact, instinctively reviving the ancient practice of the House, which was that the Government of the day got through its necessary Business with considerable expedition, and the House devoted itself to debating, usually on Petition, whatever were the topics of general public interest. I am wholly in favour of that. I believe, if this House is to keep its hold on the imagination and the interest of the public, that it is ncessary that the great questions which appeal to the nation out of doors and occupy the Press should also be the questions subject to current discussion in this House. I very much deprecate the House falling unduly into the debating of details and routine, and losing sight of its larger duty of giving guidance and encouragement to the nation and administering when required the necessary corrective to the Executive. Therefore, I consider that this practice which we have of very often disposing of Business rapidly and then having an extensive Debate upon the Adjournment, although it appears to be an innovation after the quarrels of the last 20 or 30 years, is no more than a reversion, under forms very slightly different, to the process under which the House of Commons gained its great ascendancy in the public mind.

The time-honoured ceremonial and procedure in which Crown and Parliament have played their part to-day carry with them to anxious minds the balm of confidence and serenity. When our beloved Sovereign and the Queen come from their battered palace to a building which is not without evidence of the strokes of war, when the Sovereign comes to open Parliament in person and calls his faithful Commons to the discharge of their duties, at every step, in every measure, in every formality, and in every Resolution that we pass, we touch customs and traditions which go back far beyond

9

the great Parliamentary conflicts of the seventeenth century; we feel the inspiration of old days, we feel the splendour of our political and moral inheritance.

We are frequently asked to make declarations about our war aims. Some may think that example is better than precept, and that actions speak louder than words. To-day, in inaugurating a new Session of Parliament, we proclaim the depth and sincerity of our resolve to keep vital and active, even in the midst of our struggle for life, even under the fire of the enemy, those Parliamentary institutions which have served us so well, which the wisdom and civic virtues of our forebears shaped and founded, which have proved themselves the most flexible instruments for securing ordered, unceasing change and progress; which, while they throw open the portals of the future, carry forward also the traditions and glories of the past, and which, at this solemn moment in world history, are at once the proudest assertion of British freedom and the expression of an unconquerable national will.

His Majesty's Government are conscious with gratitude that they enter upon this new Session, not only with the formal and official support of all parties, but with the general good will of the House. Immense surrenders of their hard-won liberties have been voluntarily made by the British people in order in time of war to serve the better the cause of freedom and fair play, to which, keeping nothing back, they have devoted all that they have and all that they are. Parliament stands custodian of these surrendered liberties, and its most sacred duty will be to restore them in their fullness when victory has crowned our exertions and our perseverance.

We have a long road to travel. I have never concealed from the nation or from the House the darker side of our dangers and burdens, because it is there, and because I know that it is in adversity that British qualities shine the brightest, and it is under these extraordinary tests that the character of our slowly-wrought institutions reveals its latent, invincible strength. Up to the present this war has been waged between a fully-armed Germany and a quarter- or half-armed British Empire. We have not done so badly. I look forward with confidence and hope to the time when we ourselves shall be as well armed as our antagonists, and beyond that, if need be, I look to a time when the arsenals and training-grounds and science of the New World and of the British Empire will give us that material superiority which, added to the loyalty of constant hearts, will surely bring victory and deliverance to mankind.

BRITAIN ATTACKS IN THE WESTERN DESERT

A STATEMENT TO THE HOUSE OF COMMONS
DECEMBER 10, 1940

November 20. Hungary signed Germany-Italy-Japan Three Power Pact.

De Valera declared in an interview that Eire would not hand over ports to Britain because such action would involve her directly in the war.

November 22. Greeks captured Koritza from the Italians.

November 24. Lord Craigavon, Prime Minister of Northern Ireland, died and was succeeded by Mr. J. M. Andrews.

November 27. Seven Italian warships damaged and one British cruiser slightly damaged in Mediterranean naval engagement, in which the Italians fled.

November 30. President Roosevelt announced £25,000,000 U.S. credit for China.

December 1. Total of enemy planes destroyed over the British Isles since the beginning of the war reached 3,000.

December 5. Mr. Maxton's I.L.P. amendment to the Address asking for a peace conference was rejected by the House of Commons by 341 to 4.

December 6. Marshal Badoglio, Supreme Commander of the Italian Army, resigned after further reverses for the Italians in the war with Greece. He was succeeded by Cavallero.

December 9. Britain's Middle East Army, under General Wavell, suddenly launched an attack on the Italians in the Western Desert. The Royal Navy and the Royal Air Force and Free French Troops assisted in the operation.

[December 10, 1940.

THE collapse of France seriously endangered our position in the Mediterranean, and made the task of defending Egypt from an Italian invasion one of extreme difficulty, the more so as we were compelled to face the menace of invasion ourselves at home. However, by the time the Secretary of State for War

11

[Mr. Eden] paid his important visit to the Middle East in October, reinforcements of men and material had reached Sir Archibald Wavell, commanding the British and Imperial Army of the Nile, sufficient not only to give a greater feeling of security, but to open the possibility of an assumption of the offensive. However, at this moment the Italian invasion of Greece made it necessary for us to send a considerable part of our Air Force from Egypt to aid the Greek Army in their heroic defence of their native land.

The part played by the Royal Air Force in the Greek victories has been most important, and we have received the warmest expressions of gratitude from the Greek King and Government for the aid we were able to give. The serious temporary diminution of our Air Force in Egypt made it necessary somewhat to delay the execution of the offensive plans which had been matured, and it was not until the beginning of this month that our Air Force in Egypt was once again in a position to afford the necessary support to a forward movement.

Accordingly, on the night of 7th December, a strong detachment from the Army of the Nile under Sir Maitland Wilson, comprising British and Imperial troops and a detachment from the Free French Forces, advanced towards the positions which the Italians had fortified since their incursion across the Egyptian frontier three months ago. It will be realized that the operation of advancing almost in a single bound across 75 miles of desert, is one which is by no means free from hazard and complexity when considerable forces are employed. It was with satisfaction that His Majesty's Government learned that this long and rapid approach had been successfully accomplished.

Yesterday morning, the 9th, our Forces came into contact with the enemy at various points over a wide front, stretching from Sidi Barrani on the coast into the desert. An attack was delivered against the positions of the Italian centre to the southward of Sidi Barrani. In the first defended area which was assaulted and over-run, 500 prisoners and some war material fell into our hands, the Italian General in Command was killed, and his second in command was captured. Later in the day, a further advance was made into a second and stronger and more important position nearer to the coast, and more prisoners and material were taken. Other British Forces also reached the coast between Sidi Barrani and Buq-Buq, making further captures of transport and prisoners. It is too soon to attempt to forecast either the scope or the result of the considerable operations which are in progress. But we can at any rate say that the preliminary phase has been successful.

The British Mediterranean Fleet and the Royal Air Force are, of course, co-operating closely with the Army. British warships have bombarded the various coastal positions involved in the fighting, including particularly Maktila and Sidi Barrani. Some details of the air action have been received. On the 8th a heavy attack was made by our bombers on the enemy aerodrome at Benghazi, where about 25 tons of bombs were dropped effectively on hangars and among aircraft. On the same night air attacks were made on the Italian advanced aerodromes in prelude to the morning's action; and throughout yesterday our bombers continuously harassed the Italian advanced aerodromes, while our fighter aircraft, in which Hurricane squadrons are conspicuous, made low-flying machine-gun attacks on enemy troops and motor transport, causing substantial loss.

THE VICTORY AT SIDI BARRANI

A STATEMENT TO THE HOUSE OF COMMONS
DECEMBER 12, 1940

December 11. British captured Sidi Barrani and continued to advance into Libya.

> *Lord Lothian, British Ambassador, warned the United States that Germany was concentrating on building submarines and long-distance planes for a great attack on Atlantic shipping. The next day Lord Lothian died.*

December 12. Italian prisoners in the Western Desert battle reached a total of 20,000, and the British continued to press the attack.

[December 12, 1940.

THE House evidently appreciated the full significance of the fact, which I announced, without commenting upon it, that a British column had reached the coast between Buq-Buq and Sidi Barrani. This, of course, cut the principal road by which the main body of the Italian Army which had invaded Egypt could effect a retreat. The question then was whether the encircling positions which General Wilson's Forces had capured after their brilliantly-executed desert march could be effectively maintained, and whether the net so drawn could be forced at all points to the seashore. The strong position of Sidi Barrani and various fortified posts in this neighbourhood appeared to be a considerable obstacle. However, Sidi Barrani has been captured, and the whole coastal region with the exception of one or two points still holding out is in the hands of the British and Imperial troops. Seven thousand prisoners have already reached Mersa Matruh.

We do not yet know how many Italians were caught in the encirclement, but it would not be surprising if, at least, the best part of three Italian divisions, including numerous Black Shirt formations, have been either destroyed or captured. As Sidi Barrani was the advance base for all the Italian Forces which had invaded Egypt and were preparing for a further inroad, it seems probable that considerable masses of material may be found there. The pursuit to the Westward continues with the greatest vigour, the Air Force are now bombing and the Navy are shelling the principal road open to the retreating enemy, and considerable additional captures have already been reported besides those which fell within the original encirclement.

While it is too soon to measure the scale of these operations, it is clear that they constitute a victory which, in this African theatre of war, is of the first order, and reflects the highest credit upon Sir Archibald Wavell, Sir Maitland Wilson, the staff officers who planned this exceedingly complicated operation, and the troops who performed the remarkable feats of endurance and daring which accomplished it. The whole episode must be judged upon the background of the fact that it is only three or four months ago that our anxieties for the defence of Egypt were acute. Those anxieties are now removed, and the British guarantee and pledge that Egypt would be effectually defended against all comers has been, in every way, made good.

THE OLD SCHOOL

A SPEECH TO THE BOYS OF HARROW
DECEMBER 18, 1940

December 14. Laval, Vice-Premier and Foreign Minister of the Vichy Government, dismissed by Petain and arrested. *(He was released three days later at Germany's demand.)* Flandin appointed Vichy Foreign Minister.

December 16. British forces in the Western Desert captured Sollum, Italy's last stronghold in Egypt, and Fort Capuzzo, in Libya.

December 17. President Roosevelt announced that the United States would take over and pay for all British war orders in the United States beyond those already contracted for. Planes and munitions produced by these orders would be on the same footing as those produced for U.S. defence. The proportion of arms sent to Britain would be leased or sold under mortgage to this country, and would either be returned or replaced in kind after the war.

Announced that in the month of November 4,588 civilians were killed and 6,202 were injured in air raids on Britain.

December 18. British troops pierced Bardia defences and Italian Army began retreat to Tobruk, seventy-five miles away.

NOTE

The Prime Minister visited Harrow, his old school, on December 18, 1940. He was accompanied by Mr. L. S. Amery (Secretary of State for India), Colonel J. T. C. Moore-Brabazon (Minister of Transport) and Mr. Geoffrey Lloyd (Secretary of the Petroleum Department of the Board of Trade), all old Harrovians. Mr. Churchill and his ministerial colleagues joined the boys in singing the School songs including "Giants of Old," "Boy" and "Forty Years On."

The Prime Minister then made this short speech to the boys.

[December 18, 1940.

I T is a great pleasure and a refreshing treat to me and those of my Parliamentary Ministerial colleagues who have come to Harrow with me this afternoon to join the School in singing Harrow songs. When I was here as a boy I was thrilled by them. I had a good memory and mastered the words of many of them, and they have often come back to me in after life. I feel that they are one of the greatest treasures of the school, passing as they do from one generation to another and pointing with bright hopes towards the future.

We have sung of "the wonderful giants of old" but can anyone doubt that this generation is as good and as noble as any the nation has ever produced, and that its men and women can stand against all tests? Can any one doubt that this generation is in every way capable of carrying on the traditions of the nation and handing down its love of justice and liberty and its message undiminished and unimpaired?

I like the song "Boy," although when I was at the School I did not advance to that position of authority which entitles one to make that call. The songs and their spirit form a bond between Harrovians all over the world, and they have played a great part in the influence which has been exercised in national affairs by men who have had their education here.

Hitler, in one of his recent discourses, declared that the fight was between those who have been through the Adolf Hitler Schools and those who have been at Eton. Hitler has forgotten Harrow, and he has also overlooked the vast majority of the youth of this country who have never had the advantage of attending such schools, but who have by their skill and prowess won the admiration of the whole world.

When this war is won, as it surely will be, it must be one of our aims to work to establish a state of society where the advantages and privileges which hitherto have been enjoyed only by the few shall be far more widely shared by the many, and by the youth of the nation as a whole.

It is a great time in which you are called upon to begin your life. You have already had the honour of being under the fire of the enemy, and no doubt you acquitted yourselves with befitting composure and decorum. You are here at this most important period of your lives, at a moment when our country stands forth almost alone as the champion of right and freedom all over the world. You, the young men, will be the heirs of the victory which we shall surely achieve, and perhaps some of you in this Speech Room will derive from these songs and Harrow associations the impulse to render that victory fruitful and lasting.

17

THE WAR SITUATION

A SPEECH TO THE HOUSE OF COMMONS
DECEMBER 19, 1940

December 19. *British representatives authorized to negotiate £750,000,000 new arms orders in the United States, contracts not to be placed until Congress approved the President's plan for leasing of material. Britain also ordered sixty new ships from America at a cost of £12,500,000.*

[December 19, 1940.

I TAKE the opportunity of expressing the grief which the House has felt in all quarters at the sudden untimely death of our Ambassador in the United States, Lord Lothian. He was a man of the very highest character, and of far-ranging intellectual scope. All his life his mind played about broad issues of human progress, and, whether at home or abroad, he animated an ardent philanthropy with the keenest and brightest intellectual powers. In India his work is much respected. His work in the last war was already important, as Mr. Lloyd George—whom I am very glad to see here to-day—could no doubt remind us. But all the same, when he was appointed before the war to the Embassy in the United States, the most important of all the functions outside this counry that can be discharged by any British subject, there were various opinions upon the wisdom of that choice. Very soon, however, it was seen that the new Ambassador was gaining in influence every day, that his stature rose with the greatness of the topics confided to him, and that the contacts which he established, the intimate relations which he developed, with the high personnel of the United States Administration, the friendship to which the President of the United States has himself testified—all the evidence showed the remarkable efficiency and success with which he discharged his important and extremely delicate and difficult mission.

Suddenly, he is taken from us. He passes away. But I cannot help feeling that to die at the height of a man's career, the highest

18

moment of his effort here in this world, universally honoured and admired, to die while great issues are still commanding the whole of his interest, to be taken from us at a moment when he could already see ultimate success in view—is not the most unenviable of fates. I feel that the House would have wished me to express, in these few words, the sorrow which we feel at his death, and also the very grievous and practical sense that we have of the loss we have suffered at this particular juncture in being deprived of his invaluable service.

I should like to put rather frankly to the House a difficulty which I feel about making frequent statements on the war situation. I have to be much concerned in the conduct of the war in consequence of being called upon to occupy the offices which I do as Prime Minister and Minister of Defence, and there is a danger, if one gives full and frank and frequent statements revealing one's own point of view, or the point of view of the Government or of those who are charged with the strategical and tactical decisions, that the enemy may gain an advantage. Certainly it would be very convenient if Herr Hitler or the important chiefs in Germany were to give us, every fortnight or so, an honest-to-God—if they were capable of it—statement. I am sure we should immediately set a dozen active and agile Intelligence Officers to study not only what was said but what was not said, and to read not only the lines but between the lines, and to collate any stray words with the other information which might perhaps afford a clue. Therefore, I hope the House will be indulgent to me if, although always at their service, I choose the occasions somewhat rarely, and, in the event of their desiring information at some period which I do not feel convenient, I hope the House will allow me to impart it to them as far as possible in Secret Session.

With this prelude, let me remind the House, in reinforcement of my plea for not making too many speeches, that I did say when we opened the Session that what was wanted was deeds, not words. Well, I do not think we have wholly failed to make good that hope. The Battle of the Libyan Desert is still proceeding, and I have no later news than that which is contained in the public Press at the moment. We are attacking the fort and town of Bardia with strong and increasing forces, and the situation there is not such that I can make any decided statement upon it. But I will go so far as to say that I have reason to believe it is developing favourably. This memorable battle is spread over a vast extent of desert, with swiftly-moving mechanized columns circling in and out of the camps and posts of the enemy, and with fighting taking place over an area as large, I have been told, as Yorkshire, and it is not possible to give all the details at the present time. I am, however, sure that the figure of 30,000 prisoners is, even up to the present moment, a considerable under-statement, and 100 serviceable guns and 50 tanks, together with a great quantity of invaluable stores, have also been gathered by our troops. At Sidi Omar, the day before yesterday, operations resulted in another 800 prisoners and a battery of artillery being captured, and on the same day at Giarabub Oasis, west of Siwa Oasis, which was being attacked by Australian Forces, it happened that an Australian cavalry squadron gathered both guns and transport as its trophies.

One cannot say that the Italians have shown a high fighting spirit, or quality, in this battle. In other periods of Italian history, we know, they have shown great courage; and I am certainly not going to frame a charge of lack of military qualities against a people with whom up to this time we have had—and God knows we did not seek it now—no quarrel. But perhaps their hearts are not in their work. Perhaps they have been so long controlled and disciplined and ruled, and so much relieved of all share in the government of their own country, that they have not felt those virile emotions which are the foundation for the actions of brave armies, and which are best nourished by discipline imposed upon freedom. At any rate, we have seen the spectacle of at least one whole Italian division laying down its arms to far inferior forces; and our Air Force, which has been contending at odds of three or four or five to one, has been fighting with continued success. The House will be anxious to know what in this fighting the cost has been in life and limb to our troops. Up to the night of the 16h, which is the latest return I have, the British Army, a considerable Army, which was moved so rapidly into the desert, engaged in continuous fighting all the week, lost less than 1,000 killed and wounded, of all ranks, British, Indian and Imperial troops. There have, no doubt, been other losses since. We must regard this event as highly satisfactory; and its reactions in other directions will be favourable, and should permit us to take bolder views than those which have been open to us before.

This is a case where risks have been well run. The risk in the desert was formidable. The movement across 70 or 80 miles of desert of this large force was open to very considerable hazards, and the assault upon Sidi Barrani had about it this cause of anxiety —with which I did not trouble the House at the time—that petrol and water were strictly limited in the attacking force, and that failure or delay would have entailed a serious curtailment of our operations. But these risks have been surmounted by the great skill of our Commander, General Wilson, who is reputed to be one of our finest tacticians; and General Wavell, whose figure grows upon the Eastern horizon, rises there to the very great pleasure and encouragement of all the people over here who look eagerly to see the arrival upon the scene of this great war of military, naval, and air figures to whom the Armies and the Fleets can give their enthusiasm.

I must not forget the work which has been done in this battle by Air Chief Marshal Longmore, who at the most critical moment in his preparations had to have a very large portion of his force taken away from him for Greece, but who nevertheless persevered, running additional risks, and whose handling of this situation, in co-operation with the Army, deserves the highest praise. It is, indeed, a pleasure to me personally, because when I was at the Admiralty in 1912, forming the Royal Naval Air Service, he was one of the first few fliers there, and in those days of very dubious machines he several times used to fly me about. We were personal friends as long ago as that.

I hope that the House will be contented with the present results achieved by this offensive. I do not consider that it is by any means at an end, but I think it will be better to let the future unfold as it will, without attempting to skip on ahead or in any way to forecast how the play may go. I have said that I considered that risks were well run there. They were also well run here by the General Staff of the British Army and by the War Cabinet and by the staffs who studied this matter; because it was not an easy thing in July and August—if we cast our minds back to that date—to send precious tanks of the best quality, and cannon, of which we were then so short, on that long journey around the Cape of Good Hope, in order to enable us at first to defend ourselves, and later to assume the offensive. I can only say that those were hard decisions to take, and that the Secretary of State for War and I had many anxious days in coming to those conclusions. But you will not have any means of abridging this war, or, indeed, of emerging from it safely, unless risks are run. Risks do imply that when forfeit is exacted, as it may be when a great ship is sunk or some bold attack repulsed with heavy slaughter, the House must stand by the Government and the military commanders. I have endeavoured always to say that those who launch themselves against the enemy, in any action, with vigour and violence will, whatever the upshot, receive the support of His Majesty's Government and, I doubt not, also of the House of Commons.

Another reason which makes this victory gratifying to us is that the British Army has at last had an opportunity of showing its quality. We have had hard and unfortunate experiences in this war; but in the fighting around Dunkirk all the divisions which were engaged with the enemy had the consciousness that they were fully a match for their German opponents. Several battles fought on a front of one or two divisions showed that we had not the slightest reason to shrink from contact on anything like equal terms, or even against a shade of odds, with the regular mass of the troops of the German Army. Now we have seen in Libya that our military science and our staff officers are capable of planning and executing extremely complex and daring operations with efficiency—and it is not there only that we have such officers. Therefore, I renew my advice to the House to do all possible to cultivate and develop the strength and efficiency of the great British Army now building up at home. Certainly, it will give its help in any emergency where air-raid damage occurs, but we must have here an Army on a large scale—I carefully avoid saying what the numbers should be, but on a large scale—not only to defend this Island, but for action in other theatres should they suggest themselves at any time. We must have a large Army, well found, equipped with the very best weapons, and drilled, trained and practised in what I have ventured to call all the arts and manœuvres of war.

I am sure the House will feel that this is a wise and provident provision for the year 1941, in which we shall, I trust, find opportunities of using our Forces, if not in defence of this Island, in other theatres, where we may hope that they will be able to contend with their opponents on terms of a moderate equality in number and, I trust, in terms of equality of equipment. This is the first time that we have had equal equipment. As I have said, we are still only half armed. It is no good hoping and asking for immediate conclusions. We are still a half-armed nation, fighting a well-armed nation, a fully-armed nation, a nation which has already passed the saturation point in its armaments. But in the course of 1941 we shall become a well-armed nation too, and that will open possibilities to us which have not been opened up to the present.

As Mr. Lloyd George knows so well, it takes three or four years to put the industries of a country on to a war basis. The Germans reached the saturation point, the culmination point, certainly at the end of last year, and now we ourselves are still only in the second year; but by the efforts which are being made and by the great supplies which are reaching us and will reach us from the United States, we hope that we shall become well armed during the course of 1941. It is essential that every effort should be made in the armament and munition factories to improve the supplies not only of the Air Force but of the Army, and every risk well run there under the fire of the enemy, every loyal endeavour which our united nations can procure from the workmen in those factories, who themselves are whole-hearted in the vigorous prosecution of the war, everything that can be done to accelerate and to make a more abundant production, will be a step towards victory, and towards an earlier victory than would otherwise be possible.

The House is now separating. Many Members will be visiting their constituencies. Let them use their influence wherever they can to speed the good work, to sustain the morale, if ever it were necessary, and to speed the work of production in every way they possibly can. When we come back we can indeed debate these issues of man-power and production. We are not by any means content with the results, but they are certainly on a very great and very substantial scale. We must never be content. We must continue the drive to our utmost in order to see that our men have weapons placed in their hands worthy of the task that they have to perform and worthy of the qualities and sacrifice that they bring to the discharge of that task. What I have said in respect of munitions applies with equal force to food production in all its forms. When I spoke the other day of the years 1943 and 1944, I did not mean that I believed the war would go on till then, but in matters like agriculture and shipbuilding you have to get on to steady grooves. You have to look ahead. If you do not make plans on that scale, you will not even get the first fruits in good time. Anything that can be done to increase the volume of our food production will be the wisest insurance for the later years of this war, assuming it should unhappily be prolonged to such a period, which is by no means certain.

We are separating for a short recess, and we may, I think, look with some sense of composure and even satisfaction at the progress which has been made and at the state of our affairs; but it would be a disaster if anyone supposed that the supreme dangers, the mortal dangers, are past. They are not. There are the dangers of prolonged deadlock, but there may be also more immediate dangers. The winter season offers some advantages to an invader to counterbalance those which belong to the summer season. It would be a very great lack of prudence, a lack of prudence amounting to a crime, if vigilance were relaxed in our Armies here at home, or if in any way it were assumed that the dangers of invasion had passed. Most careful preparation must continue to be made, and although it has been for some time past possible to give a proportion of leave to our troops to their homes which are close at hand, which are in this small Island, yet that should not in any way be taken as the slightest justification for supposing that we must not watch from hour to hour the dangerous menace which still exists in full force at so very short a distance away.

I may say that, of course, our defence of the beaches is complete. From the North of Scotland right round the Island enormous masses of guns and machine-guns and fortified posts, with every device of defence, have been erected and are guarded by large numbers of ardent and well-trained men. But we are not making the mistake which was made by the French General Staff when they thought that holding the Maginot Line was all that was necessary. I remember well going to Paris at that dark moment after the first defeat and asking immediately, "What are you going to do with your mass of manœuvre or general reserve?" It was with the greatest sorrow that I learned that a general reserve did not exist and had to be drawn from different parts of the line. Well, we have now got a very large Army behind in this country which is capable of moving to any place with great rapidity and going into action in the strongest counter-offensive, and, therefore, one may have good confidence in our power to beat the enemy, even supposing he should succeed in setting foot in any strength on these stores.

Nevertheless, the watchword which we carry is that vigilance must be unceasing. We should remember that Herr Hitler—and I certainly deprecate any comparison between Herr Hitler and Napoleon; I do not wish to insult the dead—who wields gigantic power and is capable of wielding it in a ruthless manner, has great need of doing something now, or soon, at any rate in the next few months. When the war began he had his plans all ready for Poland, and he doubted whether Britain and France would come in, or, if they came in, would persist. When he had destroyed Poland, he found himself faced with the war effort of Britain and France. He waited a long time in complete quiescence, as it seemed, and then struck that terrible series of blows which shattered France. He then thought that in the fall of France would be involved the fall of Britain, but it did not turn out that way; it turned out differently, and one must suppose that he is making other plans which will be particularly directed to our benefit and our address. Therefore, I am using this opportunity of addressing the House to urge not only increasing vigilance but the increasing effort of all, wherever they may be.

24

We are not afraid of any blow which may be struck against us, but we must make increasing preparations. The attacks in the air have slackened somewhat because of the weather, but they might easily have slackened in preparation for some other form of activity. I need hardly say, however, that the method of dealing with them and of fighting by night is being studied with passion and zeal by a very large number of extremely able and brilliant scientists and officers. So far we have been no more successful in stopping the German night raider than Germans have been successful in stopping our aeroplanes, which have ranged freely over Germany. We have struck very heavy blows—the blows at Mannheim appeared to be of a very heavy character—and the enemy has not found any means of preventing them. So far we have not reached any satisfactory remedy, although we have noticed a considerable improvement in various directions. We must expect a continuance of these attacks and must bear them.

The organization of shelters, the improvement of sanitation, and the endeavour to mitigate the extremely painful conditions under which many people have to get their night's rest—that is the first task of the Government at home. The Air-Raid Precautions, the Home Office, and the Ministry of Health are just as much in the front line of the battlefield as are the armoured columns which are chasing the Italians about the Libyan desert. I hope and trust, indeed, that we shall succeed in mitigating increasingly the conditions which prevail in shelters. It will not be for the want of trying or for the lack of spending money. But the difficulties of handling such great numbers of people under conditions where materials are short and labour is so fully employed on this or that other task are very great. It is a matter in which we welcome the assistance of Parliament, in either Public or Secret Session. Complaints can be made, and should be brought to the notice of Ministers in order that everything possible may be done.

The only other point I would mention is the sinkings in the Atlantic. They still continue at a very disquieting level; not so bad as in the critical period of 1917, but still we must recognize the recrudescence of the danger which, a year ago, we seemed to have mastered. We shall steadily increase, from now on, our resources in flotillas and other methods of defence, but we must regard the keeping open of this channel to the world against submarines and the long-distance aircraft which are now attacking as the first of the military tasks which lie before us at the present time.

I have spoken rather longer than I had intended, but the interest of these topics is such that one is bound to refer to them.

All I can say now is that if we look back to where we were in May and June, there is not one of us who cannot go away for Christmas —I would not say for holidays, because, so far as Ministers are concerned, any relaxation must only be the opportunity for making up arrears—or separate for the time being without a feeling of thankfulness that we have been preserved so far, and that we have made progress after a moment when many in the world, including our best friends abroad, despaired of our continued powers of resistance, that we have maintained ourselves, that our resistance has grown, that we have preserved ourselves secure in our Island home and reached out long and strong hands across the seas to discharge the obligations which we have undertaken to countries which have put their faith in us.

A CALL TO THE ITALIAN PEOPLE

A BROADCAST FROM LONDON
DECEMBER 23, 1940

December 20. British battleships bombarded Valona and other warships swept the Adriatic as far as Bari and Durazzo.

December 22. Lord Halifax appointed British Ambassador to the United States, Mr. Anthony Eden Foreign Secretary, and Capt. Margesson, former Chief Whip, Secretary of State for War.

Petain rejected Hitler's demands for the surrender of the French Fleet and the reinstatement of Laval as Foreign Minister.

Graziani, Italian Commander-in-Chief in Libya, reported to Mussolini that the British attack in the Western Desert had occurred a few days before the Italian attack was due to be launched. He admitted "crushing superiority" of British armoured units.

[December 23, 1940.

TO-NIGHT I speak to the Italian people, and I speak to you from London, the heart of the British Islands and of the British Commonwealth and Empire. I speak to you what the diplomatists call words of great truth and respect. We are at war—that is a very strange and terrible thought. Whoever imagined until the last few melancholy years that the British and Italian nations would be trying to destroy one another?

We have always been such friends. We were the champions of the Italian Risorgimento. We were the partisans of Garibaldi, the admirers of Mazzini and Cavour. All that great movement towards the unity of the Italian nation which lighted the nineteenth century was aided and was hailed by the British Parliament and public. Our fathers and our grandfathers longed to see Italy freed from the Austrian yoke, and to see all minor barriers in Italy swept away, so that the Italian people and their fair land might take an honoured place as one of the leading powers upon the Continent and as a

27

brilliant and gifted member of the family of Europe and of Christendom.

We have never been your foes till now. In the last war against the barbarous Huns we were your comrades. For fifteen years after that war we were your friends. Although the institutions which you adopted after that war were not akin to ours, and diverged, as we think, from the sovereign impulses which had commanded the unity of Italy, we could still march forward in peace and good will. Many thousands of your people dwelt with us in England; many thousands of our people dwelt with you in Italy. We liked each other; we got on well together. There were reciprocal services; there was amity; there was esteem.

And now we are at war; now we are condemned to work each other's ruin. Your aviators have tried to cast their bombs upon London; our armies are tearing and will tear your African Empire to shreds and tatters. We are now only at the beginning of this sombre tale. Who can say where it will end? Presently we shall be forced to come to much closer grips. How has all this come about, and what is it all for?

Italians, I will tell you the truth. It is all because of one man. One man and one man alone has ranged the Italian people in deadly struggle against the British Empire, and has deprived Italy of the sympathy and intimacy of the United States of America. That he is a great man I do not deny, but that after eighteen years of un-bridled power he has led your counry to the horrid verge of ruin can be denied by none. It is one man who, against the Crown and Royal Family of Italy, against the Pope and all the authority of the Vatican and of the Roman Catholic Church, against the wishes of the Italian people, who had no lust for this war, has arrayed the trustees and inheritors of ancient Rome upon the side of the ferocious pagan barbarians.

There lies the tragedy of Italian history, and there stands the criminal who has wrought the deed of folly and of shame.

What is the defence that is put forward for his action It is, of course, the quarrel about sanctions and Abyssinia. Let us look at that. Together after the last war Italy and Britain both signed the Covenant of the League of Nations, which forbade all parties to that Covenant to make war upon each other or upon fellow-members of the League, and bound all signatories to come to the aid of any member attacked by another. Presently Abyssinia came knocking at the door, asking to be a member. We British advised against it. We doubted whether they had reached a stage in their development which warranted their inclusion in so solemn a pact.

But it was Signor Mussolini who insisted that Abyssinia should become a member of the League, and who therefore bound himself and bound you and us to respect their covenanted rights. Thus the quarrel arose. It was out of this that it sprang, and thus, although no blood was shed between us, old friendships were forgotten.

But what is the proportion of this Abyssinian dispute, arising out of the Covenant of the League of Nations, to which we had both pledged our word, compared with the death-grapple in which Italy and Britain have now been engaged? I declare—and my words will go far—that nothing that has happened in that Abyssinian quarrel can account for or justify the deadly strife which has now broken out between us. Time passed. Then the great war between the British and French democracies and Prussian militarism or Nazi overlordship began again. Where was the need for Italy to intervene? Where was the need to strike at prostrate France? Where was the need to declare war on Britain? Where was the need to invade Egypt, which is under British protection? We were content with Italian neutrality. During the first eight months of the war we paid great deference to Italian interests. But this was all put down to fear. We were told we were effete, worn out, an old chatterbox people mouthing outworn shibboleths of nineteenth-century Liberalism. But it was not due to fear. It was not due to weakness.

The French Republic for the moment is stunned. France will rise again, but the British nation and Commonwealth of Nations across the globe, and, indeed, I may say the English-speaking world, are now aroused. They are on the march or on the move, and all the forces of modern progress and of ancient culture are ranged behind them.

Why have you placed yourselves, you who were our friends and might have been our brothers, in the path of this avalanche, now only just started from its base to roll forward on its predestined track? Why, after all this, were you made to attack and invade Greece? I ask why—but you may ask why, too, because you never were consulted. The people of Italy were never consulted, the army of Italy was never consulted. No one was consulted. One man and one man alone ordered Italian soldiers to ravage their neighbour's vineyard. Surely the time has come when the Italian monarchy and people, who guard the sacred centre of Christendom, should have a word to say upon these awe-inspiring issues? Surely the Italian army, which has fought so bravely on many occasions in the past, but now evidently has no heart for the job, should take some care of the life and future of Italy?

29

I can only tell you that I, Churchill, have done my best to prevent this war between Italy and the British Empire, and to prove my words I will read you the message which I sent to Signor Mussolini in the fateful days before it began. Cast your minds back to the 16th of May of this year. The French front had been broken, the French army was not yet defeated, the great battle in France was still raging. Here is the message which I sent to Signor Mussolini:

"Now that I have taken up my office as Prime Minister and Minister of Defence I look back to our meetings in Rome and feel a desire to speak words of good will to you as chief of the Italian nation across what seems to be a swiftly widening gulf. Is it too late to stop a river of blood from flowing between the British and Italian peoples? We can, no doubt, inflict grievous injuries upon one another and maul each other cruelly, and darken the Mediterranean with our strife. If you so decree, it must be so; but I declare that I have never been the enemy of Italian greatness nor ever at heart the foe of the Italian law-giver. It is idle to predict the course of the great battles now raging in Europe, but I am sure that whatever may happen on the Continent, England will go on to the end, even quite alone, as we have done before, and I believe with some assurance that we shall be aided in increasing measure by the United States and indeed by all the Americas.

"I beg you to believe that it is in no spirit of weakness or of fear that I make this solemn appeal, which will remain on record. Down the ages above all other calls comes the cry that the joint heirs of Latin and Christian civilization must not be ranged against one another in mortal strife. Hearken to it, I beseech you in all honour and respect, before the dread signal is given. It will never be given by us."

And this is the reply which I received from Signor Mussolini upon the eighteenth:

"I reply to the message which you have sent me in order to tell you that you are certainly aware of grave reasons of an historical and contingent character which have ranged our two countries in opposite camps. Without going back very far in time I remind you of the initiative taken in 1935 by your Government to organize at Geneva sanctions against Italy, engaged in securing for herself a small space in the African sun without causing the slightest injury to your interests and territories or those of others. I remind you also of the real and actual state of servitude in which Italy finds herself in her own sea. If it was to honour your signature that your Government declared war on Germany, you will understand that the same sense of honour and of respect for engagements assumed in the Italian-German treaty guides Italian policy to-day and to-morrow in the face of any event whatsoever."

That was the answer. I make no comment upon it. It was a dusty answer. It speaks for itself. Anyone can see who it was that wanted peace, and who it was that meant to have war. One man and one man only was resolved to plunge Italy after all these years of strain and effort into the whirlpool of war. And what is the position of Italy to-day? Where is it that the Duce has led his trusting people after eighteen years of dictatorial power? What hard choice is open to them now? It is to stand up to the battery of the whole British Empire on sea, in the air, and in Africa, and the vigorous counter-attack of the Greek nation; or, on the other hand, to call in Attila over the Brenner Pass with his hordes of ravenous soldiery and his gangs of Gestapo policemen to occupy, hold down, and protect the Italian people, for whom he and his Nazi followers cherish the most bitter and outspoken contempt that is on record between races.

There is where one man and one man only has led you; and there I leave this unfolding story until the day comes—as come it will—when the Italian nation will once more take a hand in shaping its own fortunes.

A TRIBUTE TO LORD HALIFAX

A SPEECH IN LONDON AT A LUNCHEON OF THE PILGRIMS IN HONOUR OF
LORD HALIFAX BEFORE HIS DEPARTURE TO TAKE UP HIS POST AS AMBASSADOR
TO THE UNITED STATES OF AMERICA.
JANUARY 9, 1941

December 25. The King, in a Christmas broadcast to the Empire, thanked the people overseas who had opened their homes to British children, and paid tribute to the courage of the people of this country in air raids.

December 26. Reported from Budapest that big German troop movements through Hungary to Rumania had started.

December 27. Sir Kingsley Wood, Chancellor of the Exchequer, announced Britain's first long-term loans of the war. Two new Government issues to be available from January 1:—2½ per cent. National War Bonds 1946-1948, and 3 per cent. Savings Bonds 1955-1965.

Darlan reported to Petain on his talks with Nazi authorities in Paris on previous day.

December 29. Great fire raid on London. Guildhall and nine City churches destroyed by incendiary bombs.

1941

January 1. Stalin announced that Soviet Russia was in "full state of mobilization" and that "Russia must hold itself in readiness to face its enemies."

January 3. Petain accepted resignation of Baudoin, Secretary of State to Vichy Government, and set up triumvirate— Darlan, Huntziger and Flandin.

Germans dropped bombs on Eire three times in twenty-four hours, and De Valera sent protest.

January 4. British captured Bardia (Libya) after 36 hours' attack, and began advance on Tobruk.

January 6. President Roosevelt declared United States would not allow defenders of freedom to surrender because of their present inability to pay for weapons needed.

The Prime Minister set up three new executives to deal with production, imports and post-war reconstruction.

32

January 8. *President Roosevelt ordered U.S. Navy to be brought up to war strength, and announced plans for three fleets—Atlantic, Pacific and Asiatic.*

[January 9, 1941.

IT is no exaggeration to say that the future of the whole world and the hopes of a broadening civilization founded upon Christian ethics depend upon the relation between the British Empire or Commonwealth of Nations and the U.S.A. The identity of purpose and persistence of resolve prevailing throughout the English-speaking world will, more than any other single fact, determine the way of life which will be open to the generations and perhaps to the centuries which follow our own.

If the co-operation between the United States and the British Empire in the task of extirpating the spirit and régime of totalitarian intolerance, wherever it may be found, were to fail, the British Empire, rugged and embattled, might indeed hew its way through and preserve the life and strength of our own country and our own Empire for the inevitable renewal of the conflict on worse terms, after an uneasy truce. But the chance of setting the march of mankind clearly and surely along the high-roads of human progress would be lost, and might never return.

Therefore we stand, all of us, upon the watch-towers of history, and have offered to us the glory of making the supreme sacrifices and exertions needed by a cause which it may not be irreverent to call sublime.

I have always taken the view that the fortunes of mankind in its tremendous journey are principally decided for good or ill—but mainly for good, for the path is upward—by its greatest men and its greatest episodes. I therefore hail it as a most fortunate occurrence that at this awe-striking climax in world affairs there should stand at the head of the American Republic a famous statesman, long versed and experienced in the work of government and administration, in whose heart there burns the fire of resistance to aggression and oppression, and whose sympathies and nature make him the sincere and undoubted champion of justice and of freedom, and of the victims of wrong-doing wherever they may dwell.

And not less—for I may say it now that the Party sruggle in the United States is over—do I rejoice that this pre-eminent figure should newly have received the unprecedented honour of being called for the third time to lead the American democracies in days of stress and storm.

His Majesty's Government placed in Washington an Ambassador, Lord Lothian, whose character and qualities were outstanding, and gained him the trust and friendship of President Roosevelt. Suddenly and unexpectedly Lord Lothian was struck down by death.

A link was broken, a gap was opened, and a loss of the highest consequence was sustained, at a very grave moment in the annals of the British and American peoples, and in the fate of those generous and wide causes which they have in their different ways and in their different situations so resolutely espoused.

We therefore thought it our duty to restore this link, to fill this gap, to repair this loss, by sending without regard to the derangement of our forces and circle here the best we could find, without regard to any other consideration whatsoever.

We chose our Foreign Secretary—who had himself chosen Lord Lothian—to fill Lord Lothian's place. Our choice was most agreeable to the President, and it commands the full confidence of nearly all of those in this country who mean to persevere in our righteous cause until its certain victorious end is reached.

In Edward Halifax we have a man of light and leading, whose company is a treat and whose friendship it is an honour to enjoy. I have often disagreed with him in the twenty years I have known him in the rough and tumble of British politics, but I have always respected him and his actions because I know that courage and fidelity are the essence of his being, and that, whether as a soldier with his regiment in the last War or as the ruler of, and trustee for, 400,000,000 in India, he has never swerved from the path of duty as he saw it shining out before him.

As a man of deep but unparaded and unaffected religious convictions and as for many years an ardent lover of the chase, he has known how to get the best out of both worlds. Like all members of the present National Government in Great Britain, most of whom seem to be gathered around this board to-day, he has vowed himself to prosecute this war against the Nazi tyranny at whatever cost until its last vestiges are destroyed.

We send the United States an envoy who comes from the very centre of our counsels and knows all our secrets. Although while Lord Halifax is serving as Ambassador out of this country he cannot be a member of the War Cabinet, he will be, if I may borrow a military term not wholly inappropriate to the times in which we live, as it were seconded from it.

He still attends all our meetings, and will continue to do so during the weeks before his departure, and should he be able to return here for consultation at any time in the summer, as I hope

34

may be possible, he will resume his full functions and responsibilities as a Minister of the Crown.

We now bid him and his brilliant and devoted wife Godspeed and all good fortune, and it is our fervent hope that he may prosper in a mission as momentous as any that the Monarchy has entrusted to an Englishman in the lifetime of the oldest of us here.

"WE WILL NOT FAIL MANKIND"

AN IMPROMPTU SPEECH AT GLASGOW DURING A TOUR OF THAT CITY'S CIVIL
DEFENCE ORGANIZATIONS, ON WHICH THE PRIME MINISTER WAS ACCOMPANIED
BY MR. HARRY HOPKINS, PERSONAL REPRESENTATIVE
OF PRESIDENT ROOSEVELT

JANUARY 17, 1941

January 13. Mr. Harry Hopkins, *personal representative of President
Roosevelt, was received by the King in London.*

January 14. *The Admiralty announced that for the first time
German dive bombers had attacked British warships in
the Mediterranean.*

January 15. *Haile Selassie entered Abyssinia.*

*Mr. Henry Morgenthau, Secretary of the U.S.
Treasury, announced that up to January 1 Britain had
paid for and taken delivery of U.S. material worth
£331,750,000.*

[January 17, 1941.

I CAN hold out no hopes of an easy passage. Before us lie
dangers—I hardly like to say as great as those through which
we have passed, but, at any rate, dangers which, if we neglect
anything, might be fatal, mortal. Before us lie many months of
having to endure bombardment of our cities and industrial areas
without the power to make equal reply. Before us lie sufferings
and tribulations. I am not one of those who pretend that smooth
courses are open to us or that our experiences during this year are
going to be deprived of terrible characteristics.

But what the end will be—about that I cannot have the
slightest doubt. The two dictators are always endeavouring to feed
their people with every kind of optimistic tale, but here we have
made up our minds; here we look at facts with unillusioned eyes,
because we are conscious of the rightness of our cause and because
we are determined that at whatever cost, whatever suffering, we
will not fail mankind at this turning point in its fortunes.

Mr. Harry Hopkins has come in order to put himself in the
closest relation with things here. He will soon return to report to

36

his famous chief the impressions he has gathered in our islands. We do not require in 1941 large armies from oversea. What we do require are weapons, ships, and aeroplanes.

All that we can pay for we will pay for, but we require far more than we shall be able to pay for. And I watch with deep emotion the stirring processes by which the Democracy of the Great American Republic is establishing its laws and formulating its decisions in order to make sure that the British Commonwealth of Nations is able to maintain, as it is maintaining at the present time, the front line of civilization and of progress.

We have a powerful army in this island. We have strongly fortified defences all around our coasts. These defences are well manned, and behind them are large mobile armies capable of advance and counter-attack upon any forces which might gain temporary lodgment on our shores.

Nevertheless I do not feel that it would be right for any of those who are responsible, or for the people of this country generally, to dismiss from their minds the possibility of an invasion.

We in this island stand four-square in the path of European dictators. Their threats will not appal us. It is certain that if Herr Hitler found the invasion of this island difficult in July, he found it more difficult in September, and if he found it difficult in September, it will not have become easier by February or March or April.

That bad man has never had so great a need as he has now to strike Great Britain from his path. He is master of a great part of Europe. His armies can move almost where they will upon the Continent. He holds down eight or ten countries by force, by the secret police, and the still more odious local Quislings. But every day that this occupation of Austria, Czechoslovakia, Poland, Norway, Denmark, Holland, Belgium, and France—and presently perhaps Italy—lasts, there is built up a volume of hatred for the Nazi creed and for the German name which generations, and perhaps centuries, will hardly efface.

Therefore it is for Herr Hitler a matter of supreme consequence to break down the resistance of Great Britain and thus rivet effectively the shackles he has prepared for the people of Europe. But it is one thing to have a need, and another to be able to satisfy that need.

But remember that the price is external vigilance. The reason why one feels a confidence that this man's concentrated hatred will not be effective against our island is because every one of us is up and doing, because there will be ceaseless attention paid

37

by all our forces to every sign of enemy preparations, and because we know that we now have millions of armed men and scores of well-equipped units capable of meeting a landing force and of engaging them with good prospects of success.

The offensive in the Middle East has succeeded beyond our dreams. Now that nearly 80,000 prisoners have been taken—and perhaps there are more to come—now that eight or nine divisions of well-equipped Italian troops have been dashed out of existence with inconceivably small losses, people may be inclined to underrate the merit of the achievement. It was a task of the greatest hazard, but it was a risk well run. The maintenance of our Island and the turning of the tables in Egypt and Libya are very important in the history of the war. They give us an opportunity to address ourselves to the problem of the perils of 1941 with far greater advantage than was at our disposal six or eight months ago. We are still a partly-armed nation, but as 1941 moves along its course, we shall gradually become a well-armed nation, and the fight will then be conducted on more equal terms.

I hope that by the end of this year or the beginning of next year we may, in the air and on the land, be at no disadvantage so far as equipment is concerned with the German foe.

My one aim is to extirpate Hitlerism from Europe. The question is such a simple one. Are we to move steadily forward and have freedom, or are we to be put back into the Middle Ages by a totalitarian system that crushes all forms of individual life and has for its aim little less than the subjugation of Europe and little more than the gratification of gangster appetites?

Do not suppose that we are at the end of the road. Yet, though long and hard it may be, I have absolutely no doubt that we shall win a complete and decisive victory over the forces of evil, and that victory itself will be only a stimulus to further efforts to conquer ourselves and to make our country as worthy in the days of peace as it is proving itself in the hours of war.

THE WAR SITUATION

A SPEECH TO THE HOUSE OF COMMONS
JANUARY 22, 1941

January 18. Announced that every man and woman between 16
and 60 is liable to be called up for compulsory A.R.P.
work, in addition to fire watching.

January 19. British launch heavy attacks against Italians in
Eritrea and Abyssinia.

Announced in Vichy that Petain and Laval had
conferred and "dissipated misunderstandings."

January 20. Officially stated that in air raids on Britain during
December 3,793 civilians had been killed and 5,044
injured.

January 21. Mr. Ernest Bevin, Minister of Labour and National
Service, announced plans for the industrial conscription
of all men and women.

Daily Worker, *Communist newspaper, closed by
the Home Secretary.*

[*January 22, 1941.*

TO try to carry on a war, a tremendous war, without the aid
and guidance of the House of Commons, would be a super-
human task. I have never taken the view that the Debates and
criticisms of this House are a drag and a burden. Far from it. I
may not agree with all the criticism—I may be stirred by it, and
I may resent it; I may even retort—but at any rate, Debates on
these large issues are of the very greatest value to the life-thrust of
the nation, and they are of great assistance to His Majesty's
Government.

Therefore, when, as we gathered, there was a wish to have a
day's discussion of large questions connected with the Home Front
—man-power, priorities, supply and so forth—I offered not only
one day, but two days. I think two are better than one, because
sometimes, when there is only one day's Debate, especially under
our rather restricted conditions of meeting, one may find that the

Minister makes a long statement and that afterwards there is nothing in the Debate but the criticism; whereas, after two days' Debate, it is possible to perceive the main character of the criticism and to endeavour, as far as possible, to reassure the House upon the points which have most been called into question.

I want to begin by communicating to the House the main ideas which I have formed, with much thought and some experience, upon the machinery for conducting war. I have reached the conclusion that in the present circumstances a War Cabinet composed of four or five men free from departmental duties would not give the best results. It may be admitted that that is a very arguable proposition. Some may say that that system assisted to carry us to victory in the last war. I saw the system at close quarters, and I do not think that it was in practice altogether what it was represented to be in theory. The War Cabinet of those days was largely an instrument designed to give the great man who then conducted our affairs wide powers to deal with matters over the whole field, and in practice the meetings of that body, theoretically so exclusive, were attended by very much larger numbers than those who now grace our council board.

Personally, I have formed the view that it is better that there should be in the responsible directing centres of Government some, at any rate, of the key Ministers. There is the Minister for Foreign Affairs, who always attended in the last war. There is the Chancellor of the Exchequer, because, after all, one must not forget that the Chancellor of the Exchequer has a function. There is the Minister of Labour, because the spontaneous, sustained, good will effort of the labouring masses of this country is the sole foundation upon which we can escape from our present difficulties. Then there is the Minister of Aircraft Production, because aircraft production is the key to survival, and, if I may say so, the Minister of Aircraft Production, who was described as an old sea raider, which is a euphemistic method of describing a pirate, is a man of altogether exceptional force and genius, who is at his very best when things are at their very worst. Then there are the Defence Ministers, the three Service Ministers. But, as the Prime Minister under this arrangement, which the House has approved, is also the Minister of Defence, he represents those Departments in the War Cabinet. We make altogether eight, and yet we hold a great many of the key offices in our body. I think it is better to work in that way than to have five Ministers, entirely divorced from their Departments, because that means that when a discussion has taken place in the Cabinet, the leaders of these Departments have to be summoned,

40

and the whole business has to be gone over again in order to learn what it is they think they can do, and to persuade them and convince them that it is necessary to do what has been decided upon.

The House must not underrate the power of these great Departments of State. I have served for over twenty years in Cabinets, in peace and war, and I can assure the House that the power of these great Departments is in many cases irresistible because it is based on knowledge and on systematized and organized currents of opinion. You must have machinery which carries to the Cabinet with the least possible friction the consent and allegiance of these great Departments. It is not a question of loyalty. It is a question of honest differences of opinion which arise, and there are many matters to be settled and decided which would not arise in the ordinary Departmental mind. There are great difficulties in dealing with Departments of State unless the key Departments are brought into the discussion in the early stages and, as it were, take part in the original formation and initiation of our designs.

As I said, the Minister of Defence represents the Service Ministers in the War Cabinet, and he, in the name of the War Cabinet and subject to its accord, directs the conduct of the war. Why then, it is asked, have we not got on the civil side another similar Minister? Why should there not be another similar Minister who would equally direct and concert the whole home front or a great part of it? The answer is this: The Minister of Defence is also Prime Minister, and he can therefore exercise his general function of superintendence and direction without impinging upon the constitutional responsibilities of the Service Ministers. If, however, a Minister of Defence were appointed who was not the Prime Minister—and I am discussing this matter quite impersonally—he would not have any real authority except, of course, a co-ordinating and conciliatory power, over the three great Service Ministries and their responsible heads. The First Lord of the Admiralty and the Secretaries of State for War and Air could at any time appeal against him in the War Cabinet, and the whole matter in dispute would then have to be argued out there once more. If at any time it becomes necessary to appoint a Minister of Defence who is not also Prime Minister, then I tell the House plainly that the Minister will have to be in fact First Lord of the Admiralty and Secretary of State for War and Air, and hold the seals or letters patent of those Departments, otherwise he will have no more power than the various Ministers for the Co-ordination of Defence have had in the years before the war and in the six months at the beginning of the war.

Let me now apply these considerations to the civil side. Here also the Departments have very strong characteristics, and the Ministers at their head have definite constitutional responsibilities to Crown and Parliament. Here also are immense volumes of specialized and organized knowledge. Where am I to find a man who, without himself being Prime Minister, would have the personal ascendancy in his nature to govern and concert the action of all those Ministers and Departments on the civil side, and drive in a happy and docile team the Minister of Supply, the Minister of Labour, and the Minister of Aircraft Production, to say nothing of the Ministers of Transport, Shipping, Agriculture, Food and Trade? I doubt if such a man exists. Certainly I do not know him. We do not live in a dictator country, where people can be brutally overruled. That is our merit. We do not want a dictator. We live in a country where His Majesty's Cabinet governs subject to the continual superintendence, correction and authority of Parliament. In the last resort, only the Cabinet can exert the necessary authority over all these Departments I have mentioned on the civil side. How, then, is this process to be achieved with the maximum of action and the minimum of friction? There is the problem for which I ventured, very respectfully, to offer a solution in the recent announcement of the formation of the Government Committees.

Let me, at this point, make a brief diversion upon the uses and abuses of committees and the possibility of administrative action by them. Four years ago I criticized the pre-war Administration for their reliance upon an elaborate network of committees. I was answered by a quotation from my own account of the organization which I set up in the Ministry of Munitions in 1917. In this quotation I was represented to have said, quite accurately, that practically all the work of the Ministry of Munitions was done by a council of committees. That seemed a very good answer in those days, when I had not the advantage of so much support in this House as I have to-day. Let me make plain to the House the difference between the Council Committees of the old Ministry of Munitions and ordinary inter-departmental committees. The Council Committees were exclusively composed of men who had under their direct control the executive and administrative branches concerned in the problem, and who bore the great responsibility for executing any agreement or any decision reached among them. That is the fact. They were like chieftains, each arriving with so many of his clan, and when the clans were joined together the Highland army was complete. The ordinary consultative and advisory committee is attended by representatives of many branches and Departments—

42

and everyone likes to have his representative on any committee that may be going; they try to agree upon forms of words for a report; and then, too often, they are inclined to pass the buck to some other futile body, equally respectable. The difference between these two kinds of committees is the difference between cheese and chalk—and cheese is much the scarcer and the more nourishing of the two.

Every British Cabinet in the last 30 or 40 years has conducted a large part of its work by Cabinet Committees. Instead of the whole Cabinet sitting there hour after hour, they appoint four or five Ministers to go into this or that particular matter, to hammer it out among themselves, and then to come back and advise the parent body. Such Committees are often based upon the Ministers, the co-ordination of whose Departments is essential to the solution of the problem. They have the strongest incentive to agree, because they are all colleagues: honourable men working for a common object; and if they do agree, they can make their Departments carry out their decisions, and carry them out with alacrity and good will. This was the system which I applied at the Ministry of Munitions in August, 1917. It was certainly generally considered to be a very great improvement and easement in organization upon what had gone before, and this is the system, which *mutatis mutandis*, I have applied now to the two extraordinarily difficult and vital spheres of our life which are covered by the Import Executive and the Production Executive.

The Import Executive consists of the five great importers from these five Departments—the Ministery of Supply, the Ministry of Aircraft Production, the Controller's Department at the Admiralty, represented by the First Lord, the Food Ministry, and the Board of Trade, which also represents the minor importers. If the men at the head of these Departments, who are among the leading and most active Ministers in the administration, could not settle among themselves how to bring in the greatest volume of imports in which they are all vitally interested, I should be very much disappointed, and indeed surprised. In order that control may be effective, the handling Departments, that is to say, the Ministry of Transport and the Ministry of Shipping, the Department responsible for ship-building and repairs, and in this connection the Ministry of Labour, whose Minister is in the Chair on the other Committee—these Departments serve them and carry out their policy. Take all this business of the docks under the attack which is being made upon them, problems of labour and transport, of turning ships round and so forth. This group of men have everything in their hands. If they can agree—and at their service are the great Departments—they can execute the policy which they put forward.

Similar principles inspired the creation of the Production Executive, the kernel of which consists of the same three Supply Ministers who are on the Import Executive and who also constitute the Committee regulating purchases in the United States. Here are these three Supply Ministers, at the root of our war production business, and naturally you meet them in all these organisms of Government. This then, is the instrumentation which I believe will produce the most effective and rapid action. I am entitled to an opinion in the matter, because, after all, the House has laid on me the responsibility, and I have the right to be judged by the results. So far as the results have gone up to the present, they have given satisfaction to all concerned, and a number of very important and practical decisions have been taken by the complete and unanimous agreement of the parties concerned, followed by immediate action in the Departments.

I see—and I am endeavouring to address myself to the pith of the argument which has been adduced—that some critics have asked. "Are you not overburdening these Ministers, each with his own Department, by making this one chairman, and these others members, of this Import or Production Executive? If they have to do all this work on these Executives, how are they going to do their own work?" But this is exactly their own work. This is the particular work they have to do. The management of these affairs and its interplay with other Departments constitute the major problem before each one of them.

I saw that someone wrote in a newspaper that this was a policy of thrusting executives upon overburdened Ministries. Well, that is like saying you are thrusting the Stock Exchange upon stockbrokers, or thrusting upon general managers of railways, at a time when railway action had to be concerted, frequent or occasional meetings together. This is the very process by which our business will be discharged. As to the Chairman of this Committee, he is not "*facile princeps*" but "*primus inter pares*," which, for the benefit of any old Etonions present, I should, if very severely pressed, venture to translate. At any rate, all these Ministries have equal and direct responsibilities. But it is asked, "Why should you not choose less busy men for these tasks?" It surely would not be any help to these busy men to burden them with the task of explaining over and over again their business to others who cannot know a tithe of what they know about it themselves, and then, when inevitable differences arise, having to carry them up to the Cabinet and fight all over again there.

The way to help busy men is to help them to come to a decision together by agreement and to give them power to make this decision promptly effective through all parts of the Government machinery at their disposal. I have my views about this, having served in so many capacities and relationships, and I can assure the House that there is no more formidable and effective organization of power than a unit of four or five consenting minds, each of which has at its disposal full and necessary powers for the discharge of the business entrusted to it. It is not for these executives to decide how many men shall be allotted to the Army, Navy or Air Force, or how much shipping shall be used to bring in food or materials, or carry troops to this campaign or that. These particular blockings-in belong in the main to the War Cabinet, and I accept the responsibility of making sure that the general policy determined by the War Cabinet is interpreted correctly by the executives. In the event of differences I hope to adjust them, and if I fail the matter must be settled, in the last resort, by the Cabinet. In no other way can business in war-time proceed with the necessary dispatch. However, it is most desirable that the Cabinet itself should not be overburdened with business. Ministers must be free when they will to stand away from the intricate machinery of government and the routine of daily work and together survey the stormy skies. Therefore, in order to diminish the number of occasions on which it is necessary to have recourse to the Cabinet, we have this Steering or Planning Committee, over which the Lord President of the Council presides, which deals with the larger issues, and also deals with questions of adjustment. It is fitted to do so, because, although it is not exactly the Cabinet, it contains a very large proportion of its members. The chairmen of the two Executive Committees, the Chancellor of the Exchequer, who at this point—having, of course, already approved departmental purchases as a matter of routine— comes in on general policy, the Minister charged with reconstruction, and the Ministers at the head of the Security and Home Departments, should be able to settle most things there without its being necessary to bring these matters to the Cabinet presided over by the Prime Minister. In this way I hope my own work, which is considerable, will be reduced and more effectively devolved.

I must say a word about the functions of the Minister charged with the study of post-war problems and reconstruction. It is not his task to make a new world, comprising a new Heaven, a new earth, and no doubt a new hell (as I am sure that would be neces-

sary in any balanced system). It is not his duty to set up a new
order or to create a new heart in the human breast. These tasks
must be undertaken by other agencies. The task is to plan in
advance a number of large practical steps which it is indispensable
to take if our society is to move forward, as it must, which steps
can be far larger and taken far more smoothly if they are made with
something of the same kind of national unity as has been achieved
under the pressure of this present struggle for life. The scope of
his task is practical, and has regard to national unity on the one
hand and about three years as a time limit on the other. There
certainly will be four or five great spheres of action in which
practical and immediate advance may be made if we can continue
on the morrow of the victory to act with the unity which we shall
have used to bring that victory about. I feel he is very well fitted
for this great task, and it gives him a grand and growing opportunity of historic national service.

Now I leave these matters of Governmental machinery, and I
turn to the larger issues. I am sure there are an awful lot of things
which could be done better, and I do not at all resent criticism, even
when, for the sake of emphasis, it for a time parts company with
reality. But are things being so very ill done here, and so much
less effectively done here, than they are in the great dictator countries? Let us look into this. At the root of all questions of man-
power lies the size of the Army. The Navy and Air Force make
gigantic demands upon us, but the great customers for man-power
are the Army and the industries which sustain the Army. The
size of the Army was settled within a few weeks of the outbreak of
war. We have not altered that decision, except to the extent of
providing for the equipment of ten more divisions. The scale of the
Army is the scale which was settled in November, 1939. I am not
going to say how many divisions it amounts to, but it is a very
large and formidable force, both in connection with sea-power and
amphibious power, and of course for the defence of these islands.
Counting the Home Guard, we have round about 4,000,000 armed
and uniformed men who would all play their part in defence of our
hearths and homes. But naturally the armies which could be put
into the field and taken overseas in formed military units would be
measured by quite different standards—the principal standard
would be fixed by the shipping tonnage available. At the time when
the scale of the Army was settled, in 1939, a vast series of factories,
plants and establishments were set on foot, sufficient to provide
this Army with all that it would require in continuous action on the
Continent of Europe against the German enemy. The bulk of these

new plants are only just beginning to come into production, and many of them are still structurally incomplete. We have a very large number of plants which are all simultaneously three-quarters or four-fifths finished. That is what happens at this period in any war when you change from peace production to war production. As these plants come into operation, the constructive services—the builders and those who lay on the water, light and power and make the communications—will depart, and the munition workers will have to be assembled. All this takes time, and you cannot go faster than a certain speed. Perhaps we might go a little faster; by all means let us try, but the stages cannot be omitted. Earl Winterton was very scornful yesterday about the Minister of Labour because he said that we had more people now employed in munitions and aircraft than we had in 1918. I was astonished that my Noble Friend, who has some experience of Government, should show himself so unaware of the slow and gradual process of munition production, because he said he had been my follower in the re-armament agitation, and I have repeatedly explained to the House in the last three or four years how lengthy and gradual this process must inevitably be.

It is not possible to make a warship go to see and fight against the enemy until the fires have been lighted under the boilers, and have got hold, until the water has got tepid, and has got warm, and finally until steam and vast power has been generated. Whilst this is going on there is no use rushing about uttering alarming cries. This is not a very good thing to do if you happen to be one of the people who did not start to warm up the boilers in good time.

I was Minister of Munitions in July, 1918, and I am therefore able to measure more or less the intensity of the effort of munitions production which was then going on. I was greatly encouraged to learn some weeks ago that in the sixteenth month of this war we had already surpassed by several hundred thousand workers the number of persons employed in munitions and aircraft production in the forty-eighth month of the last war, and it was mentioned from the Labour benches that the productivity of one pair of human hands has greatly increased in the interval. I have kept myself constantly informed of the great tide of new factories which are rising to a productive level. In the next six months we shall have for the first time an intense demand upon our man-power and woman-power. This is the problem that lies before us. We are now about to enter, for the first time in this war, the period of man-power stringency, because for the first time we are going to have the apparatus and the lay-out which this man-power and woman-

47

power will be required to handle. That is the reason for the very far-reaching declaration of which the Minister of Labour thought it necessary to apprise the House and the country.

Now is the time when the full war effort will gradually be able to be realized as the plants come into being. It is true that we have not so many women employed as we had in 1918, but there are two reasons, one, which was given, that so many more were employed already before the war situation began—that is a reason which is very important—and also the shell-filling factories are only gradually coming into being. They were only constructed after the outbreak of war.

I am, of course, aware that a mechanized army makes an enormous additional drain upon the administrative and tactical branches which lie behind the fighting vehicles. I have thought, nevertheless, for some time that the Army and the Air Force—the Navy not so much—have a great need to comb their tails in order to magnify their teeth. I have felt for some time that there was considerable scope for saving of man-power in the rearward and preparatory services in order to develop the highest economy and the highest manifestation of fighting power. I look to very considerable combings and scrapings in the Air Force and the Army, particularly the Army, not in order to cut these Forces down, but in order to reduce their demands upon the man-power market as far as possible during the coming stringent months, so that we shall be able to man the new factories and shipyards and to till the new fields which are coming into production. Both these fighting Departments are engaged in this process at the present time, and the Army in particular are making very great savings from their rearward services in order to promote the forward sharpening and expansion which is necessary.

In all this the Army problem has been greatly eased because, in the mercy of God, we have had no slaughter or wastage comparable to the last war. It is, indeed, amazing that after 16 months of war between the greatest States armed with the most deadly weapons not more than 60,000 British folks, nearly half of whom are civilians, have lost their lives by enemy action. It is a terrible figure, but it is far less than in a single protracted battle on the Western Front in 1916, 1917 or 1918. Therefore, while our Army is growing every week in power, strength, efficiency and equipment, and while a decisive expansion of the Air Force is in progress, it is the munition factories and agriculture rather than the fighting Services which will in the next five or six months make the chief demand for man-power upon the public. It is to these problems and tasks that we are now addressing ourselves.

48

Criticism is easy; achievement is more difficult. I do not pretend that there is no room for improvement and for acceleration, even apart from the methodical expansion which is going on. It is certain that the peak of our war effort has not yet been reached. It cannot be reached until the plants are all working, but my mind goes back, not to what has been said here, but to what I read outside a few weeks ago, when our critics were crying out about our inaction against Italy and wondering whose was the hidden hand that was shielding Mussolini from British wrath. At that time I endured the taunts in silence because I knew that the large and daring measures had already been taken which have since rendered possible the splendid victories in Libya—Sidi Barrani, Bardia, and it may well be that while I am speaking Tobruk and all it contains are in our hands. Apart from the Libyan victories, extremely important developments are taking place on both frontiers of Abyssinia and in Eritrea which may themselves be productive and fruitful of pregnant results.

Far be it from me to paint a rosy picture of the future. Indeed, I do not think we should be justified in using any but the more sombre tones and colours while our people, our Empire and indeed the whole English-speaking world are passing through a dark and deadly valley. But I should be failing in my duty if, on the other side, I were not to convey the true impression, namely, that this great nation is getting into its war stride. It is accomplishing the transition from the days of peace and comfort to those of supreme, organized, indomitable exertion. Still more should I fail in my duty were I to suggest that the future, with all its horrors, contains any element which justifies lassitude, despondency or despair. His Majesty's Government welcome the stimulus that the House of Commons and the Press and the public of this island give to us in driving forward our war effort, and in trying to gain an earlier inch or a more fruitful hour, wherever it may be possible; but I have no doubt that the House, in its overwhelming majority, nay almost unanimously, will wish also to give its tribute of encouragement as well as its dose of correction, and will lend the heave of its own loyal strength to the forward surges which have now begun.

A LEADER OF EMPIRE

A TRIBUTE TO THE LATE LORD LLOYD

A SPEECH TO THE HOUSE OF COMMONS
FEBRUARY 6, 1941

January 24. Lord Halifax, new British Ambassador to the United States, landed in America after a secret crossing in Britain's new battleship, King George V. *He was met personally by President Roosevelt.*

January 26. British troops penetrated into Italian Somaliland, *every part of Italy's African Empire now being invaded.*

January 29. General Metaxas, Greek Prime Minister, died and was succeeded by Korizis.

January 30. British captured Derna (Libya) and continued advance on Benghazi.

   Hitler, in Berlin speech, threatened to torpedo U.S. ships.

February 2. Great R.A.F. day air offensive against German-occupied France and Belgium is hailed as first step in pushing back air frontier.

   Admiral Darlan left Vichy for Paris to confer with Hitler's representatives.

February 4. Mr. Wendel Willkie, defeated candidate in the U.S. Presidential election, received by the King and Queen in London·

February 5. Lord Lloyd, Secretary of State for the Colonies and leader of the House of Lords, died.

February 6. Mr. John G. Winant appointed United States Ambassador to Great Britain.

   Sir Kingsley Wood, Chancellor of the Exchequer, disclosed that the war was costing Great Britain £10,500,000 a day.

[*February 6, 1941.*

THE House will have learned with sorrow of the loss, that not only His Majesty's Government, but our country and the whole Empire, have sustained in the sudden and unexpected death of the Secretary of State for the Colonies and newly-chosen Leader of the House of Lords. To me the loss is particularly painful. Lord Lloyd and I have been friends for many years and close political associates during the last twelve years. We championed several causes together which did not command the applause of large majorities; but it is just in that kind of cause, where one is swimming against the stream, that one learns the worth and quality of a comrade and friend.

The late Lord Lloyd was a man of high ability. He had energy, he had industry; and these were spurred throughout his life by a consuming desire to serve the country and uphold the British name. He had travelled far and had acquired an immense mass of special knowledge, particularly knowledge of Egypt, East Africa, Arabia and India. He was deeply versed in the affairs of the unhappy countries in the South-East of Europe, which now lie under the shadow of approaching danger and misery. In all these spheres, his opinion and advice were of the highest value. Having served under Lawrence in the Desert War, he had acquired a great love for the Arab race, and he devoted a large part of his life to their interests. His name is known and his death will be mourned in wide circles of the Moslem world. When we remember that the King-Emperor is the ruler of incomparably more Mahommedan subjects than any other Prince of Islam, we may, from this angle, measure the serious nature of the loss we have sustained.

George Lloyd fought for his country on land and in the air. As honorary commodore of an air squadron, he learned to fly a Hurricane aeroplane and obtained a pilot's certificate when almost 60 years of age, thus proving that it is possible for a man to maintain in very high efficiency eye and hand, even after a lifetime of keen intellectual work. He was a very good friend of the Royal Air Force, and, in recent years, was President of the Navy League. His was the voice which, as far back as 1934, moved a resolution at the National Union of Conservative Associations which led that body to urge upon the then Government a policy of immediate rearmament. Although an Imperialist and, in some way, an authoritarian, he had a profound, instinctive aversion from Nazism. He foresaw from the beginning the danger of Hitler's rise to power and above all to armed power, and he lived and acted during the last four or five years under a sense of the rapidly growing danger to this country.

For two long and critical periods, covering together nearly ten years, he represented the Crown, as Governor of Bombay, or as High Commissioner in Egypt. His administration of the Bombay Presidency was at once firm and progressive, and the Lloyd reservoir across the Indus River in Sind, which is the base of the largest irrigation scheme in the world and irrigates an area, formerly a wilderness, about the size of Wales—this great barrage, the Lloyd barrage, as it is called, is a monument which will link his name to the prosperity of millions yet unborn, who will see around them villages, townships, temples and fertile fields where all was formerly naught but savage scrub and sand. Lord Lloyd took over the High Commissionership of Egypt in the dark hour after the murder of Sir Lee Stack. He restored during his tenure, a very great measure of stability and tranquillity to the Nile Valley, and he achieved this without violence or bloodshed. He gained the good will of important elements in Egypt without sacrificing British interests, and our relations with Egypt have progressively improved since those days, though other hands and other points of view have played their part in that. If he, like other British statesmen, promised to protect the people of the Egyptian Delta from foreign aggression, he lived long enough to see all the obligations and undertakings of Great Britain to the Egyptian people brilliantly vindicated by the decisions of war.

When I was called upon to form the present Administration, in the heat of the great battle in France, it was a comfort to me to be able to reach out to so trusted a friend. Although his views, like perhaps some of mine, were very often opposed to the Labour party, I say, with the full assent of all his Labour colleagues, that he gained their respect and confidence and their regard in all those trying months, and that they found many deep points of agreement with him of which they had not previously been aware. The departure of Lord Halifax to the United States made it necessary to choose a new Leader for the House of Lords on behalf of the Government, and Lord Lloyd was selected for that important task. This gave him a great deal of satisfaction, and on the evening, two hours before his death, he conversed with others of his friends about the future work which lay before him in an expanding field and spoke with hopefulness and satisfaction about his ability to discharge it. Then, very suddenly, he was removed from us by death.

I should like to think, as one would like to think of every man in this House and elsewhere, that he died at the apex, at the summit, of his career. It is sometimes said that good men are scarce. It is perhaps because the spate of events with which we attempt to cope and which we strive to control have far exceeded, in this modern age, the old bounds, that they have been swollen up to giant proportions, while, all the time, the stature and intellect of man remains unchanged. All the more, therefore, do we feel the loss of this highminded and exceptionally gifted and experienced public servant. I feel I shall only be discharging my duties to the House when I express, in their name, our sympathy for his widow, who has shared so many of his journeys and all the ups and downs of his active life, and who, in her grief, may have the comfort of knowing what men and women of all parties think and feel about the good and faithful servant we have lost.

"GIVE US THE TOOLS AND WE WILL
FINISH THE JOB"

A BROADCAST ADDRESS
FEBRUARY 9, 1941

February 7. Benghazi captured by British troops, who thus held
all Eastern Libya.
February 8. "Lend and Lease" Bill passed the United States House
of Representatives.
   Mr. Malcolm MacDonald, Minister of Health,
appointed High Commissioner to Canada.
February 9. British armoured columns advanced from Benghazi to
the borders of Tripolitania.
   British warships bombarded Genoa.
   Petain appointed Darlan Vice-Premier and Foreign
Minister in Vichy Government.

[February 9, 1941.

F IVE months have passed since I spoke to the British nation and
the Empire on the broadcast. In wartime there is a lot to be
said for the motto: "Deeds, not words." All the same, it is a good
thing to look around from time to time and take stock, and certainly
our affairs have prospered in several directions during these last
four or five months, far better than most of us would have ventured
to hope.

We stood our ground and faced the two Dictators in the hour of
what seemed their overwhelming triumph, and we have shown
ourselves capable, so far, of standing up against them alone. After
the heavy defeats of the German Air Force by our fighters in
August and September, Herr Hitler did not dare attempt the
invasion of this Island, although he had every need to do so and
although he had made vast preparations. Baffled in this mighty
project, he sought to break the spirit of the British nation by the
bombing, first of London, and afterwards of our great cities. It has
now been proved, to the admiration of the world, and of our friends
in the United States, that this form of blackmail by murder and

terrorism, so far from weakening the spirit of the British nation, has only roused it to a more intense and universal flame than was ever seen before in any modern community.

The whole British Empire has been proud of the Mother Country, and they long to be with us over here in even larger numbers. We have been deeply conscious of the love for us which has flowed from the Dominions of the Crown across the broad ocean spaces. *There* is the first of our war aims: to be worthy of that love, and to preserve it.

All through these dark winter months the enemy has had the power to drop three or four tons of bombs upon us for every ton we could send to Germany in return. We are arranging so that presently this will be rather the other way round; but meanwhile, London and our big cities have had to stand their pounding. They remind me of the British squares at Waterloo. They are not squares of soldiers; they do not wear scarlet coats. They are just ordinary English, Scottish and Welsh folk—men, women and children—standing steadfastly together. But their spirit is the same, their glory is the same; and, in the end, their victory will be greater than far-famed Waterloo.

All honour to the Civil Defence Services of all kinds—emergency and regular, volunteer and professional—who have helped our people through this formidable ordeal, the like of which no civilized community has ever been called upon to undergo. If I mention only one of these services here, namely the Police, it is because many tributes have been paid already to the others. But the Police have been in it everywhere, all the time, and, as a working woman wrote to me: "What gentlemen they are!"

More than two-thirds of the winter has now gone, and so far we have had no serious epidemic; indeed, there is no increase of illness in spite of the improvised conditions of the shelters. That is most creditable to our local, medical and sanitary authorities, to our devoted nursing staff, and to the Ministry of Health, whose head, Mr. Malcolm MacDonald, is now going to Canada in the important office of High Commissioner.

There is another thing which surprised me when I asked about it. In spite of all these new wartime offences and prosecutions of all kinds; in spite of all the opportunities for looting and disorder, there has been less crime this winter and there are now fewer prisoners in our gaols than in the years of peace.

We have broken the back of the winter. The daylight grows. The Royal Air Force grows, and is already certainly master of the daylight air. The attacks may be sharper, but they will be shorter;

there will be more opportunities for work and service of all kinds; more opportunities for life. So, if our first victory was the repulse of the invader, our second was the frustration of his acts of terror and torture against our people at home.

Meanwhile, abroad, in October, a wonderful thing happened. One of the two Dictators—the crafty, cold-blooded, black-hearted Italian, who had thought to gain an Empire on the cheap by stabbing fallen France in the back, got into trouble. Without the slightest provocation, spurred on by lust of power and brutish greed, Mussolini attacked and invaded Greece, only to be hurled back ignominiously by the heroic Greek Army; who, I will say, with your consent, have revived before our eyes the glories which from the classic age gild their native land. While Signor Mussolini was writhing and smarting under the Greek lash in Albania, Generals Wavell and Wilson, who were charged with the defence of Egypt and of the Suez Canal in accordance with our treaty obligations, whose task seemed at one time so difficult, had received very powerful reinforcements of men, cannon, equipment and, above all, tanks, which we had sent from our island in spite of the invasion threat. Large numbers of troops from India, Australia and New Zealand had also reached them. Forthwith began that series of victories in Libya which have broken irretrievably the Italian military power on the African Continent. We have all been entertained, and I trust edified, by the exposure and humiliation of another of what Byron called

> Those Pagod things of sabre sway,
> With fronts of brass, and feet of clay.

Here then, in Libya, is the third considerable event upon which we may dwell with some satisfaction. It is just exactly two months ago, to a day, that I was waiting anxiously, but also eagerly, for the news of the great counter-stroke which had been planned against the Italian invaders of Egypt. The secret had been well kept. The preparations had been well made. But to leap across those seventy miles of desert, and attack an army of ten or eleven divisions, equipped with all the appliances of modern war, who had been fortifying themselves for three months, that was a most hazardous adventure.

When the brilliant decisive victory at Sidi Barrani, with its tens of thousands of prisoners, proved that we had quality, manœuvring power and weapons superior to the enemy, who had boasted so much of his virility and his military virtues, it was evident that all the other Italian forces in Eastern Libya were in great danger. They could not easily beat a retreat along the coastal road without running the risk of being caught in the open by our armoured divisions and brigades ranging far out into the desert in tremendous swoops and scoops. They had to expose themselves to being attacked piecemeal.

General Wavell—nay, all our leaders, and all their lithe, active, ardent men, British, Australian, Indian, in the Imperial Army, saw their opportunity. At that time I ventured to draw General Wavell's attention to the seventh chapter of the Gospel of St. Matthew, at the seventh verse, where, as you all know—or ought to know—it is written: "Ask, and it shall be given; seek, and ye shall find; knock, and it shall be opened unto you." The Army of the Nile has asked, and it was given; they sought, and they have found; they knocked, and it has been opened unto them. In barely eight weeks, by a campaign which will long be studied as a model of the military art, an advance of over 400 miles has been made. The whole Italian Army in the east of Libya, which was reputed to exceed 150,000 men, has been captured or destroyed. The entire province of Cyrenaica—nearly as big as England and Wales—has been conquered. The unhappy Arab tribes, who have for thirty years suffered from the cruelty of Italian rule, carried in some cases to the point of methodical extermination, these Bedouin survivors have at last seen their oppressors in disorderly flight, or led off in endless droves as prisoners of war.

Egypt and the Suez Canal are safe, and the port, the base and the airfields of Benghazi constitute a strategic point of high consequence to the whole of the war in the Eastern Mediterranean.

This is the time, I think, to speak of the leaders who, at the head of their brave troops, have rendered this distinguished service to the King. The first and foremost, General Wavell, Commander-in-Chief of all the Armies of the Middle East, has proved himself a master of war, sage, painstaking, daring and tireless. But General Wavell has repeatedly asked that others should share his fame.

General Wilson, who actually commands the Army of the Nile, was reputed to be one of our finest tacticians—and few will now deny that quality. General O'Connor commanding the 13th Corps, with General Mackay commanding the splendid Australians, and General Creagh who trained and commanded the various armoured divisions which were employed; these three men executed the complicated and astoundingly rapid movements which were made, and fought the actions which occurred. I have just seen a telegram from General Wavell in which he says that the success at Benghazi was due to the outstanding leadership and resolution of O'Connor and Creagh, ably backed by Wilson.

I must not forget here to point out the amazing mechanical feats of the British tanks, whose design and workmanship have beaten all records and stood up to all trials: and show us how closely and directly the work in the factories at home is linked with the victories abroad.

Of course, none of our plans would have succeeded had not our pilots, under Air Chief Marshal Longmore, wrested the control of the air from a far more numerous enemy. Nor would the campaign itself have been possible if the British Mediterranean Fleet, under Admiral Cunningham, had not chased the Italian Navy into its harbours and sustained every forward surge of the Army with all the flexible resources of sea-power. How far-reaching these resources are we can see from what happened at dawn this morning, when our Western Mediterranean Fleet, under Admiral Somerville, entered the Gulf of Genoa and bombarded in a shattering manner the naval base from which perhaps a Nazi German expedition might soon have sailed to attack General Weygand in Algeria or Tunis. It is right that the Italian people should be made to feel the sorry plight into which they have been dragged by Dictator Mussolini; and if the cannonade of Genoa, rolling along the coast, reverberating in the mountains, reached the ears of our French comrades in their grief and misery, it might cheer them with the feeling that friends—active friends—are near, and that Britannia rules the waves.

The events in Libya are only part of the story: they are only part of the story of the decline and fall of the Italian Empire, that will not take a future Gibbon so long to write as the original work. Fifteen hundred miles away to the southward a strong British and Indian army, having driven the invaders out of the Sudan, is marching steadily forward through the Italian colony of Eritrea, thus seeking to complete the isolation of all the Italian troops in Abyssinia. Other British forces are entering Abyssinia from the west, while the army gathered in Kenya—in the van of which we may discern the powerful forces of the Union of South Africa, organized by General Smuts—is striking northward along the whole enormous front. Lastly, the Ethiopian patriots, whose independence was stolen five years ago, have risen in arms; and their Emperor, so recently an exile in England, is in their midst to fight for their freedom and his throne. Here, then, we see the beginnings of a process of reparation and of the chastisement of wrongdoing, which reminds us that though the mills of God grind slowly, they grind exceeding small.

While these auspicious events have been carrying us stride by stride from what many people thought a forlorn position, and was certainly a very grave position in May and June, to one which permits us to speak with sober confidence of our power to discharge our duty, heavy though it be, in the future—while this has been happening, a mighty tide of sympathy, of goodwill and of effective aid, has begun to flow across the Atlantic in support of the world cause which is at stake. Distinguished Americans have come over to see things here at the front, and to find out how the United States can help us best and soonest. In Mr. Hopkins, who has been my frequent companion during the last three weeks, we have the Envoy of the President, a President who has been newly re-elected to his august office. In Mr. Wendell Willkie we have welcomed the champion of the great Republican Party. We may be sure that they will both tell the truth about what they have seen over here, and more than that we do not ask. The rest we leave with good confidence to the judgment of the President, the Congress and the people of the United States.

I have been so very careful, since I have been Prime Minister, not to encourage false hopes or prophesy smooth and easy things, and yet the tale that I have to tell to-day is one which must justly and rightly give us cause for deep thankfulness, and also, I think, for strong comfort and even rejoicing. But now I must dwell upon the more serious, darker and more dangerous aspects of the vast scene of the war. We must all of us have been asking ourselves: what has that wicked man whose crime-stained regime and system are at bay and in the toils—what has he been preparing during these winter months? What new devilry is he planning? What new small country will he overrun or strike down? What fresh form of assault will he make upon our island home and fortress; which—let there be no mistake about it—is all that stands between him and the dominion of the world?

We may be sure that the war is soon going to enter upon a phase of greater violence. Hitler's confederate, Mussolini, has reeled back in Albania; but the Nazis—having absorbed Hungary and driven Rumania into a frightful internal convulsion—are now already upon the Black Sea. A considerable Nazi German army and air force is being built up in Rumania, and its forward tentacles have already penetrated Bulgaria. With—we must suppose—the acquiescence of the Bulgarian Government, airfields are being occupied by German ground personnel numbering thousands, so as to enable the German air force to come into action from Bulgaria. Many preparations have been made for the movement of German troops into or through Bulgaria, and perhaps this southward movement has already begun.

We saw what happened last May in the Low Countries; how they hoped for the best; how they clung to their neutrality; how woefully they were deceived, overwhelmed, plundered, enslaved and since starved. We know how we and the French suffered when, at the last moment, at the urgent belated appeal of the King of the Belgians, we went to his aid. Of course, if all the Balkan peoples stood together and acted together, aided by Britain and Turkey, it would be many months before a German army and air force of sufficient strength to overcome them could be assembled in the south-east of Europe. And in those months much might happen. Much will certainly happen as American aid becomes effective, as our air power grows, as we become a well-armed nation, and as our armies in the East increase in strength. But nothing is more certain than that, if the countries of south-eastern Europe allow themselves to be pulled to pieces one by one, they will share the fate of Denmark, Holland and Belgium. And none can tell how long it will be before the hour of their deliverance strikes.

One of our difficulties is to convince some of these neutral countries in Europe that we are going to win. We think it astonishing that they should be so dense as not to see it as clearly as we do ourselves. I remember in the last war, in July, 1915, we began to think that Bulgaria was going wrong, so Mr. Lloyd George, Mr. Bonar Law, Sir F. E. Smith and I, asked the Bulgarian Minister to dinner to explain to him what a fool King Ferdinand would make of himself if he were to go in on the losing side. It was no use. The poor man simply could not believe it, or could not make his Government believe it. So Bulgaria, against the wishes of her peasant population, agains all her interests, fell in at the Kaiser's tail and got sadly carved up and punished when the victory was won. I trust that Bulgaria is not going to make the same mistake again. If they do, the Bulgarian peasantry and people, for whom there has been much regard, both in Great Britain and in the United States, will for the third time in thirty years have been made to embark upon a needless and disastrous war.

In the Central Mediterranean the Italian Quisling, who is called Mussolini, and the French Quisling, commonly called Laval, are both in their different ways trying to make their countries into doormats for Hitler and his New Order, in the hope of being able to keep, or get the Nazi Gestapo and Prussian bayonets to enforce, their rule upon their fellow-countrymen. I cannot tell how the matter will go, but at any rate we shall do our best to fight for the Central Mediterranean.

I dare say you will have noticed the very significant air action which was fought over Malta a fortnight ago. The Germans sent an entire *Geschwader* of dive-bombers to Sicily. They seriously injured our new aircraft-carrier *Illustrious*, and then, as this wounded ship was sheltering in Malta harbour, they concentrated upon her all their force so as to beat her to pieces. But they were met by the batteries of Malta, which is one of the strongest defended fortresses in the world against air attack; they were met by the Fleet Air Arm and by the Royal Air Force, and, in two or three days, they had lost, out of a hundred and fifty dive-bombers, upwards of ninety, fifty of which were destroyed in the air and forty on the ground. Although the *Illustrious,* in her damaged condition, was one of the great prizes of the air and naval war, the German *Geschwader* accepted the defeat; they would not come any more. All the necessary repairs were made to the *Illustrious* in Malta harbour, and she steamed safely off to Alexandria under her own power at 23 knots. I dwell upon this incident, not at all because I think it disposes of the danger in the Central Mediterranean, but in order to show you that there, as elsewhere, we intend to give a good account of ourselves.

But after all, the fate of this war is going to be settled by what happens on the oceans, in the air, and—above all—in this island. It seems now to be certain that the Government and people of the United States intend to supply us with all that is necessary for victory. In the last war the United States sent two million men across the Atlantic. But this is not a war of vast armies, firing immense masses of shells at one another. We do not need the gallant armies which are forming throughout the American Union. We do not need them this year, nor next year; nor any year that I can foresee. But we do need most urgently an immense and continuous supply of war materials and technical apparatus of all kinds. We need them here and we need to bring them here. We shall need a great mass of shipping in 1942, far more than we can build ourselves, if we are to maintain and augment our war effort in the West and in the East.

These facts are, of course, all well known to the enemy, and we must therefore expect that Herr Hitler will do his utmost to prey upon our shipping and to reduce the volume of American supplies entering these islands. Having conquered France and Norway, his clutching fingers reach out on both sides of us into the ocean. I have never underrated this danger, and you know I have never concealed it from you. Therefore, I hope you will believe me when I say that I have complete confidence in the Royal Navy, aided by the Air Force of the Coastal Command, and that in one way or another I am sure they will be able to meet every changing phase of this truly mortal struggle, and that sustained by the courage of our merchant seamen, and of the dockers and workmen of all our ports, we shall outwit, outmanœuvre, outfight and outlast the worst that the enemy's malice and ingenuity can contrive.

I have left the greatest issue to the end. You will have seen that Sir John Dill our principal military adviser, the Chief of the Imperial General Staff, has warned us all that Hitler may be forced, by the strategic, economic and political stresses in Europe, to try to invade these islands in the near future. That is a warning which no one should disregard. Naturally, we are working night and day to have everything ready. Of course, we are far stronger than we ever were before, incomparably stronger than we were in July, August and September. Our Navy is more powerful, our flotillas are more numerous; we are far stronger, actually and relatively, in the air above these islands, than we were when our Fighter Command beat off and beat down the Nazi attack last autumn. Our Army is more numerous, more mobile and far better equipped and trained than in September, and still more than in July.

I have the greatest confidence in our Commander-in-Chief, General Brooke, and in the generals of proved ability who, under him, guard the different quarters of our land. But most of all I put my faith in the simple unaffected resolve to conquer or die which will animate and inspire nearly four million Britons with serviceable weapons in their hands. It is not an easy military operation to invade an island like Great Britain, without the command of the sea and without the command of the air, and then to face what will be waiting for the invader here. But I must drop one word of caution; for next to cowardice and treachery, over-confidence, leading to neglect or slothfulness, is the worst of martial crimes. Therefore, I drop one word of caution. A Nazi invasion of Great Britain last autumn would have been a more or less improvised affair. Hitler took it for granted that when France gave in we should give in; but we did not give in. And he had to think again. An invasion now will be supported by a much more carefully prepared tackle and equipment of landing-craft and other apparatus, all of which will have been planned and manufactured in the winter months. We must all be prepared to meet gas attacks, parachute attacks, and glider attacks, with constancy, forethought and practised skill.

I must again emphasize what General Dill has said, and what I pointed out myself last year. In order to win the war Hitler must destroy Great Britain. He may carry havoc into the Balkan States; he may tear great provinces out of Russia; he may march to the Caspian; he may march to the gates of India. All of this will avail him nothing. It may spread his curse more widely throughout Europe and Asia, but it will not avert his doom. With every month that passes the many proud and once happy countries he is now holding down by brute force and vile intrigue are learning to hate the Prussian yoke and the Nazi name as nothing has ever been hated so fiercely and so widely among men before. And all the time, masters of the sea and air, the British Empire—nay, in a certain sense, the whole English-speaking world—will be on his track, bearing with them the swords of justice.

The other day, President Roosevelt gave his opponent in the late Presidential Election, a letter of introduction to me, and in it he wrote out a verse, in his own handwriting, from Longfellow, which he said, "applies to you people as it does to us." Here is the verse:

> . . . Sail on, O Ship of State!
> Sail on, O Union, strong and great!
> Humanity with all its fears,
> With all the hopes of future years,
> Is hanging breathless on thy fate!

What is the answer that I shall give, in your name, to this great man, the thrice-chosen head of a nation of a hundred and thirty millions? Here is the answer which I will give to President Roosevelt: Put your confidence in us. Give us your faith and your blessing, and, under Providence, all will be well.

We shall not fail or falter; we shall not weaken or tire. Neither the sudden shock of battle, nor the long-drawn trials of vigilance and exertion will wear us down. Give us the tool, and we will finish the job.

63

THE MACDONALD BILL

A SPEECH TO THE HOUSE OF COMMONS
FEBRUARY 27, 1941

February 1). Britain broke off diplomatic relations with Rumania because the Germans had been allowed to use the country as a base for an expeditionary force. German soldiers also reported penetrating into Bulgaria.

February 13. Franco and Mussolini conferred for five hours at Bordighera. Later Franco met Petain at Montpellier.

February 15. Announced that British troops had been dropped in Southern Italy and had disrupted railway communications.

February 16. R.A.F. made the longest flight of the war to Cracow and Katowice and back—1,800 miles—and dropped leaflets.

February 17. Turkey and Bulgaria signed a non-aggression pact with Britain's approval.

February 18. Strong forces of Australian troops landed at Singapore.

Announced that 1,502 civilians were killed and 2,012 injured in January air raids on Britain—the lowest monthly total since the heavy raids began.

February 20. Mr. Eden (Foreign Secretary) and General Dill (Chief of the Imperial General Staff) in Cairo to "review political and military situation in the Middle East."

February 23. Mussolini, in a speech in Rome, admitted the loss of a fifth of the Italian air force and a tenth of the Italian army.

February 24. Hitler, in a speech at Munich, threatened naval warfare "such as Britain never dreamed of."

February 26. British East and West African troops captured Mogadishu, capital of Italian Somaliland.

Mr. Eden and General Dill conferred in Ankara with Turkish leaders.

February 27. First clash between British troops and German mechanized units in Libya announced.

NOTE

When Mr. Malcolm MacDonald, Minister of Health, was appointed High Commissioner in Canada, a Bill was introduced into the House of Commons enabling him to retain his seat in Parliament. The Bill, entitled the "House of Commons Disqualification (Temporary Provisions) Bill," applied generally to members who undertook special missions during the war. The Bill was described as making "temporary provision for enabling persons required in the public interest to be employed for purposes connected with the war in offices and places under the Crown to be so employed without being disqualified for membership of the House of Commons." The Bill was passed after some opposition. This speech by the Prime Minister was made in the debate on the Second Reading of the Bill.

[*February 27, 1941.*

I MUST say that I have experienced a sensation of relief at the air of detachment which prevails in this House, and which seems to me in such very sharp contrast to some of the grave realities which are proceeding out of doors.

I must ask the House to give His Majesty's Government the minor facilities and conveniences—for that is all they are—which are afforded to us in this Bill. I must make it a question of confidence, because it touches definitely our war effort, it arises directly out of the war, and it is concerned only with the period of the war. If there is a suggestion—it has not been pressed in any quarter in any unkind manner—that the Government will abuse their powers under this Bill and proceed by mean and flagitious manœuvres to perpetuate their tenure of power, if there were such suggestions, either tacit or spoken, obviously that also would be a matter of confidence.

The Attorney-General has described the existing position and has shown the confusion of accident and anomaly, of legal fiction and Parliamentary circumnavigation, into which we have fallen over generations, quite innocently and for good reasons, and in which we now lie. This now seems to have been brought to a head by the case of the Member for Ross and Cromarty (Mr. Malcolm MacDonald). But the need for the Bill had already become imperative, even if this particular appointment had not been made.

Although this Bill is associated with a particular case, the circumstances which have rendered it necessary are far more general in their application, and I do not think it is possible to state a case against the Bill on grounds of high constitutional principle. The Member for Cambridge University (Mr. Pickthorn) seemed to seek to do so, but I should warn the House against lending countenance to the constitutional doctrine which he has

65

enunciated. He told us that the legislative functions of Parliament had ceased to be important. He even said that the control of finance had ceased to be real or important, although that is the structure around which the whole of our procedure had been built. What he considered the function of the House of Commons to be— and I took the trouble to write down his words—was

"a market upon which the price of the Prime Minister's stock is based."

I deprecate this squalid language of the bucket-shop as applied to the serious, responsible functions of the State, and I think it would be lamentable if the youth of a great centre of learning should be tempted to accept such slipshod and questionable guidance. The truth is that all the fundamental constitutional principles concerned with the holding of offices of profit and the vacation of seats— which was the real point behind this apparatus—have been blurred or effaced by decisions already taken by the House in this or previous Parliaments. Anomalies arise from the fact that positions under the Crown do or do not disqualify, according to the application or interpretation of words in old Statutes passed a long time ago in different circumstances and for different purposes.

These anomalies have continually been the target for Parliamentary attention and correction in recent years. Successive enactments have freed Ministers of the Crown from the need of re-election on appointment to office. This has been found convenient in practice, and we have lent ourselves, perhaps too readily, to those great changes. But they have been made, and made in modern times. It was a very important provision that Members, on appointment to high office, should submit themselves to re-election; it was a very important provision because it prevented a Government different from that which the electors had in mind at the time of the election from taking and holding office for a time, and filling up all its posts, without the country having a chance to challenge the matter, with different persons, of perhaps quite different policies from those the electorate had been led to contemplate, and from those that the country might wish. A Government so formed, even without a majority in the House, not daring to send a Minister that it had chosen to the process of by-election— saved from that by the legislation of the House—such a Government might take executive action which would have irrevocable consequences either in the direction of war or peace. It was a safeguard of immense consequence, but the House parted with it. It has been totally discarded by the House in my lifetime.

Now that I have shown hon. Members the camel they have

already swallowed, I hope they will address themselves with renewed sense of proportion to this somewhat inconsiderable gnat. An office of profit is, in my view—I do not speak as a lawyer—a term of art. It applies to many positions where there is no remuneration. A Junior Lord of the Treasury, unpaid, is an office of profit, but a special mission, though it may be very highly paid and may last for years, is not a disqualifying office of profit. A foreign Embassy, even though, as in the case of the Member for East Bristol (Sir Stafford Cripps), it is a formal, definite, diplomatic appointment, and not a special mission in any sense, has, according to the advice we have received, been held not to disqualify as an office of profit. That advice has not been challenged, or has not yet been challenged, by the House or by the common informer. It would make no difference if the right hon. and learned Member took a salary. He takes the fees of representation necessary to the discharge of these important duties. Even though it is a formal appointment, it has not been challenged, though I must say I should have thought it was a very doubtful case. If an office was in existence before 1705, it may be held by a Member of Parliament and profit drawn from it, unless, of course, it comes under a special ban in some later Statutes, which are numerous and obscure. The High Commissionership of one of our great Dominions, not having been in existence in 1705, thus disqualifies, whereas an Embassy to a foreign country does not. I am only putting it forward to show the anomalies.

Then there is a distinction into which I shall not trouble to plunge too deeply, though it appeals, I believe, to legal and litigious minds—a distinction between an office of profit and a place of profit. Such a distinction would smite the holder of an unpaid office of profit, and would leave unscathed the paid holder of a place of profit. That is hardly a very satisfactory logical situation for us to have reached. I have been assured that it would be possible to get out of what may be called the MacDonald difficulty in the following way: The High Commissionership in Canada would be left vacant, and the right hon. Gentleman the Member for Ross and Cromarty would be sent to Canada on a special mission, and his mission would be to discharge all the functions which would normally fall to be discharged by the High Commissioner. I am not going to play such a game as that with the House of Commons. I am sure it is very much better in this matter for the Government to come frankly to the House, tell the House their difficulties, and ask for the necessary assistance and relief. And that is what we are doing.

The House has already given to the Executive immense latitude during wartime. It allows and encourages officers in the Armed Forces to serve on full pay in any rank, and to combine their public duties with their military appointments. There is no limit except, of course, that of the general control of Parliament over the Executive. There is no legal limit at all upon the multiplication of military appointments, either at the front or the rear. Regional Commissioners, without limit of number, and deputy Regional Commissioners can, as we have been reminded, hold their duties and sit in Parliament by recent wartime legislation, without re-election, whether they are paid or unpaid. The power under the emergency legislation to create new offices and appoint additional Under-Secretaries is unlimited. There are many other facilities which have been given by the House. Why have all these facilities been accorded to the Government by the House? The reason is that the House in its wisdom does not wish the Executive to be hampered in the conduct of the war, and it is quite sure that it can by its inalienable ultimate authority correct any excessive or abusive use of these immense discretionary powers. But let me say this: There never has been a Government which had less need to hire or suborn Members of Parliament to vote for them than this present Administration at this actual time.

Therefore I make these two submissions to the House: First, that the whole of this question of offices and places of profit is in a state of great legal complexity and obscurity, and that the law may strike here or there by accident or caprice without any reference to any principal of logic or reason or constitutional doctrine. That is my submission, and I think it is a subject which may well occupy the careful deliberations and study of a Select Committee with a view to clarifying the whole position, with all due respect for tradition, and with proper regard to the interests of the modern State in times of peace or party warfare.

I am very glad that there should be a Select Committee, and I would very gladly myself, if invited, give evidence before it, when I have a little more time, upon the sound and healthy constitutional usages which should be defined, preserved and established. The terms of reference which we would suggest for this committee would be: ,

"To inquire into the existing Statutes which provide for disqualification of Members of the House of Commons by reason of their holding offices or places of profit under the Crown, and to make recommendations as to the proper principles on which future legislation in normal times of peace should be based."

This is the reference which will in due course have to be submitted to the House. If the committee completed its work before the Expiring Laws Continuance Bill came on, obviously the House would include the Measure in the Expiring Laws Continuance Bill, in the light of any report that the committee might make. If desired, the committee should not be wholly limited to the post-war period, but that is a matter which can well be discussed when the Motion for appointing the Select Committee and the terms of reference are before the House. I think I should prefer to follow the course I have indicated, because I think it is the normal course. We have introduced the principle that the Bill should only last for a year, consequently the House can bring up the point on the Bill; or, if the reference is questioned, then again on the Motion for appointment of the committee it will be possible to raise the point, and I shall have a chance of giving it more consideration, and nothing will be lost in the meanwhile.

My second submission is this: The House has already given to a wicked and unworthy Executive, if such there were, immense powers of wrongdoing, so far as legality is concerned, which wrongdoing can only be corrected by turning the Government out by a hostile vote. I hope I may be allowed to leave the legal aspect and its tangles for the wider practical considerations which arise. I think we should be wise to leave it to our Select Committee to tidy up the present state of confusion and uncertainty and meanwhile get on with the war, because, although one would hardly think it, there is a war on, and life and liberties, and even wider causes, are hanging in the balance.

Let us, therefore, look at a few simple, non-legal issues which seem to me, as a layman, relevant to the subject, and which also are involved in the practical needs of the hour. The first point is this: A Member of Parliament, when he gives service to the Crown at this time of mortal conflict, ought to be able to know whether he is doing right or not. In the White Paper which has been laid before the House there are a very large number of doubtful or borderline cases. The case of the Member for Edgbaston (Mr. Bennett) stands out. Are we to regard him as a grand constitutional criminal or not? I fear that we must if this Bill is not passed. What is the crime that may be alleged against him? He was giving his highly competent service to the Ministry of Aircraft Production in an executive office as Director-General. He does not take any remuneration. He does not even draw out-of-pocket or travelling expenses. I am assured that his work is of real value in a sphere which we all know is of critical importance. Suddenly a constituency where my hon. Friend was well known and apparently well respected, with its eyes open to the office he held and to the ties which bound him to assist the Government, elected him, and he unwittingly accepted the honour.

I am assured that he might on the action of a common informer be mulcted in financial penalties, or upon a Motion in this House his election might be declared null and void. He is not alone. The Member for Ormskirk (Commander King-Hall) and the Member for Rotherhithe (Mr. Benjamin Smith) are equally in this dangerous area, but worse may come. There may be a good many more fish in the net. The Member for Burton, in his comfortable, secure position in that constituency, has not realized that not everyone is in that position of impeccable political stability which he has so long enjoyed.

I took the trouble, working into the early hours this morning, to go through the White Paper with the Law Officers of the Crown, and I am sure that there are quite a lot of other cases, most disputable, or at any rate very doubtful and challengeable, where action might be taken by the common informer. Such action would proceed in the courts at the expense of the Member concerned. It might be carried from court to court, to his endless vexation and the detriment of his war work, and, possibly, to his heavy financial loss. I do not think any fair-minded man would expect a Government which had offered and sanctioned such appointments to permit this state of uncertainty to continue or to allow men who are giving valuable and faithful services to the State at the Government's request to lie under the menace and distress of potential persecution. I am asked why I make this a vote of confidence. This is why I felt bound to do so. If these men are to be censured, let us be censured too. If they are to be punished, let us share their misfortunes. If the House will not give to them and to us this relief, then I think the House will be taking upon its shoulders a more direct responsibility than it usually desires to do, in view of the burdens, not inconsiderable, of our present-day life. And so I put before the House, as the first of the practical objects of this Bill, fair play to individual Members, and I call upon the House to give their particular attention to this aspect and ask them, in the name of the Government, to afford to these men the relief and security which are their due.

There is a second point which ought not to be overlooked. At this time, when we are fighting for our lives, surely it is in the interests of the country that the Government responsible for the safety of the people, and for the successful emergence of the British

70

Empire from its perils, should have full freedom, as long as it retains the confidence of the House of Commons, to make the best appointments which it can devise. Let me illustrate this point by another case, that of the Member for Ross and Cromarty. He had been chosen for the High Commissionership of one of our great Dominions, and he accepted the task as a wartime duty. He made no conditions, but he expressed the earnest hope and natural desire that he might remain a Member of the House of Commons. I agreed to this so far as it rested with me, and I promised to seek from Parliament any statutory powers that might be needed. It seemed to me that if the House accepted, and indeed highly approved, the sending of two of its Members as Ambassadors to Moscow and to Madrid, no very serious, certainly no novel, constitutional issue would arise if it sent another of its Members to be High Commissioner in Canada. That was my feeling. I had never dreamed that between these two cases, the two Ambassadorships and the High Commissionership in Canada, all of which are out of this country, it could have been represented that there yawned and gaped this vast, hideous gulf of constitutional principle, and I take great shame to myself for not having appreciated the point.

I would say a word on the merits of this appointment. I attach very great importance to these High Commissionerships in the Dominions. I am anxious that in this time of war we should fill vacancies which arise in the High Commissionerships so far as possible by men of outstanding political reputation who have long experience of the House of Commons and of Cabinet government. I must admit that I may be biased in favour of the House of Commons. I have lived all my life here, and I owe any part I have been able to take in public affairs entirely to the consideration with which I have been treated by the House. But making any allowances for this bias, discounting it, as I ought, I do not hesitate to say that five or ten years' experience as a Member of this House is as fine an all-round education in public affairs as any man can obtain. Sometimes we see very able men in the great professions making public speeches which are odd and ill-judged, although they are most capable, upright men, probably possessing abilities above our average here. Why, only the other day there was a military officer with a very fine record, much respected by all those with whom he worked, who wrote a letter for which he was properly censured, a letter most awkward and unhelpful to the very work on which he was engaged. Had that officer sat here even for the lifetime of a single Parliament, and rubbed shoulders with everyone, as we do, in the lobbies and elsewhere, he would never have made

71

such a goose of himself. We get to know something about each other when we work together in this House. We see men with their qualities and defects.

In appointing a House of Commons man to a position of importance and delicacy, we are not, as it were, buying a—perhaps I had better say taking a leap in the dark, as too often has to be done, especially in time of war. Therefore, I was very glad to find in the Member for Ross and Cromarty, and also in Lord Harlech, men of proved Parliamentary and Ministerial capacity and standing, and I am very glad to find that those appointments have given the greatest satisfaction both in Canada and South Africa, and have evoked the most cordial responses from those two outstanding Empire statesmen, Mr. Mackenzie King and General Smuts. It would be a pity if, in this difficult process of selection, I should be forced to confine entirely to the House of Lords the area of my advice to the Crown. There are, no doubt, many capable men in the House of Lords with long Parliamentary experience, but I do not know why it should be considered essential to the moral and constitutional well-being of the House of Commons that choice should be confined solely to the Upper Chamber. We should take the best men at this time, those best fitted to hold appointments. There is no reason why the House of Commons should place itself under a particular ban on ability in this matter.

Now there arises the question of the rights and interests of constituents. It is a very serious question. A constituency chooses a Member to represent it in this House. The Member goes off, perhaps for a long period of time, to Moscow or Madrid or Ottawa, or it may be to Mogadishu or Benghazi. Here is a constituency, as it is said, disfranchised. Is not this a great constitutional misfortune? It certainly raises an important question, and we should look at it in some detail. It is not only in the field of service to the State that such issues arise. A sheaf of examples has been furnished to me. I will not quote names. A Member may fall a victim to a long illness which totally incapacitates him, and as a result of which, after some years, he dies; or perhaps he lingers on. A Member may become mentally deranged or feeble-minded—I am not going to cite any particular instance—and so long as that Member is not actually certified a lunatic, he can hold his seat and draw his salary. A Member may be detained in prison under wartime regulations for an indefinite period—a most painful situation for any Government to become responsible for. Or he may be sent to prison by the courts for misdemeanour without the constituency having the slightest power to compel him to resign.

An even more irritating case than this, from the point of view of the constituency, is when a Member has been elected to support a particular party or a particular policy and, after he has been returned, circumstances arise which lead him, conscientiously or otherwise, to support a different party or the opposite policy. A Member again may obviously fail to represent his constituents. He may be entirely out of harmony with their views, and he may grossly misrepresent them without having the slightest intention to do so. These cases are not numerous, but they occur sometimes, and a constituency has no redress: Of course, an honourable man actuated by good taste and good feeling, would, as is the usual practice, submit himself voluntarily for re-election, but a constituency has no power whatever to make him do so. While we are on this question of Members employed abroad, let me say I have had a written message from the Member for Ross and Cromarty, in which he says:

"I wrote on the day of the announcement of my impending appointment to Canada to the Chairman of the National Committee of my constituency, saying two things: (1) That I understood the Government were introducing legislation which, if passed, would enable me to retain my seat in the House.

(2) That, nevertheless, I would offer my resignation from Parliament to the National Committee in that constituency, and would resign forthwith if the general feeling in Ross and Cromarty was that they should have a Member of Parliament who was not absent oversea."

Returning to the general theme of my argument, I have cited a whole set of cases which could easily be extended and of which many examples could be found within living memory, where the constituency for the time being is apparently disfranchised, and it is asked: "Ought we not to provide for this?" I would not mind the Select Committee considering that aspect, but, speaking as a fairly old Parliamentarian, I am myself very doubtful whether a change in our long-established practice would be beneficial to the House of Commons. Of course, there are Parliaments like the Parliament in Soviet Russia, where the constituencies have the power of recall; that is to say, if a Member or a delegate makes speeches or asks questions or gives votes of a kind not desired by his constituency, or by the party machine, a kind of round-robin of electors can be signed, and he can be forced to submit himself for re-election. This power of recall is contrary to the best interests and dignity of Parliament, and the whole Parliamentary tradition as built up in this country, which is at once the cradle and citadel of

73

Parliamentary government, is adverse to it. I believe it would give a great deal more power to the executive Government and to the party machinery, which has in recent times often been considered to be too powerful and too efficient. The independence of all Members would be affected. They would not know whether, at any time, they might not be exposed to an agitation worked up in their constituencies, and thus forced to fight a by-election on a bad wicket. We must be very careful not to take short or impulsive views on these questions when dealing with an institution of the antiquity and vitality of the House of Commons. Once we start on this business of recall for any of the reasons I have mentioned, you will find that one will lead on to another; once we start on this business of recall, we shall have altered in a degrading sense the character of the House of Commons and the status of its Members. In attempting to avoid an occasional anomaly, we might find that we had seriously affected the health and vigour of this famous, world-honoured institution. I believe it will be found on reflection far wiser to put up with these occasional hard cases than to be drawn on to the slippery slope which would lead to the promulgation of the doctrine of recall.

I have given the best reply that I can on the subject of the disfranchisement of a constituency. But there is another important Parliamentary lesson to be borne in mind by the House. It is none of our business to declare what constituencies think and wish. We learned that in the Wilkes case. In the cases of these three eminent Members who have been appointed Ambassadors or High Commissioner, from what I can hear in this time of war, when we are all working together—or are supposed to be—and are certainly in the utmost danger, and also in a very great period of national history, these constituencies regard it as a high honour that their Members have been chosen to render these distinguished services to our country and its cause. In the same way constituencies feel proud that their representatives should go to the front on active service, and face, as many have done and are doing, the level as opposed to the vertical fire of the enemy. We shall see what view will be taken in Ross and Cromarty, but at any rate it is for them and not for us. The Members for constituencies neighbouring on those of men absent on active service or on public duty are nearly always found ready to look after local business and constituency correspondence, and the public Departments will be particularly careful in replying to such correspondence to make sure that the constituency does not suffer from the absence of its Member on what I must consider as an extremely high form of public duty.

There is, I am told, quite a lot of feeling in the country that we all ought to help as much as we can, and constituencies are glad to make a sacrifice in being inconvenienced if they think it conduces to the national advantage and safety. That is my answer to the question about the rights and interests of constituencies, and I hope that it also will be carefully considered by the House. Thus, there is the question of fair play to the individual Member, there is the question of the interest of the State in the freedom of choice and appointment, and there is the question of the alleged disadvantage to the constituency.

I come to the last issue which arises from this Bill. Is it in the interests of the House of Commons that its Members should play active, useful, and perhaps distinguished parts in the great struggle which is now going on, or ought they to confine themselves strictly to Parliamentary business and attendance upon this House? I may say that the House, or some of its Members, have shown themselves rather changeable upon this point. I remember my predecessor, the late Mr. Neville Chamberlain, drawing a very strict line against the employment of Members of Parliament, and considerable offence being given, and his modifying that line to meet the wish of the House. For my own part, I have a very clear opinion, which I expressed in the Debate on the Address last November. Here is what I said—and it met, as I thought, with general approval—

"I entirely agree with what has been said about the desirability of Members of Parliament serving not only in the military forces but in all other forms of warfare and discharging their Parliamentary duties at the same time or in alternation. No doubt, difficulties arise, but I think they are well covered, and that the good sense of the House and of hon. Members will enable these dual and occasionally conflicting functions to be discharged."

I went on to say—I abridge it a little—that the fact

"that this House should be a House of active living personalities, engaged to the hilt in the national struggle, each according to the full strength that he has to give, each according to the aptitudes which he possesses, is, I think, one of the sources of the strength of the Parliamentary institution."

I think this policy commanded the entire approval of the House. And there are many traditions which justify the desire of the Government to find useful employment for Members. In the days when the Parliamentary liberties we have gained were being fought for, Parliamentary figures, in and out of the Administration, were prominent in every field of public service and were hastening in, as they do now, from the battlefield to cast their votes and to give their counsel. It was so in the Marlborough wars, it was so under Lord Chatham, it was so in the wars against Napoleon. The Duke of Wellington, then Sir Arthur Wellesley, went out to the Army in the Peninsula while still holding the Irish Secretaryship; and when the Army went into winter quarters he returned home, and resumed his duties on the Treasury Bench. A great and respectable tradition has followed those lines.

In earlier times, I must admit, in a mood of temporary and melancholy self-abasement, or under harsh external pressure, the House of Commons passed a self-denying ordinance. That was the prelude to the dictatorship of Oliver Cromwell. In the Act of Settlement, 1702, Parliament proposed to prevent every Member of the House of Commons from holding any kind of office under the Crown. It is to the House of Lords, in the later Acts of 1705 and 1707, that we owe that immense assertion of democratic power and popular control which is secured by the presence of the principal Members of the Executive in the House of Commons, chosen mainly from its Members, and living their daily life in full intimacy and association. In the palmy days of Queen Victoria, great respect was paid to the position of a Member of Parliament. His status and authority were everywhere considered. He was much looked up to. Then there was an interlude. As the franchise became more democratic, it grew to be the fashion in certain social circles to speak with contempt about Members of Parliament as a class and as a type. They were represented as mere spouters and chatterboxes, the putters of awkward questions and the raisers of small points of procedure. Kipling wrote his poem:

"Paget, M.P., was a liar, and a fluent liar therewith."

Altogether, there was a phase in which Members of Parliament were thought to be rather a poor lot. That period is over. This White Paper is a proof that it is over. What is this White Paper? I say it is a roll of honour. The roll is not by any means necessarily final. Many things have yet to happen. This White Paper records a process reached naturally and even inevitably under the conditions of these tremendous and terrible times, and which, while it serves the interest of the nation at war, dignifies and enhances the character and quality of Parliamentary representation.

It is the policy of this present Government to raise and sustain the personal status of Members of Parliament in every possible manner. It is my deliberate policy, as Leader of the House, to do so, and always to watch very carefully—as indeed I have done—over the safety and dignity of the House, and keep it alive and effective under conditions in which it has never before been attempted to carry on Parliamentary Government in any civilized State. I am sure that, when the war is over, this institution which we cherish and serve will have gained by having in its ranks large numbers of Members who have played an important part in the great days through which we shall have passed, and who will have their share in winning the victory, the fruits of which we and other Parliaments will then enjoy.

A NEW MAGNA CARTA

A STATEMENT TO THE HOUSE OF COMMONS
ON THE PASSING OF THE UNITED STATES
"LEASE-AND-LEND" BILL
MARCH 12, 1941

March 1. Bulgaria joined the Axis and German troops marched in.
Mr. John G. Winant, the new United States Ambassador to Great Britain, arrived in England.

March 2. Turkish Government closed the Dardanelles except to ships with Turkish pilots.
Mr. Eden and General Dill flew to Athens to meet the Greek Premier, who expressed his country's determination to fight on.

March 4. Hitler sent a message, reported to be an assurance of friendship, to Turkey.
Mr. Oliver Lyttelton, President of the Board of Trade, announced a Government plan for the thinning-out of non-essential industries.

March 5. Britain broke off diplomatic relations with Bulgaria.

March 6. First news of British sloop on Lofoten Islands off Norway, factories and ships being destroyed and 215 Germans taken prisoner.

March 8. U.S. Senate passed the "Lease-Lend" Bill.
Heavy air raid on London after lull of two months. Only 789 civilians killed in February raids on Britain.

March 10. First big success of Britain's defence against the night bombers, eight raiders being destroyed.

March 11. President Roosevelt signed the "Lease-Lend" Bill.

[*March 12, 1941.*

THE Lease-Lend Bill became law yesterday, when it received the signature of the President. I am sure the House would wish me to express on their behalf, and on behalf of the nation, our deep and respectful appreciation of this monument of generous and far-seeing statesmanship.

The most powerful democracy has, in effect, declared in solemn Statute that they will devote their overwhelming industrial and financial strength to ensuring the defeat of Nazism in order that nations, great and small, may live in security, tolerance and freedom. By so doing, the Government and people of the United States have in fact written a new Magna Carta, which not only has regard to the rights and laws upon which a healthy and advancing civilization can alone be erected, but also proclaims by precept and example the duty of free men and free nations, wherever they may be, to share the responsibility and burden of enforcing them.

In the name of His Majesty's Government and speaking, I am sure, for Parliament and for the whole country, and indeed, in the name of all freedom-loving peoples, I offer to the United States our gratitude for her inspiring act of faith.

WELCOME TO MR. WINANT

A SPEECH IN LONDON AT A LUNCHEON GIVEN BY
THE PILGRIMS OF GREAT BRITAIN IN HONOUR OF
MR. JOHN G. WINANT, THE NEW UNITED STATES
AMBASSADOR
MARCH 18, 1941

March 15. President Roosevelt warned the Axis Powers: "Our Democracy has gone into action."

March 16. Mr. Ernest Bevin, Minister of Labour and National Service, announced that girls aged 20 and 21 would register for war production work.

March 17. British troops re-captured Berbera, capital of British Somaliland.

[March 18, 1941·

WE are met here to-day under the strong impression and impact of the historic declaration made on Saturday last by the President of the United States, and where could there be a more fitting opportunity than at this gathering of the Pilgrims to greet the new American Ambassador for me to express on behalf of the British nation and Empire the sense of encouragement and fortification in our resolve which has come to us from across the ocean in those stirring, august, and fateful presidential words? You have come here, Mr. Winant, to a community which is being tried and proved before mankind and history, and tried and proved to a degree and on a scale and under conditions which have not previously been known to human experience.

We have here a free society, governed through a Parliament which rests upon universal suffrage and upon the public opinion of the whole nation. We are being subjected to daily assaults which, if not effectively resisted and repelled, would soon prove mortal. We have to call upon our whole people—men, women, and children alike—to stand up with composure and fortitude to the fire of the enemy, and to accept increasing privations while making increasing efforts. Nothing like this has even been seen before.

We have our faults, and our social system has its faults, but we hope that, with God's help, we shall be able to prove for all time, or at any rate, for a long time, that a State or Commonwealth of Nations, founded on long-enjoyed freedom and steadily-evolved democracy, possesses amid the sharpest shocks the faculty of survival in a high and honourable and, indeed, in a glorious degree. At such a moment, and under such an ordeal, the words and the acts of the President and people of the United States come to us like a draught of life, and they tell us by an ocean-borne trumpet call that we are no longer alone.

We know that other hearts in millions and scores of millions beat with ours; that other voices proclaim the cause for which we strive: other strong hands wield the hammers and shape the weapons we need; other clear and gleaming eyes are fixed in hard conviction upon the tyrannies that must and shall be destroyed. We welcome you here, Mr. Winant, at the moment when a great battle in which your Government and nation are deeply interested is developing its full scope and severity. The Battle of the Atlantic must be won in a decisive manner. It must be won beyond all doubt if the declared policies of the Government and people of the United Sates are not to be forcibly frustrated. Not only German U-boats, but German battle cruisers have crossed to the American side of the Atlantic and have already sunk some of our in-dependently-routed ships not sailing in convoy. They have sunk these ships as far west as the 42nd meridian of longitude.

Over here upon the approaches to our island an intense and unrelenting struggle is being waged to bring in the endless stream of munitions and food without which our war effort here and in the Middle East—for that shall not be relaxed—cannot be maintained. Our losses have risen for the time being, and we are applying our fullest strength and resource, and all the skill and science we can command, in order to meet this potentially mortal challenge. And not only, I must remind you, does our shipping suffer by the attacks of the enemy, but also the fertility of its importing power is reduced by many of the precautions and measures which we must take to master and dominate the attacks which are made upon us.

But our strength is growing every week. The American destroyers which reached us in the autumn and winter are in-creasingly coming into action. Our flotillas are growing in number. Our air power over the island and over the seas is growing fast. We are striking back with increasing effect. Only yesterday I received the news of the certain destruction of three German U-boats. Not since October 13, 1939, had I been cheered by such delectable tidings of a triple event.

81

It is my rule, as you know, not to conceal the gravity of the danger from our people, and therefore I have a right to be believed when I also proclaim our confidence that we shall overcome them. But anyone can see how bitter is the need of Hitler and his gang to cut the sea roads between Great Britain and the United States, and, having divided these mighty Powers, to destroy them one by one. Therefore we must regard this Battle of the Atlantic as one of the most momentous ever fought in all the annals of war. Therefore, Mr. Winant, you come to us at a grand turning-point in the world's history. We rejoice to have you with us in these days of storm and trial, because we know we have a friend and a faithful comrade who will "report us and our cause aright." But no one who has met you can doubt that you hold, and embody in a strong and intense degree, the convictions and ideals which in the name of American democracy President Roosevelt has proclaimed.

In the last few months we have had a succession of eminent American citizens visiting these storm-beaten shores and finding them unconquered and unconquerable—Mr. Hopkins, Mr. Willkie, Colonel Donovan, and now to-day we have here Mr. Harriman and yourself. I have dwelt with all these men in mind and spirit, and there is one thing I have discerned in them all—they would be ready to give their lives, nay, be proud to give their lives, rather than that the good cause should be trampled down and the darkness of barbarism again engulf mankind. Mr. Ambassador, you share our purpose, you will share our dangers, you will share our anxieties, you shall share our secrets, and the day will come when the British Empire and the United Sates will share together the solemn but splendid duties which are the crown of victory.

"YUGOSLAVIA HAS FOUND ITS SOUL"

A SPEECH TO THE CENTRAL COUNCIL OF THE
NATIONAL UNION OF CONSERVATIVE AND
UNIONIST ASSOCIATIONS IN LONDON
MARCH 27, 1941

March 19. Col. Knox, United States Naval Secretary, revealed that a plan is being considered for British ships to use American naval yards for repair.

March 21. Yugoslav Cabinet split on question of signing a pact with the Axis and three Serbian Ministers resigned.

March 22. Stoyadinovitch, pro-Nazi ex-Premier of Yugoslavia, was handed over to the British "for safe custody."

March 24. R.A.F. made their heaviest raid on Berlin.

Berlin warned Yugoslavia of the consequences of signing a pact with the Axis.

March 25. Yugoslav Government signed Axis pact. Hundreds arrested in rioting which followed wave of anger throughout the country.

Graziani, Italy's leading soldier, resigned all his Army posts.

March 26. Matsuoka, Japan's Foreign Minister, arrived in Berlin.

March 27. Bloodless revolution in Yugoslavia replaced Regent Prince Paul with 17-year-old King Peter and threw out Cabinet which signed Axis pact, replacing it with a Cabinet under General Simovitch. Yugoslav Army stood ready for German attack.

British troops captured Keren (Eritre) and Harar (Abyssinia).

[*March 27, 1941.*

I THANK you for the great kindness and cordiality of your welcome. If I am a few minutes late, you will, I am sure, excuse me, because before I sit down I will tell you something which will perhaps explain that I have other business to-day to deal with.

The reason why His Majesty entrusted me in May last with the formation of a Government was because it was an almost universal opinion that national unity must be established in order to face the dangers by which we were encompassed.

You will remember how our leader, Mr. Neville Chamberlain, the moment he felt that he could not command the unity of all parties, even though he stood at the head of a great Parliamentary majority and the great mass of the Conservative party—how he, with perfect self-abnegation which for ever will be an example to public men and will long be associated with his name, stepped aside and resigned his high office. He gave me all possible help, and I was able to form in a week—in the midst of a great battle which was raging in France and the Low Countries—a Government of national union, an all-party Government. That was a dark hour, but we got through it.

Then at a later stage, Mr. Chamberlain, whose work was of the greatest assistance to the new Government, who served under his former lieutenant with perfect loyalty, was stricken by illness and died. You then invited me to be the leader of the Conservative Party. I gave at the time my reasons for accepting this very great task. I believed, and I still believe, that it is possible to reconcile the duties of the leader of the Conservative Party with those of the Prime Minister of a National Government. And, indeed, I thought I could discharge the task more easily if I were able to address myself to it on the same basis and with the same status as the leaders of the two other parties also represented in the National Government.

Nearly a year has gone by since the new Government was formed. In these times one loses the measure of time; sometimes it feels as if it were ten years and sometimes as if it were only ten days. Anyhow, however you count it or reckon it in your mental picture, here we are still, never so strong or so hopeful as we are to-day. This is because the national unity has been preserved and fortified; because we have set an example to all countries in the hour of danger.

National unity requires sacrifices from all parties, and no party has sacrificed more than the Conservative Party with its large Parliamentary majority. Many eminent men have had their careers interrupted, many Ministers of promise have seen their prospects obscured, but none has thought of himself; all have made the sacrifices, and we are proud that the Conservative Party has made the greatest sacrifices. We shall continue to make these sacrifices, and we shall preserve national unity until we have finally beaten down Satan under our feet. I cannot tell you how and when this will come, but that it will come is certain. I cannot attempt to forecast the form or character of the victory, still less what the situation in Europe and in the world, or what the mood in the minds of men may be when that victory has been won.

I hope, however, that there will be national unity in making the peace. I hope also that there will be national unity in certain practical measures of reconstruction and social advance to enable this country to recover from the war and, as one great family, get into its stride again. If this hope were not realized, if no common ground could be found on post-war policy between the parties, it would be a misfortune, because we should then have to ask the nation to decide upon the outstanding issues and party government would be the result.

I may say, however, that some of the ties and friendships which are being formed between members of the administration of all parties will not be very easy to tear asunder, and that the comradeship of dangers passed and toils endured in common will for ever exercise an influence upon British national politics far deeper than the shibboleths and slogans of competing partisans. We have found good, loyal, able comrades in our Labour and Liberal friends, and we work together with the single aim, so well expressed in your resolution to-day, of saving Europe and the world from the curse and tyranny of Nazism.

Anyone in any party who falls below the level of the high spirit of national unity which alone can give national salvation is blameworthy. I know it is provoking when speeches are made which seem to suggest that the whole structure of our decent British life and society, which we have built up so slowly and patiently across the centuries, will be swept away for some new order or other, the details of which are largely unannounced. The spirit sometimes tempts me to rejoinder, and no doubt there are many here who have experienced passing sensations of the same kind, but we must restrain those emotions; we must see things in their true proportion; we must put aside everything which hampers us in the speedy accomplishment of our common purpose.

Moreover, I do not believe that partisanship will benefit, after the war is over, those who indulge in it when the war is going on. The country will judge party men and women in every sphere of life, throughout the island, not by any partisan remarks or rejoiners they may have uttered, but by the contributions which they will have made to the common victory. There is an honourable competition in which we may all strive as parties and as individuals to win the prize. Therefore, the guidance which I offer to the Conservative Party as its leader is that we keep our party organization in good order by associating it at every point with the war effort, and that we concentrate all our thoughts and actions on the victory of the great cause we serve.

It is because of the interests of national unity that I have forborne to produce a catalogue of war aims or peace aims; every one knows quite well what we are fighting about, but if you try to set forth in a catalogue what will be the exact settlement of affairs in a period which, as I say, is unforeseeable; if you attempt to do that you will find that the moment you leave the sphere of pious platitude you will descend into the arena of heated controversy. That would militate against the efforts which we are making, and we could not in justice to our country take such a step.

I was very glad to see that the illustrious leader of the American people, President Roosevelt, is of the same opinion, though in our correspondence the topic has never been mentioned. In speaking of the mission of his new Ambassador to this country, Mr. Winant, a worthy representative of a great nation at a crucial moment—in speaking of his mission, President Roosevelt, when he was asked what instructions were given to the Ambassador about peace aims, replied that he did not see much use in talking about peace aims until Hitler had been defeated. Without taking any final or irrevocable view of what may be desirable in these matters, I may say that I think that the simplest objects are the best. Life, which is so complicated and difficult in great matters, nearly always presents itself in simple terms. For the time being the defeat of Hitler and Hitlerism is a sufficient war aim, and will open the door to every worthy peace aim.

I said that the Government was formed in a dark hour and there was worse to come. But I cannot pretend to you, my friends and supporters, that I took up my task with any other feeling than that of invincible confidence. That is the feeling which inspires me here to-day. Since then we have had the deliverance of Dunkirk, which gave us back the core and fibre of our Regular Army. Since then we have had a series of notable victories.

First of all the frustration of Hitler's invasion plan by the brilliant exploits of the Royal Air Force; secondly, the frustration of his attempt to cow and terrorize the civil population of this country by ruthless air bombing. That has recoiled, futile and shameful, from the unflinching courage of the whole of our people. Thirdly, we have had the destruction of the Italian power and Empire in Africa by our Armies there, and although they were left unsupported by our French Ally, and although we were deprived of all the strategical points necessary to maintain direct contact through the Mediterranean, nevertheless we have been able not only to defend the Nile Valley, but to remove almost all—and the rest soon—the stains which Italian tyranny has wrought on African soil.

But there is another supreme event more blessed than victories —namely, the rising of the spirit of the great American nation and its ever more intimate association with the common cause. Much of that has been accomplished by the sentiment aroused in American breasts at the spectacle of courage and devotion shown by simple and ordinary folk of this country in standing up to the fire of the enemy.

Britain could, I believe, save herself for the time being, but it will take the combined efforts of the whole of the English-speaking world to save mankind and Europe from the menace of Hitlerism and to open again the paths of progress for the people. Therefore I say that if we look back on these five events, all of which have added to our strength and our means of survival and carried us forward on our journey to success, we must see that we have much to be thankful for.

Do not let us ever suppose that our troubles are ended. There is another matter. The Battle of the Atlantic must be won so that food supplies and munitions and every form of American aid may come to us in ever-growing volume. That battle is fought against the surface raider, against the aircraft which steal up from the French and Norwegian coasts right round our islands every day, and against the U-boats. It is fought by the Royal Navy, by the Merchant Marine, by the men who are working the docks and ports and harbours, and by the women who stand at their side in equal danger. That battle is being fought. It engages the deep interest of the great peoples on both sides of the ocean, and I cannot doubt that before many months are passed I shall be able to declare to you that it has been decisively won.

But there are other difficulties and dangers which beset us, and we cannot expect to have successes unchequered by reverses. We must be ready, as we have always been ready, to take the rough with the smooth. We must have spirits so constant that we can derive from misfortune added strength, and if we are cheered by victory, we are also inspired to greater efforts by rebuffs. We cannot tell how long the road will be. We only know that it will be stony, painful, and uphill, and that we shall march along it to the end.

And now, here at this moment, I have great news for you and the whole country. Early this morning the Yugoslav nation found its soul. A revolution has taken place in Belgrade and the Ministers who but yesterday signed away the honour and freedom of the country are reported to be under arrest. This patriotic movement arises from the wrath of a valiant and warlike race at the betrayal of their country by the weakness of their rulers and the foul intrigues of the Axis Powers.

We may therefore cherish the hope—I speak, of course, only on information which has reached me—that a Yugoslav Government will be formed worthy to defend the freedom and integrity of their country. Such a government in its brave endeavour will receive from the British Empire, and, I doubt not, in its own way from the United States, all possible aid and succour. The British Empire and its Allies will make common cause with the Yugoslav nation, and we shall continue to march and strive together until complete victory is won.

THE TRADE UNIONISTS' SACRIFICES

A SPEECH AT A LUNCHEON GIVEN IN LONDON BY THE BRITISH EMPLOYERS'
CONFEDERATION AND THE TRADES UNION CONGRESS IN HONOUR
OF MR. JOHN G. WINANT, THE UNITED STATES AMBASSADOR
TO GREAT BRITAIN
MARCH 27, 1941

[March 27, 1941.

IT is a very striking thing, Mr. Winant, that the strongest organizations of capital and labour in this country should have united to do you welcome. It is explained by the high position which the Ambassador of the United States has always held; it is explained also by the gravity of the struggle in which we are engaged; but most of all it is explained by your especial personality and the services you have rendered to the joint movements of labour and industry throughout the world. It is a great pleasure to see Mr. Winant among us. He gives us the feeling that all President Roosevelt's men give me, that they would be shot stone dead rather than see this cause let down.

Now at this time we have brought into being a National Government, and a Government which rests as one of its main sources of strength upon the trade union organization of this country. In the United States during the presidency of Mr. Roosevelt enormous efforts have been made to broaden the whole basis of industry and society, and we watch them with the utmost interest and sympathy.

But I may say, and I know Mr. Winant will not think it critical and invidious if I say, that we have been several generations broadening and developing the trade union movement in this country, and we have had some differences from time to time, but every one knows, and I have been taught it all my public life, that the employers of this country are deeply thankful there is in existence a strong organized trade union movement with which they can deal, and which keeps its bargains and which moves alone a controlled and suitable path of policy.

The trade union movement has willingly accepted in this war the temporary suspension of privileges which have taken generations to win. They have been handed over to the custody and keeping of the State, and without that we should not be able to

89

produce under the severe conditions of the enemy's fire the immense output of munitions of all kinds which is needed if we are to let our soldiers, sailors, and airmen meet the enemy on even terms of equipment. It is a matter of honour to the whole country that these privileges shall be restored and resumed when this crisis has passed away, unless some other better arrangement can be made.

As for the future, I have always been a bit shy of defining war aims, but if these great communities, now struggling not only for their own lives but for the freedom and progress of the world, emerge victorious, there will be an electric atmosphere in the world which may render possible an advance towards a greater and broader social unity and justice than could otherwise have been achieved in peace-time in a score of years. We are not theorists or doctrinaires. Trade unionists are practical men aiming at practical results. I might say that our aim will be to build a society in which there will be wealth and culture, but where wealth shall not prey on commonwealth nor culture degenerate into class and pride.

To-day I have good news. It was breaking all our hearts to see the gallant Serbian and Yugoslav people signing away their souls through weak and cowardly rulers to those who, once they had them in their grip, would have shaken the life and independence out of them. But I rejoiced when I heard an hour before this luncheon that a revolution had taken place at 2 o'clock this morning, and that the Ministers who went to sign have been arrested.

Though I don't know what will happen, and one cannot be sure of anything, I believe it is reasonable to expect that we shall have a Government in Yugoslavia which will repudiate the pact which was signed the day before yesterday, and will be ready to defend the honour and the frontiers of Yugoslavia against aggression. If that be so, Great Britain will recognize that Government, Great Britain will give all the aid in her power to those who are defending their native lands; to the heroic Greeks; to the Turks if they are attacked. We will give all the aid we can. We are not as strong as we shall be when the plants have delivered their fruit, when the great factories have produced the weapons, but still we get stronger every day.

We will give all the aid we can to those who are fighting to defend their freedom and their native land, and I am quite sure that the President of the United States will be actuated by the same generous impulse to sustain those who are fighting to be free, and that according to the laws and the constitution of the United States—for, after all, as a great democratic leader, he must move with the whole march of the nation—his sympathies and aid will also be extended in full measure to the Serbian people.

Therefore this is a time when we may have good hope of the results of this war. The final result is perhaps distant, but it may be much nearer than we suppose. You cannot tell. I lived through all the last War and survived many of its political vicissitudes, including the 12½ per cent., which, at any rate, you will admit was well meant.* I remember at the Ministry of Munitions being told that we were running short of this and that, that we were running out of bauxite and steel, and so forth; but we went on, and, in the end the only thing we ran short of was Huns. One fine morning we went down to our offices to get on with the work of preparing for the campaign of 1919, and found they had all surrendered.

We must prepare ourselves for long pilgrimages and voyages, yet relief may reward patient and resolute effort.

---

* An increase of wages given by the War Cabinet in 1917 on the advice of Mr. Churchill as Minister of Munitions to the instructors of the dilutees, which led to very large temporary strikes, eventually had to be made universal throughout the war industry.

THE WAR SITUATION

A SPEECH TO THE HOUSE OF COMMONS
APRIL 9, 1941

March 28. It was announced that a total of 28,859 civilians had been killed and 40,166 seriously wounded in air raids on Great Britain to date.

March 29. Great British naval victory over the Italians in the Battle of Matapan. At least three 10,000-ton Italian cruisers and two Italian destroyers were sunk and the 35,000-ton battleship Vittorio Veneto was torpedoed.

March 30. R.A.F. made a heavy raid on Brest, where the German battleships Scharnhorst and Gneisenau were sheltering.

March 31. New bombs of "devastating power" were dropped by the R.A.F. in raids on Emden, Bremen and Rotterdam.

President Roosevelt revealed that he personally had ordered the seizing of 300,000 tons of Axis shipping in U.S. ports to defeat plan to scuttle them.

April 1. British troops captured Asmara, capital of Eritrea.

April 3. British troops evacuated Benghazi in the face of strong German-Italian forces.

Teleki, Premier of Hungary, committed suicide.

Belgrade declared an "open city" as German air units concentrated near Yugoslav frontier.

April 6. German armies attacked Yugoslavia and Greece. It was revealed that there was a British expeditionary force in Greece.

Russia and Yugoslavia signed a pact of friendship.

British troops captured Addis Ababa, capital of Abyssinia.

April 7. War Budget raised income tax to a standard rate of 10s. in the £ and cut allowance.

In the Balkans, German forces attacked down the Struma Valley towards Salonika and down the Vardar Valley, threatening the Greek left flank.

Britain broke off relations with Hungary.

April 8. Announced that in air raids on Britain in March 4,259 civilians were killed.

April 9. Allied troops were evacuating Salonika.

British troops captured Massowa (Eritrea).

I BEG to move,

"That this House on the occasion of the recent victories by sea, land and air in North Africa, Greece and the Mediterranean, records with gratitude its high appreciation of the services of all ranks of His Majesty's Forces in these brilliant operations, and also of those who by their labours and fortitude at home have furnished the means which have made these successes possible."

We are now able and indeed required to take a more general view of the war than when this Resolution of thanks was first conceived. The loss of Benghazi and the withdrawal imposed upon us by the incursion into Cyrenaica are injurious chiefly on account of the valuable airfields around Benghazi which have now passed into the enemy's hands. Apart from this important aspect, we should have been content, in view of the danger which was growing in the Balkans, to have halted our original advance at Tobruk. The rout of the Italians, however, made it possible to gain a good deal of ground easily and cheaply, and it was thought worth while to do this, although, in consequence of other obligations already beginning to descend upon us, only comparatively light forces could be employed to hold what was won. The movement of the German air forces and armoured troops from Italy and Sicily into Tripoli had begun even before we took Benghazi, and our submarines and aircraft have taken a steady toll of the transport-carrying German troops and vehicles. But that has not prevented —and could not prevent—their building-up a strong armoured force on the African shore. With this force they have made a rapid attack in greater strength than our commanders expected at so early a date, and we have fallen back upon stronger positions and more defensible country. I cannot attempt to forecast what the course of the fighting in Cyrenaica will be. It is clear, however, that military considerations alone must guide our generals, and that these problems must in no way be complicated by what are called prestige value, or by consideration of public opinion. Now that the Germans are using their armoured strength in Cyrenaica we must expect much hard and severe fighting, not only for the defence of Cyrenaica, but for the defence of Egypt.

It is fortunate, therefore, that the Italian collapse in Eritrea and Ethiopia, and in British and Italian Somaliland, is liberating progressively very subsantial forces and masses of transport to reinforce the Army of the Nile. This sudden darkening of the scene in Cyrenaica in no way detracts from the merit of the brilliant campaigns which have destroyed the Italian Empire in North-East Africa, nor does it in any way diminish our gratitude to the troops or our confidence in the commanders who have led them. On the contrary, we all show that we are no fair-weather friends, and that our hearts go out to our Armies even more warmly when they are in hard action than when they are sailing forward on the flowing tide of success. I took occasion a fortnight ago to warn the public that an unbroken continuance of success could not be hoped for, that reverses as well as victories must be expected, that we must be ready, as indeed we always are ready, to take the rough with the smooth. Since I used this language other notable episodes have been added to those that had gone before. Keren was stormed after hard fighting, which cost us about 4,000 casualties, and the main resistance of the Italian army in Eritrea was overcome. Foremost in all this fighting in Eritrea have been our Indian troops, who have at all points and on all occasions sustained the martial reputation of the sons of Hindustan.

After the fall of Keren the Army advanced. Asmara has surrendered and the port of Massowa is in our hands. The Red Sea has been virtually cleared of enemy warships, which is a matter of considerable and even far-reaching convenience. Harar has fallen, and our troops have entered and taken charge of Addis Ababa itself. The Duka of Aosta's army has retreated into the mountains, where it is being attended to by the patriot forces of Ethiopia. The complete destruction or capture of all Italian forces in Abyssinia, with a corresponding immediate relief to our operations elsewhere, may reasonably be expected. Besides these land operations, the Royal Navy, under Admiral Cunningham, splendidly aided by the Fleet Air Arm and the Royal Air Force, has gained the important sea battle of Matapan, decisively breaking the Italian naval power in the Mediterranean. When we look back upon the forlorn position in which we were left in the Middle East by the French collapses, when we remember that not only were our forces in the Nile Valley outnumbered by four or five to one by the Italian armies, that we could not contemplate without anxiety the defence of Nairobi, Khartum, Cairo, Alexandria, Jerusalem and the Suez Canal, and that this situation has been marvellously transformed, that we have taken more Italian prisoners than we had troops in the country, that the British Empire has stood alone and conquered alone, except for the aid of the gallant Free French and Belgian forces, who, although few in number, have borne their part—when all this recalls itself to our minds amid the unrelenting pressure of events, I feel confident that I can commend this Resolution to the House and that it will be most heartily and enthusiastically acclaimed.

I now turn from Cyrenaica and Abyssinia to the formidable struggle which has followed the German invasion of the Balkan Peninsula, with all its attendant savagery and science. For some months past we have witnessed and watched with growing concern the German absorption of Hungary, the occupation of Rumania, and the seduction and occupation of Bulgaria. Step by step we have seen this movement of the German military power to the South and South-East of Europe. A remorseless accumulation of German armoured and motorized divisions, and of aircraft, has been in progress in all these three countries for months, and at length we find that the Greeks and the Southern Slavs, nations and States which never wished to take part in the war and neither of which was capable of doing the slightest injury to Germany, must now fight to the death for their freedom and for the lands of their fathers.

Until Greece was treacherously and suddenly invaded in November last at the behest of the base Italian dictator, she had observed a meticulous neutrality. It may be that the sentiments of her people, like those of all free and honourable men in every country, were on our side, but nothing could have been more correct than the behaviour of her Government in diplomatic conduct and relations. We had no contacts or engagements of a military character with the Greek Government. Although there were islands like Crete, of the highest consequence to us, and although we had given Greece our guarantee against aggression, we abstained from the slightest intrusion upon her. It was only when she appealed to us for aid against the Italian invader that we gave whatever support was possible in the air and in the matter of supplies.

All this time the Germans continued to lavish friendly assurances upon Greece and to toy with the idea of a commercial treaty. German high officials, both in Athens and Berlin, expressed their disapproval of the Italian invasion and offered their sympathy to Greece. Meanwhile, since the beginning of December the movements of German forces through Hungary and Rumania towards Bulgaria became apparent to all. More than two months ago, by the traitorous connivance of the Bulgarian King and Government, advance parties of the German Air Force, in plain clothes, were gradually admitted to Bulgaria and took possession of the Bulgarian airfields. Many thousands of German airmen, soldiers and political police had already percolated into Bulgaria and were ensconced in key positions before the actual announcement of the accession of Bulgaria to the Axis was made. German troops then

95

began to pour openly into Bulgaria in very large numbers. One of the direct objectives of these forces was, plainly, Salonika, which I may mention, they entered at 4 o'clock this morning.

It has never been our policy or our interest to see the war carried into the Balkan Peninsula. In the middle of February, we sent our Foreign Secretary and the Chief of the Imperial General Staff to the Middle East, in order to see whether anything could be done to form a united defensive front in the Balkans. They went to Athens. They went to Angora. They would have gone into Belgrade, but they were refused permission by the government of Prince Paul. Of course, if these three threatened States had stood together they could have had at their disposal 60 or 70 divisions which, if a good combined plan had been made and if prompt united action had been taken in time, might have confronted the Germans with a prospect of resistance which might well have deterred them altogether, and must, in any case, have long delayed them, having regard to the mountainous and broken character of the country to be defended and the limits of the communications available in the various countries through which the German armies had forced or intrigued their way.

Although we were most anxious to promote such a defensive front, by which alone the peace of the Balkans could be maintained, we were determined not to urge the Greeks, already at grips with the Italians, upon any course contrary to their desires or judgment. The support which we can give to the peoples who are fighting, or are ready to fight, for freedom in the Balkans and in Turkey, is necessarily limited at the present time, and we did not wish to take the responsibility of pressing the Greeks to engage in a conflict with the new and terrible foe gathering upon their frontiers. However, on the first occasion when the Foreign Secretary and the Chief of the Imperial General Staff met the Greek King and Prime Minister, the Prime Minister declared spontaneously on behalf of the Government that Greece was resolved, at all costs, to defend her freedom and her native soil against any aggressor, and that even if they were left wholly unsupported by Great Britain, or by their neighbours Turkey and Yugoslavia, they would, nevertheless, remain faithful to their alliance with Great Britain, which came into play at the opening of the Italian invasion, and that they would fight to the death against both Italy and Germany.

This being so, it seemed that our duty was clear. We were bound in honour to give them all the aid in our power. If they were resolved to face the might and fury of the Huns, we had no doubts but that we should share their ordeal and that the soldiers of the

British Empire must stand in the line with them. We were advised by our generals on the spot, the Chief of the Imperial General Staff, and Generals Wavell and Papagos, both victorious commanders-in-chief, that a sound military plan, giving good prospects of success, could be made. Of course, in all these matters there is hazard, and in this case, as any one can see, without particularizing unduly, there was for us a double hazard. It remains to be seen how well those opposing risks and duties have been judged, but of this I am sure, that there is no less likely way of winning a war than to adhere pedantically to the maxim of "Safety first." Therefore, in the first weeks of March we entered into a military agreement with the Greeks, and the considerable movement of British and Imperial troops and supplies which has since developed began to take place. The House would very rightly reprove me if I entered into any details, or if while this widespread battle is going on I attempted in any way to discuss either the situation or its prospects.

I therefore turn to the story of Yugoslavia. This valiant, steadfast people, whose history for centuries has been a struggle for life, and who owe their survival to their mountains and to their fighting qualities, made every endeavour to placate the Nazi monster. If they had made common cause with the Greeks when the Greeks, having been atacked by Italy, hurled back the invaders, the complete destruction of the Italian armies in Albania could certainly and swiftly have been achieved long before the German forces could have reached the theatre of war. And even in January and February of this year, this extraordinary military opportunity was still open. But the Government of Prince Paul, untaught by the fate of so many of the smaller countries of Europe, not only observed the strictest neutrality and refused even to enter into effective Staff conversations with Greece or with Turkey or with us, but hugged the delusion that they could preserve their independence by patching up some sort of pact or compromise with Hitler. Once again we saw the odious German poisoning technique employed. In this case, however, it was to the Government rather than to the nation that the doses and the innoculations were administered. The process was not hurried. Why should it have been? All the time the German armies and air force were massing in Bulgaria. From a few handfuls of tourists, admiring the beauties of the Bulgarian landscape in the wintry weather, the German forces grew to 7, 12, 20, and finally to 25 divisions. Presently, the weak and unfortunate Prince, and afterwards his Ministers, were summoned, like others before them, to Herr Hitler's footstool, and a pact was signed which would have given Germany complete control not only over the body but over the soul of the Slav nation.

Then at last the people of Yugoslavia saw their peril, and with a universal spasm of revolt and national resurgence very similar to that which in 1808 convulsed and glorified the people of Spain, they swept from power those who were leading them into a shameful tutelage, and resolved at the eleventh hour to guard their freedom and their honour with their lives. All this happened only a fortnight ago.

A boa constrictor who had already covered his prey with his foul saliva and then had it suddenly wrested from his coils, would be in an amiable mood compared with Hitler, Goering, Ribbentrop and the rest of the Nazi gang when they experienced this bitter disappointment. A frightful vengeance was vowed against the Southern Slavs. Rapid, perhaps hurried, redispositions were made of the German forces and German diplomacy. Hungary was offered large territorial gains to become the accomplice in the assault upon a friendly neighbour with whom she had just signed a solemn pact of friendship and non-aggression. Count Teleki preferred to take his own life rather than join in such a deed of shame. A heavy forward movement of the German armies already gathered in and dominating Austria was set in motion through Hungary to the northern frontier of Yugoslavia. A ferocious howl of hatred from the supreme miscreant was the signal for the actual invasion. The open city of Belgrade was laid in ashes, and at the same time a tremendous drive by the German armoured forces which had been so improvidently allowed to gather in Bulgaria was launched westward into Southern Serbia. And as it was no longer worth while to keep up the farce of love for Greece, other powerful forces rolled forward into Greece, where they were at once unflinchingly encountered, and have already sustained more than one bloody repulse at the hands of that heroic Army. The British and Imperial troops have not up to the present been engaged. Further than this I cannot, at the moment, go. Further than this I cannot attempt to carry the tale.

Therefore, I turn for a few moments to the larger aspects of the war. I must first speak of France and of the French people, to whom in their sorrows we are united not only by memories but by living ties. I welcome cordially the declaration of Marshal Pètain that France could never take action against her former Ally or go to war with her. Such a course, so insensate, so unnatural and, on lower grounds, so improvident, might well—though, of course, it is not for me to speak for any Government but our own—alienate from France for long years the sympathies and support of the American democracy. I am sure that the French nation would, with whatever means of expression left to them, repudiate such a shameful deed. We must, however, realize that the Government of Vichy is in a great many matters, though happily not in all, in the hands of Herr Hitler acting daily through the Armistice Commission at Wiesbaden. Two million Frenchmen are prisoners in German hands. A great part of the food supply of France has been seized by Germany. Both prisoners and food can be doled out month by month in return for hostile propaganda or unfriendly action against Great Britain. Or again, the cost of the German occupation of France, for which a cruel and exorbitant toll is exacted, may be raised still further as a punishment for any manifestations of sympathy with us. Admiral Darlan tells us that the Germans have been generous in their treatment of France. All the information which we receive, both from occupied and unoccupied France, makes me very doubtful whether the mass of the French people would endorse that strange and somewhat sinister tribute. However, the generosity of the German treatment of France is a matter for Frenchmen to judge.

But I wish to make it clear that we must maintain our blockade against Germany and those rights of contraband control at sea, which have never been disputed or denied to any belligerent, and which a year ago France was exercising to the full with us. Some time ago we were ready to enter upon economic negotiations with the French. But any chance of fruitful negotiations was nipped in the bud by the generous Germans, and imperative orders were given from Wiesbaden to the Government of Vichy to break off all contact with us. Nevertheless, we have in practice allowed very considerable quantities of food to go into France out of our sincere desire to spare the French people every hardship in our power. When, however, it comes to thousands of tons of rubber and other vital war materials which pass, as we know, directly to the German armies, we are bound, even at the risk of collisions with French warships at sea, to enforce our rights as recognized by international law. There is one other form of action into which the Vichy Government might be led by the dictation of Germany, namely, the sending of powerful war vessels, which are unfinished or damaged, back from the French African ports to ports in Metropolitan France which are either under the control of the Germans, or may at very short notice fall under their control. Such movements of French war vessels from Africa to France would alter the balance of naval power, and would thus prejudice the interests of the United States as well as our own. Therefore, I trust that such incidents will be avoided, or, if they cannot be avoided, that the consequences which follow from them will be understood and fairly judged by the French nation, for whose cause we are contending no less than for our own.

I am glad to be able to report to the House a continued and marked improvement in the relative strength of the Royal Air Force as compared with that of Germany; also I draw attention to the remarkable increase in its actual strength and in its bomb-dropping capacity, and to the marked augmentation in the power and size of the bombs which we shall be using in even greater numbers. The sorties which we are now accustomed to make upon German harbours and cities are increasing in the numbers of aircraft employed and in the weight of the discharge with every month that passes, and in some cases we have already in our raids exceeded in severity anything which any single town has in a single night experienced over here. At the same time, there is a sensible improvement in our means of dealing with German raids upon this Island, and a very great measure of security has been given to this country in day-time—and we are glad that the days are lengthening. But now the moonlight periods are also looked forward to by the Royal Air Force as an opportunity for inflicting severe deterrent losses upon the raiders, as well as for striking hard at the enemy in his own territory. The fact that our technical advisers welcome the light—daylight, moonlight, starlight—and that we do not rely for our protection on darkness, clouds and mists, as would have been the case some time ago, is pregnant with hope and meaning. But, of course, all these tendencies are only in their early stages, and I forbear to enlarge upon them.

But, after all, everything turns upon the Battle of the Atlantic, which is proceeding with growing intensity on both sides. Our losses in ships and tonnage are very heavy, and vast as are the shipping resources which we control, these losses could not continue indefinitely without seriously affecting our war effort and our means of subsistence. It is no answer to say that we have inflicted upon the Germans and Italians a far higher proportion of loss compared with the scale of their merchant tonnage and the fleeting opportunities they offer us, than they have upon us, with our world-wide traffic continually maintained. We have, in fact, sunk, captured or seen scuttled over 2,300,000 tons of German and Italian shipping. But we have lost ourselves since the beginning of the war nearly 4,000,000 tons of British tonnage. As against that, we have gained under the British flag over 3,000,000 of foreign or newly-constructed tonnage, not counting the considerable foreign tonnage which has also come under our control. Therefore, at the moment our enormous fleets sail the seas without any serious or obvious diminution, as far as the number of ships is concerned.

But what is to happen in the future if these losses continue at the present rate? Where are we to find another three or four million tons to fill the gap which is being created and carry us on through 1942? We are building merchant ships upon a very considerable scale and to the utmost of our ability, having regard to other calls upon our labour. We are also making a most strenuous effort to make ready for sea the large number of vessels which have been damaged by the enemy and the still larger number which have been damaged by the winter gales. We are doing our utmost to accelerate the turn-round of our ships, remembering—-this is a striking figure—-that even ten days' saving on turn-round in our immense fleets is equal to a reinforcement of 5,000,000 tons of imports in a single year. I can assure the House that all the energy and contrivance of which we are capable have been and will continue to be devoted to these purposes, and that we are already conscious of substantial results. But, when all is said and done, the only way in which we can get through the year 1942 without a very sensible contraction of our war effort is by another gigantic building of merchant ships in the United States similar to that prodigy of output accomplished by the Americans in 1918. All this has been in train in the United States for many months past. There has now been a very large extension of the programmes, and we have the assurance that several millions of tons of new-built American shipping will be available for the common struggle during the course of the next year. Here, then, is the assurance upon which we may count for the staying power without which it will not be possible to save the world from the criminals who assail its future.

The Battle of the Atlantic must, however, be won, not only in the factories and shipyards, but upon the blue water. I am confident that we shall succeed in coping with the air attacks which are made upon the shipping in the Western and North-Western approaches. I hope that eventually the inhabitants of the sister Island may realise that it is as much in their interest as in ours that their ports and airfields should be available for the naval and air forces which must operate ever farther into the Atlantic. But, while I am hopeful that we shall gain mastery over the air attack upon our shipping, the U-boats and the surface raiders, ranging ever farther to the Westward, even nearer to the shores of the United States, constitute a menace which must be overcome if the life of Britain is not to be endangered, and if the purposes to which the Government and the people of the United States have devoted themselves are not to be frustrated. We shall, of course, make every effort in our power. The defeat of the U-boats and of the surface raiders has been proved to be entirely a question of adequate escorts for our convoys. It would be indeed disastrous if the great masses of weapons, munitions and instruments of war of all kinds, made with the toil and skill of American hands, at the cost of the United States, and loaned to us under the Aid to Britain Act, were to sink into the depths of the ocean and never reach the hard-pressed fighting line. That would be a result lamentable to us over here, and I cannot believe that it would be found acceptable to the proud and resolute people in the United States. Indeed, I am now authorized to state that ten United States Revenue cutters, fast vessels of about 2,000 tons displacement, with a fine armament and a very wide range of endurance, have already been placed at our disposal by the United States Government and will soon be in action. These vessels, originally designed to enforce prohibition, will now serve an even higher purpose.

It is, of course, very hazardous to try to forecast in what direction or directions Hitler will employ his military machine in the present year. He may at any time attempt the invasion of this Island. That is an ordeal from which we shall not shrink. At the present time he is driving south and south-east through the Balkans, and at any moment he may turn upon Turkey. But there are many signs which point to a Nazi attempt to secure the granary of the Ukraine and the oilfields of the Caucasus and thus to gain the resources wherewith to wear down the English-speaking world. All this is speculation. I will say only one thing more. Once we have gained the Battle of the Atlantic and are certain of the constant flow of American supplies which is being prepared for us, then, however far Hitler may go, or whatever new millions and scores of millions he may lap in misery, he may be sure that, armed with the sword of retributive justice, we shall be on his track.

The Prime Minister viewing damage to Coventry Cathedral, after the air raid of November 14, 1940.

The Prime Minister and the President of the United States on board H.M.S. Prince of Wales on the occasion of the signing of the Atlantic Charter, August, 1941.

A UNIVERSITY CEREMONY

MR. CHURCHILL, AS CHANCELLOR OF BRISTOL UNIVERSITY, CONFERRED THE
HONORARY DEGREE OF DOCTOR OF LAWS ON MR. JOHN G. WINANT, UNITED
STATES AMBASSADOR TO GREAT BRITAIN, DR. J. B. CONANT, PRESIDENT OF
HARVARD UNIVERSITY, AND MR. R. G.. MENZIES, PRIME MINISTER OF AUSTRALIA
APRIL 12, 1941

---

*April 10. Three British generals and 2,000 men were captured by
the Germans in Libya advance.*

[*April 12, 1941.*

HERE we are gathered in academic robes to go through a
ceremonial and repeat formulas associated with the giving
of university degrees. Many of those here to-day have been all
night at their posts, and all have been under the fire of the enemy
in heavy and protracted bombardment. That you should gather
in this way is a mark of fortitude and phlegm, of a courage and
detachment from material affairs worthy of all that we have
learned to believe of ancient Rome or of modern Greece.

I go about the country whenever I can escape for a few hours
or for a day from my duty at headquarters, and I see the damage
done by the enemy attacks; but I also see side by side with the
devastation and amid the ruins quiet, confident, bright, and smiling
eyes, beaming with a consciousness of being associated with a cause
far higher and wider than any human or personal issue. I see the
spirit of an unconquerable people. I see a spirit bred in freedom,
nursed in a tradition which has come down to us through the
centuries, and which will surely at this moment, this turning-point
in the history of the world, enable us to bear our part in such a way
that none of our race who come after us will have any reason to
cast reproach upon their sires.

Mr. Winant is the interpreter of the great Republic to us, and
he is our interpreter and friend, sending back his messages across
the ocean to them. Through him and other distinguished representatives of the United States who are with us to-day, including
Mr. Harriman, we make another tie with the illustrious President
of the United States, and with the executive of that vast com-

103

munity, at a time when great matters of consequence to all the world are being resolved. It has been to me an honour which will stand out in my twelve years' tenure of office as your Chancellor to confer this degree upon Mr. Winant.

In Dr. Conant, who is, much to his regret, not with us to-day, we have a figure widely and deeply respected throughout the United States, and particularly among the youth who attend Harvard University, holding up a clear beacon light for young men of honour and courage.

Mr. Menzies brings with him the strong assurance of the Australian Commonwealth that they will, with us, go through this long, fierce, dire struggle to the victorious end. It is, indeed, a marvellous fact that Australia and New Zealand, who are separated from us and from Europe, with all its passions and quarrels, by the great ocean spaces, should send their manhood and scatter their wealth upon this world cause. No law, no constitution, no bond or treaty pledges them to spend a shilling or send a man.

We welcome Mr. Menzies here. He has sat with us in Cabinet. He has seen every aspect of our life at home. And he is going back presently by the United States to Australia. Much will have happened by the time he returns there. Australian and New Zealand troops may well be in contact with the enemy to-day. There, to the classic scenes of the ancient lands of Greece, they will bring the valour of the sons of the Southern Cross.

TO THE PEOPLE OF YUGOSLAVIA

A MESSAGE BROADCAST IN SERBO-CROAT

APRIL 13, 1941

April 13. German armoured columns by-passed Tobruk and reached the Egyptian frontier.

Japan and Russia signed a pact of neutrality.

[*April 13, 1941.*

TO the people of Yugoslavia, to the Serbs, the Croats, and the Slovenes, I send my greetings. You have been wantonly attacked by a ruthless and barbarous aggressor. Your capital has been bombed, your women and children brutally murdered. Our cities in England, too, have been bombed by the same insensate foe. Our women and children have been murdered. Our sympathy for you therefore is heartfelt, for we are sharing the same sufferings. But as we have faith in our victory, so we have faith in yours. Do not regret the staunch courage which has brought on you this furious onslaught. Your courage will shine out in the pages of history and will, too, reap a more immediate reward. Whatever you may loose in the present, you have saved the future.

You are making an heroic resistance against formidable odds, and in doing so you are proving true to your great traditions. Serbs, we know you. You were our allies in the last War, and your arms are covered with glory. Croats and Slovenes, we know your military history. For centuries you were the bulwark of Christianity. Your fame as warriors spread far and wide on the Continent. One of the finest incidents in the history of Croatia is the one when, in the sixteenth century, long before the French Revolution, the peasants rose to defend the rights of man, and fought for those principles which centuries later gave the world democracy.

Yugoslavs, you are fighting for those principles to-day. The British Empire is fighting with you, and behind us is the great democracy of the United States, with its vast and ever-increasing resources. However hard the fight, our victory is assured.

"WESTWARD, LOOK, THE LAND IS BRIGHT"

A BROADCAST ADDRESS
APRIL 27, 1941.

April 14. German tanks were heavily repulsed in an attack on Tobruk.

April 16. British warships sank Africa-bound Axis convoy of five ships and three escorting destroyers. London had its heaviest raid of the war.

April 17. Yugoslav army asked Germany for an armistice, the situation of the Greeks being thus gravely threatened.

April 19. Korizis, Greek Prime Minister, died suddenly.
   British forces landed at Basra to safeguard Mosul oilfields.

April 21. Big withdrawals by Allied forces in Greece.

April 23. Greek Epirus army capitulated, and King George of Greece and his Cabinet removed to Crete.
   Armed merchant cruiser Rajputana sunk.

April 25. President Roosevelt announced the extension of U.S. patrol system "to the Seven Seas" if necessary, to safeguard American interests.
   Lord Gort appointed Commander-in-Chief of Gibraltar.

April 26. Air Ministry announced that the Hawker Typhoon, fastest and most powerful fighting plane in the world, is now in full production.

April 27. German troops entered Athens.

[*April 27, 1941.*

I WAS asked last week whether I was aware of some uneasiness which it was said existed in the country on account of the gravity, as it was described, of the war situation. So I thought it would be a good thing to go and see for myself what this "uneasiness" amounted to, and I went to some of our great cities and seaports which had been most heavily bombed, and to some of the places where the poorest people had got it worst. I have come back not only reassured, but refreshed. To leave the offices in Whitehall with their ceaseless hum of activity and stress, and to go out to the front, by which I mean the streets and wharves of London or Liverpool, Manchester, Cardiff, Swansea or Bristol, is like going out of a hothouse on to the bridge of a fighting ship. It is a tonic which I should recommend any who are suffering from fretfulness to take in strong doses when they have need of it.

It is quite true that I have seen many painful scenes of havoc, and of fine buildings and acres of cottage homes blasted into rubble-heaps of ruin. But it is just in those very places where the malice of the savage enemy has done its worst, and where the ordeal of the men, women and children has been most severe, that I found their morale most high and splendid. Indeed, I felt encompassed by an exaltation of spirit in the people which seemed to lift mankind and its troubles above the level of material facts into that joyous serenity we think belongs to a better world than this.

Of their kindness to me I cannot speak, because I have never sought it or dreamed of it, and can never deserve it. I can only assure you that I and my colleagues, or comrades rather—for that is what they are—will toil with every scrap of life and strength, according to the lights that are granted to us, not to fail these people or be wholly unworthy of their faithful and generous regard. The British nation is stirred and moved as it has never been at any time in its long, eventful, famous history, and it is no hackneyed trope of speech to say that they mean to conquer or to die.

What a triumph the life of these battered cities is, over the worst that fire and bomb can do. What a vindication of the civilized and decent way of living we have been trying to work for and work towards in our Island. What a proof of the virtues of free institutions. What a test of the quality of our local authorities, and of institutions and customs and societies so steadily built. This ordeal by fire has even in a certain sense exhilarated the manhood and womanhood of Britain. The sublime but also terrible and sombre experiences and emotions of the battlefield which for centuries had been reserved for the soldiers and sailors, are now shared, for good or ill, by the entire population. All are proud to be under the fire of the enemy. Old men, little children, the crippled veterans of former wars, aged women, the ordinary hard-pressed citizen or subject of the King, as he likes to call himself, the sturdy workmen who swing the hammers or load the ships; skilful craftsmen; the members of every kind of A.R.P. service, are proud to feel that they stand in the line together with our fighting men, when one of the greatest of causes is being fought out, as fought out it will be, to the end. This is indeed the grand heroic period of our history, and the light of glory shines on all.

You may imagine how deeply I feel my own responsibility to all these people; my responsibility to bear my part in bringing them safely out of this long, stern, scowling valley through which we are marching, and not to demand from them their sacrifices and exertions in vain.

I have thought in this difficult period, when so much fighting and so many critical and complicated manœuvres are going on, that it is above all things important that our policy and conduct should be upon the highest level, and that honour should be our guide. Very few people realize how small were the forces with which General Wavell, that fine Commander whom we cheered in good days and will back through bad—how small were the forces which took the bulk of the Italian masses in Libya prisoners. In none of his successive victories could General Wavell maintain in the desert or bring into action more than two divisions, or about 30,000 men. When we reached Benghazi, and what was left of Mussolini's legions scurried back along the dusty road to Tripoli, a call was made upon us which we could not resist. Let me tell you about that call.

You will remember how in November the Italian Dictator fell upon the unoffending Greeks, and without reason and without warning invaded their country, and how the Greek nation, reviving their classic fame, hurled his armies back at the double-quick. Meanwhile Hitler, who had been creeping and worming his way steadily forward, doping and poisoning and pinioning one after the other, Hungary, Rumania and Bulgaria, suddenly made it clear that he would come to the rescue of his fellow-criminal. The lack of unity among the Balkan States had enabled him to build up a mighty army in their midst. While nearly all the Greek troops were busy beating the Italians, the tremendous German military machine suddenly towered up on their other frontier. In their mortal peril the Greeks turned to us for succour. Strained as were our own resources, we could not say them nay. By solemn guarantee given before the war, Great Britain had promised them her help. They declared they would fight for their native soil even if neither of their neighbours made common cause with them, and even if we left them to their fate. But we could not do that. There are rules against that kind of thing; and to break those rules would be fatal to the honour of the British Empire, without which we could neither hope nor deserve to win this hard war. Military defeat or miscalculation can be redeemed. The fortunes of war are fickle and changing. But an act of shame would deprive us of the respect which we now enjoy throughout the world, and this would sap the vitals of our strength.

During the last year we have gained by our bearing and conduct a potent hold upon the sentiments of the people of the United States. Never, never in our history, have we been held in such admiration and regard across the Atlantic Ocean. In that great Republic, now in much travail and stress of soul, it is customary to use all the many valid, solid arguments about American interests and American safety, which depend upon the destruction of Hitler and his foul gang and even fouler doctrines. But in the long run —believe me, for I know—the action of the United States will be dictated, not by methodical calculations of profit and loss, but by moral sentiment, and by that gleaming flash of resolve which lifts the hearts of men and nations, and springs from the spiritual foundations of human life itself.

We, for our part, were of course bound to hearken to the Greek appeal to the utmost limit of our strength. We put the case to the Dominions of Australia and New Zealand, and their Governments, without in any way ignoring the hazards, told us that they felt the same as we did. So an important part of the mobile portion of the Army of the Nile was sent to Greece in fulfilment of our pledge. It happened that the divisions available and best suited to this task were from New Zealand and Australia, and that only about half the troops who took part in this dangerous expedition came from the Mother Country. I see the German propaganda is trying to make bad blood between us and Australia by making out that we have used them to do what we would not have asked of the British Army. I shall leave it to Australia to deal with that taunt.

Let us see what has happened. We knew, of course, that the forces we could send to Greece would not by themselves alone be sufficient to stem the German tide of invasion. But there was a very real hope that the neighbours of Greece would by our intervention be drawn to stand in the line together with her while time remained. How nearly that came off will be known some day. The tragedy of Yugoslavia has been that these brave people had a government who hoped to purchase an ignoble immunity by submission to the Nazi will. Thus when at last the people of Yugoslavia found out where they were being taken, and rose in one spontaneous surge of revolt, they saved the soul and future of their country: but it was already too late to save its territory. They had no time to mobilize their armies. They were struck down by the ruthless and highly-mechanized Hun before they could even bring their armies into the field. Great disasters have occurred in the Balkans. Yugoslavia has been beaten down. Only in the mountains can she continue her resistance. The Greeks have been overwhelmed. Their victorious Albanian army has been cut off and forced to surrender, and it has been left to the Anzacs and their British comrades to fight their way back to the sea, leaving their mark on all who hindered them.

I turn aside from the stony path we have to tread, to indulge a moment of lighter relief. I daresay you have read in the newspapers that, by a special proclamation, the Italian Dictator has congratulated the Italian army in Albania on the glorious laurels they have gained by their victory over the Greeks. Here surely is the world's record in the domain of the ridiculous and the contemptible. This whipped jackal, Mussolini, who to save his own skin has made all Italy a vassal state of Hitler's Empire, comes frisking up at the side of the German tiger with yelpings not only of appetite—that can be understood—but even of triumph. Different things strike different people in different ways. But I am sure there are a great many millions in the British Empire and in the United States, who will find a new object in life in making sure that when we come to the final reckoning this absurd impostor will be abandoned to public justice and universal scorn.

While these grievous events were taking place in the Balkan Peninsula and in Greece, our forces in Libya have sustained a vexatious and damaging defeat. The Germans advanced sooner and in greater strength than we or our Generals expected. The bulk of our armoured troops, which had played such a decisive part in beating the Italians, had to be refitted, and the single armoured brigade which had been judged sufficient to hold the frontier till about the middle of May was worsted and its vehicles largely destroyed by a somewhat stronger German armoured force. Our infantry, which had not exceeded one division, had to fall back upon the very large Imperial armies that have been assembled and can be nourished and maintained in the fertile delta of the Nile.

Tobruk—the fortress of Tobruk—which flanks any German advance on Egypt, we hold strongly. There we have repulsed many attacks, causing the enemy heavy losses and taking many prisoners. That is how the matter stands in Egypt and on the Libyan front.

We must now expect the war in the Mediterranean on the sea, in the desert, and above all in the air, to become very fierce, varied and widespread. We had cleaned the Italians out of Cyrenaica, and it now lies with us to purge that province of the Germans. That will be a harder task, and we cannot expect to do it at once. You know I never try to make out that defeats are victories. I have never underrated the German as a warrior. Indeed I told you a month ago that the swift, unbroken course of victories which we had gained over the Italians could not possibly continue, and that misfortunes must be expected. There is only one thing certain about war, that it is full of disappointments and also full of mistakes. It remains to be seen, however, whether it is the Germans who have made the mistake in trampling down the Balkan States and in making a river of blood and hate between themselves and the Greek and Yugoslav peoples. It remains also to be seen whether they have made a mistake in their attempt to invade Egypt with the forces and means of supply which they have now got. Taught by experience, I make it a rule not to prophesy about battles which have yet to be fought out. This, however, I will venture to say, that I should be very sorry to see the tasks of the combatants in the Middle East exchanged, and that General Wavell's armies should be in the position of the German invaders. That is only a personal opinion, and I can well understand you may take a different view. It is certain that fresh dangers besides those which threaten Egypt may come upon us in the Mediterranean. The war may spread to Spain and Morocco. It may spread eastward to Turkey and Russia. The Huns may lay their hands for a time upon the granaries of the Ukraine and the oil-wells of the Caucasus. They may dominate the Black Sea. They may dominate the Caspian. Who can tell? We shall do our best to meet them and fight them wherever they go. But there is one thing which is certain. There is one thing which rises out of the vast welter which is sure and solid, and which no one in his senses can mistake. Hitler cannot find safety from avenging justice in the East, in the Middle East, or in the Far East. In order to win this war, he must either conquer this Island by invasion, or he must cut the ocean life-line which joins us to the United States.

Let us look into these alternatives, if you will bear with me for a few minutes longer. When I spoke to you last, early in February, many people believed the Nazi boastings that the invasion of Britain was about to begin. It has not begun yet, and with every week that passes we grow stronger on the sea, in the air, and in the numbers, quality, training and equipment of the great Armies that now guard our Island. When I compare the position at home as it is to-day with what it was in the summer of last year, even after making allowance for a much more elaborate mechanical preparation on the part of the enemy, I feel that we have very much to be thankful for, and I believe that provided our exertions

111

and our vigilance are not relaxed even for a moment, we may be confident that we shall give a very good account of ourselves. More than that it would be boastful to say. Less than that it would be foolish to believe.

But how about our life-line across the Atlantic? What is to happen if so many of our merchant ships are sunk that we cannot bring in the food we need to nourish our brave people? What if the supplies of war materials and war weapons which the United States are seeking to send us in such enormous quantities should in large part be sunk on the way? What is to happen then? In February, as you may remember, that bad man in one of his raving outbursts threatened us with a terrifying increase in the numbers and activities of his U-boats and in his air attack—not only on our Island but, thanks to his use of French and Norwegian harbours, and thanks to the denial to us of the Irish bases—upon our shipping far out into the Atlantic. We have taken and are taking all possible measures to meet this deadly attack, and we are now fighting against it with might and main. That is what is called the Battle of the Atlantic, which in order to survive we have got to win on salt water just as decisively as we had to win the Battle of Britain last August and September in the air.

Wonderful exertions have been made by our Navy and Air Force; by the hundreds of mine-sweeping vessels which with their marvellous appliances keep our ports clear in spite of all the enemy can do; by the men who build and repair our immense fleets of merchant ships; by the men who load and unload them; and need I say by the officers and men of the Merchant Navy who go out in all weathers and in the teeth of all dangers to fight for the life of their native land and for a cause they comprehend and serve. Still, when you think how easy it is to sink ships at sea and how hard it is to build them and protect them, and when you remember that we have never less than two thousand ships afloat and three or four hundred in the danger zone; when you think of the great armies we are maintaining and reinforcing in the East, and of the world-wide traffic we have to carry on—when you remember all this, can you wonder that it is the Battle of the Atlantic which holds the first place in the thoughts of those upon whom rests the responsibility for procuring the victory?

It was therefore with indescribable relief that I learned of the tremendous decisions lately taken by the President and people of the United States. The American Fleet and flying boats have been ordered to patrol the wide waters of the Western Hemisphere, and to warn the peaceful shipping of all nations outside the combat zone of the presence of lurking U-boats or raiding cruisers belonging to the two aggressor nations. We British shall therefore be able to concentrate our protecting forces far more upon the routes nearer home, and to take a far heavier toll of the U-boats there. I have felt for some time that something like this was bound to happen. The President and Congress of the United States, having newly fortified themselves by contact with their electors, have solemnly pledged their aid to Britain in this war because they deem our cause just, and because they know their own interests and safety would be endangered if we were destroyed. They are taxing themselves heavily. They have passed great legislation. They have turned a large part of their gigantic industry to making the munitions which we need. They have even given us or lent us valuable weapons of their own. I could not believe that they would allow the high purposes to which they have set themselves to be frustrated and the products of their skill and labour sunk to the bottom of the sea. U-boat warfare as conducted by Germany is entirely contrary to international agreements freely subscribed to by Germany only a few years ago. There is no effective blockade, but only a merciless murder and marauding over wide, indiscriminate areas utterly beyond the control of the German sea-power. When I said ten weeks ago: "Give us the tools and we will finish the job", I meant, *give* them to us: put them within our reach—and that is what it now seems the Americans are going to do. And that is why I feel a very strong conviction that though the Battle of the Atlantic will be long and hard, and its issue is by no means yet determined, it has entered upon a more grim but at the same time a far more favourable phase. When you come to think of it, the United States are very closely bound up with us now, and have engaged themselves deeply in giving us moral, material, and, within the limits I have mentioned, naval support.

It is worth while therefore to take a look on both sides of the ocean at the forces which are facing each other in this awful struggle, from which there can be no drawing back. No prudent and far-seeing man can doubt that the eventual and total defeat of Hitler and Mussolini is certain, in view of the respective declared resolves of the British and American democracies. There are less than seventy million malignant Huns—some of whom are curable and others killable—many of whom are already engaged in holding down Austrians, Czechs, Poles, French, and the many other ancient races they now bully and pillage. The peoples of the British Empire and of the United States number nearly two hundred millions in their homelands and in the British Dominions alone. They possess

113

the unchallengeable command of the oceans, and will soon obtain decisive superiority in the air. They have more wealth, more technical resources, and they make more steel, than the whole of the rest of the world put together. They are determined that the cause of freedom shall not be trampled down, nor the tide of world progress turned backwards, by the criminal Dictators.

While therefore we naturally view with sorrow and anxiety much that is happening in Europe and in Africa, and may happen in Asia, we must not lose our sense of proportion and thus become discouraged or alarmed. When we face with a steady eye the difficulties which lie before us, we may derive new confidence from remembering those we have already overcome. Nothing that is happening now is comparable in gravity with the dangers through which we passed last year. Nothing that can happen in the East is comparable with what is happening in the West.

Last time I spoke to you I quoted the lines of Longfellow which President Roosevelt had written out for me in his own hand. I have some other lines which are less well known but which seem apt and appropriate to our fortunes to-night, and I believe they will be so judged wherever the English language is spoken or the flag of freedom flies:

> For while the tired waves, vainly breaking,
>   Seem here no painful inch to gain,
> Far back, through creeks and inlets making,
>   Comes silent, flooding in, the main.
>
> And not by eastern windows only,
>   When daylight comes, comes in the light;
> In front the sun climbs slow, how slowly!
>   But westward, look, the land is bright.

A MESSAGE TO THE POLISH PEOPLE

A BROADCAST ADDRESS
MAY 3, 1941

April 29. *President Roosevelt announced that U.S. patrols were now ranging 2,000 miles out into the Atlantic.*

April 30. *It was officially announced that 48,000 of the original force of 60,000 British troops in Greece had been evacuated.*

President Roosevelt ordered the pooling of 2,000,000 tons of shipping to aid Britain.

May 1. *Lord Beaverbrook, Minister of Aircraft Production, appointed Minister of State. The Ministries of Shipping and Transport were merged.*

May 2. *War flared up in Irak, where Rashid Ali, pro-German usurper, attacked British air base near Bagdad and appealed to Germany for help.*

May 3. *It was announced in Washington that the United States Navy would shadow Axis raiders in the Atlantic and report their positions by radio.*

[May 3, 1941.

TO-NIGHT I am speaking to the Polish people all over the world. This is the hundred-and-fiftieth anniversary of the adoption by your Parliament of the Constitution.

You are right to keep this day as a national holiday, because your Constitution of 1791 was a pattern, when it was framed, of enlightened political thought. Your neighbours in those bygone days saw in the adoption of this system the beginning of the regeneration of Poland. They hastened to perpetrate the partition of your country before the Polish nation could consolidate its position.

The same tragedy, the same crime, was repeated in 1939. The Germans became alarmed at the success achieved by the Polish nation in setting its house in order. They saw that their aggressive designs would be thwarted by the growth of a strong, independent Polish State. At the time of the brutal German attack in September, 1939, your country had in the face of tremendous difficulties

115

achieved notable progress during the twenty years of its revived national existence.

To complete this work of national reconstruction, you needed, and you hoped for, a similar period of peaceful development. When the call came, Poland did not hesitate. She did not hesitate to risk all the progress she had made rather than compromise her national honour; and she showed in the spontaneous response of her sons and daughters that spirit of national unity and of self-sacrifice which has maintained her among the great nations of Europe through all her many trials and tribulations.

I know from talks I have had with Poles now in this country how magnificently the mass of the Polish nation answered the appeal to duty in the hour of need. I have been deeply moved by what I have heard of the inhabitants of Warsaw during the three weeks of the siege, and of their continued strenuous resistance to the alien oppressor who now occupies their city.

We in this country who are conscious that our strength is built on the broad masses of the British nation appreciate and admire the Polish nation for its noble attitude since the outbreak of the war. Mainly for geographical reasons, personal contacts between our two peoples have been restricted in the past; and fighting as we are at opposite ends of Europe against our common foe, this war has not yet provided an opportunity for personal contacts on any large scale between you and my own countrymen.

The fortunes of war have, however, brought to these shores your President, your Government and many thousands of brave Polish soldiers, airmen, sailors and merchant seamen. Their bearing has won them universal admiration in this country, and cast further lustre, if that were possible, upon the proud, heroic traditions of Poland.

It has been my privilege to come to know your Prime Minister and Commander-in-Chief, General Sikorski, whose leadership, energy, and unfaltering confidence are a source of great encouragement to all who meet him. I have visited your soldiers in Scotland while they were waiting to repel the invader, and while they were longing in their hearts above all to carry back the flag of freedom to their fellow-countrymen at home.

I have seen your pilots, who have by their prowess played a glorious part in the repulse of the German air hordes. Meanwhile, your sailors have been earning the respect and high regard of their comrades in the Royal Navy and Merchant Marine, with whom they are sharing the task of maintaining those contacts with America and with the outside world through which will come the liberation of your country. The presence here of your Government and armed forces has enabled us to get to know each other better, and to build a foundation for Anglo-Polish relations after our common victory and the restoration of your freedom.

Our thoughts go out to-night not only to those valiant exiled Poles whom we have learned to like and respect in the British Islands and who stand armed in the ranks of the armies of liberation, but even more to those who are gripped at home in the merciless oppression of the Hun.

All over Europe, races and States whose culture and history made them a part of the general life of Christendom in centuries when the Prussians were no better than a barbarous tribe, and the German Empire no more than an agglomeration of pumpernickel principalities, are now prostrate under the dark, cruel yoke of Hitler and his Nazi gang. Every week his firing parties are busy in a dozen lands. Monday he shoots Dutchmen; Tuesday Norwegians; Wednesday, French or Belgians stand against the wall; Thursday it is the Czechs who must suffer. And now there are the Serbs and the Greeks to fill his repulsive bill of executions. But always, all the days, there are the Poles. The atrocities committed by Hitler upon the Poles, the ravaging of their country, the scattering of their homes, the affronts to their religion, the enslavement of their man-power, exceed in severity and in scale the villainies perpetrated by Hitler in any other conquered land.

It is to you Poles, in Poland, who bear the full brunt of the Nazi oppression—at once pitiless and venal—that the hearts of the British and American Democracies go out in a full and generous tide. We send you our message of hope and encouragement to-night, knowing that the Poles will never despair, and that the soul of Poland will remain unconquerable.

This war against the mechanized barbarians, who, slave-hearted themselves, are fitted only to carry their curse to others—this war will be long and hard. But the end is sure; the end will reward all toil, all disappointments, all suffering in those who faithfully serve the cause of European and world freedom. A day will dawn, perhaps sooner than we now have a right to hope, when the insane attempt to found a Prussian domination on racial hatred, on the armoured vehicle, on the secret police, on the alien overseer, and on still more filthy Quislings, will pass like a monstrous dream. And in that morning of hope and freedom, not only the embattled and at last well-armed Democracies, but all that is noble and fearless in the New World as well as in the Old, will salute the rise of Poland to be a nation once again.

117

THE WAR SITUATION

A SPEECH TO THE HOUSE OF COMMONS
MAY 7, 1941

May 4. Hitler, in a speech to the Reichstag, threatened to drop 100 bombs for each British bomb until Britain got rid of Winston Churchill.

British air defences made a record by destroying sixteen German night bombers.

May 6. Stalin became Prime Minister of Soviet Russia in place of Molotov, who remained Foreign Commissar and became Vice Premier.

May 7. Darlan signed an agreement with Germany lightening Armistice restrictions, but did not disclose the price he paid.

[May 7, 1941.

THIS Debate, as I think will be agreed on all hands, has been marked by a high sense of discretion and a high degree of responsibility in all who have taken part in it. If there were any speech I could single out especially for praise, it would, I think, be the last, to which we have just listened. The Member for Derby (Mr. Noel-Baker) is a great devotee of the Greek cause, and all that he has said has shown how deeply he has studied the articulation of their defences and, of course, their fortunes. If there were any speech which I felt was not particularly exhilarating, it was the speech of the Member for Carnarvon Boroughs (Mr. Lloyd George), who honoured us by one of his always deeply important and much valued appearances in the House. He made complaints, first of all, of the speech of the Foreign Secretary yesterday because he did not refer to Spain, Russia, Vichy and Turkey. But this was not a Debate on foreign policy, although no doubt such might well be arranged, in public or in private; and I do not think the speech of the Foreign Secretary can be judged entirely by what he said. Rather might it be judged by what he did not say.

If he did not refer to Spain, it was not because we have not plenty of information about Spain or because there are not a lot of things that could be said about Spain. I am not sure how those

118

things which could be said about Spain could be couched in a vein which would be helpful to our affairs. Again, much might be said about Russia; but I am not quite sure that we should gain any advantage by saying it, and I am not quite certain we should receive any thanks from the Soviet Government. It should be possible no doubt to dilate at length upon the sad and sorry and squalid tale of what is going on at Vichy, but I really do not think we should profit ourselves well if we tarried very long to examine and dissect that tragic spectacle. With regard to Turkey, I thank him for the great restraint with which he spoke about that country, whose relations are so highly valued by us, and whose part in this great world conflict is of the greatest importance. But there are two points on which I think I can a little relieve his fears and anxieties about Turkey. First of all, he said they had allowed ships which carried the German troops to the Greek Islands to come through the Dardanelles. They had no right to stop them. While at peace, they had no right whatever to stop them. That would be a decision to quit their neutrality. Article 4 of the Convention reads as follows:

"In time of war, Turkey not being belligerent, merchant vessels under any flag or with any kind of cargo shall enjoy freedom of transit and navigation in the Straits."

It is evident that a decision by Turkey to stop these vessels would have been of very great consequence to her. I said merchant vessels. I believe that one of them may have been used in the occupation of the Islands, but there were other vessels in possession of the Germans and Italians which may equally have been used for that purpose. At any rate, the question of the interpretation of their neutrality is a matter obviously of supreme consequence to Turkey. I do not think we should make a reproach upon that subject.

Then Mr. Lloyd George said that he had read how Turkey had made some agreement with the Iraki Government, and he asked about that. I always thought it was a most unfortunate and most tiresome thing when both Persia and Mesopotamia changed their names at about the same time to two names which were so much alike—Iran and Iraq. I have endeavoured myself in the domestic sphere to avoid such risks by naming the new Minister a Minister of State in order that there should be no confusion between him and the Minister without Portfolio. That unfortunate procedure on the part of these two neighbouring States has led Mr. Lloyd George into needless anxiety. I am very happy to be able to relieve him. It appears that the arrangement is between Turkey and Persia, and that it relates to measures to strengthen the Turco-Persian border, which we knew all about, which have been prepared for some time, and which are now put into force as from 4th May, 1941. I hope I have relieved his anxiety on that score, which indeed was entirely excusable owing to the unhappy similarity of the names of these two countries.

I must, however, say that I did not think Mr. Lloyd George's speech was particularly helpful at a period of what he himself called discouragement and disheartenment. It was not the sort of speech which one would have expected from the great war leader of former days, who was accustomed to brush aside despondency and alarm, and push on irresistibly towards the final goal. It was the sort of speech with which, I imagine, the illustrious and venerable Marshal Pètain might well have enlivened the closing days of M. Reynaud's Cabinet. But in one respect I am grateful to my right hon. Friend for the note which he struck, because if anything could make it clearer that we ought to close our Debate by a Vote of Confidence, it is the kind of speech which he delivered, and the kind of speeches we have heard from some of the ablest and most eminent Members of the House. I think the Government were right to put down a Motion of Confidence, because after our reverses and disappointments in the field, His Majesty's Government have a right to know where they stand with the House of Commons, and where the House of Commons stands with the country. Still more is this knowledge important for the sake of foreign nations, especially nations which are balancing their policy at the present time, and who ought to be left in no doubt about the stability or otherwise of this resolved and obstinate war Government. Questions are asked, conversations take place in the Lobbies, paragraphs are written in the political columns of the newspapers, and before you know where you are, you hear in all the Embassies with which we are in relation queries, "Will the Government last?—Are they going to break up?—Will there be a change of administration and a change of policy?"

I think it is essential, considering the tremendous issues which are at stake, and, not to exaggerate, the frightful risks we are all going to run, and are running, that we should have certitude on these matters. In enemy countries they take a lively interest in our proceedings, and I flatter myself that high hopes are entertained that all will not go well with His Majesty's present advisers. The only way in which these doubts can be removed and these expectations disappointed is by a full Debate followed by a Division, and the Government are entitled to ask that such a Vote shall express itself in unmistakeable terms. I see that one of the newspapers, which is described as a supporter of the Government, and which supports us by being the most active in keeping us up to the mark —like the Noble Lord the Member for Horsham (Earl Winterton), now relieved from all necessity of keeping himself up to the mark —has deplored the fact of this Motion of Confidence being proposed, because such a procedure might lead some Members to make speeches in favour of the Government, whereas it would be much more useful if the Debate consisted entirely of informative criticism. I am not one, and I should be the last, unduly to resent unfair criticism, or even fair criticism, which is so much more searching. I have been a critic myself—I cannot at all see how I should have stood the test of being a mere spectator in the drama which is now passing. But there is a kind of criticism which is a little irritating. It is like that of a bystander who, when he sees a team of horses dragging a heavy wagon painfully up a hill, cuts a switch from the fence, and there are many switches, and belabours them lustily. He may well be animated by a benevolent purpose, and who shall say the horses may not benefit from his efforts, and the wagon gets quicker to the top of the hill?

I think that it would be a pity if this important and critical Debate, at this moment which my right hon. Friend describes as disheartening and discouraging, consisted solely of critical and condemnatory speeches, because, apart from the inartistic monotony, it would tend to give a distorted impression to many important and interested foreign observers who are not very well acquainted with our Parliamentary or political affairs. Therefore I ask the House for a Vote of Confidence. I hope that those, if such there be, who sincerely in their hearts believe that we are not doing our best and that they could do much better, I hope that they will carry their opinion to its logical and ultimate conclusion in the Lobby. Here I must point out, only for the benefit of foreign countries, that they would run no risk in doing so. They are answerable only to their consciences and to their constituents. It is a free Parliament in a free country. We have succeeded in maintaining, under difficulties which are unprecedented, and in dangers which, in some cases, might well be mortal, the whole process and reality of Parliamentary institutions. I am proud of this. It is one of the things for which we are fighting. Moreover, I cannot imagine that any man would want to bear, or consent to bear, the kind of burden which falls upon the principal Ministers in the Government, or upon the head of the Government in this terrible war, unless he were sustained, and continually sustained, by strong convinced support, not only of the House of Commons, but of the nation to which the House of Commons is itself responsible.

It is very natural that the House should not be entirely satisfied with the recent turn of events in the Middle East, and that some Members should be acutely disappointed that we have not been able to defend Greece successfully against the Italian or German armies, and that we should have been unable to keep or extend our conquests in Libya. This sudden darkening of the landscape, after we had been cheered by a long succession of victories over the Italians, is particularly painful. For myself, I must confess that I watched the fate of Greece, after her repulse of the Italian invader, with agony. The only relief I feel is that everything in human power was done by us and that our honour as a nation is clear. If anything could add a pang to this emotion, it would be the knowledge we had of the approaching and impending outrage, with so little power to avert from this heroic and famous people a fate so hideous and so undeserved.

My right hon. Friend the Member for Devonport (Mr. Hore-Belisha) and some others, have spoken of the importance in war of full and accurate Intelligence of the movements and intentions of the enemy. That is one of those glimpses of the obvious and of the obsolete with which his powerful speech abounded. So far as the German invasion of the Balkans is concerned, we had long and ample forewarning of what was in prospect. It is three months since I stated publicly in a broadcast that the Bulgarian airfields were being occupied with the knowledge of the Bulgarian Government by the advance parties and agents of the German air force. Talk of our diplomacy being idle—our diplomacy has never ceased for one moment to try to apprise countries of the dangers and perils that were coming on them, and to urge them to common action by which alone their own security and safety could be maintained. Every week one watched the remorseless movement of vast German forces through Hungary, through Rumania and into Bulgaria, or towards the Croatian frontier of Yugoslavia, until at last no fewer than forty German divisions, five of which were armoured, were massed upon the scene. Hitler has told us that it was a crime in such circumstances on our part to go to the aid of the Greeks. I do not wish to enter into argument with experts. This is not a kind of crime of which he is a good judge.

When the first request for a Debate began to be made about a fortnight ago, I understood that our critics wished to argue that we were wrong to go to Greece, especially in view of what had happened in Libya. Therefore, we put the question of aid to Greece in the forefront of this Motion of Confidence. We cannot judge our aid to Greece without the consequential effect on the position in Libya. Looking back on the sad course of events, I can only feel, as the Prime Minister of New Zealand has so nobly declared, that if we had again to tread that stony path, even with the knowledge we possess to-day, I for one would do the same thing again; and that is the view of my colleagues in the War Cabinet and on the Defence Committee, and I believe that view is almost universally sustained by the House. Military operations must be judged by the success which attends them rather than by the sentiments which inspired them, though these, too, may play their part in the verdict of history and in the survival of races. It remains to be seen whether the Italian dictator, in invading Greece, and the German dictator, in coming to his rescue and trampling her into a bloody welter, will in fact have gained an advantage or suffered a loss when the full story of the war is completed.

Even in a strictly military view, the addition of the whole of the Balkan peoples to the number of ancient and independent States and Sovereignties which have now fallen under the Nazi yoke, and which have to be held down by force or by intrigue, may by no means prove a source of strength to the German Army. This vast machine, which was so improvidently allowed to build itself up again during the last eight years, has now spread from the Arctic to the Aegean and from the Atlantic Ocean to the Black Sea. That is no source of strength, and, returning from the military to the political aspect, nothing can more surely debar the Germans from establishing and shaping the new Europe—and one will certainly emerge—than the fact that the German name and the German race have become and are becoming more universally and more intensely hated among all the peoples in all the lands than any name or any race of which history bears record.

Some have compared Hitler's conquests with those of Napoleon. It may be that Spain and Russia will shortly furnish new chapters to that theme. It must be remembered, however, that Napoleon's armies carried with them the fierce, liberating and equalitarian winds of the French Revolution, whereas Hitler's Empire has nothing behind it but racial self-assertion, espionage, pillage, corruption, and the Prussian boot. Yet Napoleon's Empire, with all its faults, and all its glories, fell, and flashed away like snow at Easter till nothing remained but His Majesty's ship *Bellerophon*, which awaited its suppliant refugee. So I derive confidence that the will-power of the British nation, expressing itself through a stern, steadfast, unyielding House of Commons, once again will perform its liberating function and humbly exercise and execute a high purpose among men; and I say this with the more confidence because we are no longer a small Island lost in the Northern mists, but around us gather in proud array all the free nations of the British Empire, and this time from across the Atlantic Ocean the mighty Republic of the United States proclaims itself on our side, or at our side, or, at any rate, near our side.

I do not intend to-day to discuss the large, complicated questions of munitions or food production. On a future occasion, probably in secret session, the Minister of Supply will make a considerable statement to the House. My right hon. Friend the Member for Devonport (Mr. Hore-Belisha), who is so far-seeing now that we have lost his services and who told us at the end of November, 1939, that we were comfortably winning the war, had the temerity yesterday to raise the subject of our admitted shortage of tanks. There is one very simple point about tanks, which I think he might have mentioned to us, in the years preceding the war when he was at the head of the War Office and had the opportunity of the highest technical advice. In the last war, tanks were built to go three or four miles an hour and to stand up to rifle or machine-gun bullets. In the interval the process of mechanical science had advanced so much that it became possible to make a tank which could go 15, 20 or 25 miles an hour and stand up to cannon fire. That was a great revolution, by which Hitler has profited. That is a simple fact which was perfectly well known to the military and technical services three or four years before the war. It did not spring from German brains. It sprang from British brains, and from brains like those of General de Gaulle in France, and it has been exploited and turned to our grievous injury by the uninventive but highly competent and imitative Germans. The German Tank Corps knew all about it and wrote it down, but apparently my right hon. Friend did not take it in—at any rate, he did not mention it to us in those simple terms, and, indeed, it may be that the point may not have struck him until now. It would have been a very valuable contribution to our pre-war preparations. My right hon. Friend played a worthy part in bringing in compulsory service. I should not have referred to this matter if he had not endeavoured to give the House a sort of idea of his super-prevision and super-efficiency and shown himself so aggressive when, I think, with all good will, he sometimes stands in need of some humility in regard to the past.

Let me tell him that we are now making every month as many heavy tanks as there existed in the whole British Army at the time he left the War Office—and that we shall very soon, before the end of this year, be producing nearly double that number. This takes no account of the immense productive efforts in the United States. I only say this to him by way of reassuring him that the good work which he did, the foundations which he laid, have not been left to stand where they were when he went out of office. He must learn to "forgive us our trespasses as we forgive them that trespass against us."

My right hon. Friend the Member for Carnarvon Boroughs (Mr. Lloyd George) made his usual criticisms about the composition and character of the Government, of the war control and of the War Cabinet, and the House is entitled to know, has a right to know, who are responsible for the conduct of the war. The War Cabinet consists of eight members, five of whom have no regular Department, and three of whom represent the main organisms of the State, to wit, Foreign Affairs, Finance and Labour, which in their different ways come into every great question that has to be settled. That is the body which gives its broad sanction to the main policy and conduct of the war. Under their authority, the Chiefs of Staff of the three Services sit each day together, and I, as Prime Minister and Minister of Defence, convene them and preside over them when I think it necessary, inviting, when business requires it, the three Service Ministers. All large issues of military policy are brought before the Defence Committee, which has for several months consisted of the three Chiefs of Staff, the three Service Ministers, and four members of the War Cabinet, namely, myself, the Lord Privy Seal, who has no Department, the Foreign Secretary, and Lord Beaverbrook. This is the body, this is the machine; it works easily and flexibly at the present time, and I do not propose to make any changes in it until further advised.

My right hon. Friend spoke of the great importance of my being surrounded by people who would stand up to me and say, "No, No, No." Why, good gracious, has he no idea how strong the negative principle is in the constitution and working of the British war-making machine? The difficulty is not, I assure him, to have more brakes put on the wheels; the difficulty is to get more impetus and speed behind it. At one moment we are asked to emulate the Germans in their audacity and vigour, and the next moment the Prime Minister is to be assisted by being surrounded by a number of "No-men" to resist me at every point and prevent me from making anything in the nature of a speedy, rapid and, above all, positive constructive decision.

However, I must say that, in this whole business of Libya and Greece, I can assure the House that no violence has been done to expert military opinion, either in the Chiefs of Staff Committee at home or in the generals commanding in the field. All decisions have been taken unitedly and freely and in good will, in response to the hard pressure of events. I would make it clear, however, that, in certain circumstances or emergencies, the responsible political Minister representing the Government of the country would not hesitate to assume responsibility for decisions which might have to be taken, and I, personally, as head of the Government, obviously assume that responsibility in the most direct personal form. It follows, therefore, when all is said and done, that I am the one whose head should be cut off if we do not win the war. I am very ready that this should be so, because, as my hon. Friend the Member for Seaham (Mr. Shinwell) feelingly reminded us yesterday, most of the Members of the House would probably experience an even more unpleasant fate at the hands of the triumphant Hun.

I notice a tendency in some quarters, especially abroad, to talk about the Middle East as if we could afford to lose our position there and yet carry on the war to victory on the oceans and in the air. Stated as an academic and strategic fact, that may be true, but do not let anyone underrate the gravity of the issues which are being fought for in the Nile Valley. The loss of the Nile Valley and the Suez Canal and the loss of our position in the Mediterranean, as well as the loss of Malta, would be among the heaviest blows which we could sustain. We are determined to fight for them with all the resources of the British Empire, and we have every reason to believe that we shall be successful. General Wavell has under his orders at the present moment nearly 500,000 men. A continual flow of equipment has been in progress from this country during the last ten months, and, now that the Italian resistance in Abyssinia, East Africa and the Somalilands is collapsing, a steady concentration northwards of all these Forces is possible, and, indeed, it has been for many weeks rapidly proceeding; and General Smuts has ordered the splendid South African Army forward to the Mediterranean shores.

Warfare in the Western Desert or, indeed, in all the deserts which surround Egypt, can only be conducted by comparatively small numbers of highly-equipped troops. Here, the fortunes of war are subject to violent oscillation, and mere numbers do not count. On the contrary, the movement in the desert of large numbers would, if things went wrong, lead only to disaster on a larger scale. That is what happened to the Italians. For many months last year a steady flow of Italian troops moved forward day by day from west to east along the coastal roads of Libya, in order to build up an army for the invasion of Egypt. In December those masses were ripe for the sickle; 180,000 men lay along the North African shore, from Benghazi to the Egyptian frontier. Once the head of this force was chopped and broken, it was not physically possible for this great army to retreat. It had been built up bit by bit. It could not retreat all at once; the single coastal road could not carry it, and the transport available could not feed it on the move. The victory of Sidi Barrani, as I told the House some months ago, settled the fate of the troops in Cyrenaica. They did not possess command of the sea, they were beaten in the air, and no course was open to them but to be pinned against the sea and destroyed in detail at Bardia, Tobruk and Benghazi.

The same thing, with important modifications, might well have happened to us when the German armoured forces defeated, dispersed and largely destroyed our single armoured brigade which was guarding the advanced frontier of the Province of Cyrenaica. There are no exact accounts of what happened at Agedabia and Mechili. The generals have been taken prisoner through running undue risks in their personal movements, risks which they could run against the Italians, but not against the Germans. The remnants of the armoured brigade are now fighting in Tobruk. Events are moving so fast, people have so much to do, and the intensity of the war is such, that there is not much time to be spared to dwell upon the past. But there are certain broad features which will interest the House. It may surprise the House to learn that the German armoured force was not much larger than our own. But tactical mistakes were committed and mischances occurred, and with very little fighting our armoured force became disorganized. However, the troops we had in Benghazi only amounted to a division, and this division, by a rapid retreat, gained the fortress of Tobruk in good order and unmolested, and there joined the large garrison. There, a month ago, it stood at bay, and there it stands at bay to-day.

The Germans, as we now know from the examination of prisoners, had no expectation of proceeding beyond Agedabia. They meant to engage our armoured troops and create a diversion to prevent the dispatch of reinforcements to Greece, while they were bringing over larger forces from Italy and Sicily and building up their supplies and communications; but when they won their surprising success, they exploited it with that organized, enterprising audacity which ranks so high in the military art. They pushed on into the blue—I might say into the yellow ochre—of the desert, profiting by their easy victory as they have done in so many countries, and for the morrow they took, in this case, little thought either what they should eat or what they should drink. They pushed on until they came up against Tobruk. There they met their prop, a hard and heavy prop, not the less important because, like all these desert operations, it was on a small scale. They pushed on until they came in contact also with the large forces which guard the frontiers of Egypt and which lie there securely based on the road, railway and sea communications. There, for the present moment, they stop.

I shall not attempt to carry the story further this afternoon. To do so would be foolish and might be harmful, but this I will say, that so long as the enemy has a superiority in armoured vehicles they will have an advantage in desert warfare, even though at the present time the air forces are about equal. But as I said, this desert warfare must be conducted only by small forces. Thirty or forty thousand men is the most that can be supplied in the desert, and it is very doubtful whether even this number can be attained. For the invasion of Egypt, for an invasion in main force such as the Italians contemplated last autumn, enormous preparations would be required, great supplies would have to be built up and maintained, a pipeline might have to be made to carry an artificial river forward with the troops. We, on the other hand, lying back on our fertile delta, which incidentally is the worst ground in the world for armoured vehicles, and enjoying the command of the sea, confront the enemy with problems far more difficult, because on a far larger scale, than any he has yet solved in Africa. All the more true is this while we defend, as we intend to do to the death and without thought of retirement, the valuable and highly offensive outposts of Crete and Tobruk. Crete has not yet been attacked, but Tobruk has already been the scene of a most stubborn and spirited defence by the Australian and British troops gathered within these widespread fortified lines, under the command of the Australian General Morshead. The strategic significance of Tobruk was obvious from the first, and anyone can see now how irresistibly it has imposed itself as a magnet on the enemy.

I have gone into all this military detail, not in order to burden the House with it, but in order to give Members an indication of what happened, and why, and what were the various factors. I have gone into all these details because I want to make it clear that we intend to fight with all our strength for the Nile Valley and its surrounding country and for the command of the Mediterranean. We have every reason to believe that our troops and resources will give a good account of themselves. Let there be no feather-headed or defeatist talk about cutting our losses in the Middle East. I agree with my right hon. Friend the Member for Devonport in that. But, as I said early in December, when our situation in Egypt was far more critical than it is now, it is a case of deeds, not words. We must allow the story to unfold. My hon. and gallant Friend the Member for Petersfield (Sir G. Jeffreys), in a speech to which I listened with great interest, asked a very fair question: how was it that this very large number of Germans got across to Libya without our Intelligence or generals knowing about it? Perhaps they did know about it; or perhaps the numbers were not so very large, after all. It depends on what you call "very large." At any rate, our generals on the spot believed that no superior German force could advance as far across the desert towards Egypt, as soon or as effectively as they did; and, secondly, that if they did advance, they would not be able to nourish themselves. That was a mistake. But anyone who supposes that there will not be mistakes in war is very foolish. I draw a distinction between mistakes. There is the mistake which comes through daring, what I call a mistake towards the enemy, in which you must always sustain your commanders, by sea, land or air. There are mistakes from the safety-first principle, mistakes of turning away from the enemy; and they require a far more acid consideration.

In the first belief to which I have just referred our generals were proved wrong; the second has not been decided. It has not yet been seen how the forces that advance will fare in the desert fighting, with all its chances and hazards, which still lies at no great distance before us. I will allow the speech of my hon. and gallant Friend the Member for Petersfield to detain me a moment longer on military issues, because it illustrates some of the points in the Debate. He reminded us of Frederick the Great's maxim, that it was pardonable to be defeated but that it was not pardonable to be surprised. On the other hand, when your enemy has five or six times as large a regular army as you have, much more amply equipped, and a good deal stronger in the air and far stronger in tanks; and when he lies in the centre of the war scene, and can strike out in any one, two or three different directions simultaneously, out of a choice of seven or eight, it is evident that your problems become very difficult. It is also evident, I think, that you would not solve your problem, as Frederick the Great's maxim and his remarks seem to suggest, by being prepared at every point to resist not only what is probable but what is possible. In such circumstances, upon which there is no need to enlarge, it is not possible to avoid repeated rebuffs and misfortunes, and these, of course, we shall very likely have to go through for quite a long time. Therefore, the right hon. Gentleman the Member for Devonport, the hon. Member for Seaham and any others of our leading lights in the embryonic all-party Opposition to the Government are not likely to run short of opportunities where they will be able to point to our lack of foresight and to the failure of our Intelligence service, of which I will only say that it was thought to be the best in the world in the last war, and it is certainly not the worst in the world to-day.

Some have pointed to what has happened in Iraq as another instance of the failure of our Intelligence and our diplomacy. My hon. and gallant Friend the Member for Wycombe (Sir A. Knox), though in a perfectly friendly way, has inquired about that. We have been told that the Foreign Office never knows anything that is going on in the world, and that our organization is quite unadapted to meet the present juncture. But we have known only too well what was going on in Iraq, and as long ago as last May, a year ago, the Foreign Office began to ask for troops to be sent there to guard the line of communications. We had not the troops. All that we could send had to go to the Nile Valley. In default of troops, it was very difficult to make head against the pronounced pro-Axis intrigues of Rashid Ali, who eventually, after his removal from power at our instance, staged a *coup d'ctat* against the Regent and the lawful Government of the country. Obviously, his object was to have everything ready for the Germans as soon as they could reach Iraq according to programme. However, in this case the ill-informed slothful, kid-gloved British Government, as it has no doubt become since it has been deprived of the abilities of some valuable Members, actually forestalled this plot. Three weeks ago strong British forces, which are continually being reinforced from India, were landed at Basra, and they assumed control of that highly important bridgehead in the East for which we shall, no doubt, have to fight hard and long.

Rashid Ali, having consented to the first stage of this action, was led into a more violent course. He attacked the British air cantonment at Habbaniyah, and for several days we were very anxious about the people there. We are very anxious about them even yet. They had, however, been reinforced beforehand. Air Forces from Egypt and Palestine were able to give powerful assistance, and I am glad to inform the House that yesterday the garrison sallied out and attacked the besiegers, with the result that they completely routed them and put them to flight. Twenty-six Iraqi officers and 408 men were taken prisoners, and the total enemy casualties were estimated at 1,000. While this was going on, our Air Force attacked and largely destroyed the reinforcing convoy of lorries and ammunition which was on its way to the besiegers. Other operations are in progress, and I shall not predict their results. But we shall try to make headway against all our foes, wherever they present themselves and from whatever quarter they come. A combative spirit in all directions is essential. It may be that the Germans will arrive before we have crushed the revolt, in which case our task will become more difficult. It may be that the revolt went off at half-cock in consequence of our forestalling action in landing at Basra. I would, therefore, enjoin caution on some of our critics, who may perhaps find that they have been premature in saying that we were too tardy, and too soon in saying that we were too late. We are not at war with Iraq; we are dealing with a military dictator who attempted to subvert the constitutional Government, and we intend to assist the Iraqis to get rid of him and get rid of the military dictatorship at the earliest possible moment.

I ask you to witness, Mr. Speaker, that I have never promised anything or offered anything but blood, tears, toil and sweat, to which I will now add our fair share of mistakes, shortcomings and disappointments, and also that this may go on for a very long time, at the end of which I firmly believe—though it is not a promise or a guarantee, only a profession of faith—that there will be complete, absolute and final victory.

Now—I think there is just time for it—we come to the Battle of the Atlantic. It is a mistake to say that the Battle of the Atlantic is won. First of all, how is it won? It would be quite easy to reduce our losses at sea to vanishing point by the simple expedient of keeping our ships in harbour, or to reduce them markedly by overloading our ships with precautions. The Admiralty, on whom the first burden rests, naturally measure their struggle by the ships which they bring safely into port; but that is not the test by which those responsible for the highest direction of the country have to be guided. Our test is the number of tons of imports brought into this island in a given quarter or a given year. At present we are maintaining great traffics, although with heavy losses. We try to meet these losses by building new ships, repairing damaged ships, by repairing them more speedily, and by acceleration of the turn-round of our ships in our ports and in foreign ports. We have made great progress in these spheres since the beginning of the year, but there is much more to do in that field.

With the continued flow of assistance which has already been given to us by the United States, and promise to us, we can probably maintain our minimum essential traffic during 1941. As for 1942, we must look for an immense construction of merchant ships by the United States. This is already in full swing, and since I last mentioned this subject to the House a month ago, I have received assurances that the construction of merchant vessels by the United States, added to our own large programme of new building and repair, should see us through the year of 1942. It may be that 1943, if ever we have to endure it as a year of war, will present easier problems. The United States patrol, announced by President Roosevelt, on which the American Navy and Air Force are already engaged, takes a very considerable part of the Atlantic Ocean, in a certain degree, off our hands; but we need a good deal more help, and I expect we shall get a good deal more help in a great many ways. In fact, it has been declared that we are to have all the help that is necessary; but here I speak with very great caution, for it is not for a British Minister to forecast, still less to appear to prescribe, the policy of the United States. So far, in our relations with that great Republic, which began so well under the auspices of Lord Lothian, I do not think we have made any serious mistakes. Neither by boasting nor by begging have we offended them. When a mighty democracy of 130,000,000 gets on the move, one can only await the full deployment of these vast psychological manifestations and their translation into the physical field. Anyone can see Hitler's fear of the United States from the fact that he has not long ago declared war upon them.

In some quarters of the House, or at any rate among some Members, there is a very acute realization of the gravity of our problems and of our dangers. I have never underrated them. I feel we are fighting for life and survival from day to day and from hour to hour. But, believe me, Herr Hitler has his problems, too, and if we only remain united and strive our utmost to increase our exertions, and work like one great family, standing together and helping each other, as 5,000,000 families in Britain are doing to-day under the fire of the enemy, I cannot conceive how anyone can doubt that victory will crown the good cause we serve. Government and Parliament alike have to be worthy of the undaunted and unconquerable people who give us their trust and who give their country their all.

It is a year almost to a day since, in the crash of the disastrous Battle of France, His Majesty's present administration was formed. Men of all parties, duly authorized by their parties, joined hands together to fight this business to the end. That was a dark hour, and little did we know what storms and perils lay before us, and little did Herr Hitler know, when in June, 1940, he received the total capitulation of France and when he expected to be master of all Europe in a few weeks and the world in a few years, that ten months later, in May, 1941, he would be appealing to the much-tried German people to prepare themselves for the war of 1942. When I look back on the perils which have been overcome, upon the great mountain waves through which the gallant ship has driven, when I remember all that has gone wrong, and remember also all that has gone right, I feel sure we have no need to fear the tempest. Let it roar, and let it rage. We shall come through.

[Editor's Note: *The vote of confidence in the Government was then carried by 447 to 3.*

This was Mr. Churchill's last speech in the old House of Commons, which was totally destroyed in the air raid three days later.]

TO THE INVADED COUNTRIES

MESSAGES SENT TO THE PRIME MINISTER OF HOLLAND,
THE PRIME MINISTER OF BELGIUM AND THE FOREIGN
MINISTER OF LUXEMBURG
MAY 10, 1941

(The anniversary of the German invasion of the Low Countries)

---

*May 8. Rashid Ali fled from Iraq after a series of successes by
British troops.*

*Hitler reported to have demanded permission from
Vichy Government to land troops in Syria.*

*May 9. President Roosevelt warned Vichy Government that
United States would stop wheat supplies if Vichy adopted
a policy favourable to Germany.*

*May 10. R.A.F. night fighters scored their greatest success, 33
German raiders being shot down in big London raid
in which the House of Commons was devastated.*

*Officially announced that the Axis had lost 612,000
tons of shipping in six weeks.*

[*May 10, 1941.*

[TO HOLLAND]

ON the anniversary of the barbarous, brutal, unprovoked
invasion of the Netherlands by the German armed forces, I
wish to express the gratitude of H.M. Government for the aid which
the Netherlands Government has given to the Allied cause throughout this grievous year.

The presence in this country of Her Majesty the Queen of the
Netherlands and of Her Majesty's Government and the support
given by the Netherlands Empire and the Netherlands armed forces
and merchant marine have been most valuable sources of strength
to the common cause.

Nor do we forget brave Dutchmen who fought so gallantly in
the battle of the Netherlands and who now under Nazi yoke continue to oppose tyranny.

The sympathy and admiration of H.M. Government and of the

British people go out in a special measure to the people of the Netherlands who by their courage and endurance play so firm a part in the war against the hated enemy.

[TO BELGIUM]

On the anniversary of the day when in violation of the most solemn undertakings the German Government, without cause or provocation, launched their armed forces against the territory of Belgium, I wish to acknowledge in the name of H.M. Government the effective help which the Belgian Government, the Belgian Empire, and the Belgian armed forces and merchant marine have given to the Allied cause throughout the past year.

We remember also your soldiers who resisted the invader in the battle of Belgium and who now in their homes oppose his will.

The sympathy and admiration of H.M. Government and of the British people go out in special measure to the Belgian people now under the hateful Nazi tyranny, who by their courage and endurance daily contribute to the defence of freedom.

[TO LUXEMBURG]

On the anniversary of the day when the barbarous German hordes overran the territory of your Grand Duchy in violation of their solemn oath, I desire to express to Your Excellency the sympathy and admiration of H.M. Government and of the British people for the peaceful and industrious people of the Grand Duchy once again so cruelly subjected to the tyranny of a foreign aggressor. The unfaltering gallantry and endurance which Her Royal Highness the Grand Duchess and Her Royal Highness's Government and the whole people of Luxemburg have displayed since that dark day, has given encouragement and support to the Allied cause.

TO HAILE SELASSIE

A MESSAGE OF CONGRATULATION TO THE EMPEROR OF
ABYSSINIA ON HIS RETURN TO HIS CAPITAL, ADDIS ABABA,
MAY 10, 1941

[May 10, 1941.

IT IS WITH DEEP AND UNIVERSAL PLEASURE THAT THE BRITISH NATION AND EMPIRE HAVE LEARNED OF YOUR IMPERIAL MAJESTY'S WELCOME HOME TO YOUR CAPITAL AT ADDIS ABABA. YOUR MAJESTY WAS THE FIRST OF THE LAWFUL SOVEREIGNS TO BE DRIVEN FROM HIS THRONE AND COUNTRY BY THE FASCIST AND NAZI CRIMINALS, AND IS NOW THE FIRST TO RETURN IN TRIUMPH. YOUR MAJESTY'S THANKS WILL BE DULY CONVEYED TO THE COMMANDERS, OFFICERS AND MEN OF THE BRITISH AND EMPIRE FORCES WHICH HAVE AIDED THE ETHIOPIAN PATRIOTS IN THE TOTAL AND FINAL DESTRUCTION OF THE ITALIAN MILITARY USURPATION. HIS MAJESTY'S GOVERNMENT LOOK FORWARD TO A LONG PERIOD OF PEACE AND PROGRESS IN ETHIOPIA AFTER THE FORCES OF EVIL HAVE BEEN FINALLY OVERTHROWN.

THE WAR SITUATION

TWO STATEMENTS MADE TO THE HOUSE OF COMMONS
MAY 20, 1941

May 12. World sensation caused by the announcement that Rudolph Hess, Deputy Fuhrer of Germany, had flown from Germany in a plane piloted by himself and landed by parachute in Scotland.

May 14. Mr. Winant, United States Ambassador to Great Britain, called for British-U.S. collaboration, saying: "This is not Britain's fight alone."

Enemy troops which penetrated 30 miles into Egypt thrown back to Sollum.

May 15. Mr. Eden announced that the Germans were using French air bases in Syria, and warned Vichy Government that Britain would take appropriate action.

May 16. R.A.F. raided three airfields in Syria.

United States seized the Normandie and other French ships and cancelled food shipments.

British troops made a surprise attack on German armoured units on the Libya border.

May 17. It was officially announced that 6,065 people were killed in air raids on Britain in April.

May 20. Germany launched a great attack on Crete, dropping large numbers of parachute troops and landing other forces by air troop carriers and gliders.

[*May 20, 1941.*

SINCE we last were together several important events have happened on which perhaps I might presume to say a few words to the House. The victory of Amba Alagi has resulted in the surrender of the Duke of Aosta and his whole remaining forces, and must be considered to bring major organized resistance by the Italians in Abyssinia to an end. No doubt other fighting will continue for some time in the south, but this certainly wears the aspect of the culmination of a campaign which I think is one of the most remarkable ever fought by British or Imperial arms. It reflects the utmost credit on Generals Cunningham and Platt, who discharged so well the task assigned to them by the Commander-in-Chief in the Middle East, Sir Archibald Wavell. When we look back to January, I find that the best expert opinion fixed the middle or end of May as the earliest date at which we could advance upon Kismayu, and anyone who has acquainted himself with the geography will see the enormous achievements, beyond anything that could have been hoped for, which have been accomplished by audacious action and by extraordinary competence in warfare in those desolate countries.

I take this opportunity of pointing out that in this campaign the South African Army, strong forces raised in the Union of South Africa, have played a most distinguished part. They were ordered by General Smuts to go forward, and, now that this theatre is closing down, they are to move northward to the Mediterranean. But also two British Indian divisions have gained laurels in the fighting at Kassala and all the way from Kassala to Keren and in the final event. These Indian divisions consist of six Indian and three British battalions. I am assured that the greatest admiration is felt at the extraordinary military qualities displayed by the Indian troops, and that their dash, their ardour and their faithful endurance of all the hardships have won them the regard of their British comrades. Sometimes we have seen cases where not a single British officer remained, and the battalion conducted itself in the most effective manner. Altogether this campaign is one which reflects very high honour upon the soldiers of India of all castes and creeds who were engaged. I feel that I could not refer to it without bringing this matter in a direct and emphatic manner to the attention of the House.

The second event which has occurred since we were last here is the sharp and well-sustained action at Sollum. This is of interest because it was fought exclusively between British and German troops. It has not, I suppose, been found worth while to maintain Italian troops at the end of such a long and precarious line of communications. Fighting was severe but, of course, not on a very large scale. Several of our motorized brigades, supported by armoured brigades and strong artillery, advanced about 30 miles from the position where they had been deployed for some weeks past, and attacked the enemy, taking Sollum, Halfaya Pass and Fort Capuzzo, and the armoured troops then got round the tanks and were very well situated about one o'clock on the 17th. The Germans launched a resolute counter-attack by about 40 tanks and recaptured Capuzzo. That entailed the withdrawal of the armoured brigade from the advantageous position which it had attained.

The operation, therefore, was indecisive. The Germans claim 100 British prisoners, but we have 500 Germans in our hands, and the losses in tanks and in personnel on their side are certainly as heavy, if not heavier, than on ours. These operations must be regarded on the background that for more than six weeks past the Germans have been proclaiming that they would shortly be in Suez, and have been making much credit with the neutral world by spreading at large statements of this kind. It is, therefore, satisfactory for us to see that we have retained strong offensive power, and that the fighting is being maintained, at any rate, on even terms in the advance areas of the approaches to Egypt.

The third matter is not yet known to the House. For the last few days our reconnoitring aeroplanes have noticed very heavy concentrations of German aircraft of all kinds on the aerodromes of Southern Greece. We have attacked them night after night, inflicting considerable damage. It is now clear that these concentrations were the prelude to an attack upon Crete. An air-borne attack in great strength started this morning, and what cannot fail to be a serious battle has begun and is developing. Our troops there —British, New Zealand and Greek Forces—are under the command of General Freyberg, and we feel confident that most stern and resolute resistance will be offered to the enemy.

[Editor's Note: *Later the same day Mr. Churchill made this additional statement on the situation in Crete.*]

As I mentioned to the House this morning that a serious attack had been begun upon the Island of Crete by air-borne troops, I thought that the House would like to know, before it separated, what is the latest information in the possession of the Government. But I cannot pretend that the statement is of momentous importance. It is only because we are all together in this matter that I thought that the House would be most anxious to be kept fully informed, as it is my duty to do whatever possible. After a good deal of intense bombing of Suda Bay and the various aerodromes in the neighbourhood, about 1500 enemy troops wearing New Zealand battle dress [Editor's Note: *This point was corrected by Mr. Churchill in a speech made on June 10*] landed by gliders, parachutes and troop-carriers in the Canea-Maleme area. This message was sent at 12 o'clock to-day, when the military reported that the situation was in hand. Apparently the capture of Maleme aerodrome was the enemy's object, and this has so far failed.

A later report at 3 o'clock says that there is continuous enemy reconnaissance, accompanied by sporadic bombing and machine-gunning, chiefly against anti-aircraft defence. The military hospital between Canea and Maleme, captured by the enemy, has now been recaptured. There is reported to be a fairly strong enemy party south of the Canea-Maleme Road, which has not yet been mopped up, but other parties are reported to be accounted for. Heraklion was bombed, but there has been no landing so far. I must apologize to the House for intruding on them, but I thought they would like to hear how the action has so far developed.

THE FIGHTING IN CRETE

A STATEMENT IN THE HOUSE OF COMMONS
MAY 22, 1941

---

*May 21. The Duke of Aosta, Italian Viceroy of Abyssinia, and
five other generals, surrendered at Amba Alagi.*
*May 22. Fierce fighting in Crete. The British foiled German
attempts to land sea-borne troops.*

May 22, 1941.

THIS is a somewhat indeterminate moment in the battle for
Crete on which to make a statement, and I can only give a
very provisional account. Fighting is continuing with intensity,
and, although the situation is in hand, the Germans have gained
some local successes, at heavy cost. They are using large numbers
of air-borne and parachute troops, and these are being increased
daily. The position at Heraklion is that our troops are still holding
the aerodrome, although the Germans are now in what is called
occupation of the town, which probably means that they are
ensconced in certain buildings in the town. In the Retimo district
there is no report of any particular fighting, although an attempt
by the enemy to attack an aerodrome early yesterday morning was
successfully held. In the Canea-Suda Bay sector heavy enemy air
attacks in the early morning of yesterday were followed, in the
course of the day, by further parachute landings south-west of
Canea, which were heavily engaged by our artillery and machine-
guns. At Maleme Aerodrome, 10 miles south-west of Canea, it
appears that the enemy are now in occupation of the aerodrome
and the area to the west of it, but the aerodrome is still under our
fire. Elsewhere in this sector the coastal line remains in our hands.

The fighting is going on, deepening in intensity, and will certainly continue for some time. Last night the enemy began to try
seaborne landings, but a convoy, making for Crete, was intercepted
by our naval forces, and two transports and a number of caiques,
Greek boats, which probably contained troops intended for landing
operations, were sunk, and an enemy destroyer, which was escorting the convoy, was also sunk. But during the course of to-day,

very much larger attempts have been made by the enemy to carry an army into Crete, and a convoy of 30 vessels was discerned this morning by our forces, and was presumably attacked by them. My information is not complete on that point. The convoy had turned away towards the Islands of the Archipelago, and was being attacked by our destroyers and light forces. I have not received any further information as to what happened, except that there has been a great deal of fighting during the day, with the enemy air forces attacking our ships, and our forces attacking the convoy. I am sorry to say that I have got no definite information as to the results, but I feel they can hardly be other than satisfactory, in view of the naval forces of which we dispose in the Mediterranean sphere.

It is a most strange and grim battle that is being fought. Our side have no air, because they have no aerodromes, and not because they have no aeroplanes, and the other side have very little or no artillery or tanks. Neither side has any means of retreat. It is a desperate, grim battle. I will certainly send the good wishes of the House, and the encouragement and approval of the House, to these men who are fighting what is undoubtedly a most important battle which will affect the whole course of the campaign in the Mediterranean.

THE WAR SITUATION

A SPEECH TO THE HOUSE OF COMMONS
MAY 27, 1941

May 23. Darlan told the French people that the Vichy Government had "freely chosen" collaboration with Germany.

May 24. Hood, *Britain's biggest warship, was sunk by the new German battleship* Bismarck, *which was then pursued by other British ships and aircraft.*

May 25. King George of Greece and his Cabinet arrived in Egypt from Crete.

May 27. Bismarck *trapped 400 miles from Brest and sunk by torpedoes.*

President Roosevelt declared a state of "unlimited emergency" in the United States.

[*May 27, 1941.*

THE battle in Crete has now lasted for a week. During the whole of this time our troops have been subjected to an intense and continuous scale of air attack, to which, owing to the geographical conditions, our Air Forces have been able to make only a very limited, though very gallant, counterblast. The fighting has been most bitter and severe, and the enemy's losses up to the present have been much heavier than ours. We have not, however, been able to prevent further descents of air-borne German reinforcements, and the enemy's attack and the weight of this attack has grown from day to day. The battle has swayed backwards and forwards with indescribable fury at Canea, and equally fiercely, though on a smaller scale, at Retimo and Heraklion. Reinforcements of men and supplies have reached and are reaching General Freyberg's Forces, and at the moment at which I am speaking the issue of their magnificent resistance hangs in the balance.

So far, the Royal Navy have prevented any landing of a seaborne expedition, although a few shiploads of troops in caiques may have slipped through. Very heavy losses have been inflicted by our submarines, cruisers and destroyers upon the transports and the small Greek ships. It is not possible to state with accu-

143

racy how many thousands of enemy troops have been drowned, but the losses have been very heavy. The services rendered by the Navy in the defence of Crete have not been discharged without heavy losses to them. Our Fleet has been compelled to operate constantly without air protection within effective range of the enemy airfields. Claims even more exaggerated than usual have been made by the German and Italian wireless, which it has hitherto not been thought expedient to contradict. I may state, however, that we have lost the cruisers *Gloucester* and *Fiji* and the destroyers *Juno*, *Greyhound*, *Kelly* and *Kashmir*, by far the greater part of their crews having been saved. Two battleships and several other cruisers have been damaged, though not seriously, either by hits or near misses, but all will soon be in action again, and some are already at sea. The Mediterranean Fleet is to-day relatively stronger, compared to the Italian Navy, than it was before the Battle of Cape Matapan. There is no question whatever of our naval position in the Eastern Mediterranean having been prejudicially affected. However the decision of the battle may go, the stubborn defence of Crete, one of the important outposts of Egypt, will always rank high in the military and naval annals of the British Empire.

In Iraq, our position has been largely re-established, and the prospects have greatly improved. There have been no further adverse developments in Syria. In Abysinnia, the daily Italian surrenders continue, many thousands of prisoners and masses of equipment being taken.

While this drama has been enacted in the Eastern Mediterranean, another episode of an arresting character has been in progress in the Northern waters of the Atlantic Ocean. On Wednesday of last week, 21st May, the new German battleship, the *Bismarck*, accompanied by the new 8-in. gun cruiser *Prince Eugen*, was discovered by our air reconnaissance at Bergen, and on Thursday, 22nd May, it was known that they had left. Many arrangements were made to intercept them should they attempt, as seemed probable, to break out into the Atlantic Ocean with a view to striking at our convoys from the United States. During the night of 23rd to 24th our cruisers got into visual contact with them as they were passing through the Denmark Strait between Iceland and Greenland. At dawn on Saturday morning the *Prince of Wales* and the *Hood* intercepted the two enemy vessels. I have no detailed account of the action, because events have been moving so rapidly, but the *Hood* was struck at about 23,000 yards by a shell which penetrated into one of her magazines, and blew up, leaving only very few survivors. This splendid vessel, designed 23 years ago, is a serious loss to the Royal Navy, and even more so are the men and officers who manned her.

During the whole of Saturday our ships remained in touch with the *Bismarck* and her consort. In the night aircraft of the Fleet Air Arm from the *Victorious* struck the *Bismarck* with a torpedo, and arrangements were made for effective battle at dawn yesterday morning; but as the night wore on the weather deteriorated, the visibility decreased, and the *Bismarck*, by making a sharp turn, shook off the pursuit. I do not know what has happened to the *Prince Eugen*, but measures are being taken in respect of her. Yesterday, shortly before midday, a Catalina aircraft—one of the considerable number of these very far-ranging scouting aeroplanes which have been sent to us by the United States—picked up the *Bismarck*, and it was seen that she was apparently making for the French ports—Brest or Saint Nazaire. On this, further rapid dispositions were made by the Admiralty and by the Commander-in-Chief, and, of course, I may say that the moment the *Bismarck* was known to be at sea the whole apparatus of our ocean control came into play, very far-reaching combinations began to work, and from yesterday afternoon—I have not had time to prepare a detailed statement—Fleet Air Arm torpedo-carrying seaplanes from the *Ark Royal* made a succession of attacks upon the *Bismarck*, which now appears to be alone and without her consort. About midnight we learned that the *Bismarck* had been struck by two torpedoes, one amidships and the other astern. This second torpedo apparently affected the steering of the ship, for not only was she reduced to a very slow speed, but she continued making uncontrollable circles in the sea. While in this condition she was attacked by one of our flotillas, and hit by two more torpedoes, which brought her virtually to a standstill, far from help and far outside the range at which the enemy bomber aircraft from the French coast could have come upon the scene. This morning, at daylight or shortly after daylight, the *Bismarck* was attacked by the British pursuing battleships. I do not know what were the results of the bombardment; it appears, however, that the *Bismarck* was not sunk by gunfire, and she will now be dispatched by torpedo. It is thought that this is now proceeding, and it is also thought that there cannot be any lengthy delay in disposing of this vessel.

Great as is our loss in the *Hood*, the *Bismarck* must be regarded as the most powerful, as she is the newest, battleship in the world; and this striking of her from the German Navy is a very definite simplification of the task of maintaining the effective mastery of the Northern seas and the maintenance of the Northern blockade.

I daresay that in a few days it will be possible to give a much more detailed account, but the essentials are before the House, and although there is shade as well as light in this picture, I feel that we have every reason to be satisfied with the outcome of this fierce and memorable naval encounter.

Later Mr. Churchill rose again in the House of Commons to add:

I do not know whether I might venture, with great respect, to intervene for one moment. I have just received news that the *Bismarck* is sunk.

TO THE PEOPLE OF CANADA

A MESSAGE BROADCAST IN CONNECTION WITH THE
LAUNCHING OF CANADA'S 1941 VICTORY LOAN
JUNE 2, 1941

---

*May 30. Big Allied withdrawals in Crete, and the situation de-
scribed as "delicate and serious."*

> *Rashid Ali, Iraqi usurper, fled as British troops closed
in on Bagdad.*

May 31. Iraqi rebels asked for an Armistice.

> *Darlan made a violent anti-British speech.*

*June 1. Clothes and footwear rationed, each person being allowed
66 coupons a year.*

> *War Office revealed that 15,000 British troops had been
evacuated from Crete, and that our losses were "severe."*

> *New Constitutional government set up in Iraq.*

*June 2. Hitler and Mussolini had a five-hour conference in the
Brenner Pass.*

[June 2, 1941.

I AM glad to have an opportunity of speaking again to the people of Canada. Your comradeship in this mortal struggle cheers and fortifies the people of these islands. To Nazi tyrants and gangsters it must seem strange that Canada, free from all compulsion or pressure, so many thousands of miles away, should hasten forward into the van of the battle against the evil forces of the world. These wicked men cannot understand the deep currents of loyalty and tradition that flow between the different self-governing nations of the British Empire. The people of Great Britain are proud of the fact that the liberty of thought and action they have won in the course of their long, romantic history should have taken root throughout the length and breadth of a vast continent, from Halifax to Victoria.

But the Canadians are the heirs of another tradition: the true tradition of France, a tradition of valour and faith which they keep alive in these dark days and which we are confident will in the end bring back again to life France itself.

147

The people of this country know that the prayers, the toil and the anxious thought of all Canadians are with them in their severe ordeal. Canada has given abundant proofs of her purpose. Canadian troops are becoming a familiar sight in the towns and villages of England. I have met many men of the Canadian forces, and I have never seen a finer body of troops. It has not fallen to them as yet to be engaged with the enemy, but they have been allotted a task of vital importance, to play their part in the defence of the heart of the Empire, and to meet the enemy, should he venture to come, upon the very threshold of the land. And when the test comes, and if the test comes—and come it may—I know they will prove that they are worthy sons of those who stormed the Vimy Ridge twenty-four years ago.

But this war will not be won by valour in action alone. It will be won also by a hard, persevering effort in field and in factory. It will not be won without a multitude of minor, prosaic, unnoticed sacrifices.

I have heard from your Prime Minister, my friend—my old friend, Mr. Mackenzie King—of the remarkable organization which has been built up in Canada, to raise this, the greatest war loan in her history; and I am confident that this tremendous effort will be crowned by success.

I speak to you this afternoon from No. 10 Downing Street, here in the capital and the governing centre of this battered but indomitable city and island. Our people have been through much in the last few months. They have learned much—and some things they will never forget. But above all they have learned their own strength. They have tested their resolve under heavy hardship and danger. None of them, none of us, doubts that together with the whole Empire together, with the Old World and the New World together—no one doubts that we can or that we shall see it through; and that when at length we march again back into the light of happier and easier days, Canada will play her just part in laying the foundations of a wider and a better world.

THE WAR SITUATION

A SPEECH TO THE HOUSE OF COMMONS
JUNE 10, 1941

June 3. While German troops continued to filter into Syria, Vichy Government announced that they would defend the country "without German help" against British attack.

June 4. R.A.F. raided petrol stores at Beirut (Syria).

   The ex-Kaiser died at Doorn, aged 82.

June 5. Germans made their first heavy air attack on Alexandria and killed more than 150.

June 6. President Roosevelt accused German sympathizers in the United States of spreading "collapse and peace proposals" stories.

June 7. It was revealed that the R.A.F. had sunk 83 enemy ships in twelve weeks of daylight raids.

June 8. British and Free French forces invaded Syria, and pledges of Syrian independence were given.

June 9. It was officially announced that 17,000 British troops had been evacuated from Crete.

   The Germans torpedoed the U.S. cargo ship Robin Moor.

   President Roosevelt ordered United States troops to break aircraft factory strike in California.

[June 10, 1941.

I DO not think anyone, however Ministerially-minded, could possibly complain of the tone, temper and matter of this Debate. The kind of criticism we have had to-day, some of it very searching, is the kind of criticism that the Government not only accept but welcome. All the same, the House will permit me perhaps to point out that the way in which this Debate came about was calculated to give one the feeling of a challenge to the security of the Administration, and, from the point of view of the advantage to the country, that raises serious considerations. There were all kinds of paragraphs and reports which appeared in the papers about the grave uneasiness and unrest, stating that a Debate on Crete must take place. The parties were demanding it, the Labour party, the Liberal party and members of the Conservative party were demanding it, and there must be a full accounting, an inquest held, and so forth. That being so, one is bound to take a serious view because of the interests which are confided to our care.

I think that it would be a mistake if the House got into the habit of calling for explanations on the varying episodes of this dangerous and widespread struggle and asking for an account to be given of why any action was lost or any part of the front was beaten in. In the first place, no full explanations can possibly be given without revealing valuable information to the enemy, information not only about a particular operation which is over, but about the general position and also about the processes of thought which are followed, such as they may be, by our war direction and our high command. There is always a danger that a Minister in my position, in seeking to vindicate the course we have pursued, might inadvertently say something which may supply the enemy with some essential, with some seemingly innocent fact, about which the enemy is in doubt, and thus enable the enemy to construct a comprehensive and accurate picture of our state of mind and the way in which we are looking at things. The heads of the Dictator Governments are not under any similar pressure to explain or excuse any ill-success that may befall them. Far be it from me to compare myself or the office I hold or the functions I discharge with those of these pretentious and formidable potentates. I am only the servant of the Crown and Parliament, and am always at the disposal of the House of Commons, where I have lived my life.

Still the House, and I think I may say also the country, have placed very considerable responsibilities upon me, and I am sure they would not wish any servant they have entrusted with such duties to be at a disadvantage against our antagonists. I have not heard, for instance, that Herr Hitler had to attend the Reichstag and tell them why he sent the *Bismarck* on her disastrous cruise, when by waiting for a few weeks, and choosing his opportunity, when perhaps our capital ships were dispersed on convoy duty, she might have gone out accompanied by the *Tirpitz*, another 45,000-ton ship, and offered a general sea battle. Neither have I heard any very convincing statement by Signor Mussolini of the reasons why the greater part of his African Empire has been conquered and more than 200,000 of his soldiers are prisoners in our hands.

I must say, quite frankly, to the House that I should feel myself under a needless disadvantage if it were understood that I should be obliged, in public Debate, to give an account, possibly a controversial account, of our operations irrespective of whether the times were suitable or not. It would, for instance, have been a nuisance if Parliament had demanded a Debate on the loss of the *Hood* before we were in a position to tell the House what measures we had taken to secure the destruction of the *Bismarck*. I always take —and I am sure that what I say will be accepted—very great pains to serve the House, and on all occasions to associate the House in the fullest possible manner with the conduct of the war; but I think it would be better, and I submit it to the House, if in the future I were permitted on behalf of His Majesty's Government to choose the occasions for making statements about the war, which I am most anxious to do.

There is another general reason why I should have deprecated a Debate upon the Battle of Crete. It is only one part of the very important and complicated campaign which is being fought in the Middle East, and to select one particular sector of our widely extended front for Parliamentary Debate is a partial, lopsided and misleading method of examining the conduct of the war. A vast scene can only be surveyed as a whole, and it ought not to be exposed and debated piecemeal, especially at a time when operations which are all related to one another are wholly incomplete. Into the general survey of the war come all sorts of considerations about the gain and loss of time and its effect upon the future. There also comes into the picture the entire distribution of our available resources to meet the many calls that are made upon them. For instance, my hon. Friend the Member for Kidderminster (Sir J. Wardlaw-Milne), who has just spoken, asked why it was that when we had Crete in our possession for more than six months we had wasted all that time for constructing numerous airfields and placing them in the highest state of defence, and he reminded us how very efficiently the Germans would have done a work like that if Crete had fallen into their hands. Everyone will, I dare say, admit that it would have been a mistake to make a great number of airfields in Crete unless we could find the anti-aircraft guns, both of high and low ceiling, and the aircraft to defend those airfields, for that would simply have facilitated the descent of the enemy's air-borne troops upon the island.

Why then, first of all, I must ask, were enough guns not provided for the two serviceable airfields which existed in Crete? To answer that question one would have to consider how many guns we have and whether we could afford to spare them for that purpose. That leads us to a wider sphere. All this time, the Battle of the Atlantic has been going on, and a very great number of the guns which might have usefully been employed in Crete have been, and are being, mounted in the merchant vessels to beat off the attacks of the Fokke Wulf and Heinkel aircraft, whose depredations have been notably lessened thereby.

Again, we must consider, on the subject of these guns, whether our airfields at home, our air factories, or the ports and cities in our Islands, which are under heavy and dangerous attack, should have been further denuded or stinted of guns, in the last six or seven months, for the sake of the war in the Middle East. Further, it must be remembered—I did not notice that this was mentioned —that everything we send out to the Middle East is out of action for the best part of three months, as it has to go round the Cape. We have run very great risks and faced very serious maulings in this Island, in order to sustain the war in the Mediterranean, and no one, I venture to submit, can be a judge of whether we should have run more risks or exposed ourselves to heavier punishment at home, for the sake of fortifying and multiplying the Cretan airfields, without having full and intimate knowledge of all our resources and making a complete survey of the various claims upon them.

We did, however, from the moment that the Greek Government invited us into Crete, take steps to defend the anchorage of Suda Bay, as an important naval base, to develop the aerodrome nearby, and to provide the base and the aerodrome with the largest quantity of high and low ceiling guns which we thought it fit to divert from other strategic points in the Mediterranean. We provided, in fact, a deterrent to the enemy attack sufficient to require a major effort on his part; but, of course, there are a great many islands and strategic points in the seas, and to attempt to be safe everywhere is to make sure of being strong nowhere.

Therefore it may well be that if the House were able to go into these matters, which I am afraid is not possible, hon. Members would feel that a reasonable and right disposition of our Forces was made; but without going into the facts and figures, which I am sure no one would wish me to do, even in Secret Session, let alone in Public Session, it is quite impossible for the House, or even for the newspapers, to arrive at a justly-proportioned and level judgment on this affair. There is, however, this much that I should like to say: A man must be a perfect fool who thinks that we have large quantities of anti-aircraft guns and aircraft lying about unused at the present time. I will speak about aircraft in a moment, but, so far as anti-aircraft guns are concerned, large and expanding as is our present production, every single gun is in action at some necessary point or other, and all future production for many

152

months ahead is eagerly competed for by rival claimants with, very often, massive cases behind each one of them.

This goes back a long way, but four years ago, in March, 1937, I mentioned to the House that the Germans had already got 1,500 mobile anti-aircraft guns—mobile and formed in batteries—in addition to the whole of their static artillery of anti-aircraft defence. Since then they have been making them at a great rate, and they have also conquered more than all they want from the many countries they have overthrown, so that our position is very different from that. The right hon. Member for Devonport (Mr. Hore-Belisha) has made to-day a very cogent and moderate, well-informed and thoughtful contribution to the Debate, but he used a different mood and tone in a speech which he recently delivered in the country, and that at any rate makes it necessary for me to say that the state in which our Army was left when the right hon. Gentleman had ended his two years and seven months' tenure of the War Office, during the greater part of which he was also responsible for production and supply, was lamentable. We were short of every essential supply, but most particularly of those modern weapons, those special classes of weapons, the anti-aircraft gun, the anti-tank gun and the tank itself, which have proved themselves the vital necessities of modern war, a fact which he is now prepared to suggest we are so purblind and out-dated as not to be able to comprehend.

The equipment of our Army at the outbreak of war was of the most meagre and deficient character, and the deficiencies made themselves most marked—and still make themselves most marked —in the very type of weapons for which there is the greatest possible demand. I could give facts and figures upon this point if we were in private which would, I think, leave no dispute upon the subject. I am not throwing all the blame for this upon my right hon. Friend at all—certainly not—but I think it is only fair, when he himself comes forward and sets himself up as an arbiter and judge, and speaks so scornfully of the efforts of some others who have inherited his dismal legacy, I think when he speaks in this way—he has a great responsibility in the matter—it is only fair to point out to him that he is one of the last people in this country entitled to take that line.

An hon. Gentleman said something about no recriminations, but extremely violent and hostile speeches have been spread about, doing a great deal of harm, and about which I have received information from different countries and capitals, showing the uncertainty and disturbance which are caused by them; and certainly, if we are attacked, we shall counter-attack.

So much for the difficulty in which we stand in the matter of the anti-aircraft guns. The output is at last rapidly expanding, but the fact remains that our outfits are incomparably inferior in numbers to those possessed by the Germans, and every claim has to be weighed against every other claim. Another general question which may fairly be asked is, "Why have we not got much stronger and much larger air forces in the Middle East?" I can only say this: From the moment when the Battle of Britain was decided in our favour, in September and October of last year, by the victories of our fighters, we have been ceaselessly sending aircraft as fast as possible to the Middle East, by every route and by every method. During the present year, as our strength in the air has grown, we have not been hampered in this matter, as we were in the case of the anti-aircraft guns, by lack of aircraft. The problem has been to send them to the Eastern theatre of war.

Anyone can see how great are the Germans' advantages, and how easy it is for the Germans to move their Air Force from one side of Europe to another. They can fly along a line of permanent airfields. Wherever they need to alight and refuel, there are permanent airfields in the highest state of efficiency, and, as for the services and personnel and all the stores which go with them—without which the squadrons are quite useless—these can go by the grand continental expresses along the main railway lines of Europe. One has only to compare this process with the sending of aircraft packed in crates, then put on ships and sent across the great ocean spaces until they reach the Cape of Good Hope, then taken to Egypt, set up again, trued-up and put in the air when they arrive—to see that the Germans can do in days what takes us weeks, or even more. This reflection, I say, has its bearing upon the possibility of a German movement back from the East to the West, which certainly could be executed very swiftly if they were to resolve upon an assault upon this country. I can give an assurance to the House that we have done, are doing, and will do, our utmost to build up the largest possible Air Force in the Middle East. It is not aircraft, but transportation, which is the limiting factor at this end. I have dealt with anti-aircraft guns; I have dealt with aircraft. As to the disposition of our Forces in the Middle East, it is primarily a matter for the Commanders-in-Chief in the Middle East, although His Majesty's Government share to the full their responsibility for whatever is done. I might refer again to what was said by my hon. and gallant Friend the Member for Lewes (Rear-Admiral Beamish) about the importance of co-ordination between the Services. It is carried to a very high pitch.

The Chief Air Officer lives in the same house in Cairo as the Commander-in-Chief. They are there side by side. The Naval Commander-in-Chief has to be at sea very often. He has to be at Alexandria. But the very closest association exists between these branches. The idea that any one of these problems would be studied by one of these commanders only, without the closest association with the other two, is quite an illusory idea, and I can really reassure my hon. Friend on that point. No disagreement that I know of has arisen. Obviously, the Army is the main factor in that business, and the Fleet is preserving the security of the Army on the seas, and preserving the command of the seas, and the Air is assisting the Army and the Fleet in all their functions. But in the event of any differences, they cannot be settled in a few hours by reference here. These Commanders-in-Chief have to settle them among themselves, although we share to the full responsibility for whatever is done. It must not be forgotten that apart from the effort we made in Greece, which was very costly in aircraft, the situation in Iraq, in Palestine, and potentially in Syria, as well as the winding-up of the Abyssinian story, all made very heavy demands upon our aircraft, and the situation in the Western Desert had also to be considered. Before any rational judgment could be formed upon the disposition of our Air Force and the consequent failure to supply an adequate Air Force for Crete, it would be necessary, as in the case of the anti-aircraft guns, to know not only what are our whole resources, but also what was the situation in these other theatres, which were all intimately interrelated, and it is no use trying to judge these matters without full knowledge, and that full knowledge obviously cannot be made public, and ought not to be spread outside the narrowest circle compatible with the execution of operations.

I come to the next stage of my argument, because I am offering the House an argument, if they will bear with me as I unfold it. I have shown them the foundations upon which we started, and I now go a step forward. In March we decided to go to the aid of Greece in accordance with our Treaty obligations. This, of course, exposed us to the danger of being attacked in the Western Desert, and also to defeat by overwhelming numbers in Greece, unless Yugoslavia played her part, or unless the Greek Army could be extricated to hold some narrower line than that actually chosen. If Greece was overrun by the enemy, it seemed probable that Crete would be the next object of attack. The enemy, with his vast local superiority in air power, was able to drive our aircraft from the airfields of Greece, and adding this to his enormously superior anti-aircraft batteries, he was able to make those airfields rapidly available for his own use. Moreover, as the season was advancing, many more airfields became available to him as the weather improved and dried them up. It was evident, therefore, that the attack upon Crete, if it were made, would be primarily an airborne attack, for which, again, a vastly superior hostile air force would be available.

The question then arose as to whether we should try to defend Crete or yield it without a fight. No one who bears any responsibility for the decision to defend Crete was ignorant of the fact that conditions permitted of only the most meagre British air support to be provided for our troops in the island or for our Fleet operating round the island. It was not a fact that dawned upon the military and other authorities after the decision had been taken; it was the foundation of a difficult and harsh choice, as I shall show. The choice was: Should Crete be defended without effective air support, or should the Germans be permitted to occupy it without opposition? There are some, I see, who say that we should never fight without superior or at least ample air support and ask when will this lesson be learned? But suppose you cannot have it? The questions which have to be settled are not always questions between what is good and bad; very often it is a choice between two very terrible alternatives. Must you, if you cannot have this essential and desirable air support, yield important key points, one after another?

There are others who have said to me, and I have seen it in the newspapers, that you should defend no place that you cannot be sure you can hold. Then, one must ask, can one ever be sure how the battle will develop before it has ever been fought? If this principle of not defending any place you cannot be sure of holding were adopted, would not the enemy be able to make an unlimited number of valuable conquests without any fighting at all? Where would you make a stand and engage them with resolution? The further question arises as to what would happen if you allowed the enemy to advance and overrun, without cost to himself, the most precious and valuable strategic points? Suppose we had never gone to Greece and had never attempted to defend Crete. Where would the Germans be now? Suppose we had simply resigned territory and strategic islands to them without a fight. Might they not, at this early stage of the campaign in 1941, already be masters of Syria and Iraq and preparing themselves for an advance into Persia?

The Germans in this war have gained many victories. They have easily overrun great countries and beaten down strong Powers with little resistance offered to them. It is not only a question of the time that is gained by fighting strongly, even if at a disadvantage, for important points. There is also this vitally important principle of stubborn resistance to the will of the enemy. I merely throw out these considerations to the House in order that they may see that there are some arguments which deserve to be considered before you can adopt the rule that you have to have a certainty of winning at any point, and that if you have not got it beforehand you must clear out. The whole history of war shows the fatal absurdity of such a doctrine. Again and again, it has been proved that fierce and stubborn resistance, even against heavy odds and under exceptional conditions of local disadvantage, is an essential element in victory. At any rate, the decision was taken to hold Crete. The decision to fight for Crete was taken with the full knowledge that air support would be at a minimum, as anyone can see—apart from the question of whether you have adequate supplies or not—who measures the distances from our airfields in Egypt and compares them with the distances from enemy airfields in Greece, and who acquaints himself with the radius of action of dive-bombers and aircraft.

Of course, I take the fullest personal responsibility for that decision, but the Chiefs of Staff, the Defence Committee and General Wavell, the Commander-in-Chief, all in turn and in their various situations not only thought that Crete ought to be defended in the circumstances, which were fully before them, but that, in spite of the lack of air support, we had a good chance of winning the battle. No one had any illusions about the scale of the enemy air-borne attack. We knew it would be gigantic and intense. The reconnaissances over the Greek aerodromes showed the enormous mass of aircraft which were gathering there—many hundreds— and it turned out that the enemy was prepared to pay an almost unlimited price for this conquest, and his resources when concentrated upon any particular point may often be overwhelming at that point.

My right hon. Friend the Member for Devonport referred to the broadcasts which were given by the spokesman of the War Office, Major-General Collins, and by the spokesman of the Air Ministry, Air-Commodore Goddard. I take no responsibility for those statements. I take no responsibility for those or any others that may be made. It is very convenient to bring them up in the course of Debate, but the officers who give these broadcasts are not acquainted with the control of affairs and with what is decided or thought or felt in the Chiefs of Staff Committee or the Defence Committee. How can they be? One does not spread things about in that way. I should have liked very much to have stopped the broadcasts, and in some cases I have reduced them in number. I think it is a very risky thing to ask a professional officer, naval, military or air, to give a weekly expatiation on the war when, in the nature of things, although he may be very accomplished in his profession, he cannot know and ought not to know the facts as they are understood at the secret meetings.

I am very glad to see the feeling in the House on the subject, because, on the other side, one is appealed to ceaselessly to give more information, to make the war more interesting to the people, and to tell them more about what is going on. But it is not possible for the head of the Government or even for the Chiefs of Staff to vet—to use a slang term—beforehand these detailed weekly statements which are made. I think the matter must certainly be reconsidered. As I have said, no one had any illusions about the tremendous scale of the air-borne attack, the greatest ever delivered in the world, but we thought that we should resist it without any but the most restricted air support on our side. That is the fact. It is not a nice case, but it is the fact. Let us look at the anatomy of this battle of Crete which was undertaken in those bleak circumstances. We hoped that the 25,000 to 30,000 good troops—I am making it a little vague—with artillery and a proportion of tanks, aided by the Greek forces, would be able to destroy the parachute and glider landings of the enemy and prevent him from using the airfields or the harbours.

Our Army was to destroy the air-borne attacks, while the Navy held off or destroyed the sea-borne attacks. But there was a time limit. The action of the Navy in maintaining the Northern sea guard without adequate air defence was bound to be very costly. We could only stand a certain proportion of naval losses before the Northern sea guard of the Fleet would have to be withdrawn. If meanwhile the Army could succeed in biting off the head of the whole terrific apparatus of the air-borne invasion before the naval time limit, or loss limit, was reached, then the enemy would have to begin all over again, and, having regard to the scale of the operation, the enormous, unprecedented scale of the operation, and the losses he would have to incur, he might well for the time being have at least broken it off—at any rate, there would have been a long delay before he could have mounted it again. That was the basis on which the decision was taken.

I wonder what would have been said by our critics if we had given up the island of Crete without firing a shot. We should have been told that this pusillanimous flight had surrendered to the enemy the key of the Eastern Mediterranean, that our communications with Malta and our power to interrupt the enemy's communications with Libya were grievously endangered. There is only too much truth in all that, although perhaps it will not in the end turn out so badly. Crete was an extremely important salient in our line of defence. It was like Fort Douaumont at Verdun, in 1916; it was like Kemmel Hill, in 1918. These were taken by the Germans, but in each case the Germans lost the battle and also the campaign, and in the end they lost the war. But can you be sure the same result would have been achieved if the Allies had not fought for Douaumont, and had not fought for Kemmel Hill? What would they have fought for if they had not fought for them? These battles can only be judged in their relation to the campaign as a whole.

I have been asked a lot of questions. For instance, why were the Cretan airfields not mined beforehand? Or again, why were they not commanded by long-range gunfire, or why were not more tanks allotted to their defence? There are many other questions like that. I can give answers to these questions, but I do not propose to discuss tactics here, because I am sure it is quite impossible for us to fight battles in detail, either beforehand or afterwards, from Whitehall or from the House of Commons. His Majesty's Government in their responsibility to Parliament choose the best generals they can find, set before them the broad strategic objects of the campaign, offer them any advice or counsel that may seem fitting, ask searching questions which are very necessary in respect of particular plans and proposals, and then they support them to the best of their power in men and munitions, and also, so long as they retain their confidence, they support them with loyal comradeship in failure or success.

It is impossible to go into tactical details, and I never remember in the last war, in those great battles which cost something like 40,000, 50,000 or 70,000 men—I am talking of battles of a single day—in which sometimes there were very grave errors made, that they were often made the subject of the arraignment of the Government in the House of Commons. It is only where great strategic issues of policy come that it is fitting for us here to endeavour to form a final opinion. Defeat is bitter. There is no use in trying to explain defeat. People do not like defeat, and they do not like the explanations, however elaborate or plausible, which are given of them. For defeat there is only one answer. The only answer to defeat is victory. If a Government in time of war gives the impression that it cannot in the long run procure victory, who cares for its explanations? It ought to go—that is to say, if you are quite sure you can find another which can do better. However, it must be remembered that no Government can conduct a war unless it stands on a solid, stable foundation, and knows it stands on that foundation, and, like a great ship, can win through a period of storms into clearer weather. Unless there is a strong impression of solidarity and strength in a Government in time of war, that Government cannot give the support which is necessary to the fighting men and their commanders in the difficult periods, in the disheartening and disappointing periods. If the Government has always to be looking over its shoulder to see whether it is going to be stabbed in the back or not, it cannot possibly keep its eye on the enemy.

There is another point of some difficulty which presents itself to me whenever I am asked to make a statement to the House. Ought I to encourage good hopes of the successful outcome of particular operations, or ought I to prepare the public for serious disappointments? From the purely British standpoint, there is no doubt that the second of these courses is to be preferred, and this is the course that I have usually followed. It is the course which, no doubt, would commend itself to my noble Friend [Earl Winterton]. He has been urging us to look on the gloomy side of things—a kind of inverted Couèism. When you get up in the morning you say to yourself "we can easily lose this war in the next four months," and you say it with great emphasis and go on your daily task invigorated. I must point out that the British nation is unique in this respect. They are the only people who like to be told how bad things are, who like to be told the worst, and like to be told that they are very likely to get much worse in the future and must prepare themselves for further reverses. But when you go to other countries—oddly enough I saw a message from the authorities who are most concerned with our Arab problem at present, urging that we should be careful not to indulge in too gloomy forecasts. The Arabs do not understand the British character of meeting trouble long before it comes, and they think it is much better to go on putting a bold face on things and then meet the disaster when it arrives. Any statements of a pessimistic character which are used here are calculated to discourage our friends and to spread alarm and despondency over wide regions, to affect the nicely-balanced neutrals, and to encourage the enemy, who, of course, seizes upon any phrase or any gloomy allusion and repeats its myriad-fold in his strident propaganda.

It is a nice question whether the increase in our war effort which would result from my Noble Friend administering this austere mental treatment to himself in the mornings would counterbalance the undoubted harm which would be done when a phrase torn from its context, and probably with an alteration of the verb, is sent throughout the world—"Admission in the House of Commons by an eminent nobleman and ex-Minister: We are going to lose the war," or something like that. I am not blaming him at all. I feel just like him about it, and it is very much safer. It makes me wonder very much whether Members of Parliament have not got to pick their words a little carefully. After all, in this deadly war in which we are gripped, with dangers which are measureless, as they are unprecedented, closing upon us in so many quarters, with so much to defend and such limited resources, so many chances which may turn ill against us—when we think of this position, it is a great pity if statements are made which add nothing to the informative criticism which is so valuable, but can be taken from their context and placarded all over the world as a sign that we are not united or that our case is much worse than it is.

There is one thing I regret very much, and that is that the brunt of this fighting in the Middle East—I quite agree it is a very foolish expression, "in the Middle East"—or in the East should have fallen so heavily on the splendid Australian and New Zealand troops. I regret it for this reason among others, that the German propaganda is always reproaching us for fighting with other people's blood, and they mock us with the insulting taunt that England will fight to the last Australian or New Zealander. I was very glad to see that Mr. Menzies, in his noble speech of Sunday night, dealt with this vile propaganda as it deserved. There have been, in fact, during 1941, almost as many British as there are Australian and New Zealand troops engaged in all the operations in the Western Desert, in Greece and in Crete. The losses during this year compared with the numbers engaged are slightly heavier for the British than for the Dominion troops.

In Crete also, the numbers were almost exactly equal, and the British loss again was slightly heavier. These figures include killed, wounded and missing. They exclude Indian or non-British troops. In order to turn the edge of this German propaganda, I have asked the Secretary of State for War to endeavour to have mentioned more frequently the names of British regiments, when this can be done without detriment to the operations. The following British regiments and units, for instance, fought in Crete: The Rangers, the Black Watch, the Argyll and Sutherland Highlanders, the Leicestershire Regiment, the Welch Regiment, the York and Lancaster Regiment, the Royal Artillery, the Royal Engineers and numbers of the Royal Marines, who formed the rearguard and suffered the most heavily of all. In fact, of 2,000 Royal Marines landed in Crete, 1,400 became casualties or prisoners. Naval losses of life in these operations exceeded 500 officers and men, and while this was going on, we also lost 1,300 men in the *Hood*. Out of 90,000 lives lost so far in this war at home and abroad, at least 85,000 come from the Mother Country. Therefore, I repel and repudiate the German taunt, both on behalf of the Mother Country and of the Dominions of Australia and New Zealand.

It might well be asked—I am trying to look at the questions which might fairly be asked—why, having begun the battle for Crete, did you not persist in the defence of the island? If you could bring off 17,000 men safely to return to Egypt, why could you not have reinforced with 17,000 men to carry on the battle? I have tried to explain in a simple way that the moment it was proved that we could not crush the air-borne landings before the Fleet, losses became too heavy to hold off longer a sea-borne landing. Crete was lost, and it was necessary to save what was possible of the Army. It is one thing to take off 17,000 men as we did, with their rifles and side arms, and quite another to land them in a fighting condition with guns and materials. It is a wonderful thing that as many as 17,000 got away in face of the enemy's overwhelming command of the air.

I do not consider that we should regret the Battle of Crete. The fighting there attained a severity and fierceness which the Germans have not previously encountered in their walk through Europe. In killed,, wounded, missing and prisoners we have lost about 15,000 men. This takes no account of the losses of the Greeks and Cretans, who fought with the utmost bravery and suffered so heavily. On the other hand, from the most careful and precise inquiries I have made, and which have been made by the Commanders-in-Chief on the spot, we believe that about 5,000 Germans were drowned in trying to cross the sea and at least 12,000 killed or wounded on the island itself. In addition, the air force the Germans employed sustained extraordinary losses, above 180 fighter and bomber aircraft being destroyed, and at least 250 troop-carrying aeroplanes. This, at a time when our air strength is overtaking the enemy's, is important. I am sure it will be found that this sombre, ferocious battle, which was lost, and lost, I think, upon no great margin, was well worth fighting, and that it will have an extremely important effect on the whole defence of the Nile Valley throughout the present year. I do not think there are any of those responsible for it who would not take the same decision again, although no doubt, like our critics, we should be wiser in many ways after the event.

It is asked, Will the lessons of Crete be learned, and how will they affect the defence of this Island? Officers who took part in the thickest of the fighting in responsible positions, including a New Zealand brigadier, are already approaching this country. At the same time, very full appreciations have been made by the Staff in the Middle East, and are now being extended in detail. All this material will be examined by the General Staff here and placed at the disposal of General Sir Alan Brooke, who commands the several millions of armed men we have in this Island, including of course, the Home Guard. Every effort will be made to profit by it. There are, however, two facts to be borne in mind in comparing what happened in Crete with what might happen here. In the first place, we rely upon a strong superiority in air power, and certainly upon a much greater air power, both actually and relatively, than was proved sufficient last autumn. This not only sustains the land defence but liberates again the power of the Navy from the thraldom in which it was held round Crete. In the second place, the scale of the effort required from the Germans in attack would have to be multiplied many times over from what was necessary in Crete, and this might prove to be beyond the capacity of their resources or their schemes. Everything, however, will be done to meet an airborne and sea-borne attack launched upon a vast scale and maintained with total disregard of losses.

We shall not be lulled by the two arguments I have put forward into any undue sense of security. An attack by parachute troops and gliders may be likened to an attack by incendiary bombs, which, if not quickly extinguished one by one, may lead not only to serious fires but to an enormous conflagration. We are making many improvements in the defence of our airfields and in the mobility of the forces which will be employed upon that and other tasks. Nothing will be stinted, and not a moment will be lost. Here I ought to say that it is not true that the Germans clothed their parachute troops who attacked Crete in New Zealand uniforms. I gave that report to the House as it reached me from the Commander-in-Chief in the Middle East, but he now informs me that this was a mistake. Parachute troops, after landing at one point, drove a number of New Zealand walking wounded before them and along with them in their attack, and consequently the cry arose that they themselves were in New Zealand uniforms. There is no objection to the use of parachute troops in war so long as they are properly dressed in the uniform of their country and so long as

163

that uniform is in itself distinctive. This kind of fighting is, however, bound to become very fierce as it breaks out behind the
fronts and lines of the armies, and the civil population is almost
immediately involved.

. . . .

Last year, when we were considering our affairs, the great need
was to multiply fighters and bombers. This became an enormously
important matter. Nevertheless, while considerable portions of the
Army co-operation squadrons were associated with the military
forces, this was not done on the scale or to the extent which was
desirable. I think it is of the utmost consequence that every
division, especially every armoured division, should have a chance
to live its daily life and training in a close and precise relationship
with a particular number of aircraft that it knows and that it can
call up at will and need.

It was not possible last year to fulfil this requirement on a
sufficient scale without trenching on other domains which were
more vital to our safety, but it is the intention to go forward upon
that path immediately and to provide the Army with a large
number, a considerably larger number, of aeroplanes exactly suited
to the work they have to do, and above all to the development of
that wireless connection between the ground forces and the air
which the Germans have carried to such an extraordinary point of
perfection. Any attempt to use this method in Crete must have
failed, because the number of machines suitable for co-operating
with the troops was not large enough to have altered the results.

The member for Devonport asked me who it was who decided
that the air forces on the aerodromes in Crete were to be withdrawn. It was decided by the Commander-in-Chief of the Air
Force in the Middle East, on the recommendation of General
Freyberg, concurred in by the R.A.F. officer commanding on the
spot, Group-Captain Beamish. The numbers were small, and if they
had not been withdrawn, they would have been blown off the
aerodromes without having been able in the slightest degree to
affect the course of events.

Now I come to the Syrian operation. Let me repeat that we
have no territorial designs in Syria or anywhere else in French
territory. We seek no Colonies or advantages of any kind for
ourselves in this war. Let none of our French friends be deceived
by the blatant German and Vichy propaganda. On the contrary,
we shall do all in our power to restore the freedom, independence
and rights of France. I have written, in a letter to General de
Gaulle, of "the rights and the greatness of France"; we shall do all

in our power to restore her freedom and her rights, but it will be for the French to aid us in restoring her greatness. There can be no doubt that General de Gaulle is a more zealous defender of France's interests than are the men of Vichy, whose policy is that of utter subservience to the German enemy.

It did not take much intelligence to see that the infiltration into Syria by the Germans and their intrigues in Iraq constituted very great dangers to the whole Eastern flank of our defence in the Nile Valley and the Suez Canal. The only choice before us in that theatre for some time has been whether to encourage the Free French to attempt a counter-penetration by themselves or, at heavy risk in delay, to prepare, as we have done, a considerable force of our own. It was also necessary to restore the position in Iraq before any serious advance in Syria could be made. Our relations with the Vichy Government and the possibilities of an open breach with it evidently raised the military and strategic significance of these movements to the very highest point. Finally, and above all, the formidable menace of the invasion of Egypt by the German Army in Cyrenaica, supported by large Italian forces with German stiffening, remains our chief pre-occupation in the Middle East.

The advance by the German army forces into Egypt has been threatened for the last two months, and there would not be much use in attempting to cope with the situation in Syria if, at the same time, our defences in the Western Desert were beaten down and broken through. We had to take all these things into consideration, and I was very glad indeed when General Wavell reported that he was in a position to make the advance which began on Sunday morning, and which, so far as I have been informed up to the present, is progressing favourably and with very little opposition. The position in Syria was very nearly gone. The German poison was spreading through the country, and the revolt in Iraq, perhaps beginning prematurely, enabled us to take the necessary measures to correct the evil; but, as I say, we must not rejoice or give way to jubilation while we are engaged in operations of this difficulty and while the reaction of the Germans still remains to us obscure and unknown.

It is very easy, if I may say so, for critics, without troubling too much about our resources and even without a sense of the features of time and distance, to clamour for action now here and now there: "Why do you not go here? what," as I think an hon. Member said, "are you dithering about? why do you not go in there?" and so on. Indeed, one can see how many attractive strategic propositions there are, even with the most cursory examination of the atlas. But the House will, I am sure, best guard its own dignity and authority by refraining from taking sweeping or superficial views. Others have said that we must not follow a hand-to-mouth strategy, that we must regain the initiative, and impart to all our operations that sense of mastery and design which the Germans so often display. No one agrees with that more than I do, but it is a good deal easier said than done, especially while the enemy possesses vastly superior resources and many important strategical advantages. For all those reasons I have never, as the House knows, encouraged any hope of a short or easy war.

None the less, it would be a mistake to go to the other extreme and to belittle the remarkable achievements of our country and its Armed Forces. There are many things for which we may be thankful. The air attack on this Island has not overwhelmed us; indeed, we have risen through it and from it strengthened and glorified. There is no truth in the statement which my right hon. Friend the Member for Devonport made in his speech in the country, that productivity in our factories is falling off at an alarming rate. It may not be going as fast as we should like, and if anyone can do anything to make it go faster, or tell us how to do it, he will be rendering a great service. But it is not simply a question of giving very strident orders and demands. There is a great deal more than that in making the whole of our factories go properly, but it is certainly the exact reverse of the truth to say that productivity is falling off at an alarming rate. In guns and heavy tanks, for instance, the monthly average for the first quarter of 1941 was 50 per cent. greater than in the last quarter of 1940. The output for the month of May, a four-week month, was the highest yet reached, and more than double the monthly rate for the last quarter of 1940.

I felt I must contradict his statement to-day, because it happens that I have heard from two foreign countries in the course of the morning of the very serious effect which this statement produced upon opinion there; how it was published rapidly throughout Spain, for instance, and given the greatest prominence, coming as it did from an ex-Secretary of State. It was said to be exercising a bad effect.

I do not think we are in a sufficiently safe position to allow ourselves the full luxuries of vehement statement upon these very grave matters. As I say, we have many things we may be thankful for. In the first place, we have not been overwhelmed by the air attack; and our production, far from being beaten down by the disorganization of that attack, has been increasing at a very high rate.

The Battle of the Atlantic is also being well maintained. In January, Herr Hitler mentioned March as the peak month of his effort against us on the sea. We were to be exposed to attacks on a scale never before dreamed of, and there were rumours of hundreds of U-boats and masses of aircraft to be used against us. These rumours were spread throughout the world, and a very alarming impression was produced. March has gone, April has gone, May has gone, and now we are in the middle of June. Although serious losses were incurred in the Mediterranean, May was the best month we have had for some time in the Atlantic. Prodigious exertions were made to bring in the cargoes and to protect the ships, and these exertions have not failed. It is much easier to sink ships than to build them or to bring them safely across the ocean. We have lately been taking a stronger hand in this sinking process ourselves. It is a most astonishing fact that in the month of May we sank, captured or caused to be scuttled no less than 257,000 tons of enemy shipping, although they present us with a target which is perhaps one-tenth as great as we present to them. While they slink from port to port under the protection of their air umbrella, and make short, furtive voyages from port to port across the seas, we maintain our whole world-wide traffic, with never less than 2,000 ships on the seas or less than 400 in the danger zones on any day. Yet the losses we inflicted upon them in the month of May were, I think, in the nature of three-quarters of the losses they inflicted upon us. This also has a bearing on the possibility of sea-borne invasion, because the destruction of enemy tonnage is proceeding at a most rapid and satisfactory rate.

Nor need these solid grounds for thankfulness and confidence fall from us when we look at the aspect of the war in the Middle East. We have been at war for 21 months. Almost a year has passed since France deserted us and Italy came in against us. If anybody had said in June last that we should to-day hold every yard of the territories for which Great Britain is responsible in the Middle East; that we should have conquered the whole of the Italian Empire of Abyssinia, Eritrea and East Africa; that Egypt, Palestine and Iraq would have been successfully defended, he would have been thought a very foolish visionary. But that is the position at the moment. It is more than three months since the Germans gave out that they would be in Suez in a month, and were telling the Spaniards that when Suez fell they would have to come into the war. Two months ago many people thought that we should be driven out of Tobruk, or forced to capitulate there. The last time we had a Debate on the war in this House, so instructed a commentator as my hon. and gallant Friend the Member for

Petersfield (Sir G. Jeffreys) warned us gravely of the danger of a German thrust at Assiout, at the head of the Delta.

Six weeks ago all Iraq was aflame, and Habbaniyah was declared to be in the direst jeopardy. Women and children were evacuated by air. It was reported from enemy quarters that a surrender would be forced. A hostile insurgent Government ruled in Bagdad, in closest association with the Germans and the Italians. Our forces were pinned in Basra, having only just landed. Kirkuk and Mosul were in enemy hands. All has now been regained. We are advancing into Syria in force. Our front at Mersa Matruh in the Western Desert is unbroken, and our defensive lines there are stronger than ever. The large forces which were occupied in the conquest of Abyssinia are now set free, with an immense mass of transport, and large numbers are on their way to, or have already reached, the Delta of the Nile.

I think it would be most unfair and wrong, and very silly, in the midst of a defence which has so far been crowned with remarkable success, to select the loss of the Crete salient as an excuse and pretext for branding with failure or belittling with taunt the great campaign for the defence of the Middle East, which has so far prospered beyond all expectation, and is now entering upon an even more intense and critical phase.

I give no guarantee, I make no promise or prediction for the future. But if the next six months, during which we must expect even harder fighting and many disappointments, should find us in no worse position than that in which we stand to-day; if, after having fought so long alone, single-handed against the might of Germany, and against Italy, and against the intrigues and treachery of Vichy, we should still be found the faithful and unbeaten guardians of the Nile Valley and of the regions that lie about it, then I say that a famous chapter will have been written in the martial history of the British Empire and Commonwealth of Nations.

"UNTIL VICTORY IS WON"

A SPEECH TO A CONFERENCE OF DOMINION HIGH COMMISSIONERS
AND ALLIED COUNTRIES' MINISTERS AT ST. JAMES'S PALACE,
LONDON, JUNE 12, 1941

---

*June 11. News of heavy concentrations of German troops on the
Russian frontier. Sir Stafford Cripps, British Ambassador
to Russia, returned to London for conference.*
*June 12. Several hundred R.A.F. bombers made "heaviest ever"
raid on the Ruhr.*
    *The United States made a strong protest to Germany
about the sinking of the* Robin Moor.

[June 12, 1941.

I N the twenty-second month of the war against Nazism we meet
here in this old Palace of St. James's, itself not unscarred by the
fire of the enemy, in order to proclaim the high purposes and
resolves of the lawful constitutional Governments of Europe whose
countries have been overrun; and we meet here also to cheer the
hopes of free men and free peoples throughout the world. Here
before us on the table lie the title-deeds of ten nations or States
whose soil has been invaded and polluted, and whose men, women,
and children lie prostrate or writhing under the Hitler yoke. But
here also, duly authorized by the Parliament and democracy of
Britain, are gathered the servants of the ancient British Monarchy
and the accredited representatives of the British Dominions beyond
the seas, of Canada, Australia, New Zealand, and South Africa, of
the Empire of India, of Burma, and of our Colonies in every quarter
of the globe. They have drawn their swords in this cause. They
will never let them fall till life is gone or victory is won. Here we
meet, while from across the Atlantic Ocean the hammers and lathes
of the United States signal in a rising hum their message of
encouragement and their promise of swift and ever-growing aid.

What tragedies, what horrors, what crimes have Hitler and all
that Hitler stands for brought upon Europe and the world! The
ruins of Warsaw, of Rotterdam, of Belgrade are monuments which

will long recall to future generations the outrage of the unopposed air-bombing applied with calculated scientific cruelty to helpless populations.   Here in London and throughout the cities of our Island, and in Ireland, there may also be seen the marks of devastation.   They are being repaid, and presently they will be more than repaid.

But far worse than these visible injuries is the misery of the conquered peoples. We see them hounded, terrorized, exploited. Their manhood by the million is forced to work under conditions indistinguishable in many cases from actual slavery. Their goods and chattels are pillaged, or filched for worthless money. Their homes, their daily life are pried into and spied upon by the all-pervading system of secret political police which, having reduced the Germans themselves to abject docility, now stalk the streets and byways of a dozen lands. Their religious faiths are affronted, persecuted, or oppressed in the interests of a fantastic paganism devised to perpetuate the worship and sustain the tyranny of one abominable creature.   Their traditions, their culture, their laws, their institutions, social and political alike, are suppressed by force or undermined by subtle, coldly-planned intrigue.

The prisons of the Continent no longer suffice. The concentration camps are overcrowded. Every dawn the German volleys crack. Czechs, Poles, Dutchmen, Norwegians, Yugoslavs and Greeks, Frenchmen, Belgians, Luxembourgers, make the great sacrifice for faith and country. A vile race of quislings—to use the new word which will carry the scorn of mankind down the centuries —is hired to fawn upon the conqueror, to collaborate in his designs, and to enforce his rule upon their fellow-countrymen, while grovelling low themselves.   Such is the plight of once glorious Europe, and such are the atrocities against which we are in arms.

It is upon this foundation that Hitler, with his tattered lackey Mussolini at his tail and Admiral Darlan frisking by his side, pretends to build out of hatred, appetite, and racial assertion a new order for Europe. Never did so mocking a fantasy obsess the mind of mortal man. We cannot tell what the course of this fell war will be as it spreads remorseless through ever-wider regions. We know it will be hard, we expect it will be long; we cannot predict or measure its episodes or its tribulations. But one thing is certain, one thing is sure, one thing stands out stark and undeniable, massive and unassailable, for all the world to see.

It will not be by German hands that the structure of Europe will be rebuilt or the union of the European family achieved. In every country into which the German armies and the Nazi police have

170

broken there has sprung up from the soil a hatred of the German name and a contempt for the Nazi creed which the passage of hundreds of years will not efface from human memory. We cannot yet see how deliverance will come, or when it will come, but nothing is more certain than that every trace of Hitler's footsteps, every stain of his infected and corroding fingers will be sponged and purged and, if need be, blasted from the surface of the earth.

We are here to affirm and fortify our union in that ceaseless and unwearying effort which must be made if the captive peoples are to be set free. A year ago His Majesty's Government was left alone to face the storm, and to many of our friends and enemies alike it may have seemed that our days too were numbered, and that Britain and its institutions would sink for ever beneath the verge. But I may with some pride remind your Excellencies that, even in that dark hour when our Army was disorganized and almost weaponless, when scarcely a gun or a tank remained in Britain, when almost all our stores and ammunition had been lost in France, never for one moment did the British people dream of making peace with the conqueror, and never for a moment did they despair of the common cause. On the contrary, we proclaimed at that very time to all men, not only to ourselves, our determination not to make peace until every one of the ravaged and enslaved countries was liberated and until the Nazi domination was broken and destroyed.

See how far we have travelled since those breathless days of June a year ago. Our solid, stubborn strength has stood the awful test. We are masters of our own air, and now reach out in ever-growing retribution upon the enemy. The Royal Navy holds the seas. The Italian fleet cowers diminished in harbour, the German Navy is largely crippled or sunk. The murderous raids upon our ports, cities, and factories have been powerless to quench the spirit of the British nation, to stop our national life, or check the immense expansion of our war industry. The food and arms from across the oceans are coming safely in. Full provision to replace all sunken tonnage is being made here, and still more by our friends in the United States. We are becoming an armed community. Our land forces are being perfected in equipment and training.

Hitler may turn and trample this way and that through tortured Europe. He may spread his course far and wide, and carry his curse with him: he may break into Africa or into Asia. But it is here, in this island fortress, that he will have to reckon in the end. We shall strive to resist by land and sea. We shall be on his track wherever he goes. Our air power will continue to teach the German homeland that war is not all loot and triumph.

We shall aid and stir the people of every conquered country to resistance and revolt. We shall break up and derange every effort which Hitler makes to systematize and consolidate his subjugation. He will find no peace, no rest, no halting-place, no parley. And if, driven to desperate hazards, he attempts the invasion of the British Isles, as well he may, we shall not flinch from the supreme trial. With the help of God, of which we must all feel daily conscious, we shall continue steadfast in faith and duty till our task is done.

This, then, is the message which we send forth to-day to all the States and nations bond or free, to all the men in all the lands who care for freedom's cause, to our allies and well-wishers in Europe, to our American friends and helpers drawing ever closer in their might across the ocean: this is the message—Lift up your hearts. All will come right. Out of the depths of sorrow and sacrifice will be born again the glory of mankind.

"THE BIRTH THROES OF A SUBLIME RESOLVE"

A RADIO SPEECH TO AMERICA ON RECEIVING THE HONORARY DEGREE
OF DOCTOR OF LAWS OF THE UNIVERSITY OF ROCHESTER
NEW YORK, JUNE 16, 1941

---

*June 13. Air raid casualties in May announced as 5,394 killed and
5,181 injured.*
*June 14. President Roosevelt ordered the "freezing" of all German
and Italian money in the United States.*
*June 15. British troops captured Sidon (Syria) after 24 hours'
shelling by the Navy.*
*June 16. President Roosevelt ordered the closing of all German
consulates in the United States and the expulsion of
nationals employed by them.*

[June 16, 1941.

I AM grateful, President Valentine, for the honour which you
have conferred upon me in making me a Doctor of Laws of
Rochester University in the State of New York. I am extremely
complimented by the expressions of praise and commendation in
which you have addressed me, not because I am or ever can be
worthy of them, but because they are an expression of American
confidence and affection which I shall ever strive to deserve.

But what touches me most in this ceremony is that sense of
kinship and of unity which I feel exists between us this afternoon.
As I speak from Downing Street to Rochester University and
through you to the people of the United States, I almost feel I have
the right to do so, because my mother, as you have stated, was born
in your city, and here my grandfather, Leonard Jerome, lived for
so many years, conducting as a prominent and rising citizen a
newspaper with the excellent eighteenth-century title of the *Plain
Dealer.*

The great Burke has truly said, "People will not look forward to
posterity who never look backward to their ancestors," and I feel
it most agreeable to recall to you that the Jeromes were rooted for
many generations in American soil, and fought in Washington's
Armies for the independence of the American Colonies and the

173

foundation of the United States. I expect I was on both sides then. And I must say I feel on both sides of the Atlantic Ocean now.

At intervals during the last forty years I have addressed scores of great American audiences in almost every part of the Union. I have learnt to admire the courtesy of these audiences; their sense of fair play; their sovereign sense of humour, never minding the joke that is turned against themselves; their earnest, voracious desire to come to the root of the matter and to be well and truly informed on Old World Affairs.

And now, in this time of world storm, when I have been called upon by King and Parliament and with the support of all parties in the State to bear the chief responsibility in Great Britain, and when I have had the supreme honour of speaking for the British nation in its most deadly danger and in its finest hour, it has given me comfort and inspiration to feel that I think as you do, that our hands are joined across the oceans, and that our pulses throb and beat as one. Indeed I will make so bold as to say that here at least, in my mother's birth city of Rochester, I hold the latchkey to American hearts.

Strong tides of emotion, fierce surges of passion, sweep the broad expanses of the Union in this year of fate. In that prodigious travail there are many elemental forces, there is much heart-searching and self-questioning; some pangs, some sorrow, some conflict of voices, but no fear. The world is witnessing the birth throes of a sublime resolve. I shall presume to confess to you that I have no doubts what that resolve will be.

The destiny of mankind is not decided by material computation. When great causes are on the move in the world, stirring all men's souls, drawing them from their firesides, casting aside comfort, wealth, and the pursuit of happiness in response to impulses at once awe-striking and irresistible, we learn that we are spirits, not animals, and that something is going on in space and time, and beyond space and time, which, whether we like it or not, spells duty.

A wonderful story is unfolding before our eyes. How it will end we are not allowed to know. But on both sides of the Atlantic we all feel, I repeat, all, that we are a part of it, that our future and that of many generations is at stake. We are sure that the character of human society will be shaped by the resolves we take and the deeds we do. We need not bewail the fact that we have been called upon to face such solemn responsibilities. We may be proud, and even rejoice amid our tribulations, that we have been born at this cardinal time for so great an age and so splendid an opportunity of service here below.

174

Wickedness, enormous, panoplied, embattled, seemingly triumphant, casts its shadow over Europe and Asia. Laws, customs, and traditions are broken up. Justice is cast from her seat. The rights of the weak are trampled down. The grand freedoms of which the President of the United States has spoken so movingly are spurned and chained. The whole stature of man, his genius, his initiative, and his nobility, is ground down under systems of mechanical barbarism and of organized and scheduled terror.

For more than a year we British have stood alone, uplifted by your sympathy and respect and sustained by our own unconquerable will-power and by the increasing growth and hopes of your massive aid. In these British islands that look so small upon the map we stand, the faithful guardians of the rights and dearest hopes of a dozen States and nations now gripped and tormented in a base and cruel servitude. Whatever happens we shall endure to the end.

But what is the explanation of the enslavement of Europe by the German Nazi règime? How did they do it? It is but a few years ago since one united gesture by the peoples, great and small, who are now broken in the dust, would have warded off from mankind the fearful ordeal it has had to undergo. But there was no unity. There was no vision. The nations were pulled down one by one while the others gaped and chattered. One by one, each in his turn, they let themselves be caught. One after another they were felled by brutal violence or poisoned from within by subtle intrigue.

And now the old lion with her lion cubs at her side stands alone against hunters who are armed with deadly weapons and impelled by desperate and destructive rage. Is the tragedy to repeat itself once more? Ah no! This is not the end of the tale. The stars in their courses proclaim the deliverance of mankind. Not so easily shall the onward progress of the peoples be barred. Not so easily shall the lights of freedom die.

But time is short. Every month that passes adds to the length and to the perils of the journey that will have to be made. United we stand. Divided we fall. Divided, the dark age returns. United, we can save and guide the world.

"THE FOURTH CLIMACTERIC"

A BROADCAST ADDRESS ON THE GERMAN
INVASION OF RUSSIA
JUNE 22, 1941

June 17. British launched an attack on the Libya-Egypt frontier and a fierce battle was fought around Halfaya Pass.

Air Ministry revealed that Britain was using a new radio device to locate enemy planes.

June 18. Turkey signed friendship pact with Germany, but without prejudice to existing treaty obligations with Britain.

British troops withdrew after battle with German forces on Libya-Egypt frontier, taking hundreds of prisoners.

June 19. Germany announced closing of all United States consulates in Axis territory.

June 20. German-Russian crisis grew more serious, and Field-Marshal List, Nazi blitzkrieg expert, set up H.Q. in Rumania.

June 21. British troops captured Damascus.

King Peter of Yugoslavia flew to England.

June 22. Germany attacked Russia on a front of 1,500 miles from Finland to the Black Sea, and Mr. Churchill announced all possible help to Russia.

[June 22, 1941.

I HAVE taken occasion to speak to you to-night because we have reached one of the climacterics of the war. The first of these intense turning-points was a year ago when France fell prostrate under the German hammer, and when we had to face the storm alone. The second was when the Royal Air Force beat the Hun raiders out of the daylight air, and thus warded off the Nazi invasion of our island while we were still ill-armed and ill-prepared. The third turning-point was when the President and Congress of the United States passed the Lease-and-Lend enactment, devoting nearly 2,000 millions sterling to the wealth of the New World to help us to defend our liberties and their own. Those were the three climacterics. The fourth is now upon us.

At four o'clock this morning Hitler attacked and invaded Russia. All his usual formalities of perfidy were observed with scrupulous technique. A non-aggression treaty had been solemnly signed and was in force between the two countries. No complaint had been made by Germany of its non-fulfilment. Under its cloak of false confidence, the German armies drew up in immense strength along a line which stretches from the White Sea to the Black Sea; and their air fleets and armoured divisions slowly and methodically took their stations. Then, suddenly, without declaration of war, without even an ultimatum, German bombs rained down from the air upon the Russian cities, the German troops violated the frontiers; and an hour later the German Ambassador, who till the night before was lavishing his assurances of friendship, almost of alliance, upon the Russians, called upon the Russian Foreign Minister to tell him that a state of war existed between Germany and Russia.

Thus was repeated on a far larger scale the same kind of outrage against every form of signed compact and international faith which we have witnessed in Norway, Denmark, Holland and Belgium, and which Hitler's accomplice and jackal Mussolini so faithfully imitated in the case of Greece.

All this was no surprise to me. In fact I gave clear and precise warnings to Stalin of what was coming. I gave him warning as I have given warning to others before. I can only hope that this warning did not fall unheeded. All we know at present is that the Russian people are defending their native soil and that their leaders have called upon them to resist to the utmost.

Hitler is a monster of wickedness, insatiable in his lust for blood and plunder. Not content with having all Europe under his heel, or else terrorized into various forms of abject submission, he must now carry his work of butchery and desolation among the vast multitudes of Russia and of Asia. The terrible military machine, which we and the rest of the civilized world so foolishly, so supinely, so insensately allowed the Nazi gangsters to build up year by year from almost nothing, cannot stand idle lest it rust or fall to pieces. It must be in continual motion, grinding up human lives and trampling down the homes and the rights of hundreds of millions of men. Moreover it must be fed, not only with flesh but with oil.

So now this bloodthirsty guttersnipe must launch his mechanized armies upon new fields of slaughter, pillage and devastation. Poor as are the Russian peasants, workmen and soldiers, he must steal from them their daily bread; he must devour their harvests; he must rob them of the oil which drives their ploughs; and thus produce a famine without example in human history. And even the carnage and ruin which his victory, should he gain it—he has not gained it yet—will bring upon the Russian people, will itself be only a stepping-stone to the attempt to plunge the four or five hundred millions who live in China, and the three hundred and fifty millions who live in India, into that bottomless pit of human degradation over which the diabolic emblem of the Swastika flaunts itself. It is not too much to say here this summer evening that the lives and happiness of a thousand million additional people are now menaced with brutal Nazi violence. That is enough to make us hold our breath. But presently I shall show you something else that lies behind, and something that touches very nearly the life of Britain and of the United States.

The Nazi régime is indistinguishable from the worst features of Communism. It is devoid of all theme and principle except appetite and racial domination. It excels all forms of human wickedness in the efficiency of its cruelty and ferocious aggression. No one has been a more consistent opponent of Communism than I have for the last twenty-five years. I will unsay no word that I have spoken about it. But all this fades away before the spectacle which is now unfolding. The past with its crimes, its follies and its tragedies, flashes away. I see the Russian soldiers standing on the threshold of their native land, guarding the fields which their fathers have tilled from time immemorial. I see them guarding their homes where mothers and wives pray—ah yes, for there are times when all pray—for the safety of their loved ones, the return of the breadwinner, of their champion, of their protector. I see the ten thousand villages of Russia, where the means of existence was wrung so hardly from the soil, but where there are still primordial human joys, where maidens laugh and children play. I see advancing upon all this in hideous onslaught the Nazi war machine, with its clanking, heel-clicking, dandified Prussian officers, its crafty expert agents fresh from the cowing and tying-down of a dozen countries. I see also the dull, drilled, docile, brutish masses of the Hun soldiery plodding on like a swarm of crawling locusts. I see the German bombers and fighters in the sky, still smarting from many a British whipping, delighted to find what they believe is an easier and a safer prey.

Behind all this glare, behind all this storm, I see that small group of villainous men who plan, organize and launch this cataract of horrors upon mankind. And then my mind goes back across the years to the days when the Russian armies were our allies against the same deadly foe; when they fought with so much valour and constancy, and help to gain a victory from all share in which, alas, they were—through no fault of ours—utterly cut off. I have lived through all this, and you will pardon me if I express my feelings and the stir of old memories.

But now I have to declare the decision of His Majesty's Government—and I feel sure it is a decision in which the great Dominions will, in due course, concur—for we must speak out now at once, without a day's delay. I have to make the declaration, but can you doubt what our policy will be? We have but one aim and one single, irrevocable purpose. We are resolved to destroy Hitler and every vestige of the Nazi règime. From this nothing will turn us—nothing. We will never parley, we will never negotiate with Hitler or any of his gang. We shall fight him by land, we shall fight him by sea, we shall fight him in the air, until with God's help we have rid the earth of his shadow and liberated its peoples from his yoke. Any man or state who fights on against Nazidom will have our aid. Any man or state who marches with Hitler is our foe. This applies not only to organized states but to all representatives of that vile race of quislings who make themselves the tools and agents of the Nazi règime against their fellow-countrymen and the lands of their birth. They—these quislings—like the Nazi leaders themselves, if not disposed of by their fellow-countrymen, which would save trouble, will be delivered by us on the morrow of victory to the justice of the Allied tribunals. That is our policy and that is our declaration. It follows, therefore, that we shall give whatever help we can to Russia and the Russian people. We shall appeal to all our friends and allies in every part of the world to take the same course and pursue it, as we shall, faithfully and steadfastly to the end.

We have offered the Government of Soviet Russia any technical or economic assistance which is in our power, and which is likely to be of service to them. We shall bomb Germany by day as well as by night in ever-increasing measure, casting upon them month by month a heavier discharge of bombs, and making the German people taste and gulp each month a sharper dose of the miseries they have showered upon mankind. It is noteworthy that only yesterday the Royal Air Force, fighting inland over French territory, cut down with very small loss to themselves 28 of the Hun fighting machines in the air above the French soil they have invaded, defiled and profess to hold. But this only a beginning. From now forward the main expansion of our Air Force proceeds with gathering speed. In another six months the weight of the help we are receiving from the United States in war materials of all kinds, and especially in heavy bombers, will begin to tell.

This is no class war, but a war in which the whole British

179

Empire and Commonwealth of Nations is engaged without distinction of race, creed or party. It is not for me to speak of the action of the United States, but this I will say: if Hitler imagines that his attack on Soviet Russia will cause the slightest division of aims or slackening of effort in the great Democracies who are resolved upon his doom, he is woefully mistaken. On the contrary, we shall be fortified and encouraged in our efforts to rescue mankind from his tyranny. We shall be strengthened and not weakened in determination and in resources.

This is no time to moralize on the follies of countries and governments which have allowed themselves to be struck down one by one, when by united action they could have saved themselves and saved the world from this catastrophe. But when I spoke a few minutes ago of Hitler's blood-lust and the hateful appetites which have impelled or lured him on his Russian adventure, I said there was one deeper motive behind his outrage. He wishes to destroy the Russian power because he hopes that if he succeeds in this, he will be able to bring back the main strength of his army and air force from the East and hurl it upon this Island, which he knows he must conquer or suffer the penalty of his crimes. His invasion of Russia is no more than a prelude to an attempted invasion of the British Isles. He hopes, no doubt, that all this may be accomplished before the winter comes, and that he can overwhelm Great Britain before the fleet and air power of the United States may intervene. He hopes that he may once again repeat, upon a greater scale than ever before, that process of destroying his enemies one by one, by which he has so long thrived and prospered, and that then the scene will be clear for the final act, without which all his conquests would be in vain—namely the subjugation of the Western Hemisphere to his will and to his system.

The Russian danger is therefore our danger, and the danger of the United States, just as the cause of any Russian fighting for his hearth and home is the cause of free men and free peoples in every quarter of the globe. Let us learn the lessons already taught by such cruel experience. Let us redouble our exertions, and strike with united strength while life and power remain.

UNITED STATES OCCUPATION OF ICELAND

A STATEMENT TO THE HOUSE OF COMMONS
JULY 9, 1941

June 23. Russia accepted the offer of British aid against Germany. Germans captured Brest Litovsk.

June 24. President Roosevelt supported Britain by promising aid to Russia.

June 25. German attack on Russia developed into four thrusts towards key points of Leningrad, Moscow, Kiev and Odessa.

June 26. R.A.F. carrying out day and night raids on Western Germany and German-occupied territory.

June 27. Sir Stafford Cripps, British Ambassador, arrived in Moscow with British Military Mission.

June 28. Russia reported that 4,000 tanks were engaged round Minsk in the biggest tank battle in history.

June 29. Lord Beaverbrook appointed Minister of Supply in drive for more tanks.

July 1. General Wavell, Commander-in-Chief in the Middle East, exchanged posts with General Auchinleck, Commander-in-Chief in India.

July 3. Stalin, in broadcast speech, admitted loss of Russian territory, but expressed confidence in ultimate victory He ordered, in the event of a retreat, destruction of everything useful to the enemy.

British troops captured Palmyra (Syria).

July 5. Russians started a counter-attack to bar the way to Leningrad.

July 6. Roman Catholic bishops in Germany made a stern attack on the Nazi attitude towards the Church.

July 7. President Roosevelt announced that the United States forces had begun to occupy Iceland and Greenland.

July 8. Russian military mission arrived in London.

July 9. General Dentz asked for terms of an Armistice in Syria after British troops had fought their way to Beirut.

July 9, 1941.

THE military occupation of Iceland by the forces of the United States is an event of first-rate political and strategic importance; in fact, it is one of the most important things that have happened since the war began. It has been undertaken by the United States in pursuance of the purely American policy of protecting the Western Hemisphere from the Nazi menace. I understand that in the view of the American technical authorities modern conditions of war, especially air war, require forestalling action, in this case especially in order to prevent the acquisition by Hitler of jumping-off grounds from which it would be possible, bound by bound, to come to close quarters with the American Continent. It is not for me to comment on these American views, although I may say they seem fairly obvious to anyone who takes an intelligent interest in what is going on.

The seizure of Iceland by Hitler would be of great advantage to him in bringing pressure to bear both on Great Britain and the United States. We have for some time past, with the assent of the Icelandic people and the Legislature, maintained a strong garrison in the Island, and the arrival of powerful United States forces will greatly reduce the danger to Iceland. This measure of American policy is therefore in complete harmony with British interests, and we have found no reason on any occasion to object to it; indeed, I cannot see that we should have had any grounds for doing so in view of the invitation extended to the United States by the Icelandic Government. We still propose to retain our Army in Iceland, and, as British and United States Forces will both have the same object in view, namely, the defence of Iceland, it seems very likely they will co-operate closely and effectively in resistance to any attempt by Hitler to gain a footing. It would obviously be foolish for the United States to have one plan for defending Iceland and for the British Forces to have another.

If any issue of principle arises, it may be safely left to the British and American naval, military and Air Force authorities concerned, who will, I have no doubt, study each other's convenience to the utmost. Looked at from every point of view, I have been unable to find any reason for regretting the step which the United States have taken, and which in the circumstances they have been forced to take; indeed, I think I may almost go so far as to say, on behalf of the House of Commons as well as of His Majesty's Government, that we really welcome it. Whether similar satisfaction will be aroused in Germany is another question, and one which hardly concerns us this morning.

The second principle of United States policy, which I understand has led them to the occupation of Iceland, has been the declared will and purpose of the President, Congress and people of the United States, not only to send all possible aid in warlike munitions and necessary supplies to Great Britain, but also to make sure we get them. Here again is a course of action for which the United States must take the full responsibility. Apart from this, the position of the United States Forces in Iceland will, of course, require their being sustained or reinforced by sea from time to time. These consignments of American supplies for American Forces on duty overseas for the purposes of the United States will, of course, have to traverse very dangerous waters, and, as we have a very large traffic constantly passing through these waters, I daresay it may be found in practice mutually advantageous for the two navies involved to assist each other, so far as is convenient, in that part of the business. I really do not think I have anything further to say about a transaction which appears at every point to be so very plain and simple.

[SYRIA]

We have received a formal application from the French High Commissioner in Syria, General Dentz, for a discussion of terms leading to an armistice. I need hardly say how very glad His Majesty's Government will be to see an end brought to this distressing conflict, in which 1,000 to 1,500 British, Australian and Indian soldiers who volunteered to join the Army in order to defend France have fallen, killed or wounded, under French bullets as the result of the lamentable confusion into which the affairs of so many good people in so many parts of the world have been thrown by the victories of Hitler's Army. I, therefore, should welcome the negotiations, and I trust they may reach a speedy conclusion. Pending any formal arrangement being made, military operations must, of course, continue without abatement.

CIVILIANS ON PARADE

A SPEECH TO 6,000 MEN AND WOMEN OF LONDON'S
CIVIL DEFENCE SERVICES AT A REVIEW IN HYDE
PARK, JULY 14, 1941

July 10. *Russia claimed that the German offensive had been
stemmed "along a fairly stable line."*
  *Heavy R.A.F. raids on Le Havre, Cherbourg, Cologne
and Naples.*

July 11. *Russia appointed Marshals Timoshenko, Voroshilov and
Budenny to take over three main sectors of the 1,500
mile front.*
  *Vichy Government rejected Britain's terms for an
Armistice in Syria, but gave a free hand to General Dentz
to negotiate further.*

July 12. *"Cease Fire" order in Syria.*
  Anglo-Russian military agreement signed.

July 14. *Russia claimed that twenty-six enemy troopships and
three destroyers had been set on fire in the Baltic.*

July 14, 1941.

MEMBERS of the Civil Defence Forces, it is a good thing
that to-day we should assemble here representatives of the
vast army which conducts the civil defence of London, and which
is itself typical of all those similar forces which have been called
into being and have acquitted themselves with distinction in every
city, in every town, and in every village of our land.

I see before me an array of men and women who have just come
out of one long, hard battle and may at any moment enter upon
another. The defence of London last winter against Hitler's act of
terror showed decisively that the assault upon our lives and homes,
launched indiscriminately upon men, women, and children, military
and civil, old and young alike, failed utterly in its purpose of breaking the British spirit.

The defence of London, in which you bore your part, was the
counterpart of the defeat of the German air force by our fighters a

184

few weeks earlier in the Battle of Britain. These two events, which were imitated and rivalled in every part of the country, showed that the weapon of indiscriminate air attack upon these Islands, which had produced such frightful consequences at Warsaw and at Rotterdam, could not prevail against British tenacity and resolution.

In this war, so terrible in many aspects and yet so inspiring, men and women who have never thought about fighting or being involved in fighting before have been proud to emulate the courage of the bravest regiments of His Majesty's armies, and proud to find that, under the fire of the enemy, they could comport themselves with discipline and with composure. It is that quality, universally spread among our people, which gives us the foundation from which we shall prosecute to the end this righteous war for the freedom and future of mankind.

We shall not turn from our purpose, but we can only achieve that purpose if we have behind us a nation sound at the core and in every fibre. For the moment there is a lull, but we must expect that before long the enemy will renew his attacks upon us. It is true that some of his forces are away attacking the lives and rights of another vast branch of the human family; but he still has very large forces close at hand, and if he has not come recently to London it is certainly not because he likes us better.

The courage of Londoners, and the organization of our many defence and municipal services under unexampled strain, not only enable us to come through what many might have thought a mortal peril, but impressed itself in every country, upon the minds of every country in the world, and gained us scores of millions of friends in the United States. I do not hesitate to say that the enormous advance in United States opinion towards making their contribution to British resistance thoroughly effective has been largely influenced by the conduct of Londoners and of the men and women in our provincial cities in standing up to the enemy's bombardments.

We must certainly prepare ourselves to receive other visits in the future. We shall be ready. We shall be more ready than we have ever been before, but whether the enemy comes again here or not will not alter our course of action. We are now bombing him at a heavier rate in discharge of tons of bombs than he has in any monthly period bombed us.

This is only a beginning. We shall continue the process, and upon a growing scale, month after month, until at last we have beaten down this horrible tyranny which has reared itself against our life and against the honour of every free people in the world.

185

Therefore it is of the utmost consequence that you should regard yourselves as constantly in action, that every preparation should be brought to an even higher pitch of efficiency, and that the utmost vigilance should be maintained in all formations.

It has given me great pleasure to see you here this beautiful summer morning, and to thank you in the name of His Majesty's Government not only for the memorable services you have rendered in the past but for the spirit which will enable you to confront and overcome whatever menaces the future may contain.

"DO YOUR WORST—AND WE WILL DO OUR BEST"

A SPEECH AT A LUNCHEON GIVEN BY THE LONDON COUNTY
COUNCIL AT THE COUNTY HALL AFTER THE REVIEW OF THE
CIVIL DEFENCE SERVICES IN HYDE PARK
JULY 14, 1941

July 14, 1941.

IT seems to me odd that it should have taken the stresses of a great world war to bring me for the first time to the County Hall, and I am very glad indeed to find that by the time the call came the hall had not already ceased to exist. You have taken in this building some of the blows and scars which have fallen upon London, but like the rest of London you carry on.

The impressive and inspiring spectacle we have witnessed in Hyde Park this morning displays the vigour and efficiency of the civil defence forces of London. They have grown up in the stress of emergency. They have been shaped and tempered by the fire of the enemy, and this morning we saw them all, in their many grades and classes—the wardens, the rescue and first-aid parties, the casualty services, the decontamination squads, the fire services, the report and control centre staffs, the highways and public utility services, the messengers, the police. All these we have seen on a lovely English summer morning, marching past, men and women in all the pomp and panoply—not of war, though it is war—but of their civic duties. There they marched, and as one saw them passing by no one could but feel how great a people, how great a nation we have the honour to belong to.

How complex, sensitive, resilient, is the society we have evolved over centuries, and how capable of withstanding the most unexpected strain! Those whom we saw this morning were the representatives of nearly a quarter of a million organized functionaries and servants in the defence of London, who, in one way or another, stand to their posts or take an active part in the maintenance of the life of London and Greater London against an attack which, when it began and while it was at its pitch, was unexampled in history.

And what we saw to-day in Hyde Park was only symbolic of what can be produced, though on a smaller scale, throughout the length and breadth of this country—a competent and embattled Island.

In September last, having been defeated in his invasion plans by the R.A.F., Hitler declared his intention to raze the cities of Britain to the ground, and in the early days of that month he set the whole fury of the Hun upon London.

None of us quite knew what would be the result of a concentrated and prolonged bombardment of this vast centre of population. Here in the Thames Valley, over 8,000,000 people are maintained at a very high level of modern civilization. They are dependent from day to day upon light, heat, power, water, sewerage, and communications on the most complicated scale.

The administration of London in all its branches was confronted with problems hitherto unknown and unmeasured in all the history of the past. Public order, public health, the maintenance of all the essential services, the handling of the millions of people who came in and out of London every day; the shelter—not indeed from the enemy's bombs, for that was beyond us, but from their blast and splinters—the shelter of millions of men and women, and the removal of the dead and wounded from the shattered buildings; the care of the wounded when hospitals were being ruthlessly bombed, and the provision for the homeless—sometimes amounting to many thousands in a single day, and accumulating to many more after three or four days of successive attacks—all these things, with the welfare and the education amid these scenes of our great numbers of children here—all these presented tasks which, viewed in cold blood beforehand, might well have seemed overwhelming.

Indeed, before the war, when the imagination painted pictures of what might happen in the great air raids on our cities, plans were made to move the Government, to move all the great controlling services which are centred in London, and disperse them about the countryside, and also it was always considered a very great danger that a sudden wave of panic might send millions of people crowding out into the countryside along all the roads.

Well, when you are doing your duty and you are sure of that, you need not worry too much about the dangers or the consequences. We have not been moved in this war except by the promptings of duty and conscience, and therefore we do not need to be deterred from action by pictures which our imagination or careful forethought painted of what the consequences would be.

I must, however, admit that when the storm broke in September, I was for several weeks very anxious about the result. We were then not prepared as we are now. Our defences had not the advantages they have since attained, and again I must admit that I greatly feared injury to our public services, I feared the ravages of fire, I feared the dislocation of life and the stoppage of work, I feared epidemics of serious disease or even pestilence among the crowds who took refuge in our by no means completely constructed or well equipped shelters.

I remember one winter evening travelling to a railway station—which still worked—on my way north to visit troops. It was cold and raining. Darkness had almost fallen on the blacked-out streets. I saw everywhere long queues of people, among them hundreds of young girls in their silk stockings and high-heeled shoes, who had worked hard all day and were waiting for bus after bus, which came by already overcrowded, in the hope of reaching their homes for the night. When at that moment the doleful wail of the siren betokened the approach of the German bombers, I confess to you that my heart bled for London and the Londoners.

All this sort of thing went on for more than four months with hardly any intermission. I used to hold meetings of my Ministerial colleagues and members of the authorities concerned every week in Downing Street in order to check up and see how we stood. Sometimes the gas had failed over large areas—the only means of cooking for great numbers of people; sometimes the electricity. There were grievous complaints about the shelters and about conditions in them. Water was cut off, railways were cut or broken, large districts were destroyed by fire, 20,000 people were killed, and many more thousands were wounded.

But there was one thing about which there was never any doubt. The courage, the unconquerable grit and stamina of the Londoners showed itself from the very outset. Without that all would have failed. Upon that rock, all stood unshakable. All the public services were carried on, and all the intricate arrangements, far-reaching details, involving the daily lives of so many millions, were carried out, improvised, elaborated and perfected in the very teeth of the cruel and devastating storm.

I am very glad to come here to-day to pay my tribute and to record in the name of the Government our gratitude to all the civil authorities of London who, first under Sir John Anderson, and through the darkest moments under the courageous and resourceful leadership of Mr. Herbert Morrison—so long master of the London County Council, and now acting in an even higher sphere—to all who carried out their duties faithfully, skilfully, and devotedly, so that at last we made our way through the tempest, and came for the time being, at any rate, into a calm spell.

189

During her long ordeal London was upheld by the sympathy and admiration of the other great cities of our Island—and let us not forget here loyal Belfast, in Northern Ireland—and when after the enemy wearied of his attack upon the capital and turned to other parts of the country, many of us in our hearts felt anxiety lest the weight of attack concentrated on those smaller organisms should prove more effective than when directed on London, which is so vast and strong that she is like a prehistoric monster into whose armoured hide showers of arrows can be shot in vain. But in the event, the staunchness and vigour of London were fully matched by the splendid behaviour of our ports and cities when they in turn received the full violence and frightful cruelty of the enemy's assault; and I say here that, while we are entitled to speak particularly of London, we honour them for their constancy in a comradeship of suffering, of endurance, and of triumph. That comradeship in this hideous, unprecedented, novel pressure has united us all, and it has proved to the world the quality of our Island life.

I have no doubt whatever, as I said to the civil defence forces in Hyde Park this morning, that the behaviour of the British people in this trial gained them conquests in the mind and spirit and sympathy of the United States of America which swept into an ignominious corner all the vilest strokes of Goebbels' propaganda.

We have to ask ourselves this question: Will the bombing attacks of last autumn and winter come back again? We have proceeded on the assumption that they will. Some months ago I requested the Home Secretary and Minister of Home Security and his principal colleagues, the Minister of Health and others, to make every preparation for the autumn and winter war as if we should have to go through the same ordeal as last year, only rather worse. I am sure that everything is being done in accordance with those directions. The shelters are being strengthened, improved, lighted and warmed. All arrangements for fire-control and fire-watching are being perpetually improved.

Many new arrangements are being contrived as a result of the hard experience through which we have passed and the many mistakes which no doubt we have made—for success is the result of making many mistakes and learning from experience. If the lull is to end, if the storm is to renew itself, London will be ready, London will not flinch, London can take it again.

We ask no favours of the enemy. We seek from them no compunction. On the contrary, if to-night the people of London were asked to cast their vote whether a convention should be entered

190

into to stop the bombing of all cities, the overwhelming majority would cry, "No, we will mete out to the Germans the measure, and more than the measure, that they have meted out to us." The people of London with one voice would say to Hitler: "You have committed every crime under the sun. Where you have been the least resisted there you have been the most brutal. It was you who began the indiscriminate bombing. We remember Warsaw in the very first few days of the war. We remember Rotterdam. We have been newly reminded of your habits by the hideous massacre of Belgrade. We know too well the bestial assault you are making upon the Russian people, to whom our hearts go out in their valiant struggle. We will have no truce or parley with you, or the grisly gang who work your wicked will. You do your worst—and we will do our best." Perhaps it may be our turn soon; perhaps it may be our turn now.

We live in a terrible epoch of the human story, but we believe there is a broad and sure justice running through its theme. It is time that the Germans should be made to suffer in their own homeland and cities something of the torment they have twice in our lifetime let loose upon their neighbours and upon the world.

We have now intensified for a month past our systematic, scientific, methodical bombing on a large scale of the German cities, seaports, industries, and other military objectives. We believe it to be in our power to keep this process going, on a steadily rising tide, month after month, year after year, until the Nazi régime is either extirpated by us or, better still, torn to pieces by the German people themselves.

Every month as the great bombers are finished in our factories or sweep hither across the Atlantic Ocean we shall continue the remorseless discharge of high explosives on Germany. Every month will see the tonnage increase, and, as the nights lengthen and the range of our bombers also grows, that unhappy, abject, subject province of Germany which used to be called Italy will have its fair share too.

In the last few weeks alone we have thrown upon Germany about half the tonnage of bombs thrown by the Germans upon our cities during the whole course of the war. But this is only the beginning, and we hope by next July to multiply our deliveries manifold.

It is for this reason that I must ask you to be prepared for vehement counter-action by the enemy. Our methods of dealing with the German night raiders have steadily improved. They no longer relish their trips to our shores. It is not true to say they did

191

not come this last moon because they were all engaged in Russia. They have a bombing force in the West quite capable of making very heavy attacks. I do not know why they did not come, but, as I mentioned in Hyde Park, it is certainly not because they have begun to love us more. It may be because they are saving up, but even if that be so, the very fact that they have to save up should give us confidence by revealing the truth of our steady advance from an almost unarmed position to a position at least of equality, and soon of superiority to them in the air.

But all engaged in our civil defence forces, whether in London or throughout the country, must prepare themselves for further heavy assaults. Your organization, your vigilance, your devotion to duty, your zeal for the cause must be raised to the highest intensity.

We do not expect to hit without being hit back, and we intend with every week that passes to hit harder. Prepare yourselves, then, my friends and comrades in the Battle of London, for this renewal of your exertions. We shall never turn from our purpose, however sombre the road, however grievous the cost, because we know that out of this time of trial and tribulation will be born a new freedom and glory for all mankind.

"THE SOUL OF FRANCE CAN NEVER DIE"

A MESSAGE TO GENERAL DE GAULLE, LEADER OF THE FREE FRENCH FORCES,
ON THE DAY OF THE "FRENCH NATIONAL FETE" (THE ANNIVERSARY OF THE
STORMING OF THE BASTILLE)
JULY 14, 1941

July 14, 1941.

TWO years ago I stood in the Champs Elysèes and watched with emotion the splendid parade of the French Army and Empire. Many catastrophies have filled these two terrible years. Many States have been trampled down and cast into Nazi bondage. Millions of Frenchmen have found themselves for the time being in positions of insuperable difficulty. Some have broken under the strain, and have let themselves slide into the bottomless pit of despair. But the soul of France can never die, and the spirit of the French people will rise again from all the ruin and the misery, purified and rejuvenated by what it has undergone.

To you and your gallant comrades I send this message of greeting and good will.

I send a message to tell all true Frenchmen and Frenchwomen, wherever they may be, however hard their lot, that the British nation and Empire is always on the march along the great road which leads to victory. I feel sure that most of us will live to see another Fourteenth of July when the glories of France will be restored, and when, amid the roar of liberated Europe, we shall celebrate a festival of peace and freedom.

Hard, stern years lie before us, but the end is certain, and the end will make amends for all.

It is a good augury that this Fourteenth of July should witness the liberation of Syria from the control of Wiesbaden, and cleanse it from the intrigues and infiltrations of the Huns.

By British and French hands independence and sovereignty can now be restored to the Arab peoples, and the historic interests of France in Syria can be recognized and preserved.

Thus encouraged, thus fortified, we can turn again to our toils and to our duty.

WAR PRODUCTION AND THE WAR SITUATION

STATEMENTS TO THE HOUSE OF COMMONS
JULY 15, 1941

July 15. Armistice signed in Syria.
June shipping losses announced as 329,296 tons—the lowest for five months.

July 15, 1941.

I AM somewhat concerned at the effects produced abroad and overseas by the two days' Debate on Production. Statements that our industry is only working 75 per cent. of some unspecified standard and that the Ministry of Aircraft Production is in chaos from top to bottom tend to give a general impression in the United States and the Dominions, particularly Australia, that things are being very ill-managed here and that we are not trying our best. It is impossible for the newspapers to report our Debates except in a very abridged form, but these kind of sensational statements telegraphed all over the world do serious harm to our cause wherever they go. Moreover, they do not at all represent the immense and well-directed effort which is yielding remarkable results in almost every field of war production, and they do far from justice to the admirable tenure of the Ministry of Supply by my right hon. Friend the present President of the Board of Trade. I much regret that it was not possible for me, because of the many other things I have to do, to be present in the House except during the closing speeches of that Debate. It is obviously not possible for considered Ministerial answers to be submitted to these charges on the spur of the moment. It is not like ordinary party, peace-time fighting, when any score handed across the Table is good enough for the purposes of the occasion. These are very serious times in which we live. I have, however, read thoroughly the Official Report of the two days' Debate, and I have given directions that all allegations of any serious substance shall be sent to the various Departments concerned in order that the facts may be ascertained. On the Third Sitting Day after 20th July I propose to set up the same Votes as were under discussion last week and have a third day's

Debate, in Public Session. I will myself endeavour to make a full and comprehensive statement on the whole question of production so far as the public interest permits. I hope by this course, which is inspired by the greatest possible respect for the House, to remove any mistaken and evil impression which may be doing us harm in any part of the world.

I propose to initiate the Debate myself, and it will then be open for anyone to take up the quarrel, if they think there is any public advantage in so doing.

. . . .

Towards the end of last week it became possible to make a solemn agreement between the British and Russian Governments, carrying with it the full assent of the British and Russian people and all the great Dominions of the Crown, for united action against the common foe. Both the British and Russian Governments have undertaken to continue the war against Hitlerite Germany to the utmost of their strength, to help each other as much as possible in every way, and not to make peace separately. My right hon. Friend the Foreign Secretary and the right hon. Member for East Bristol (Sir Stafford Cripps), our Ambassador in Moscow, were indefatigable in carrying matters to a swift conclusion. The Agreement which has been signed, the text of which has been published, cannot fail to exercise a highly beneficial and potent influence on the future of the war. It is, of course, an Alliance, and the Russian people are now our Allies. General Smuts has, with his usual commanding wisdom, made a comment which, as it entirely represents the view of His Majesty's Government, I should like to repeat now. He says:

"Let no one say that we are now in league with communists and are fighting the battle of Communism. More fitly can neutralists and fence-sitters be charged with fighting the battle of Nazism. If Hitler, in his insane megalomania, has driven Russia to fighting in self-defence, we bless her arms and wish her all success without for a moment identifying ourselves with her communistic creed. Hitler has made her his enemy and not us friendly to her creed, just as previously he treacherously made her his friend without embracing her Communism."

My right hon. Friend the Foreign Secretary, in these busy days, has also been instrumental in bringing about a very great measure of agreement between the Russian Soviet State and the Polish Republic. These negotiations have not yet reached their conclusion, but I am very hopeful that, aided by the statesmanship of General

Sikorski, another important step will soon be taken in the marshalling of all the peoples of the world against the criminals who have darkened its life and menaced its future.

The House will also have read, I have no doubt, the good news from Syria. A military Convention has been signed, in a cordial spirit on both sides, putting an end to a period of fratricidal strife between Frenchmen and Frenchmen, and also between Frenchmen and British, Australian and Indian soldiers, all of whom drew the sword of their own free will in defence of the soil of France. The fact that our relations, such as they are, with the Vichy Government have not been worsened during these weeks of distressing fighting, when the forces on both sides acquitted themselves with so much discipline, skill and gallantry, is a proof of the deep comprehension by the French people of the true issues at stake in the world. It is a manifestation of that same spirit which leads them to wave encouragement to our bombing aircraft, although the bombs have, in the hard fortune of war, to be cast on French territory because it is in enemy hands.

We seek no British advantage in Syria. Our only object in occupying the country has been to beat the Germans and help to win the war. We rejoice that with the aid of the forces of General de Gaulle, led by General Catroux and General Legentilhomme, we have been able to bring to the peoples of Syria and the Lebanon the restoration of their full sovereign independence. We have liberated the country from the thraldom exercised by the German Armistice Commission at Wiesbaden, and from the dangerous German intrigues and infiltrations which were in progress. The historic interests of France in Syria, and the primacy of those interests over the interests of other European nations, are preserved without prejudice to the rights and sovereignty of the Syrian races.

The conclusion of this brief Syrian campaign reflects credit upon all responsible—upon General Wavell, who was able to spare the force, first to put down the revolt in Iraq, and afterwards to act in Syria, while at the same time making vigorous head against the German and Italian Army and its strong armoured elements which have for so many months been attempting unsuccessfully to invade the Nile Valley. The actual conduct of the campaign was in the hands of General Sir Maitland Wilson, who, it will be remembered, was the General who extricated our Forces from the very great dangers by which they were encompassed in Greece. He did not tell us much about what was going on in either sphere, but in both his operations constitute an admirable example of military skill. I hope it will soon be possible to give fuller accounts to the public than they have yet received of the Syrian fighting, marked as it was by so many picturesque episodes, such as the arrival of His Majesty's Lifeguards and Royal Horse Guards, and the Essex Yeomanry, in armoured cars, across many hundreds of miles of desert, to surround and capture the oasis of Palmyra. There are many episodes of that kind, of great interest, which I trust may soon be made public.

We are entitled to say that the situation in the Nile Valley has for the time being, at any rate, been considerably improved. If any one had predicted two months ago, when Iraq was in revolt and our people were hanging on by their eyelids at Habbaniyah, and our Ambassador was imprisoned in his Embassy at Bagdad, and when all Syria and Iraq began to be overrun by German tourists and were in the hands of forces controlled indirectly but none the less powerfully by German authority—if anyone had predicted that we should already, by the middle of July, have cleaned up the whole of the Levant and re-established our authority there for the time being, such a prophet would have been considered most imprudent. The heavy and indecisive fighting at Sollum by our desert Army, and the stubborn defence of Crete, in which such heavy losses were inflicted on the enemy's air power, must be judged to have played their part in arriving at the general result.

V FOR VICTORY

A MESSAGE TO THE PEOPLES OF EUROPE ON THE LAUNCHING
OF THE "V FOR VICTORY" PROPAGANDA CAMPAIGN
JULY 20, 1941

July 16. Japanese Cabinet resigned.
   *Russia admitted fierce fighting in the Smolensk sector,
   indicating German advance.*
*July 18. Mr. Harry Hopkins, Administrator of the United States
   Lend Lease Act, announced encouraging figures of
   American war production, and said: "This War just
   cannot be lost."*
*July 20. Mr. Churchill launched a great European "V for Victory"
   propaganda campaign with a message which was broad-
   cast to occupied countries.*

July 20, 1941.

THE V sign is the symbol of the unconquerable will of the
occupied territories, and a portent of the fate awaiting the
Nazi tyranny. So long as the peoples of Europe continue to refuse
all collaboration with the invader, it is sure that his cause will
perish, and that Europe will be liberated.

WAR PRODUCTION

A SPEECH TO THE HOUSE OF COMMONS
JULY 29, 1941

July 21. Mr. Brendan Bracken became Minister of Information in succession to Mr. Duff Cooper, appointed to a special co-ordinating mission to the Far East.

Germans made their first heavy air raid on Moscow. Russians claimed it was a failure and that 22 planes had been destroyed.

July 23. Vichy Government signed agreement allowing Japan to take over "military protection" of Indo-China, and alleged that a British military force menaced the country.

July 24. New American "Flying Fortresses" used at stratosphere heights by the R.A.F. in great raid on German naval bases in Occupied France.

July 25. Britain and the United States froze all Japanese credits and instituted a trade blockade.

R.A.F. bombed Berlin.

July 26. United States placed the Philippines on a war footing as a move against Japanese occupation of Indo-China.

Secret Italian torpedo boats made a mass attack on Malta, but all were destroyed.

July 27. Mr. Harry Hopkins, United States Lend-Lease Act Administrator, broadcasting from London, said that British and American warships were now patrolling the Atlantic in "parallel lines."

Second offensive in the German attack on Russia brought to a halt.

July 28. Finland, fighting with Germany against Russia, broke off diplomatic relations with Great Britain.

July 29. Mr. Churchill revealed the great advance in the nation's war production, and said he would not appoint a special Minister of Production.

Mr. Anthony Eden warned the country of a coming "peace campaign" by Germany, and pledged "no peace with Hitler."

[July 29, 1941.

O N 22nd January of this year I explained to the House the system of administration and production which it was proposed to adopt. I then described it in detail and at length, and I hope my statement may be studied again by those who have forgotten it, because it is the system we have followed since, and it is the system to which, in general and in principle, I propose to adhere. Changes in personnel are caused from time to time by the march of events and by the duty of continual improvement. Changes in machinery are enjoined by experience, and, naturally, while we live we ought to learn. Change is agreeable to the human mind, and gives satisfaction, sometimes short-lived, to ardent and anxious public opinion. But, if Parliament is convinced, and those to whom it has given its confidence are convinced, that the system is working well and smoothly, then I say change for the sake of change is to be deprecated. In wartime especially, in vast, nation-wide, and in some respects world-wide organization, continuity and stability must not be underrated. It we were perpetually to be altering our system or lending ourselves too lightly to that process, we might achieve the appearance of energy and reform only at the expense of the authority of individuals and only to the detriment of the smooth working of the machinery, and at a heavy cost in output, which is the sole objective. Therefore, it is at the point where I left off this subject when I discussed it with the House in January that I take up my theme to-day.

There are two main aspects in which production must be considered. First, the organization of planning and control, and, secondly, the actual conditions present in the factories. Let us see first of all what was, and what is, the system upon which the high administrative control of our war effort proceeds. The foundation must, of course, be a single co-ordinated plan for the programmes of the three Services based upon our strategic needs. In my capacity as Minister of Defence, without which I could not bear the responsibilities entrusted to me for bringing about a successful outcome of the war, in that capacity, I prepared for the War Cabinet during the first three months of this year a revised general scheme, bringing together the whole of our munition production and import programme, and prescribing the highest reasonable target at which we ought to aim. For this purpose I was furnished with the forward programmes of the various fighting Departments, very much in the same way as the Service Estimates are brought before the Cabinet and the Treasury in the autumn in time of peace. I discussed these programmes orally and in writing with the Ministers and Service Chiefs of those Departments. The programmes were also examined by my own statistical Department under Professor Lindemann, now Lord Cherwell, and through the machinery of the Office of the Minister of Defence, which, as the House knows, embodies the peace-time Committee of Imperial Defence organization. The work of these organizations proceeds ceaselessly. The strategic aspect of production is also continually considered by the Chiefs of Staff Committee, which meets every day to advise upon or direct the conduct of the war. The general scheme, or War Supply Budget, for the year 1941, a series of printed documents agreed with the Service Ministers and comprising a perfectly clear apportionment of resources and tasks, received the final approval of the War Cabinet on 31st March, and thereafter became mandatory on all Departments. There is, of course, no absolute finality in this scheme. Within its general framework revision and adjustment under the pressure of events are continuous.

So much for the framework of the general lay-out. The execution of this scheme on the military side is confided to the three great Supply Departments, namely, the Controller's Department of the Admiralty, the Ministry of Supply, and the Ministry of Aircraft Production. The work has been parcelled out, and it remains for them to do it. The picture so luridly drawn of the chaotic and convulsive struggles of the three Supply Departments, without guidance or design, is one which will no doubt be pleasing to our enemies, but happily has no relation to the facts. The question however arises whether in their execution of the approved scheme the three Supply Departments have either been wanting in energy, or, on the contrary, through excess of zeal have quarrelled with each other or have trespassed upon each other's domain. There are no doubt instances of friction at the fringe of these powerful organizations, but I do not believe they bear any proportion worth mentioning to their individual and concerted efforts. It must be remembered that a very high proportion of our war production is carried out in factories working solely for one Department. That is true of aircraft factories, naval shipbuilding firms, ordnance factories, automobile factories and many others.

A system has also been worked out for the allocation of the capacity of private engineering firms, either to single Departments, or, in other cases, to two or more Departments in stated proportions. Probably half the factories concerned and certainly more than three-quarters of the men employed are working now, at this time, for one single Department. The Admiralty has its many firms, with their factories dating from long ago and kept alive during our quiet periods by Admiralty orders. The Air Ministry has been striving for a great many years to build up an aircraft industry in this island pending the day when Parliament should decide to have an Air Force equal to any within striking distance of these shores. The War Office, always in time of peace the drudge and starveling of British defence, had its own ordnance factories and was at last on the eve of the war accorded a Ministry of Supply, and this Ministry of Supply has of course extended over a very large part of the remaining British industry.

At the point which we have now reached in our munitions development, almost all firms and factories are working under the complete control of the Government at the fulfilment of the approved and concerted programmes. They are either working directly or indirectly in the sphere of war production, or they are ministering to our domestic and other needs. In this domestic field also, however, a very complete and searching organization under Government control has been instituted. At the present moment, the whole industry of the country, with inconsiderable exceptions, which may soon be linked up and absorbed, is assigned its function under Government authority. There are no doubt a number of minor aspects of our national life which have not yet been effectively regimented. When and as they are wanted, their turn will come. We are not a totalitarian State, but we are steadily, and I believe as fast as possible, working ourselves into total war organization. When we are given vivid instances of lack of organization or of inter-departmental rivalry in some of the shops and factories, and when these are all bunched together to make an ill-smelling posy, it is just as well to remember that the area of disputation is limited, circumscribed and constantly narrowing.

In order to regulate the imports of commodities from abroad in accordance with the policy prescribed by the War Cabinet, we have, as I explained six months ago, the Import Executive comprising the heads of the Importing Departments, and presided over by my right hon. Friend the President of the Board of Trade, and formerly by him when he was Minister of Supply. This is working very smoothly, and I am not aware of any troubles or disputes which have arisen. I should certainly hear of these soon enough if there were any. By the side of this Import Executive we have the North American Supply Committee with its elaborate corresponding organization in the United States. We are always trying to tighten up and make more precise and definite the work of our Purchasing Commissions in the United States. I should certainly not pretend that there is not a great deal of room for improvement and refinement, but it would be a mistake to suppose that the efficiency of our Purchasing Commissions under the supreme control of Mr. Purvis has not reached a very high level or that it is not constantly being shaped and sharpened. A year ago, six months ago, there were a lot of troubles and discordances; but latterly, although again I should be the first to hear of them, my information is that they have very largely died away.

We have of course to come to very clear-cut agreements with our American friends and helpers. They are making an immense effort for the common cause, and they naturally ask for the fullest and clearest information about what is happening to their goods and whether there is waste or misdirection. It is our duty to satisfy them that there is no muddle, or that muddle is reduced to a minimum, and that they are getting value for their money. We welcome their criticism because it is at once searching, friendly and well-informed. The improvement in the ordering of imports and of the British purchases in the United States, and in the relations of the very large number of competent persons who work night and day on both sides of the ocean in this sphere is, I am glad to say, steady and progressive.

Now I come to the home scene. What are the relations of the three Supply Departments in the vast fertile production field of this busy Island? I have already said that for their chief production each of the Fighting Services through its Supply Department or Ministry to an overwhelming extent commands its own factories and labour. Nevertheless, there is an inevitable region of debatable ground, of firms which serve several Departments at once. Many of them are small sub-contracting firms, or firms which make components. Besides this, a process of change is continually going forward to meet the rapidly-varying demands of the war. A firm is resigned by the Admiralty and can be transferred either to the Ministry of Aircraft Production or to the Ministry of Supply. Particular lines of production acquire special urgency or importance as we gain experience from the fighting or as new ideas come along. One line of production dries up because it is no longer needed; another opens or grows in scale. Obviously there is rivalry in this part of the field between the Supply Departments. There ought to be rivalry, and there ought to be zealous competition within the limits of the programme prescribed. It is this zealous competition, limited though it be to a fraction of our industry, which presents the hard cases and sometimes the bad instances of which so much is made.

203

It is among other things for the purpose of resolving the disputes and rivalries of the Departments in this limited field that the Production Executive was called into being in January. The Minister of Labour, himself a contributory factor in that capacity to the work of the rest of the Executive, and himself a Member of the War Cabinet, presides over a committee of six, three of whom are the heads of the Supply Departments, the other two being the President of the Board of Trade and the Minister of Works and Buildings. As I explained to the House six months ago, all the members of this body have every interest to agree. They may have different interests to advocate because they have different duties to discharge, but it is a delusion to suppose that they do not feel a corporate responsibility and try to work together for the common purpose and for the execution of the approved programmes entrusted to them. If they agree they have the power to act. Each can make his contribution to the common action immediately, and the movement of labour and materials can be ordered there and then. If there is a difference which cannot be settled by agreement or compromise, any Minister of Cabinet rank, and they are all such, has the right of appeal to the War Cabinet, or, as between the Service Supply Departments, in the first instance to me as Minister of Defence. During my tenure I have seen some very sharp differences, but those differences have never been so sharp as they were, as I well remember having lived through it, in the days of the last war. All I can say now is that for the last four months no question of departmental rivalry or dispute has been brought to me or the War Cabinet from the Production Executive. I give the assurance to the House to-day that in the high controlling organization there is now no dispute in progress about priorities of labour, raw materials, factory space or machine tools. Do not suppose however that this remarkable fact is the result of inertia or decay. On the contrary, as I shall show before I sit down—I am afraid I shall have to make a somewhat prolonged demand on patience, the subject is of great importance and must be dealt with comprehensively—production in all its forms is gaining steadily and swiftly, not only in volume, but, even at its present high altitude, in momentum.

I may say, while I am on the point, that much of this talk about the difficulties of settling priorities is a back number. The whole business of priorities has undergone a complete transformation. We have no more of those arrogant, absolute priorities in virtue of which one Department claimed all that there was of a particular commodity and left nothing for the lesser but indispensable needs of others. Although the 1A priority is still maintained largely for psychological reasons, for certain particular spheres of production such as aircraft, and now tanks, it is no longer exercised in the crude manner of the last war or the early months of this one. The method of allocation of labour, materials, and facilities has modified and to a large extent replaced the scale of priorities. Allocation is the governing principle, and priorities are becoming little more than a stimulus upon its detailed assignments.

It is at this point and in this setting that I shall deal with the suggestion that a Ministry of Production should be formed. Several speakers referred to this in the recent Debate, and apparently it is regarded by some of our most important newspapers as an easy and speedy solution of our difficulties. There is however a difference among the advocates of a Ministry of Production. Some ask that there should be a complete merging of the Supply Departments of the Admiralty, the Air Ministry and the War Office, and that there should be one great common shop, a vast Department or emporium, serving all fighting needs. That would be very pretty if we were not at war. Others, recoiling from the frightful disturbance and confusion which would accompany the transition and the danger of upsetting so much in the midst of war, are content to ask for one Minister, presumably assisted by a secretarial staff, who should be interposed between the Prime Minister and Minister of Defence and the three Supply Departments. Nothing would be easier than for me to gratify this request by asking one of my colleagues in the War Cabinet to call himself Minister of Production and to duplicate the work of general apportionment which I already do. But, so far from helping me in my task, or helping the Departments in theirs, this would be an additional complication, burden and cause of delay.

Moreover, the relations of this Minister of Production with the three Supply Departments would be most unsatisfactory. He would either have to trust them and use them, as I do, for the purpose of executing the prescribed programmes, or he would be left to break into these Departments, interfere with their work and try to get things done by his personal exertions. The Ministers at the head of these Departments are men of energy, experience and knowledge. They work night and day, and they have powerful, far-reaching, swift-running machinery at their disposal. If, in the sphere assigned to them, they cannot execute the programmes with which they are charged, I do not myself see how a super-Minister from outside, with his skeleton staff, could do it for them. If the new Minister's control were nominal, and did not affect the Ministerial responsibility of the heads of the Supply Departments, it would be a farce and a fraud upon the public to which I will not stoop. If, on the other hand, the Minister of Production attempted to lay strong hands on the internal administration and day-to-day work of these Departments, they would confront him with a knowledge superior to his own and far more intimate, and all the resulting differences would have to come to me, with very great friction to the administrative machine and additional burdens upon the head of the Government.

Furthermore, these matters cannot be considered without reference to the personalities involved. I have not been told who is to be this superman who, without holding the office of Prime Minister, is to exercise an overriding control and initiative over the three Departments of Supply and the three Ministers of Supply. Where is the super-pensonality who, as one of the members of the War Cabinet, will dominate the vast, entrenched, established, embattled organization of the Admiralty to whose successful exertions we owe our lives? Where is the War Cabinet Minister who is going to teach the present Minister of Aircraft Production how to make aircraft quicker and better than they are being made now? Who is the War Cabinet Minister who is going to interfere with Lord Beaverbrook's control and discharge of the functions of Minister of Supply duly and constitutionally conferred upon him? When you have decided on the man, let me know his name, because I should be very glad to serve under him, provided that I were satisfied that he possessed all the Napoleonic and Christian qualities attributed to him. In the conduct of vast, nation-wide administration there must be division of functions, and there must be proper responsibility assigned to the departmental chiefs. They must have the power and authority to do their work, and be able to take a proper pride in it when it is done, and be held accountable for it if it is not done.

Moreover, as I have tried to show, such difficulties as exist are not found at the summit, but out in the country in a minority of smaller firms and factories. I do not for a moment deny that there are many things that go wrong and ought to be put right, but does anyone in his senses suggest that this should be the task of the super-Minister, that he should take up the hard cases and breakdowns by direct intervention from above? All he could do would be to refer complaints or scandals that came to his notice to the heads of the three Supply Departments, and, if he did not get satisfaction, he, having no power to remove or change the Ministers involved, would have to come to me, on whom rests the responsibility of advising His Majesty in such matters.

For good or ill, in any sensible organization you must leave the execution of policies already prescribed to the responsible Ministers and Departments. If they cannot do it, no one can. It is to them that complaints should be addressed. It is to them that Members should write. Any case of which full particulars are provided—I must add that proviso—will be searchingly examined. We do not stand here to defend the slightest failure of duty or organization. But let us have the facts. A kind of whispering campaign has been set on foot; there is a flood of anonymous letters. Vague and general charges are made. And all this fills our shop windows, greatly to our detriment. It is impossible for me, within the limits of this Debate, to deal with various specific allegations which were made by Members in different parts of the House in the two preceding days of this Debate. Such a treatment of the matter would be entirely out of proportion, and I should have to trespass upon the Committee altogether unduly.

I turn aside, however, for a moment to deal with one particular aspect of the problem of production, namely machine tools. *The Times*, in its leading article this morning, makes the valuable suggestion that a census of machine tools throughout the country should be held. There have already been three—in June, 1940, in November, 1940, and a partial census of the principal firms in June, 1941. The Supply Ministers are responsible for the use of machine tools to the best advantage. There is, however, a controller of machine tools, Mr. Mills, a business man of the highest repute, whose sole duty is to supervise their employment by all Departments. By the joint agreement and good will of the three Supply Departments, this gentleman has independent powers. He has his own representatives throughout the country. Although he is actually under the Ministry of Supply, he can remove any machine tool that is idle from any Department or factory and transfer it to another, and he is continually exercising these powers. He exercised them on several occasions against the late Minister of Aircraft Production before the recent changes in the Government took place. This functionary is given these powers with good will by people who wish to submit their Departments to his use of them.

There are, however, three limiting factors in the use of machine tools. The first is any shortage that may exist of skilled labour, which we are striving by every method to overcome. The second is the undoubted difficulty we have found in working to the full extent night shifts under conditions of air attack. It is the third limiting factor which gives rise to the complaints which are made. I am not an expert in these matters, but I am told that there are between 200 and 300 kinds of machine tools in our census. Their effective use is governed by certain precision machine tools of which there is a shortage. I need not say how intense are the efforts to break down these vexatious bottle-necks. Moreover, the precision tools of which there is a shortage vary sometimes with the varying demands of war production, and sometimes the block is found here and sometimes there. Thus, when people go about the country and see at some garage or factory or in some small firm a number of machine tools of the lower grades, or of peace-time specialized types, lying idle and write to their Member about it, the explanation is not that the supply of machine tools is not organized to the highest degree, nor that the Government do not know about these machine tools, where they are and what they are, nor that they do not in general know about them and have them on their census list: it is because, owing to the shortage of key points of special precision types, many of these tools cannot be brought into action, and there would be no sense in crowding out the factories with redundant machinery.

That is a digression which I have made because I have read with some interest the thoughtful article which appears in *The Times* this morning. Hardly any part of our common organization for war production has been more thoroughly and precisely examined than the question of machine tools. No one can be engaged, as my right hon. Friend the Member for Carnarvon Boroughs (Mr. Lloyd George) knows, in munition production for one day without feeling that this is, as it were, the ganglion nerve, the centre of the whole of supply. I said just now that I cannot go into details of many of the cases which hon. Members brought up in the Debate. If they will write about them, they will be gone into in detail.

There was, however, one charge made by my hon. Friend the Member for North Aberdeen (Mr. Garro Jones) which, as it has had wide publicity and as it affects the United States supplies, requires to be answered. My hon. Friend said:

"The sad feature of the United States supply of aircraft is that whereas orders were energetically placed in the last two years or more for airframes and engines, those who placed them forgot at the same time to ensure that supplies of maintenance equipment and ancillary equipment were provided. What is the result? Of one type of aircraft imported from the United States, complete and operationally ready, there are several hundreds—or were a few weeks ago—lying unpacked in inland warehouses, in their crates, for the sole reason that those who placed the orders on behalf of the Ministry of Aircraft Production did not order the necessary ancillary equipment."

So far as aircraft on British orders are concerned, this statement is quite untrue. All British orders for American aircraft have always been placed with spare engines and spares for airframes. There has been no failure or oversight of this kind in ordering British aircraft.

The mistake into which my hon. Friend has fallen arose from an exceptional event. When the French collapsed, all their contracts for aircraft in the United States were taken over immediately, for what they were worth, by the Minister of Aircraft Production. There was not an hour's delay. These aircraft had to be accepted in the condition in which they were prepared for the French, under French orders. This is the case to which I am sure reference was made in this passage of my hon. Friend's speech. They had to be accepted in the condition in which the French had specified them and in which they were delivered by the American manufacturers. This was a windfall, but it had its drawbacks. For instance, the French Tomahawks arrived without spare engines or spares for their airframes, exactly as my hon. Friend pointed out. They were built to take French guns. Their wireless sets did not tune with ours. Their instruments were on the metric system. They were not armoured according to our conditions. They differed in many ways from our methods of control and manœuvre. Instead of pushing some lever forwards, you had to pull it backwards, which our pilots found most inconvenient.

As swiftly as possible these aircraft have been modified and brought into use. The "cannibal" system was frequently resorted to of necessity, leaving lots of them partly gutted, but practically all of these French American aeroplanes are in use and have been most satisfactory in operation. Now there is the whole of that story that has been paraded as a typical scandal and example of how we do our business.

Everything that has been ordered on British account has been ordered complete. The aeroplanes ordered on French account were lacking in equipment. An inquiry addressed to the Minister concerned would have elicited an immediate explanation, but when allegations of this sort are given the utmost publicity in Parliament by a Member speaking from the Front Bench opposite, uninformed American readers—here is where the serious part comes—must come to the conclusion that there is disorganization and incapacity in the conduct of our munitions business, and this opinion, so damaging to us, would be based entirely on misconception and misunderstanding. It is not, I am glad to say, shared by the American authorities. I presided at a recent meeting attended by Mr. Harry

Hopkins, the Lease-Lend authority, to whose words we listened with so much comfort the other night. He, with his full knowledge and attended by expert American officers, dwelt upon the trials and difficulties attending the modification of aircraft from the United States on French account and expressed satisfaction with the arrangements we had made to overcome them. But outside this circle, who know all the facts, inside the United States, where there is a vigorous campaign against the policy pursued by the President and the majority, I fear that harm has been done, and it cannot be easily overtaken or healed.

What are the other elements which produce oscillations or discordances in the process of production? They arise, of course, out of the changing conditions of the war. As new needs arise, new directions have to be given, which undoubtedly cause disturbances in the flow of production, but I must say I have the feeling that the British machinery of production, vast and intricate though it be, is capable not only of flexible adaptation but of sustaining successfully a number of inevitable jerks. These take place, for instance, largely in the sphere of aircraft production. The Minister of Aircraft Production explained to the House on the second day of this Debate the constant changes in the design of aircraft which arose from the progress of our aeronautics and our experience of manufacture and war. He showed how it was sometimes inevitable that there should be a break in the continuity of production because one type had failed and another had proved itself, because one type was being faded out and another being worked in, and how this must happen when you run the risk of ordering off the drawing-board and carrying out large orders on the basis of the pilot model without having the time to go through all the processes which in peace-time make the completion of the aeroplane from the moment of its conception a matter of five or six years.

It is a difficult question to decide when the mass production of a particular type, should be discarded in favour of a new and better type, and to what intensity such a process of transformation should be carried. I think on the whole, at this moment, we have carried it a bit far. Aircraft of a particular type which slowly work up to the peak of production may be discarded after too short a run at the peak level—no doubt for very good reasons, very fine reasons, greater bomb capacity, greater speed and so forth. Simplification and continuity of serial production are, of course, the basic factors necessary in securing flow of output, and it is a question of balancing between the two sides. All the same, believe me, mastery

210

of the air, leadership and command in design, cannot possibly be achieved except by a process of interminable trial and error and the scrapping of old types. Something better comes along. You cannot afford to miss it, even if you have to pay, and pay heavily, in numbers of output or dislocation in a section of the workshops. The struggle for air mastery requires vast numbers, but those vast numbers could not succeed alone unless the forward leading types constantly achieved the highest level of enterprise and perfection. Combat in the air is the quintessence of all physical struggle. To lose primacy in the quality of the latest machines would be incompatible with the attainment of that command of the air in quality and in quantity upon which a large part of our confidence is founded.

I am glad to tell the Committee that our spring and summer fashions in aircraft are this year farther ahead of contemporary German production than they were last year. The enemy borrowed many ideas from our fighter aeroplanes when he felt their mettle a year ago, and we borrowed from him too, but in the upshot we have confronted him in 1941 with fighter aircraft which in performance, speed, ceiling and, above all, gun armaments have left our pilots with the old, and even an added, sense of technical superiority. It would take too long to describe, as I easily could do, some of the smaller causes of oscillation which affect the execution of the Navy and Army supply programmes. I could show in a way which I think would satisfy the House that a certain measure of change, with resulting dislocation, is inevitable under the strenuous conditions of war, but I do not propose to enter upon either of those fields to-day.

Let me come, on the other hand, to an example of criticism which is helpful and constructive. I have read the Seventeenth Report of the Select Committee on National Expenditure. It deals with the conditions in the filling factories. These are admittedly far from satisfactory. Since the war began great factories have been built in out-of-the-way districts, without time to meet the needs and amenities of the working population. They have not by any means yet reached their full capacity and proper standards. Although we have been making many millions of shells, there are still several millions of shells and their components, including fuses, which are not yet filled. But there is no need for alarm, but rather for greater exertion, because in this war we are firing shells at men and not, as in the last war, so largely at ground. Nor have we a great battlefront continuously engaged. We are making on an enormous scale, but we are not firing on any great scale. It is important to remember in the battles in the desert the difficulties of getting ammunition to the places where the guns are, and since the front in France broke down there is no field of fire for our artillery. Therefore, what we have witnessed is not, as in the last war, as I know so well and as did my right hon. Friend before me, the feeling of intense effort to feed the guns from day to day; but we are piling up large and satisfactory reserves with no corresponding outflow to drain them off at the present time. Let me say nothing which would in any way remove from the minds of those engaged in the filling factories the view that catching up with the filling of the already large stores of components, fuses and shell-cases is a work of high and prime order and of national importance.

Representatives of the Select Committee visited the filling factories in June, and they produced a number of extremely shrewd and valuable suggestions dealing with transport, hostels, canteens, Sunday work and piece-work. We agree with nearly all of them. We shall adopt almost all of them. We agree with them the more readily and we can adopt them the more speedily because, as I see from the records, on 7th January and on 5th February, in my capacity as Minister of Defence, I presided over two successive meetings of the Supply Committee on this very subject. Almost every one of these proposals had already been ordered to be put into operation months before, and has been or is being carried into effect with very great improvement, in spite of the many difficulties attendant upon the bringing into action of these great new plants in out-of-the-way districts under the conditions which prevailed last winter.

I have here a detailed account of all that had been set on foot or that had been done before the Select Committee visited the factories. I will send it to the chairman of the Committee for their further observations. It is too long for me to read in detail, but it shows that great minds sometimes think alike, and that the Government great minds had a good long start of the great minds of the Select Committee. The report of the Select Committee is the kind of criticism that one wants—not mere vague abuse and prejudice, in which only bad citizens and bad people indulge in times like these, but helpful and constructive suggestions, many of which were contained in the speeches made from the Front Bench opposite.

I leave the first part of this subject, dealing with discordances and shortcomings alleged to be attributable to faults or weaknesses in the high control, and I come to the more general charges of slackness and inefficiency in the factories themselves, whether due to local lack of management or to lack of zeal in the workpeople. There is a certain class of member of all parties—you can count them on your fingers and toes—who feel, no doubt quite sincerely, that their war work should be to belabour the Government and portray everything at its worst, in order to produce a higher efficiency. I see that a Motion has been put on the Paper calling specifically for the appointment of a Minister of Production. I consider that to be a perfectly proper step for the Members concerned to take. I regret only that the Motion cannot be moved in this form to-day. If the Members who have fathered it do not feel satisfied with the reasons I have given against creating a Minister or a Ministry of Production, I hope that they will not hesitate to go to a Division by moving a nominal reduction of one of the Votes we are discussing. That is the straightforward and manly course. No one should be deterred in wartime from doing his duty merely by the fact that he will be voting against the Government, and still less because the party Whips are acting as tellers.

We are often told that "the House of Commons thinks this" or "feels that." Newspapers write: "The general feeling was of grave uneasiness," "There was much disquiet in the Lobby," etc. All this is telegraphed all over the world and produces evil effects. No one has a right to say what is the opinion of the House of Commons. We suffer now from not having divisions. We have Debates, to which a very small minority of Members are able to contribute, because of the time available. They express their anxiety and grievances and make our affairs out as bad as they possibly can, and these views bulk unduly in the reports which reach the public or are heard abroad. These Members do not represent the opinion of the House of Commons or of the nation, nor do their statements give a true picture of the prodigious war effort of the British people. Parliament should be an arena in which grievances and complaints become vocal. The Press also should be a prompt and vigilant alarm bell, ringing when things are going right. But it is a very heavy burden added to the others we have to bear if, without a vote being cast, the idea should be spread at home and abroad that it is the opinion of the House of Commons that our affairs are being conducted in an incompetent and futile manner and that the whole gigantic drive of British industry is just one great muddle and flop.

People speak of workmen getting £6, £7, or £8 a week and not giving a fair return to the State. It is also asserted, on the other hand, that the workmen are eager to work, but that the mismanagement from the summit is such that they are left for weeks or even

213

months without the raw material, or the particular component or the special direction which they require for their task. We may be quite sure that in an organization which deals with so many millions of people under all the stresses of the present time, including the inevitable oscillations of wartime which I have mentioned, there are a great many faults; but we must try sedulously to eradicate those faults and to raise the harmony and cohesion of our whole productive effort. Here again, it is important to preserve a sense of proportion, and not to be led away into thinking that hard cases, wrong deeds and minor or local discordances represent more than a very small fraction of our war performance. It is no less important—indeed, in a way it is even more important—not to sum up and condemn the whole effort of the nation as if it were expressed in these discordances and failures. That is my complaint about the recent Debate, and the use made of it by certain sections of the Press. When I read it, I was distressed to realize the effect it might have on our own self-confidence, and still more upon opinion, friendly, hostile, or balancing, in foreign countries. I therefore ventured to ask the House to resume the Debate in order that I might present a complete picture; and I should be glad to have the matter brought to a plain issue. It is on this footing and with these preliminaries to dealing with the second branch of my subject, namely, what is going on in the factories, that I come to the remark of my hon. Friend the Member for Kidderminster (Sir J. Wardlaw-Milne), who said that "our people are only working up to 75 per cent. of their possible efficiency." I am well aware that in making that statement my hon. Friend did not wish to attack the Government or in any way to embarrass the national defence. In fact, he has been ill-used: this particular sentence has been wrested from its context and from the whole character of his speech. Nevertheless, as Chairman of the Select Committee on National Expenditure, he holds a very responsible position and is credited with exceptional knowledge. A statement like this, coming from him, although uttered with the best of motives, is dangerous when it is broadcast apart from its context. I have to think of its effect in Australia, for instance, where party politics are pursued with the same robust detachment as was exhibited by our forerunners in this House in the seventeenth and eighteenth centuries. A statement like this, taken out of its context, or in a very summarized version of what was said, becomes the subject of lively discussion out there.

Australian troops are bearing with great distinction much of the brunt of the fighting in the Middle East, and it must be very painful to Australians to be told that we are only making a three-quarter effort here at home to put proper weapons in their hands. In America, such a statement is meat and drink to the Isolationist forces. Americans are being asked to pay much heavier taxes, to give up their food, to alter their daily lives, and to reduce their motor cars, indulgences and pleasures of all kinds, in order to help Britain; and I cannot help being deeply disturbed when they are told on what seems to be high British authority that we are making only a three-quarter-hearted effort to help ourselves. My hon. Friend's allegation has been wrested from its context. I have no quarrel with him, but it has gone to all parts of the country and to all quarters of the world; but nothing can be done about that.

What is important is whether it is true; but how difficult to decide—because, after all, this is a double expression of opinion—first, whether it is 75 per cent. or not, and, secondly, 75 per cent. of what? I have tried to find a datum line, and I take as the datum line the three months after Dunkirk. Then, it will be admitted, our people worked to the utmost limit of their moral, mental and physical strength. Men fell exhausted at their lathes, and workmen and working women did not take their clothes off for a week at a time. Meals, rest, and relaxation all faded from their minds, and they just carried on to the last ounce of their strength. Thus there was a great spurt in June, July and August of last year. Immense efforts were made, and every semi-finished weapon was forced through to completion, very often at the expense of future production; and the result was an altogether abnormal inflation. So let us take those three months as the datum line; you could not have a harder test.

Now is it true that we are only working 75 per cent. of that? There are certainly one or two reasons why we cannot wholly recapture and maintain indefinitely the intense personal efforts of a year ago. First of all, if we are to win this war—and I feel solidly convinced that we shall—it will be largely by staying power. For that purpose you must have reasonable minimum holidays for the masses of the workers: there must, as my hon. Friend himself urged in his speech, be one day in seven of rest as a general rule; and there must be, subject to coping with bottle-necks and with emergencies which know no law, a few breaks and where possible one week's holiday in the year. Since what I will call the Dunkirk three-months datum period, we have undoubtedly relaxed to that extent. Sunday work is practically eliminated, and brief periods of leisure have been allowed to break the terrible routine strain of continuous employment. I am quite sure that if we had not done

215

so, we should have had a serious crack which would have cost far more in production than these brief periods of rest from labour.

Next, allowances must be made for the very severe change in the diet of the heavy manual worker. It is quite true that no one has gone short of food; there has been no hunger, there has not been the confusion of some periods of the last war; but no one can pretend that the diet of the British people and especially of their heavy workers has not become far less stimulating and interesting than it was a year ago. Except for our Fighting Services, we have been driven back to a large extent from the carnivore to the herbi-vore. That may be quite satisfactory to the dietetic scientists who would like to make us all live on nuts, but undoubtedly it has produced, and is producing, a very definite effect upon the energetic output of the heavy worker. We want more meat in the mines and the foundries, and we want more cheese. Why should that gratify Lord Haw-Haw? Lord Haw-Haw should also bear in mind the statement of Mr. Harry Hopkins the other day, on the intention of the United States to see that we get our food, and to keep clear the sea-lanes by which our food will be brought. I know of the great arrangements which have been made to send us nourishing, varied and more interesting food in vast quantities. Therefore there is no need to tell me I am helping Lord Haw-Haw. If he never gets any more consolation than he gets from me, his lot will be as hard as he deserves. Every effort will be made, and is being made, to supplement this deficiency; and I share the hope of the Minister of Food and the Minister of Agriculture that our rations in 1942 will be more stimulating and more intensely nourishing than in 1941.

That is the second reason. The first is the need for some relaxation; then there is this question of food, which has come upon us gradually, and which is serious. I wish it to be known all over the United States that it is serious, because it encourages them in their actions. The third reason is this: Look at all the dilution we have had. It is estimated that one-third more people are working in the war industries than there were a year ago. A great many of these are trainees and newcomers. It would not be wonder-ful if they failed to preserve the same level of output per pair of human hands as was achieved by the skilled craftsmen of a year or eighteen months ago. Naturally they will improve. They are improving, but dilution means a reduction in efficiency per pair of human hands in the earlier stages.

Then, fourthly, there has been great dislocation by reason of the air raids, by which the Germans hoped to smash up our industries and break down our power of resistance last autumn and winter. Air-raid destruction, extraordinary blitzes on our ports and manufacturing centres, the restrictions of the black-out, the interruptions and delays of transportation, all played their retarding and dislocating parts. The remedy and counter-measure which was proposed and carried through when possible with such extreme vigour by the Supply Departments, with Lord Beaverbrook and the Ministry of Aircraft Production in the van as the inspiring force, took the form of dispersion. This was a matter of life and death, in the aircraft industry as well as in other key war industries. The great Bristol firm, for instance, was dispersed into nearly 45 such centres. I could give you—and the enemy too—a score of instances of the dispersion of firms to 20, 30 or 40 such centres. All this has been an obstacle to the smooth running of production. It has placed us, however, in a position in which we are immune from mortal damage from enemy air raids on our aircraft production and other branches of munitions. We may suffer, we may be retarded, we can no longer be destroyed. When a great firm like the Bristol firm is divided and dispersed, consider the trials of the workpeople and the problems of the management. Workpeople by the thousand have to be moved from their homes, plant has to be shifted, ruined factories have to be reconditioned, domestic affairs have to somehow or other to be adjusted, often with great sacrifice and hardship, and it is a marvel what has been done to overcome these grievous and novel difficulties. That they should hamper the pace and intensity of production was inevitable.

I have now described to the Committee a number of solid factors which have arisen since the Dunkirk period, all of which have tended to obstruct and reduce output. I should like to give the Committee some facts and figures to show how far we have succeeded, by improved organization and by the smoother running of our expanding machinery, in overcoming these adverse currents which I have set out at length. But here I encounter a new difficulty. I am told we cannot have these Debates in Secret Session; they must be in public. The Germans must read in two or three days every word we say, and therefore I cannot give actual figures. In addition, I am told by my hon. Friends to "Let us have none of these comparative percentages; let us not be told that we are producing half as much again or double what we produced this time last year, because we were producing nothing last year or something like it." As my hon. Friend said, it is a Lancashire saying that "Twice nowt is nowt." So, according to these critics, I am inhibited from all vindicatory comparisons.

I must not say how much better we are than at this time last year, when, after all, we had been at war for 10 or 11 months, and so were presumably making something. I must not say how much better we are than at the twenty-third month of the last war, nor how our output compares with the peak of the last war, because it is contended conditions have changed. This is rather easy money for the critics. A handful of Members can fill a couple of days' Debate with disparaging charges against our war effort, and every ardent or disaffected section of the Press can take it up, and the whole can cry a dismal cacophonous chorus of stinking fish all round the world. But no answer must be made, nothing must be said to show the giant war effort, the prodigy of national zeal, which excites the astonishment of friend and foe, which will command the admiration of history, and which has kept us alive.

I defy these tyrannical prohibitions. I intend to make comparisons, both with the Dunkirk datum period and with the similar and peak periods of the last war. Despite all the troubles I have enumerated, the Ministry of Supply output in the last three months has been one-third greater than in the three months of the Dunkirk period. Though our Navy, Army and Air Force are larger, the Ministry has one-third more people working in its factories. Thus, despite dilutions, dispersion, reduced food, the black-out, and all the troubles I have described, each man is turning out, on the whole, each day, as much as he did in that time of almost super-human effort. Let me present the balance-sheet. One-third more workers and one-third more output is quits. But all the adverse factors I have described have somehow or other been cancelled out by superior development of our machinery and organization. We have made, in the last three months, more than twice the field guns we made in the Dunkirk period. The ammunition we are turning out is half as much again. The combined merchant and naval shipbuilding now in active progress is bigger, not only in scale but in current daily volume of execution, than it was at any period in the last war, and, of course, the work now is immeasurably more complex than it was then.

In aircraft production it is foolish to calculate only by the number of machines, though these have largely increased, because one machine takes 5,000 man-hours, and another, 75,000 man-hours. Judged, however, either by the test of numbers or man-hours eventuating in aircraft production, the increase even above the spurt period of a year ago is substantial. The increase since this Government took office is enormous, and I should be proud to tell what it is. I am not going to do so, because the enemy do not tell

218

us their figures, much as we should like to have them. Therefore, be content with my assurance that progress and expansion on a great scale are continuous, and are remorselessly spurred on. This progress has been accomplished under the fire of the enemy, under air assault, which Hitler was led to believe would shatter our industries and reduce us to impotence and subjection. It has been done in spite of the difficulties of dispersion, and not only with no sacrifice in quality but with a gain in quality, both actual and relative. Now that the air battles are developing again in scale and intensity, we can claim that our fighters are at least as much ahead of the enemy as when we defeated him a year ago.

As for the bombers, in the year that has passed, in British production alone, taking no account of the now rapidly expanding United States imports, we have doubled our power of bomb discharge on Germany at 1,500 miles range; and in the next three months, though this time taking account of the American reinforcements, we shall double it again. In the six months after that we shall redouble it. Besides all this we have ploughed the land, and, by the grace of God, have been granted the greatest harvest in living memory, perhaps the greatest we have even known in these Islands. So much for comparison with the high level of the Dunkirk period.

Now I turn to some comparisons with the last war. That was a terrible war. It lasted 52 months; there was frightful slaughter; there was an immense British effort; there was a complete final victory. We are now in the twenty-third month. We have lost large stocks of equipment on the beaches of Dunkirk, our food has been rationed, our meat reduced, we have been bombed and blacked out, and yet, even in this seventh quarter of the war, our total output of war-like stores has been nearly twice as great as our total output of production in the corresponding seventh quarter of the last war, and has equalled our production in the fourteenth and culminating quarter of the last war. We have rather more workers in the metal industry than we had then. When all those now working to complete and equip our new factories become available, and the Ministry of Labour has completed its task of collecting workers from unessential industries, we shall produce even more. But to reach, in two years, the level only achieved in the fourth year of the last war is, I venture to submit, an achievement which deserves something better than flouts and jeers.

We are told how badly labour is behaving, and then a lot of people who never did a day's hard work in their lives are out after them. Again I claim to look back to the last war. In that war we

219

had many bitter and devastating strikes, and in the final two years nearly 12,000,000 working days were lost through labour disputes. So far, in the whole 23 months of this war, we have lost less than 2,000,000 days. I was anxious to have the latest information about trade disputes in the country. I received, a few minutes before I rose to speak, a report that at 11 o'clock to-day there was no stoppage of work of any kind arising from a trade dispute in any part of Great Britain. It is the fashion nowadays to abuse the Minister of Labour. He is a workman, a trade union leader. He is taunted with being an unskilled labourer representing an un-skilled union. I daresay he gives offense in some quarters; he has his own methods of speech and action. He has a frightful load to carry; he has a job to do which none would envy. He makes mistakes, as I do, though not so many or so serious—he has not the same opportunities. At any rate he is producing, at this moment, though perhaps on rather expensive terms, a vast and steady volume of faithful effort, the like of which has not been seen before. And if you tell me that the results he produces do not compare with those of totalitarian systems of government and society, I reply by saying, "We shall know more about that when we get to the end of the story."

I daresay that some of our critics will not like this kind of talk. They call it complacency. Living in comparative idleness, they wish to lash the toilers of body and mind to further exertions. To state facts which are true and encouraging is to be accused of a cheap and facile optimism. Our critics do not like it; neither do the Germans, though for different reasons. But I consider that if, for days on end, the whole national effort is disparaged and insulted, and if, all over the world, we are depicted by our friends and countrymen as slack, rotten and incompetent, we are entitled, nay, it becomes a pressing duty to restore the balance by presenting the truth.

A number of Votes have been put down as a basis of this Debate. I do not think I shall be out of Order if I place our discussion in its relation to the general aspects of the war before we separate for a short Recess, during which Members will be able to regain contact with their constituents, and Ministers to give un-divided attention to their work. When I look out upon the whole tumultuous scene of this ever-widening war, I feel it my duty to conclude by giving a very serious warning to the House and to the country. We must be on our guard equally against pessimism and against optimism. There are, no doubt, temptations to optimism. It is the fact that the mighty Russian State, so foully and treacherously assaulted, has struck back with magnificent strength and courage, and is inflicting prodigious and well-deserved slaughter for the first time upon the Nazi armies. It is the fact that the United States, the greatest single Power in the world, is giving us aid on a gigantic scale and advancing in rising wrath and conviction to the very verge of war. It is the fact that the German air superiority has been broken, and that the air attacks on this country have for the time being almost ceased. It is the fact that the Battle of the Atlantic, although far from won, has, partly through American intervention, moved impressively in our favour. It is the fact that the Nile Valley is now far safer than it was twelve months ago or three months ago. It is the fact that the enemy has lost all pretence of theme or doctrine, and is sunk ever deeper in moral and intellectual degradation and bankruptcy, and that almost all his conquests have proved burdens and sources of weakness.

But all these massive, towering facts, which we are entitled to dwell on, must not lead us for a moment to suppose that the worst is over. The formidable power of Nazi Germany, the vast mass of destructive munitions that they have made or captured, the courage, skill and audacity of their striking forces, the ruthlessness of their centralized war-direction, the prostrate condition of so many great peoples under their yoke, the resources of so many lands which may to some extent become available to them—all these restrain rejoicing and forbid the slightest relaxation. It would be madness for us to suppose that Russia or the United States is going to win this war for us. The invasion season is at hand. All the Armed Forces have been warned to be at concert pitch by 1st September, and to retain the utmost vigilance meanwhile. We have to reckon with a gambler's desperation. We have to reckon with a criminal who by a mere gesture has decreed the death of three or four million Russian and German soldiers. We stand here still the champions. If we fail, all fails, and if we fall, all will fall together. It is only by a superb, intense and prolonged effort of the whole British Empire that the great combination of about three-quarters of the human race against Nazidom will come into vehement and dynamic life. For more than a year we have been all alone: all alone, we have had to guard the treasure of mankind. Although there have been profound and encouraging changes in the situation, our own vital and commanding responsibilities remain undiminished; and we shall discharge them only by continuing to pour out in the common cause the utmost endeavours of our strength and virtue, and, if need be, to proffer the last drop of our heart's blood.

A TRIBUTE TO THE MERCHANT SEAMEN

A MESSAGE SENT TO THE JOURNAL OF THE
MERCHANT SEAMEN'S UNION
JULY, 1941

July 30. Russo-Polish Pact, signed in London, recognised pre-War boundaries and freed 200,000 Poles held in Russia to form an Allied Army against Germany.

    Fleet Air Arm planes bombed German-occupied ports of Kirkenes and Petsamo.

July 31. Mr. Harry Hopkins, United States Lend-Lease Act Administrator, met Stalin in Moscow and assured him of "all possible aid."

[July, 1941.

THE Merchant Navy, with Allied comrades, night and day, in weather fair or foul, face not only the ordinary perils of the sea but the sudden assaults of war from beneath the waters or from the sky. Your first task is to bring to port the cargoes vital for us at home or for our armies abroad, and we trust your tenacity and resolve to see this stern task through.

We are a seafaring race, and we understand the call of the sea. We account you in these hard days worthy successors in a tradition of steadfast courage and high adventure, and we feel confident that that proud tradition of our island will be upheld to-day wherever the ensign of a British merchantman is flown.

THE EIGHT POINTS

A JOINT DECLARATION BY MR. WINSTON CHURCHILL AND
PRESIDENT ROOSEVELT AT THEIR MEETING IN THE ATLANTIC
AUGUST 14, 1941

*August 1. Russians launched a counter-attack in an effort to fore-
stall the Germans' third offensive.*

*August 2. R.A.F. opened its new bombing offensive on Germany
with heavy raids on Berlin, Hamburg and Kiel.*

*August 3. The Germans switched the main drive of their attack to
the Ukraine, menacing Kiev with a pincers movement.*

*August 5. Strong forces of British and Indian troops reached
Singapore, threatened by Japanese moves.*

*August 6 Mr. Anthony Eden, Foreign Secretary, warned Japan
to keep out of Thailand, and advised Iran to get rid of
German agents in that country.*

*August 7. Russian planes made their first attack on Berlin while
the R.A.F. bombed Krupps works at Essen.*

*August 9. Hitler reported to have ordered preparations for a
winter campaign against Russia after favourable defensive positions had been established.*

*It was revealed in Washington that hundreds of
U.S. planes had been ear-marked for Russia, and some
were actually on their way.*

*August 10. The Queen broadcast a message of thanks to the women
of the United States of America for their help in war
work.*

*August 11. In the Far East Japan announced general mobilization,
Thailand reinforced its Indo-China frontier, and the
Australian Cabinet held a twelve-hour "crisis" meeting.*

*August 12. R.A.F. carried out its most devastating air raids of
the war on Germany.*

*Fighting in the Ukraine reached a critical stage, and
the Germans claimed they were encircling Odessa.*

*Russia and Britain gave a joint pledge to go to the
aid of Turkey if attacked.*

*Petain took the pro-German step of appointing
Darlan virtual dictator of France.*

August 13. *After five weeks of heroic defence, Smolensk admitted by the Russians to have been evacuated.*

Announced that in the month of July 501 people were killed in air raids on Great Britain—the second lowest figure since the heavy raids started.

August 14. *First announcement of the historic meeting of Mr. Winston Churchill and President Roosevelt. An eight-point declaration was signed giving the common policies of the two countries and promising, after the final destruction of Nazi tyranny and the disarmament of the aggressors, to work for a peace that would ensure "that all men may live out their lives in freedom from want and fear."*

It was also announced that important staff talks had accompanied the meeting of Mr. Churchill and President Roosevelt.

Mr. A. B. Purvis, head of the British Purchasing Commission in the United States, killed in plane crash.

[*August 14, 1941.*

THE President of the United States and the Prime Minister, Mr. Churchill, representing His Majesty's Government in the United Kingdom, being met together, deem it right to make known certain common principles in the national policies of their respective countries on which they base their hopes for a better future for the world.

FIRST, their countries seek no aggrandisement, territorial or other.

SECOND, they desire to see no territorial changes that do not accord with the freely expressed wishes of the peoples concerned.

THIRD, they respect the right of all peoples to choose the form of Government under which they will live; and they wish to see sovereign rights and self-government restored to those who have been forcibly deprived of them.

FOURTH, they will endeavour, with due respect for their existing obligations, to further enjoyment by all States, great or small, victor or vanquished, of access, on equal terms, to the trade and to the raw materials of the world which are needed for their economic prosperity.

FIFTH, they desire to bring about the fullest collaboration between all nations in the economic field, with the object of securing for all improved labour standards, economic advancement, and social security.

SIXTH, after the final destruction of Nazi tyranny, they hope to see established a peace which will afford to all nations the means of dwelling in safety within their own boundaries, and which will afford assurance that all the men in all the lands may live out their lives in freedom from fear and want.

SEVENTH, such a peace should enable all men to traverse the high seas and oceans without hindrances.

EIGHTH, they believe all of the nations of the world, for realistic as well as spiritual reasons, must come to the abandonment of the use of force. Since no future peace can be maintained if land, sea, or air armaments continue to be employed by nations which threaten, or may threaten, aggression outside of their frontiers, they believe, pending the establishment of a wider and permanent system of general security, that the disarmament of such nations is essential. They will likewise aid and encourage all other practicable measures which will lighten for peace-loving peoples the crushing burden of armament.

A MESSAGE TO PREMIER STALIN

MR. WINSTON CHURCHILL AND PRESIDENT ROOSEVELT, FROM THEIR ATLANTIC
CONFERENCE, SENT THIS JOINT MESSAGE TO THE PRESIDENT OF THE SOVIET
OF PEOPLE'S COMMISSARS OF THE U.S.S.R.
AUGUST 15, 1941

---

*August 15. Following the meeting between Mr. Churchill and
President Roosevelt, a joint message was sent to Stalin
suggesting a three-power conference in Moscow to co-
ordinate war supplies and strategy.*

*In the Ukraine, Marshal Budenny continued a big
retirement from the line of the Dnieper River in face
of dangerous German thrusts.*

*It was announced that R.A.F. bombers had cut the
Corinth Canal.*

[*August 15, 1941.*

WE have taken the opportunity afforded by the consideration
of the report of Mr. Harry Hopkins on his return from
Moscow to consult together as to how best our two countries can
help your country in the splendid defence that you are making
against the Nazi attack. We are at the moment co-operating to
provide you with the very maximum of supplies that you most
urgently need. Already many shiploads have left our shores and
more will leave in the immediate future.

We must now turn our minds to the consideration of a more
long-term policy, since there is still a long and hard path to be
traversed before there can be won that complete victory without
which our efforts and sacrifices would be wasted.

The war goes on upon many fronts and before it is over there
may be further fighting fronts that will be developed. Our resources
though immense are limited, and it must become a question as to
where and when those resources can best be used to further to the
greatest extent our common effort. This applies equally to manufactured war supplies and to raw materials.

The needs and demands of your and our armed services can only
be determined in the light of full knowledge of the many factors

which must be taken into consideration in the decisions that we make. In order that all of us may be in a position to arrive at speedy decisions as to the apportionment of our joint resources, we suggest that we prepare for a meeting to be held in Moscow, to which we would send high representatives who could discuss these matters directly with you. If this conference appeals to you, we want you to know that pending the decisions of that conference we shall continue to send supplies and material as rapidly as possible.

We realize fully how vitally important to the defeat of Hitlerism is the brave and steadfast resistance of the Soviet Union, and we feel therefore that we must not in any circumstances fail to act quickly and immediately in this matter of planning the programme for the future allocation of our joint resources.

TO THE PEOPLE OF ICELAND

A SPEECH MADE AT REYKJAVIK (ICELAND) ON THE JOURNEY BACK TO
ENGLAND AFTER THE ATLANTIC MEETING WITH PRESIDENT ROOSEVELT,
AUGUST, 1941

---

*August 16. President Roosevelt said that he had reached complete
agreement with Mr. Churchill, but denied that the
United States was any nearer to entry into the War.
He expressed confidence that Russia would hold out
through the winter.*

> *Stalin welcomed the offer of a three-power con-
ference in Moscow.*

*August 18. Germans renewed their thrust at Leningrad, and the
Russians evacuated the key town of Kingisepp, 75 miles
away.*

*August 19. Mr. Churchill arrived back in London from his meeting
with President Roosevelt, having broken his journey
to inspect British and American troops in Iceland.*

> *Revealed that in five weeks Germany and Italy had
lost 616,000 tons of shipping, their heaviest losses
of the war.*

[*August, 1914.*

I AM glad to have an opportunity to visit the nation which for so
long has loved democracy and freedom. We, and later the
Americans, have undertaken to keep war away from this country.
But you will all realize that if we had not come others would.

We will do all in our power to make sure that our presence here
shall cause as little trouble as possible in the lives of the Icelanders.
But at the moment your country is an important base for the
protection of the rights of the nations.

When the present struggle is over, we, and the Americans, will
ensure that Iceland shall receive absolute freedom. We come to
you as one cultured nation to another, and it is our aim that your
culture in the past may be joined to your progress in the future
as a free people. I have pleasure in wishing you happiness and
good luck in time to come.

THE MEETING WITH PRESIDENT ROOSEVELT

A BROADCAST ADDRESS
AUGUST 24, 1941

August 20. *Germany's third offensive against Russia reached its peak with fierce battles at three key points—at Novgorod (in the Leningrad sector), at Gomel (midway between Smolensk and Kiev) and around Odessa.*

August 21. *Voroshilov made a stirring appeal to the people of Leningrad to rally to the defence of the threatened city.*

Mr. Mackenzie King, Prime Minister of Canada, arrived in London. In Australia there was a widening of the Parliamentary split on the question of Mr. Menzies representing Australia in London.

Iran crisis developed, and it was reported the Iran Government had given an unsatisfactory answer to the demand by Britain and Russia that German agents should be turned out of the country.

August 22. *Mr. A. V. Alexander, First Lord of the Admiralty, described the country's July shipping losses as "easily the best" for a year.*

August 23. *Marshal Voroshilov issued an Order of the Day stating that the "decisive moment" had arrived in the battle for Leningrad.*

August 24. *Mr. Churchill broadcast to the world his story of the meeting with President Roosevelt.*

[August 24, 1941.

I THOUGHT you would like me to tell you something about the voyage which I made across the ocean to meet our great friend, the President of the United States. Exactly where we met is a secret, but I don't think I shall be indiscreet if I go so far as to say that it was "somewhere in the Atlantic."

In a spacious, landlocked bay which reminded me of the West Coast of Scotland, powerful American warships protected by strong flotillas and far-ranging aircraft awaited our arrival, and, as it were, stretched out a hand to help us in. Our party arrived in the newest or almost the newest, British battleship, the *Prince of Wales*, with a modern escort of British and Canadian destroyers; and there for three days I spent my time in company, and I think I may say in comradeship, with Mr. Roosevelt; while all the time the chiefs of the staff and the naval and military commanders both of the British Empire and of the United States sat together in continual council.

President Roosevelt is the thrice-chosen head of the most powerful state and community in the world. I am the servant of King and Parliament at present charged with the principal direction of our affairs in these fateful times, and it is my duty also to make sure, as I have made sure, that anything I say or do in the exercise of my office is approved and sustained by the whole British Commonwealth of Nations. Therefore this meeting was bound to be important, because of the enormous forces at present only partially mobilized but steadily mobilizing which are at the disposal of these two major groupings of the human family : the British Empire and the United States, who, fortunately for the progress of mankind, happen to speak the same language, and very largely think the same thoughts, or anyhow think a lot of the same thoughts.

The meeting was therefore symbolic. That is its prime importance. It symbolizes, in a form and manner which everyone can understand in every land and in every clime, the deep underlying unities which stir and at decisive moments rule the English-speaking peoples throughout the world. Would it be presumptuous for me to say that it symbolizes something even more majestic—namely, the marshalling of the good forces of the world against the evil forces which are now so formidable and triumphant and which have cast their cruel spell over the whole of Europe and a large part of Asia?

This was a meeting which marks for ever in the pages of history the taking-up by the English-speaking nations, amid all this peril, tumult and confusion, of the guidance of the fortunes of the broad toiling masses in all the continents; and our loyal effort without any clog of selfish interest to lead them forward out of the miseries into which they have been plunged back to the broad highroad of freedom and justice. This is the highest honour and the most glorious opportunity which could ever have come to any branch of the human race.

When one beholds how many currents of extraordinary and terrible events have flowed together to make this harmony, even the most sceptical person must have the feeling that we all have

Mr. Churchill speaking before Members of Congress at a joint session in the Senate Chamber, Washington, December 26, 1941.

Mr. Churchill inspecting the guard of honour provided by the Canadian Army, outside Parliament Buildings, Ottawa, December 30, 1941.

the chance to play our part and do our duty in some great design, the end of which no mortal can foresee. Awful and horrible things are happening in these days. The whole of Europe has been wrecked and trampled down by the mechanical weapons and barbaric fury of the Nazis; the most deadly instruments of war-science have been joined to the extreme refinements of treachery and the most brutal exhibitions of ruthlessness, and thus have formed a combine of aggression the like of which has never been known, before which the rights, the traditions, the characteristics and the structure of many ancient honoured states and peoples have been laid prostrate and are now ground down under the heel and terror of a monster. The Austrians, the Czechs, the Poles, the Norwegians, the Danes, the Belgians, the Dutch, the Greeks, the Croats, and the Serbs, above all the great French nation, have been stunned and pinioned. Italy, Hungary, Rumania, Bulgaria have bought a shameful respite by becoming the jackals of the tiger, but their situation is very little different and will presently be indistinguishable from that of his victims. Sweden, Spain and Turkey stand appalled, wondering which will be struck down next.

Here, then, is the vast pit into which all the most famous states and races of Europe have been flung and from which unaided they can never climb. But all this did not satiate Adolf Hitler; he made a treaty of non-aggression with Soviet Russia, just as he made one with Turkey, in order to keep them quiet till he was ready to attack them, and then, nine weeks ago to-day, without a vestige of provocation, he hurled millions of soldiers, with all their apparatus, upon the neighbour he had called his friend, with the avowed object of destroying Russia and tearing her in pieces. This frightful business is now unfolding day by day before our eyes. Here is a devil who, in a mere spasm of his pride and lust for domination, can condemn two or three millions, perhaps it may be many more, of human beings, to speedy and violent death. "Let Russia be blotted out—Let Russia be destroyed. Order the armies to advance." Such were his decrees. Accordingly from the Arctic Ocean to the Black Sea, six or seven millions of soldiers are locked in mortal struggle. Ah, but this time it was not so easy.

This time it was not all one way. The Russian armies and all the peoples of the Russian Republic have rallied to the defence of their hearths and homes. For the first time Nazi blood has flowed in a fearful torrent. Certainly a million-and-a-half, perhaps two millions of Nazi cannon-fodder have bit the dust of the endless plains of Russia. The tremendous battle rages along nearly two thousand miles of front. The Russians fight with magnificent

231

devotion; not only that, our generals who have visited the Russian front line report with admiration the efficiency of their military organization and the excellence of their equipment. The aggressor is surprised, startled, staggered. For the first time in his experience mass murder has become unprofitable. He retaliates by the most frightful cruelties. As his armies advance, whole districts are being exterminated. Scores of thousands—literally scores of thousands—of executions in cold blood are being perpetrated by the German police-troops upon the Russian patriots who defend their native soil. Since the Mongol invasions of Europe in the sixteenth century, there has never been methodical, merciless butchery on such a scale, or approaching such a scale. And this is but the beginning. Famine and pestilence have yet to follow in the bloody ruts of Hitler's tanks. We are in the presence of a crime without a name.

But Europe is not the only continent to be tormented and devastated by aggressions. For five long years the Japanese military factions, seeking to emulate the style of Hitler and Mussolini, taking all their posturing as if it were a new European revelation, have been invading and harrying the five hundred million inhabitants of China. Japanese armies have been wandering about that vast land in futile excursions, carrying with them carnage, ruin and corruption and calling it the "Chinese Incident." Now they stretch a grasping hand into the southern seas of China; they snatch Indo-China from the wretched Vichy French; they menace by their movements Siam; menace Singapore, the British link with Australasia; and menace the Philippine Islands under the protection of the United States. It is certain that this has got to stop. Every effort will be made to secure a peaceful settlement. The United States are labouring with infinite patience to arrive at a fair and amicable settlement which will give Japan the utmost reassurance for her legitimate interests. We earnestly hope these negotiations will succeed. But this I must say: that if these hopes should fail we shall of course range ourselves unhesitatingly at the side of the United States.

And thus we come back to the quiet bay somewhere in the Atlantic where misty sunshine plays on great ships which carry the White Ensign, or the Stars and Stripes. We had the idea, when we met there—the President and I—that without attempting to draw up final and formal peace aims, or war aims, it was necessary to give all peoples, and especially the oppressed and conquered peoples, a simple, rough and ready wartime statement of the goal towards which the British Commonwealth and the United States mean to make their way, and thus make a way for others to march with them upon a road which will certainly be painful, and may be long.

There are, however, two distinct and marked differences in this joint declaration from the attitude adopted by the Allies during the latter part of the last war; and no one should overlook them. The United States and Great Britain do not now assume that there will never be any more war again. On the contrary, we intend to take ample precautions to prevent its renewal in any period we can foresee by effectively disarming the guilty nations while remaining suitably protected ourselves.

The second difference is this: that instead of trying to ruin German trade by all kinds of additional trade barriers and hindrances as was the mood of 1917, we have definitely adopted the view that it is not in the interests of the world and of our two countries that any large nation should be unprosperous or shut out from the means of making a decent living for itself and its people by its industry and enterprise. These are far-reaching changes of principle upon which all countries should ponder. Above all, it was necessary to give hope and the assurance of final victory to those many scores of millions of men and women who are battling for life and freedom, or who are already bent down under the Nazi yoke. Hitler and his confederates have for some time past been adjuring, bullying and beseeching the populations whom they have wronged and injured, to bow to their fate, to resign themselves to their servitude, and for the sake of some mitigations and indulgences, to "collaborate"—that is the word—in what is called the New Order in Europe.

What is this New Order which they seek to fasten first upon Europe and if possible—for their ambitions are boundless—upon all the continents of the globe? It is the rule of the *Herrenvolk*— the master-race—who are to put an end to democracy, to parliaments, to the fundamental freedoms and decencies of ordinary men and women, to the historic rights of nations; and give them in exchange the iron rule of Prussia, the universal goose-step, and a strict, efficient discipline enforced upon the working-classes by the political police, with the German concentration camps and firing parties, now so busy in a dozen lands, always handy in the background. There is the New Order.

Napoleon in his glory and his genius spread his Empire far and wide. There was a time when only the snows of Russia and the white cliffs of Dover with their guardian fleets stood between him and the dominion of the world. Napoleon's armies had a theme: they carried with them the surges of the French Revolution.

233

Liberty, Equality and Fraternity—that was the cry. There was a sweeping away of outworn medieval systems and aristocratic privilege. There was the land for the people, a new code of law. Nevertheless, Napoleon's Empire vanished like a dream. But Hitler, Hitler has no theme, nought but mania, appetite and exploitation. He has, however, weapons and machinery for grinding down and for holding down conquered countries which are the product, the sadly perverted product, of modern science.

The ordeals, therefore, of the conquered peoples will be hard. We must give them hope; we must give them the conviction that their sufferings and their resistances will not be in vain. The tunnel may be dark and long, but at the end there is light. That is the symbolism and that is the message of the Atlantic meeting. Do not despair, brave Norwegians: your land shall be cleansed not only from the invader but from the filthy quislings who are his tools. Be sure of yourselves, Czechs: your independence shall be restored. Poles, the heroism of your people standing up to cruel oppressors, the courage of your soldiers, sailors and airmen, shall not be forgotten: your country shall live again and resume its rightful part in the new organization of Europe. Lift up your heads, gallant Frenchmen: not all the infamies of Darlan and of Laval shall stand between you and the restoration of your birthright. Tough, stout-hearted Dutch, Belgians, Luxemburgers, tormented, mishandled, shamefully cast-away peoples of Yugoslavia, glorious Greece, now subjected to the crowning insult of the rule of the Italian jackanapes: yield not an inch! Keep your souls clean from all contact with the Nazis; make them feel even in their fleeting hour of brutish triumph that they are the moral outcasts of mankind. Help is coming; mighty forces are arming in your behalf. Have faith. Have hope. Deliverance is sure.

There is the signal which we have flashed across the water; and if it reaches the hearts of those to whom it is sent, they will endure with fortitude and tenacity their present misfortunes in the sure faith that they, too, are still serving the common cause, and that their efforts will not be in vain.

You will perhaps have noticed that the President of the United States and the British representative, in what is aptly called the "Atlantic Charter," have jointly pledged their countries to the final destruction of the Nazi tyranny. That is a solemn and grave undertaking. It must be made good; it will be made good. And, of course, many practical arrangements to fulfil that purpose have been and are being organized and set in motion.

The question has been asked: how near is the United States to war? There is certainly one man who knows the answer to that question. If Hitler has not yet declared war upon the United States, it is surely not out of his love for American institutions; it is certainly not because he could not find a pretext. He has murdered half-a-dozen countries for far less. Fears of immediately redoubling the tremendous energies now being employed against him is no doubt a restraining influence. But the real reason is, I am sure, to be found in the method to which he has so faithfully adhered and by which he has gained so much.

What is that method? It is a very simple method. One by one: that is his plan; that is his guiding rule; that is the trick by which he has enslaved so large a portion of the world. Three-and-a-half years ago I appealed to my fellow countrymen to take the lead in weaving together a strong defensive union within the principles of the League of Nations, a union of all the countries who felt themselves in ever-growing danger. But none would listen; all stood idle while Germany re-armed. Czechoslovakia was subjugated; a French Government deserted their faithful ally and broke a plighted word in that ally's hour of need. Russia was cajoled and deceived into a kind of neutrality or partnership, while the French Army was being annihilated. The Low Countries and the Scandinavian countries, acting with France and Great Britain in good time, even after the war had begun, might have altered its course, and would have had, at any rate, a fighting chance. The Balkan States had only to stand together to save themselves from the ruin by which they are now engulfed. But one by one they were undermined and overwhelmed. Never was the career of crime made more smooth.

Now Hitler is striking at Russia with all his might, well knowing the difficulties of geography which stand between Russia and the aid which the Western Democracies are trying to bring. We shall strive our utmost to overcome all obstacles and to bring this aid. We have arranged for a conference in Moscow between the United States, British and Russian authorities to settle the whole plan. No barrier must stand in the way. But why is Hitler striking at Russia, and inflicting and suffering himself or, rather, making his soldiers suffer, this frightful slaughter? It is with the declared object of turning his whole force upon the British Islands, and if he could succeed in beating the life and the strength out of us, which is not so easy, then is the moment when he will settle his account, and it is already a long one, with the people of the United States and generally with the Western Hemisphere. One by one, there is the process; there is the simple, dismal plan which has served Hitler so well. It needs but one final successful appli-

235

cation to make him the master of the world. I am devoutly thankful that some eyes at least are fully opened to it while time remains. I rejoiced to find that the President saw in their true light and proportion the extreme dangers by which the American people as well as the British people are now beset. It was indeed by the mercy of God that he began eight years ago that revival of the strength of the American Navy without which the New World to-day would have to take its orders from the European dictators, but with which the United States still retains the power to marshal her gigantic strength, and in saving herself to render an incomparable service to mankind.

We had a Church parade on the Sunday in our Atlantic bay. The President came on to the quarter-deck of the *Prince of Wales*, where there were mingled together many hundreds of American and British sailors and marines. The sun shone bright and warm, while we all sang the old hymns which are our common inheritance and which we learned as children in our homes. We sang the hymn founded on the psalm which John Hampden's soldiers sang when they bore his body to the grave, and in which the brief, precarious span of human life is contrasted with the immutability of Him to Whom a thousand ages are but as yesterday, and as a watch in the night. We sang the sailors' hymn "For those in peril"—and there are very many—"on the sea." We sang "Onward Christian Soldiers." And indeed I felt that this was no vain presumption, but that we had the right to feel that we were serving a cause for the sake of which a trumpet has sounded from on high.

When I looked upon that densely-packed congregation of fighting men of the same language, of the same faith, of the same fundamental laws and the same ideals, and now to a large extent of the same interests, and certainly in different degrees facing the same dangers, it swept across me that here was the only hope, but also the sure hope, of saving the world from measureless degradation.

And so we came back across the ocean waves, uplifted in spirit, fortified in resolve. Some American destroyers which were carrying mails to the United States marines in Iceland happened to be going the same way too, so we made a goodly company at sea together.

And when we were right out in mid-passage one afternoon a noble sight broke on the view. We overtook one of the convoys which carry the munitions and supplies of the New World to sustain the champions of freedom in the Old. The whole broad horizon seemed filled with ships; seventy or eighty ships of all kinds and sizes, arrayed in fourteen lines, each of which could have

236

been drawn with a ruler, hardly a wisp of smoke, not a straggler, but all bristling with cannons and other precautions on which I will not dwell, and all surrounded by their British escorting vessels, while overhead the far-ranging Catalina air-boats soared—vigilant, protecting eagles in the sky. Then I felt that, hard and terrible and long drawn-out as this struggle may be, we shall not be denied the strength to do our duty to the end.

CANADA AND THE WAR

A SPEECH AT A MANSION HOUSE LUNCHEON GIVEN BY
THE CITY OF LONDON IN HONOUR OF MR. MACKENZIE
KING, THE PRIME MINISTER OF CANADA
SEPTEMBER 4, 1941

August 25. British and Soviet troops invaded Iran following an unsatisfactory reply to a request for the expulsion of German agents.

August 26. British and Soviet forces made rapid advances into Iran, the British using some air-borne troops. Oil installations and Axis ships were captured.

August 27. Laval and Deat, leading pro-Nazis in France, were shot and critically wounded in anti-Communist rally at Versailles.

August 28. New Iranian Government ordered all opposition to British and Soviet advances to stop.

Russians evacuated Dnepropetrovsk in face of increased German pressure, and also admitted they had blown up the great Dnieper Dam, the greatest engineering achievement in the Soviet Union.

Mr. R. G. Menzies resigned the position of Prime Minister of Australia, and was succeeded by Mr. A. W. Fadden.

August 29. Germans captured Talinn, Soviet outpost in Esthonia,

August 30. President Roosevelt warned the United States that they might be forced into war by the Axis.

Anglo-Soviet terms handed to Iran Government, while Mr. Eden pledged Iranian integrity.

August 31. Soviet troops were withdrawn to old Finnish frontier in Karelian Isthmus, the move being interpreted as a peace gesture to the Finns.

September 1. British and Soviet troops joined forces in Iran.

Second anniversary of Germany's march into Poland, which caused the outbreak of the War.

September 3. British official estimate of the losses of German planes since the outbreak of the War given as 8,020, not counting those lost in the campaign against the Soviet. British losses given as 3,089.

September 4. Mr. Mackenzie King, speaking at a luncheon given in his honour in London, made a direct appeal to America to come into the War.

It was announced that the U.S. destroyer Greer, *bound for Iceland, had been attacked by a U-boat.*

[*September 4, 1941.*

M Y Lord Mayor, nothing in your year of office shall stand out more vividly in your mind than this entertainment held to-day of so many military representatives of the Dominions to give a hearty welcome and do all honour to the Prime Minister of Canada, Mr. Mackenzie King.

I have, as Mr. Mackenzie King has reminded us, known him for a great many years. I remember, as a young Under-Secretary for the Colonies, negotiating with him the details of some Canadian legislation about which there was some hitch in the days when he was here at the side of that great Canadian, Sir Wilfrid Laurier. That is now 35 or 36 years ago, and ever since then I have enjoyed the honour and the pleasure of his friendship and have followed with close attention the long, consistent political message which he has delivered to his country, to the Empire, and to the times in which we live.

To-day you have listened to a memorable and momentous declaration made here amid our ruins of London, but it resounds throughout the Empire, and is carried to all parts of the world by the marvellous mechanism of modern life and of modern war. You have listened to a speech which, I think, all those who have heard it will feel explains the long-continued authority which Mr. Mackenzie King has wielded while, during more than 15 years, he has been Prime Minister of the Dominion of Canada.

He has spoken of the great issues of the war and of the duty which lies before free men in all parts of the world to band together lest their heritage be wasted. He has spoken of the immense burden we have to bear, of our unflinching resolve to persevere in carrying forward our standard in common, and he has also struck that note, never absent from our minds, that no lasting or perfect solution of the difficulties with which we are now confronted— with which the whole world is now confronted—no diversion of that sad fate by which the whole world is menaced, can be achieved without the full co-operation in every field of all the nations which as yet lie outside the range of the conqueror's power.

In Mr. Mackenzie King we have a Canadian statesman who has always preserved the most intimate relations with the great Republic of the United States, and whose name and voice are honoured there as they are on this side of the Atlantic. I had the opportunity of meeting the President of the United States a few weeks ago, and I know from him the great esteem in which Mr. Mackenzie King is held and how much he has contributed to joining together in close sympathetic action the Republic of the United States and the Dominion of Canada.

I am grateful to Mr. Mackenzie King to-day for having put in terms perhaps more pointed than I, as a British Minister, would use, that overpowering sense we have that the time is short, that the struggle is dire, and that all the free men of the world must stand together in one line if humanity is to be spared a deepening and darkening and widening tragedy which can lead only, as Mr. Mackenzie King has said, to something in the nature of immediate world chaos.

I hope, Mr. Mackenzie King, during your all too brief visit here, a visit which in a few weeks must draw to its close, you have found yourself able to see with your own eyes what we have gone through, and also to feel that unconquerable uplift of energy and of resolve which will carry this old island through the storm and carry with it also much that is precious to mankind.

You have seen your gallant Canadian Corps and other troops who are here. We have felt very much for them that they have not yet had a chance of coming to close quarters with the enemy. It is not their fault, it is not our fault, but there they stand and there they have stood through the whole of the critical period of the last fifteen months at the very point where they would be the first to be hurled into a counter-stroke against an invader. No greater service can be rendered to this country, no more important military duty can be performed by any troops in all the Allied forces. It seems to me that although they may have felt envious that Australian, New Zealand, and South African troops have been in action, the part they have played in bringing about the final result is second to none.

You have a great knowledge of the flexible organization, a system ever changing and expanding, yet ever growing into a greater harmony, by which the British Commonwealth of Nations is conducted. You have also a knowledge of your own people, and your association with them is so long and so intimate that it has enabled you to realize and express in these hours of trouble a more complete unity of Canada than has ever before been achieved. The

240

war effort of Canada during this war has not happily so far required effusion of blood upon a large scale, but that effort in men, in ships, in aircraft, in air training, in finance, in food, constitutes an element in the resistance of the British Empire without which that resistance could not be successfully maintained.

Canada is the linchpin of the English-speaking world. Canada, with those relations of friendly, affectionate intimacy with the United States on the one hand and with her unswerving fidelity to the British Commonwealth and the Motherland on the other, is the link which joins together these great branches of the human family, a link which, spanning the oceans, brings the continents into their true relation and will prevent in future generations any growth of division between the proud and the happy nations of Europe and the great countries which have come into existence in the New World.

For all these reasons we are all the better that you, my Lord Mayor, have bidden us to come here to-day. You have had a strange tenure of office. Buildings have fallen about your ears and been laid in ruins, but you carry on; you carry on unflinching and unwearying.

You carry forward the proud traditions of the City of London, always in the van in the struggle for Britain, and once again I have no doubt you will, as Lord Mayor of London, have played a worthy part in carrying our latest grievous ordeal to a happy ending.

THE WAR SITUATION

A SPEECH TO THE HOUSE OF COMMONS
SEPTEMBER 9, 1941

September 5. President Roosevelt ordered a "shoot at sight" search for the U-boat which attacked the U.S. destroyer Greer.

September 7. Berlin had its heaviest raid of the war on the anniversary of the first blitz on London.

September 8. News released of a great British raid on Spitzbergen, in which coal mines were wrecked and radio installations destroyed.

September 9. Mr. Churchill gave a heartening survey of the War to the House of Commons.

[September 9, 1941.

LATE in July I learned that the President of the United States would welcome a meeting with me in order to survey the entire world position in relation to the several and common interests of our respective countries. As I was sure that Parliament would approve, I obtained His Majesty's permission to leave the country. I crossed the Atlantic Ocean in one of our latest battleships to meet the President at a convenient place. I was, as the House knows, accompanied by the First Sea Lord, the Chief of the Imperial General Staff, and the Vice-Chief of the Air Staff, together with the Permanent Secretary to the Foreign Office and others. We were, therefore, in a position to discuss with the President and with his technical advisers every question relating to the war and to the state of affairs after the war.

Important conclusions were reached on four main topics. First of all, on the Eight-Point Declaration of the broad principles and aims which guide and govern the actions of the British and United States Governments and peoples amid the many dangers by which they are beset in these times. Secondly, on measures to be taken to help Russia to resist the hideous onslaught which Hitler has made upon her. Thirdly, the policy to be pursued towards Japan in order, if possible, to put a stop to further encroachment in the Far East likely to endanger the safety or interests of Great Britain or the United States and thus, by timely action, prevent the spreading of the war to the Pacific Ocean. Fourthly, there was a large number of purely technical matters which were dealt with, and close personal relations were established between high naval, military and air authorities of both countries. I shall refer to some of these topics in the course of my statement.

I have, as the House knows, hitherto consistently deprecated the formulation of peace aims or war aims—however you put it—by his Majesty's Government, at this stage. I deprecate it at this time, when the end of the war is not in sight, when the conflict sways to and fro with alternating fortunes and when conditions and associations at the end of the war are unforeseeable. But a Joint Declaration by Great Britain and the United States is a process of a totally different nature. Although the principles in the Declaration, and much of the language, have long been familiar to the British and American democracies, the fact that it is a united Declaration sets up a milestone or monument which needs only the stroke of victory to become a permanent part of the history of human progress. The purpose of the Joint Declaration signed by President Roosevelt and myself on 12th August is stated in the Preamble to be:

"To make known certain common principles in the national policies of our respective countries on which they base their hopes for a better future for the world."

No words are needed to emphasize the future promise held out to the world by such a Joint Declaration by the United States and Great Britain. I need only draw attention, for instance, to the phrase in Paragraph 6

"after the final destruction of the Nazi tyranny"

to show the profound and vital character of the solemn agreement into which we have jointly entered. Questions have been asked, and will no doubt be asked, as to exactly what is implied by this or that point, and explanations have been invited. It is a wise rule that when two parties have agreed a statement one of them shall not thereafter, without consultation with the other, seek to put special or strained interpretations upon this or that passage. I propose, therefore, to speak to-day only in an exclusive sense.

First, the Joint Declaration does not try to explain how the broad principles proclaimed by it are to be applied to each and every case which will have to be dealt with when the war comes to an end. It would not be wise for us, at this moment, to be drawn into laborious discussions on how it is to fit all the manifold problems with which we shall be faced after the war. Secondly, the Joint Declaration does not qualify in any way the various statements of policy which have been made from time to time about the development of constitutional government in India, Burma or other parts of the British Empire. We are pledged by the Declaration of August, 1940, to help India to obtain free and equal partnership in the British Commonwealth with ourselves, subject, of course, to the fulfilment of obligations arising from our long connection with India and our responsibilities to its many creeds, races and interests. Burma also is covered by our considered policy of establishing Burmese self-government and by the measures already in progress. At the Atlantic meeting we had in mind, primarily, the restoration of the sovereignty, self-government and national life of the States and nations of Europe now under the Nazi yoke, and the principles governing any alterations in their territorial boundaries which may have to be made. So that is quite a separate problem from the progressive evolution of self-governing institutions in the regions and peoples which owe allegiance to the British Crown. We have made declarations on these matters which are complete in themselves, free from ambiguity, and related to the conditions and circumstances of the territories and peoples affected. They will be found to be entirely in harmony with the high conception of freedom and justice which inspired the Joint Declaration.

Since we last met the Battle of the Atlantic has been going on unceasingly. In his attempt to blockade and starve out this Island by U-boat and air attack and the very formidable combination of U-boat and air attacks, the enemy continually changes his tactics. Driven from one beat, he goes to another. Chased from home waters, driven from the approaches to this Island, he proceeds to the other side of the Atlantic. Increasingly hampered by United States patrols in the North Atlantic, he develops his malice in the South. We follow hard upon his track, and sometimes we anticipate his tactics. But it is not desirable to give him too precise or, above all, too early information of the success or failure of each of his various manœuvres, and it was therefore decided that the publication of our shipping losses at regular monthly intervals should cease. Accordingly, no statement of losses has been published for July and August, and I do not think the time has come to give the actual figures yet. The public, and indeed the whole world, have however derived the impression that things have gone much better in those two months. I cannot deny that this is so.

244

The improvement in the sea war manifests itself in two directions. In the first place, there is a very great falling-off in the sinkings of British and Allied ships, with a corresponding increase in the tonnage of invaluable cargoes safely landed on our shores. The estimates which I made at the beginning of the year of the volume of our importations for 1941, and which I mentioned to the House on another occasion, to which it would be improper to refer, look to me as if they would be not only made good but exceeded. The second improvement is the extraordinary rise during the last three months in the destruction of German and Italian shipping. This has been achieved very largely by the development of new and brilliant tactics by the Coastal Command and by the Royal Air Force bombing squadrons, acting with the Coastal Command. To the exploits of the Air Force must be added those of our submarines. The destruction of enemy shipping by both these forms of attack has been enormous. In fact, I may say—and I should like the House to pay attention to this statement because it is really an extraordinary one for anyone to be able to make—the sinkings of British and Allied ships by enemy action in July and August, added together, do not amount to much more than one-third of the German and Italian tonnage which we have sunk by our aircraft and our submarines. How remarkable that statement is may be judged when we remember that we present perhaps ten times, or it may be even twenty times, the target to hostile attack upon the seas that is presented to us by the shipping of the enemy. His ships make short voyages, darting across a narrow strip of water or slinking along the coast from one defended port to another under air protection, while we carry on the gigantic world-wide trade of Britain with, as has often been stated and can hardly be too often repeated, never less than 2,000 ships at sea and never less than 400 in the danger zone.

I have for some time looked for an opportunity of paying a tribute to our submarines. There is no branch of His Majesty's Forces which in this war has suffered the same proportion of fatal loss as our Submarine Service. It is the most dangerous of all the Services. That is perhaps the reason why the First Lord tells me that entry into it is keenly sought by officers and men. I feel the House would wish to testify its gratitude and admiration for our submarine crews, for their skill and devotion, which have proved of inestimable value to the life of our country. During 1941 British submarines have sunk or seriously damaged 17 enemy warships. Some of them were U-boats. Besides the warships, 105 supply ships have fallen to their torpedoes. This is an average of 15 ships a month, or one ship every two days. The ships which

245

have been torpedoed varied between large liners of 20,000 tons and caiques and schooners loaded with troops and military stores. They also included a considerable number of laden troop transports and tankers, most of which were passing across the Mediterranean, through the British submarine attack, in order to keep alive the enemy's armies in Libya. Submarines of the Royal Netherlands Navy and the Free French Naval Forces have been operating in combination with our submarines, and have contributed in a most gallant manner to these results.

There are other perils which have been overcome and other labours of splendid quality which have been performed unknown, or almost unknown, to the public. I mentioned some of these to the House upon a private occasion, and it has been suggested to me that this particular reference should also obtain publicity. The first deals with the anti-mining service. We do not hear much about the mine menace now. Yet almost every night 30 or 40 enemy aeroplanes are casting these destructive engines, with all their ingenious variations, at the most likely spots to catch our shipping. The attack, which began in November, 1939—which began, indeed, when the war opened—with the ordinary moored mine laid by night in the approaches to our harbours, was succeeded before the end of 1939 by the magnetic mine, with all its mysterious terrors, and is now waged continually by the acoustic mine as well as the magnetic in many dangerous combinations. We do not hear much about all this now, because, by the resources of British science and British organization, it has been largely mastered. We do not hear much about it, because 20,000 men and 1,000 ships toil ceaselessly with many strange varieties of apparatus to clear the ports and channels every morning of the deadly deposits of the night. You will remember the lines of Kipling:

> "Mines reported in the fairway,
> Warn all traffic and detain.
> Sent up Unity, Claribel, Assyrian,
> Stormcock, and Golden Gain."

This is going on night after night, day after day, and it may well be imagined, as the work has to be performed in all weathers and constantly under the attack of the enemy, how excellent is the service rendered by the brave and faithful men engaged in it. We do not hear much about them because this work is done in secret and in silence, and we live on. We take it as a matter of course, like the feats of the salvage service, to which I must also refer. The salvage service has recovered, since the beginning of the war, in every circumstance of storm and difficulty, upwards of 1,000,000 tons of shipping which would otherwise have been cast away. These marvellous services of seamanship and devotion and the organization behind them prove at every stage and step the soundness of our national life and the remarkable adaptiveness of the British mind and the tenacity of the British character by which we shall certainly be saved, and save others.

Although, as I have admitted, there has been a very great improvement in our losses at sea in July and August, it would be a very foolish mistake to assume that the grave dangers which threaten us are at an end. The enemy has been employing a greater number of U-boats and also of long-range aircraft than ever before, and we must expect further increases. We have made prodigious exertions, and our resources are continually growing. The skill and science of the Admiralty staff and their commanders, working in perfect harmony with the Royal Air Force, have gained these successes; but the Admiralty would be the last to guarantee their continuance as a matter of course, and certainly the slightest relaxation of vigilance, of exertion, and of contrivance would be followed swiftly by very serious relapses. It must be remembered also that the Germans are much hampered in the American parts of the Atlantic, which are very extensive, by the fear of trouble with the powerful American Naval forces which ceaselessly patrol the approaches to the Western Hemisphere. This has been a great help to us. I could wish it might be a greater help. But here again, the enemy's tactics may change. No doubt Hitler would rather finish off Russia and then Britain before coming to close quarters with the United States. That would be in accordance with his habitual technique of one by one. Hitler has, however, also the greatest possible need to prevent the precious munition supplies, now streaming across the Atlantic in pursuance of the policy of the United States Government, from reaching our shores. Should he do so the area of the danger zones would again become ocean-wide. In the meanwhile, let us hear no vain talk about the Battle of the Atlantic having been won. We may be content with the successes which have rewarded patience and exertion, but war is inexhaustible in its surprises, and very few of those surprises are of an agreeable character.

It was with great pleasure that on my homeward voyage I visited Iceland, where we were received with the utmost cordiality by the Government and the people, and where I had the honour of reviewing large numbers of the strong British and United States Forces which, no doubt for entirely different reasons and in pursuance of separate duties, happen to be engaged jointly in defending this all-important island and stepping-stone across the Atlantic from Nazi intrusion and attack. Very considerable British and United States Air and Naval Forces are also assembled in Iceland in the harbours and on the airfields. The spacious airfields which we have constructed, and which we are expanding there and in Newfoundland, will play an ever-increasing part, not only in the control of the broad waters, but in the continual flow of that broadening stream of heavy bombers, now attacking Germany night after night, which will play the decisive part, or one of the decisive parts, in the final victory.

Our affairs have also prospered in the Eastern theatre of the war. Our relations with Iraq are governed by the Treaty of Alliance, which in time of war or other emergency accords to us wide powers for the purposes of defence both in Iraqian and British interests. The Germans had, of course, practised their usual methods of building-up by infiltration and intrigue a pro-German party in Bagdad, and on 2nd April the pro-German leader, Rashid Ali, carried out a *coup d'état* in Bagdad, forcing the constitutional ruler of the country, the Regent, to fly from the capital. This move did not find us wholly unprepared. We had the right and the duty to protect our lines of communication through Iraq, and orders were at once given to send to the Port of Basra, at the head of the Persian Gulf, an Indian division which was held in readiness for this emergency. This division disembarked at Basra on 18th April, without opposition. Hoping perhaps to secure from us recognition for his illegal régime, Rashid Ali even pretended to welcome the arrival of our troops. Soon, however, instigated by the Germans and lured on by promises of prompt and powerful air support, he resorted to open war against us in utter breach of the Treaty. Our air-training station at Habbaniyah, where about 1,500 airmen and soldiers were stationed, was attacked on 2nd May by the Iraqian Army, and the position seemed for some days most critical. Reinforcements were sent through Basra and India by air, and strong mobile columns moved from Palestine to relieve Habbaniyah by land. Before they could reach Habbaniyah, however, the reinforced garrison, aided by the aircraftsmen in training, turned the tables on its attackers in the most spirited manner, and, in spite of a superiority of three to one, drove the enemy off with heavy losses. By a bold stroke the bridge across the Euphrates was then captured intact, and, in spite of difficulties due to floods, our troops reached Bagdad on 30th May, thus liberating our gifted and resolute Ambassador from his virtual blockade in the British Embassy.

While all this was going on, Rashid Ali appealed constantly to the Germans to make good their promises, but only 30 or 40 German aeroplanes arrived from Syria and endeavoured tentatively to install themselves at Bagdad and also to the north of Mosul. But meanwhile there was an explanation for this failure of the Germans. The German parachute and air-borne corps, which no doubt was to have operated in Iraq and would have been assisted on its journey across Syria by the Vichy French, had been largely exterminated in the Battle of Crete. Over 4,000 of these special troops were killed, and very large numbers of carrier aircraft were destroyed. This specialist corps were so mauled in the ferocious fighting that, although they forced us to evacuate Crete, they were themselves in no condition for further operations. We therefore suppressed the revolt of Rashid Ali, and he and his partisans fled to Persia—I like to call it Persia, and I hope the House will permit me to indulge myself in that fashion—and the exiled Regent was able to return and to re-establish a lawful Government in Iraq. With this Government we have been able to revert to the basis of friendly co-operation which we have followed for a good many years, and which we propose still to follow. The Treaty is now being loyally observed on both sides. Our ground and air forces have been accorded full facilities throughout Iraq, and the situation which in April had appeared so disastrous was fully restored by the end of May. There are still dangers in Iraq which require attention, but which need cause no serious anxiety.

The intrigues of the Germans with the Vichy French in Syria had meanwhile been in full swing, and the Vichy French Governor, General Dentz, in a base and treacherous manner was striving his utmost to further the German interests. We were ourselves hard pressed. Our Armies in Greece had been evacuated, having lost much of their equipment, our Western Front in Cyrenaica had been beaten in by the incursion of General Rommel's German Africa Corps, and we had the revolt in Iraq to put down. Nevertheless, we found it possible, in conjunction with the Free French, to invade Syria on 8th June. The Sixth Free French Battalion under General Legentilhomme fought gallantly and co-operated with our Forces, which ultimately reached the equivalent of about four Divisions. The Australian and Indian troops distinguished themselves repeatedly in action. Although the Vichy French forces in their antagonism to the Free French movement fought with unusual vigour, by 11th July the conquest of Syria was complete and all Germans had been driven out. The occupation of Syria by the Army of the Nile carried with it the means of securing the safety of Cyprus, which until then, as anyone can see, had been in great danger from the air forces which the Germans were trying to build up in Syria in order to cut Cyprus off from naval protection. All this part of the Levant thus came into a far more satisfactory condition. Our naval and air control over the Eastern end of the Mediterranean became effective, and we obtained direct contact with our Turkish friends, and the control of the pipe line and other resources.

This is the point at which it will be convenient for me to explain our position in Syria. We have no ambitions in Syria. We do not seek to replace or supplant France, or substitute British for French interests in any part of Syria. We are only in Syria in order to win the war. However, I must make it quite clear that our policy, to which our Free French Allies have subscribed is that Syria shall be handed back to the Syrians, who will assume at the earliest possible moment their independent sovereign rights. We do not propose that this process of creating an independent Syrian Government, or Governments—because it may be that there will not be only one Government—should wait until the end of the war. We contemplate constantly increasing the Syrian share in the administration. There is no question of France maintaining the same position which she exercised in Syria before the war, but which the French Government had realized must come to an end. On the other hand, we recognize that among all the nations of Europe the position of France in Syria is one of special privilege, and that in so far as any European countries have influence in Syria, that of France will be pre-eminent. That is the policy which we have decided to adopt. We did not go there in order to deprive France of her historic position in Syria, except in so far as is necessary to fulfil our obligations and pledges to the Syrian population. There must be no question, even in wartime, of a mere substitution of Free French interests for Vichy French interests. The Syrian peoples are to come back into their own. This is fully recognized in the documents which have been exchanged between the Minister of State and the representatives of the Free French.

I was asked a question about our relations with Iraq. They are special; our relations with Egypt are special, and, in the same way, I conceive that France will have special arrangements with Syria. The independence of Syria is a prime feature in our policy.

While all this was going on in the Levant, on the Eastern flank of the Army of the Nile, that Army struck two heavy blows at the German and Italian forces which had recaptured Cyrenaica. These forces found themselves unable to advance upon Egypt, as had been foreseen, without destroying the stronghold of Tobruk, which was firmly held by Australian and British troops. The heavy attacks made by our Forces in the Western Desert in the middle of May and the middle of June, while they did not succeed, as we had hoped, in forcing the enemy to retreat, played a great part in bringing him to a standstill. All the German boasts which they had widely circulated throughout Europe and the East that they would be in Suez by the end of May have thus proved to be vain. Powerful reinforcements have reached the Army of the Nile in the interval, and I feel considerable confidence that we shall be able to defend Egypt successfully from German invasion across the Western Desert. Thus the position both on the Western and on the Eastern flanks of the Nile has been greatly improved. A marked recovery has been made from the unfortunate setback coming after the victories over the Italians which occurred at the beginning of April. Altogether we are entitled to be content with these favourable developments.

Now I turn to a far wider field. The magnificent resistance of the Russian Armies and the skilful manner in which their vast front is being withdrawn in the teeth of Nazi invasion make it certain that Hitler's hopes of a short war with Russia will be dispelled. Already in three months he has lost more German blood than was shed in any single year of the last war. Already he faces the certainty of having to maintain his armies on the whole front from the Arctic to the Black Sea, at the end of long, inadequate, assailed and precarious lines of communication, through all the severity of a Russian winter, with the vigorous counter-strokes which may be expected from the Russian Armies. From the moment, now nearly 80 days ago, when Russia was attacked, we have cast about for every means of giving the most speedy and effective help to our new Ally. I am not prepared to discuss the military projects which have been examined. Such a discussion would be harmful to our interests, both by what was said and by what was not said. Nor will it be possible for anyone representing the Government to enter upon any argument on such questions. In the field of supply more can be said. I agreed with President Roosevelt upon the message which was sent to Premier Stalin, the terms of which have already been made public. The need is urgent, and the scale heavy. A considerable part of the munition industry and the iron and steel production of Russia has fallen into the hands of the enemy. On the other hand, the Soviet Union disposes of anything from ten to fifteen million soldiers, for nearly all of whom they have equipment and arms. To aid in the supply of these masses, to enable them to realize their long-continuing force, and to organize the operation of their supply, will be the task of the Anglo-American-Russian Conference.

There has been no unavoidable delay in arranging for this conference or in choosing the personnel of the British Mission. Some people seem to think nothing has been done, nothing has been sent, and nothing is going on. The study of the whole problem has been ceaselessly proceeding, both in the United States and here, and we are waiting the arrival of the American Mission under Mr. Harriman, which I trust will soon be here. This Mission contains important representatives of the United States Fighting Services. Our Mission will be headed by Lord Beaverbrook, who has already visited the United States and has been in the closest conference with the President and his advisers and officers. It must be remembered that we already have a Military Mission with officers of high rank in Moscow. Those whom Lord Beaverbrook takes with him will therefore supplement those who are already there, and during the conference he will be in charge of all of them. The names are already selected and will be published in due course. It is obviously undesirable to announce the date when the Mission will start for the conference, but no time will be lost. Meanwhile, many very important emergency decisions are being taken, and large supplies are on the way.

We must be prepared for serious sacrifices in the munitions field in order to meet the needs of Russia. The utmost exertion and energy will therefore be required from all concerned in production in order not only to help Russia but to fill the gaps which must now be opened in our longed-for and at last arriving supply. It must be remembered that everything that is given to Russia is subtracted from what we are making for ourselves, and in part at least from what would have been sent us by the United States. In terms of finished munitions of war the flow of our own production in this country and the Empire is still rising. It will reach full flood during this third year of our wartime munitions production. If the United States are to fulfil the task they have set themselves, very large new installations will have to be set up or converted, and there will have to be a further curtailment over there, as they fully recognize, of civilian consumption. We must ourselves expect a definite reduction in the military supplies from America on which we have counted, but within certain limits we are prepared to accept these facts and their consequences.

Other limiting factors are also present. There is time, there is distance, there is geography. These impose themselves upon us. There are the limitations of transport and of harbour facilities.

Above all, there is the limitation of shipping. Only three routes are open—the Arctic route by Archangel, which may be hampered by the winter ice; the Far Eastern route via Vladivostok, which is scowled upon by the Japanese and operates only over 7,000 miles of railway line; and finally the route across Persia, which leads over a 500-mile stretch from the Persian Gulf to that great inland sea, the Caspian, upon which the Russians maintain a strong naval force and which again gives access to the very heart of Russia, the Volga Basin.

The Germans were, of course, busy betimes in Persia with their usual tricks. German tourists, technicians and diplomatists were busy suborning the people and Government of Persia with the object of creating a Fifth Column which would dominate the Government at Teheran, and not only seize or destroy the oilfields, which are of the highest consequence, but—a fact to which I attach extreme importance—close the surest and shortest route by which we could reach Russia. We thought it necessary, therefore, to make sure that these machinations did not succeed. Accordingly, we demanded of the Persian Government the immediate expulsion of their Teutonic visitors. When under local duress the Persian Government failed to comply with our request, British and Russian Forces entered Persia from the south and from the north in sufficient and indeed overwhelming strength.

The Persian Government, having made such resistance as they thought fit, sued for peace. We must have the surrender into our hands of all the Germans and Italians who are on the premises; we must have the expulsion of the German and Italian Legations, whose diplomatic status we, of course, respect; and we must have the unquestioned control and maintenance of the through communications from the warm-water port of Basra to the Caspian Sea. It is from this point particularly that American and British supplies can be carried into the centre of Russia in an ever-widening flow, and naturally every effort will be made, and is being made, to improve the railway communications and expand the volume of supplies that can be transported over the existing British-gauge railway, which has happily only recently been completed and now requires only large accessions of rolling stock and locomotives to expand it greatly as a line of supply.

The House will, I have no doubt, approve the somewhat drastic measures we thought it right to take to achieve these important objects, and the further measures we may have to take. The occupation of Persia enables us to join hands with the Southern flank of the Russian Armies and to bring into action there both military and air forces. It also serves important British objects in presenting a shield which should bar the eastward advance of the German invader. In this the Armies of India, whose military quality has become shiningly apparent, will play an increasing part, and in so doing will keep the scourge of war a thousand miles or more from the homes of the peoples of India. One must, therefore, expect that very considerable deployments of British, Indian, and Dominion Forces will gradually manifest themselves in these enormous and desolate or ill-developed regions. The Allied front now runs in an immense crescent from Spitzbergen in the Arctic Ocean to Tobruk in the Western Desert, and our section of this front will be held by the British and Empire Armies with their growing strength fed and equipped by ocean-borne supplies from Great Britain, from the United States, from India and from Australasia. I am glad to say that adequate naval power will be at hand in both the Atlantic and the Indian Ocean to secure the sea routes against attack.

If we now look back for a moment, we can measure the solid improvement in our position in the Middle East or East which has been achieved since the French suddenly fell out of the war and the Italians made haste so eagerly to come in against us. At that date all we had in those parts was from 80,000 to 100,000 men, starved of munitions and equipment, which had all been sent to the French front, always first to claim the best we had. We had lost our means of safe communication through the Mediterranean and almost all the main bases on which we relied. We were anxiously concerned for our defence of Nairobi, Khartoum, British Somaliland and, above all, of the Nile Valley and Palestine, including the famous cities of Cairo and Jerusalem. None was safe; but nevertheless, after little more than a year we have managed to gather very large and well-equipped Armies, which already begin to approach 750,000, which possess and are being supplied with masses of equipment of all kinds. We have developed an Air Force almost as large as that we had in Great Britain when the war began, an Air Force which is rapidly expanding. We have conquered the whole of the Italian Empire in Abyssinia and Eritrea, and have killed or taken prisoner the Italian armies of over 400,000 men by which these regions were defended. We have defended the frontiers of Egypt against German and Italian attack. We have consolidated our positions in Palestine and Iraq. We have taken effective control of Syria and provided for the security of Cyprus. Finally, by the swift, vigorous campaign in Persia which has taken place since the House last met we have joined hands with our Russian Allies, and stand in the line to bar the further eastward progress of the enemy. I cannot help feeling that these are achievements which, whatever the future may contain, will earn the respect of history and deserve the approval of the House.

Thus far then have we travelled along the terrible road we chose at the call of duty. The mood of Britain is wisely and rightly averse from every form of shallow or premature exultation. This is no time for boasts or glowing prophecies, but there is this—a year ago our position looked forlorn and well nigh desperate to all eyes but our own. To-day we may say aloud before an awe-struck world, "We are still masters of our fate. We still are captain of our souls."

THE WEAPON OF SCIENCE

A MESSAGE TO THE INTERNATIONAL CONFERENCE OF SCIENTISTS
ORGANIZED BY THE BRITISH ASSOCIATION
SEPTEMBER 26, 1941

September 10. *Martial law declared in Oslo owing to growing unrest in Norway.*

September 11. *President Roosevelt, in a world broadcast, announced that the United States fleet had been ordered to destroy Axis forces operating in American "defensive waters," and that all merchant ships in those waters would be protected by patrolling vessels and planes.*

September 12. *Another United States ship was torpedoed on its way to Iceland.*

September 14. *It was revealed that a complete wing of the R.A.F. was already in action in Russia.*

September 15. *Col. Knox, Secretary of the United States Navy, announced a "shoot first" policy against German raiders.*

Lord Beaverbrook stated that every tank made in Britain in the following week would go straight to Russia.

September 16. *The Shah of Iran abdicated, following protests by Britain and Russia about his protection of Germans in his country. Allied troops marched on Teheran, the capital.*

September 17. *Son of the former Shah took oath to rule Iran as a constitutional monarch.*

September 18. *German armies, held at Leningrad and Smolensk, shifted main attack to Kiev and the Crimea.*

September 20. *R.A.F. carried out its greatest daylight attack of the war on Germany and occupied territory.*

September 21. *Russia admitted the evacuation of Kiev, and claimed to have counter-attacked in the Smolensk area.*

September 22. *British and American delegates to the Three-Power Conference with Soviet Russia arrived in Moscow.*

King George of Greece and his Government arrived in London.

September 23. M. Maisky, Soviet Ambassador in London, claimed that the German losses in the campaign against Russia were 3,000,000 men and 8,500 planes, and criticized those who thought the winter would halt the campaign.

President Roosevelt stated he would ask Congress to permit arming of all American and U.S.-protected ships.

September 24. It was revealed that General Wavell had been in London for staff talks affecting the campaign in the Middle East.

[September 26, 1941.

ONE of our objects in fighting this war is to maintain the right of free discussion and the interchange of ideas. In contrast to the intellectual darkness which is descending on Germany, the freedom that our scientists enjoy is a valuable weapon to us, for superiority in scientific development is a vital factor in the preparation of victory. The presence of the representatives of so many different nations is striking proof of that universal desire for liberty of thought which all the power of the Gestapo will never entirely stamp out. It will take a long time for the civilized powers to repair the trail of material and moral havoc which the Germans leave behind them. It will require all the resources of science. But I look forward to the day when the scientists of every nation can devote all their energies to the common task, and I wish you every success in the work you are undertaking now.

THE WAR SITUATION

A SPEECH TO THE HOUSE OF COMMONS
SEPTEMBER 30, 1941

September 27. *Heydrich, German Gestapo chief, replaced Von Neurath in Czechoslovakia to smash growing sabotage.*

September 28. *Lord Beaverbrook (for Great Britain) and Mr. Harriman (for the United States) began Aid-to-Russia conferences in Moscow.*

September 30. *Mr. Churchill reviewed the War Situation and warned the country that, although Germany had been weakened in the air, she was still capable of carrying on simultaneous campaigns on land.*

September 30, 1941.

THE House will remember that in June last I deprecated the making of too frequent expositions of Government policy and reviews of the war situation by Ministers of the Crown. Anything that is said which is novel or pregnant will, of course, be studied attentively by the enemy and may be a help to him in measuring our affairs. The House will have noticed how very silent the Nazi leaders have fallen. For seven months Hitler has said nothing about his war plans. What he blurted out in January and February certainly proved helpful to us.

"In the spring," he said, "our submarine warfare will begin in earnest, and our opponents will find that the Germans have not been sleeping. The Luftwaffe and the entire German defence forces will, in this way or that, bring about the ultimate decision."

And again:

"In March and April naval warfare will start such as the enemy had never expected."

We were, therefore, led to expect a crescendo of attacks upon our lifeline of supplies. Certainly the Germans have used an ever larger force of U-boats and long-range aircraft against our shipping. However, our counter-measures, which were undertaken in good time on the largest scale, have proved very successful. For reasons which I have explained very fully to the House, we have since June abandoned the practice of publishing statements at regular monthly intervals of our shipping losses, and I propose to continue this salutary practice. But, apart from anything that may happen during this afternoon, the last day of the month, I may make the following statement to the House. The losses from enemy action of British, Allied and neutral merchant ships during the quarter July, August and September have been only one-third of those losses during the quarter April, May and June. During the same period our slaughter of enemy shipping, German and Italian, has been increasing by leaps and bounds. In fact, it is about one and a half times what it was in the previous three months. So we have at one end a reduction in average monthly losses of about a third and at the other an increase in the losses inflicted upon the enemy of half as much again.

These important results enable us to take a more expansive view of our import programme. Very few important ships carrying munitions have been lost on the way. Our reserves of food stand higher than they did at the outbreak of war, and far higher than a year or eighteen months ago. The Minister of Food, who has a pretty tough job, now finds himself able to make some quite appreciable improvements in the basic rations of the whole country, and in particular to improve the quantity and variety of the meals available for the heavy worker during the coming winter. There will be better Christmas dinners this year than last, and at the same time more justification behind those dinners. It seems likely now that we shall bring in several million tons more than the import total which I mentioned in private to the House earlier in the year, which total was itself sufficient to keep us going. We are now within measurable distance of the immense flow of American new building, to which, together with our own construction, we look to carry us through 1942 and on progressively till the end of the war.

I deprecate premature rejoicings over these considerable facts, and I indulge in no sanguine predictions about the future. We must expect that the enemy U-boat warfare, now conducted by larger numbers of U-boats than ever before, supported by scores of Fokke Wulfs, will be intensified. The U-boats will be beaten, and kept beaten, only by a corresponding intensification of our own measures and also, to put it very plainly, by that assistance which we are receiving in increasing degree from other quarters. We must not, I repeat, relax for an instant; nevertheless, the facts that I have stated must be regarded as not entirely unsatisfactory, and certainly they are most stultifying to Hitler, who so obligingly warned us of his hopes and plans. This is, I think, an apt illustration of the dangers which should prevent those who are engaged in the high conduct of the war from having to make too many speeches about what they think is going to happen or would like to happen or what they intend to try and do. All the more is this habit important when we have to deal not only with our own affairs but with those of other great allied or associated nations.

Here I may perhaps be pardoned for making an observation of a somewhat encouraging character. We are no longer alone. Little more than a year ago we seemed quite alone, but, as time has passed, our own steadfast conduct, and the crimes of the enemy, have brought two other very great States and nations into most intimate and friendly contact and concert with us. Whether we look to the East or whether we look to the West, we are no longer alone. Whether we look at the devoted battle lines of the Russian Armies or at the majestic momentum of United States resolve and action, we may derive comfort and good cheer in our struggle which, nevertheless, even if alone, we should carry on inflexibly, unwearyingly, and with steadily increasing resources. The fact, however, that at every stage we have to consider the interests of our Russian Ally and also the outlook, wishes and actions of the United States, makes it all the more necessary, imperative even, that I and my colleagues should be particularly careful about any pronouncements, explanations or forecasts in which we might otherwise be tempted to indulge. I feel sure that the House of Commons, which is the solid foundation of the British war effort and which is resolved to prosecute the war as sternly and implacably as did our forerunners in bygone days, will expect and require from the Ministers who are its servants a particular measure of caution and restraint in all their utterances about the war.

We have climbed from the pit of peril on to a fairly broad plateau. We can see before us the difficult and dangerous onward path which we must tread. But we can also feel the parallel movement of convergence of the two mighty nations I have mentioned, Russia and the United States. We feel around us the upsurge of all the enslaved countries of Europe. We see how they defy Hitler's firing parties. Far away in the East we see the faithful, patient, inexhaustible spirit of the Chinese race, who also are battling for home and freedom. We are marching in company with the vast majority of mankind, all trending, bearing, forging, steadily forward towards a final goal which, though distant, can already be plainly seen.

When we reflect upon the magnitude of modern events compared with the men who have to try to control or cope with them, and upon the frightful consequences of these events on hundreds of millions, the importance of not making avoidable mistakes grows impressively upon the mind.

For these reasons I could not attempt to discuss at the present time questions of future strategy. They are discussed every day in the newspapers, in an exceedingly vivid and often well-informed manner, but I do not think that His Majesty's Government ought to take any part just now in such debates. Take, for instance, the question of whether we should invade the Continent of Europe in order to lift some of the weight off Russia, whether we ought to take advantage of the lull now that Hitler is busy in Russia to strike him in the West. I shall be guilty of no indiscretion if I admit that these are questions which have several times occurred to those responsible for the conduct of the war. But what could I say about them that would be useful? If I were to throw out dark hints of some great design, no one would have any advantage but the enemy. If, on the other hand, I were to assemble the many cogent reasons which could be ranged on the other side, I should be giving altogether gratuitous reassurance to Hitler.

Such confidences are not reciprocated by the enemy. They have told us nothing since Hitler's speech in February. We are in complete ignorance at this moment about what he is going to do. We do not know how far he will attempt to penetrate the vast lands of Soviet Russia in the face of the valiant Russian defence, or how long his people will endure their own calamitous losses, or, again, whether he will decide to stand on the defensive and exploit the territory of immense value which he has conquered. Should he choose this last, we do not know whether he will turn a portion of his vast armies southwards, towards the Valley of the Nile, or whether he will attempt to make his way through Spain into North-West Africa, or whether, using the great Continental railways of Europe and the immense chains of airfields which are in excellent order, he will shift his weight to the West and assemble an extensive army with all the special craft that he has constructed for an attempted invasion of the British Isles. It would certainly be in his power, while standing on the defensive in the East, to undertake all three of these hazardous enterprises, on a great scale, together, at one time.

The enemy's only shortage is in the air. This is a very serious shortage, but, for the rest, he still retains the initiative. We have not the force to take it from him. He has the divisions, he has the weapons, and on the mainlands of Europe he has ample means of transport. If he does not tell us his plans, I do not see why we should tell him ours. But I can assure the House that we study and ponder over these dangers and possibilities, and on how best to dispose our resources to meet them, every working day, and all days are working days, from dawn to far past midnight. We also have the advantage of following very closely all the arguments which are used about them in the public Press and of considering every helpful suggestion which reaches us from any quarter. More than that I really cannot say, and I feel sure that the House would reprove me if I were by any imprudence or desire to be interesting to say anything which afterwards was seen to be harmful.

There is, however, one matter upon which I may speak a little more freely, namely, the material assistance in the way of munitions and supplies which we and the United States are giving to Russia. The British and United States Missions are now in conference with the chiefs of the Soviet at Moscow. The interval which has passed since President Roosevelt and I sent our message from the Atlantic to Premier Stalin has been used in ceaseless activity on both sides of the ocean. The whole ground has been surveyed in the light of the new events, and many important supplies have already been dispatched. Our representatives and their American colleagues have gone to Moscow with clear and full knowledge of what they are able to give to Russia month by month from now onward. The Soviet Government have a right to know what monthly quotas of weapons and supplies we can send and they can count upon. It is only when they know what we can guarantee to send, subject, of course, to the hazards of war, that they themselves can use their vast resources and reserves to the best possible advantage. It is only thus that they can best fill the gap between the very heavy losses sustained and the diminution of munitions-making power which they have suffered on the one hand, and the arrival of really effective quantities of British and American supplies on the other. I may say at once, however, that in order to enable Russia to remain indefinitely in the field as a first-class war-making power, sacrifices of the most serious kind and the most extreme efforts will have to be made by the British people, and enormous new installations or conversions from existing plants will have to be set up in the United States, with all the labour, expense and disturbance of normal life which these entail.

We have just had a symbolic Tank Week for Russia, and it has, I feel—in fact I know—given an added sense of the immediate importance of their work to the toiling men and women in our factories. The output of Tank Week is only a very small part of the supplies which Britain and the United States must send to

Russia, and must send month after month upon a growing scale and for an indefinite period. It is not only tanks, the tanks for which we have waited so long, that we have to send, but precious aircraft and aluminium, rubber, copper, oil, and many other materials vital to modern war, large quantities of which have already gone. All these we must send and keep sending to Russia. It is not only the making and the giving of these commodities, but their transportation and reception, which have to be organized. It may be that transportation rather than our willingness or ability to give will prove in the end the limiting factor. All this is now being discussed and planned with full authority and full knowledge by our representatives and the American representatives in conclave in Moscow with Premier Stalin and his principal commanders. It would certainly not be right for me in public Session, or even in Secret Session, at the present time to make any detailed or definite statements upon these subjects. The veriest simpleton can see how great is our interest, to put it no higher, in sustaining Russia by every possible means.

There are, however, other interests which have to be remembered at the same time. In some respects the problems we now have to face are similar to those which rent our hearts last year, when we had, for instance, to refuse to send away from this country for the help of France the last remaining squadrons of fighter aircraft upon which our whole future resistance depended; or again, they remind one of the occasion when, rightly judging Hitler's unpreparedness for invasion in the summer of 1940, we took the plunge of sending so many of our tanks and trained troops all round the Cape to the Valley of the Nile in order to destroy the Italian Armies in Libya and Abyssinia. If it is now thought that we solved those problems correctly, we should hope that there might be grounds for confidence that in these new problems His Majesty's Government and their professional advisers will not err either in the direction of reckless improvidence or through want of courage. Anyone who, without full knowledge, should attempt to force the hands of those responsible would act without proper warrant and also—I say it with great respect—would not achieve any useful purpose, because in the discharge of the duties which the House has confided to us we are determined to take our own decisions and to be judged accordingly.

Here I must say a few words about the British Army. There is a current of opinion, which finds frequent expression, that the brass hats and Colonel Blimps and, of course, the much abused War Office, are insisting on building up a portentous, distended and bloated mass of soldiers in this Island at the expense of the manufacture of those scientific weapons and appliances which are the main strength of victory in modern war. The truth is far different. We have never had, and never shall have, an Army comparable in numbers to the armies of the Continent. At the outbreak of war our Army was insignificant as a factor in the conflict. With very great care and toil and time, we have now created a medium-sized, but very good Army. The cadres have been formed, the battalions, batteries, divisions and corps have taken shape and life. Men have worked together in the military units for two years. Very severe training was carried out all through last winter. It will continue all through this winter. The Army is hardened, nimble and alert. The commanders and staff have had opportunities and are having opportunities of handling large-scale movements and manœuvres.

Our Army may be small compared with the German or Russian armies. It has not had the repeated successful experiences of the German army, which are a formidable source of strength. Nevertheless, a finely-tempered weapon has been forged. It is upon this weapon, supported by nearly 2,000,000 of armed and uniformed Home Guard, that we rely to destroy or hurl into the sea an invader who succeeded in making a number of successive or simultaneous lodgments on our shores. When I learned about the absolutely frightful, indescribable atrocities which the German police troops are committing upon the Russian population in the rear of the advance of their armoured vehicles, the responsibility of His Majesty's Government to maintain here at home an ample high-class force to beat down and annihilate any invading lodgment from the sea or descent from the air comes home to me in a significantly ugly and impressive form. I could not reconcile such responsibilities with breaking-up or allowing to melt away the seasoned, disciplined fighting units which we have now at last laboriously and so tardily created.

As our Army must inevitably be small compared with European standards, it is all the more necessary that it should be highly mechanized and armoured. For this purpose a steady flow of skilled tradesmen and technicians will be required in order to use the weapons which the factories are now producing in rapidly growing quantities. There is no question of increasing the numbers of the Army, but it is indispensable that the normal wastage—considerable even when troops are not in contact with the enemy—should be made good, that the ranks should be kept filled, and that the battalions, the batteries, and the tank regiments should be at their proper strength. Above all, we cannot have the existing formations pulled to pieces and gutted by taking out of every platoon and section trained men who are an essential part of these living entities, on which one of these fine or foggy mornings the whole existence of the British nation may depend.

I hope, indeed, that some of our ardent critics out of doors—I have nothing to complain of here—will reflect a little on their own records in the past, and by searching their hearts and memories will realize the fate which awaits nations and individuals who take an easy and popular course or who are guided in defence matters by the shifting winds of well-meaning public opinion. Nothing is more dangerous in wartime than to live in the temperamental atmosphere of a Gallup Poll, always feeling one's pulse and taking one's temperature. I see that a speaker at the week-end said that this was a time when leaders should keep their ears to the ground. All I can say is that the British nation will find it very hard to look up to leaders who are detected in that somewhat ungainly posture. If to-day I am very kindly treated by the mass of the people of this country, it is certainly not because I have followed public opinion in recent years. There is only one duty, only one safe course, and that is to try to be right and not to fear to do or say what you believe to be right. That is the only way to deserve and to win the confidence of our great people in these days of trouble.

Our hearts go out to our British Army, not only to those who in the Mediterranean and in the East may soon have to bear the brunt of German fury and organization, but also to that splendid, but not too large, band of men here at home whose task is monotonous and unspectacular, whose duty is a long and faithful vigil, but who must be ready at any hour of any day to leap at the throat of the invader. It may well be the occasion will never come. If that should be the final story, then we may be sure that the existence of the kind of army we have created would be one of the reasons why once again in a war which has ravaged the world our land will be undevastated and our homes inviolate.

Of course we strive to profit from well-informed criticism, whether friendly or spiteful, but there is one charge sometimes put forward which is, I think, a little unfair. I mean the insinuation that we are a weak, timid, lethargic Government, usually asleep, and in our waking hours always held back by excessive scruples and inhibitions, and unable to act with the vehemence and severity which these violent times require. People ask, for instance, "Why don't you bomb Rome? What is holding you back? Didn't you say you would bomb Rome if Cairo were bombed?" What is the answer? One answer is that Cairo has not yet been bombed. Only military posts on the outskirts have been bombed. But, of course, we have as much right to bomb Rome as the Italians had to bomb London last year, when they thought we were going to collapse; and we should not hesitate to bomb Rome to the best of our ability and as heavily as possible if the course of the war should render such action convenient and helpful.

Then there is the case of Persia. I see complaints that we have acted feebly and hesitatingly in Persia. This surprises me very much. I do not know of any job that has been better done than that. With hardly any loss of life, with surprisng rapidity, and in close concert with our Russian Ally, we have rooted out the malignant elements in Teheran; we have chased a dictator into exile, and installed a constitutional Sovereign pledged to a whole catalogue of long-delayed, sorely-needed reforms and reparations; and we hope soon to present to the House a new and loyal alliance made by Great Britain and Russia with the ancient Persian State and people, which will ratify the somewhat abrupt steps we were forced to take, and will associate the Persian people with us not only in their liberation but in the future movement of the war. It must, indeed, be a captious critic who can find a pretext to make a quarrel out of that. The Persian episode, so far as it has gone, would seem to be one of the most successful and well-conducted affairs in which the Foreign Office has ever been concerned. It ill deserves the treatment it has received from our natural and professional crabbers.

In conclusion, let me once again repeat to the House that I cannot give them any flattering hopes, still less any guarantee, that the future will be bright or easy. On the contrary, even the coming winter affords no assurance, as the Russian Ambassador has candidly and shrewdly pointed out, that the German pressure upon Russia will be relaxed; nor, I may add, does the winter give any assurance that the danger of invasion will be entirely lifted from this island. Winter fog has dangers of its own, and, unlike last year, the enemy has now had ample time for technical preparation. We must certainly expect that in the spring, whatever happens in the meanwhile, very heavy fighting, heavier than any we have yet experienced in this war, will develop in the East, and also that the menace to this island of invasion will present itself in a very grave and sharp form. Only the most strenuous exertions, a perfect unity of purpose, added to our traditional unrelenting tenacity, will enable us to act our part worthily in the prodigious world drama in which we are now plunged. Let us make sure these virtues are forthcoming.

TO THE AIRCRAFT WORKERS

A MESSAGE SENT TO THE MINISTER OF AIRCRAFT PRODUCTION
OCTOBER 6, 1941

October 1. *Three-Power Conference ended in Moscow, and it was announced that Russia would be granted practically every requirement asked for to carry on the War.*

October 3. *Hitler, in his first speech for seven months, said he had attacked Russia because he could not hope to beat Britain with Russian armies massed in his rear.*

Mr. John Curtin, Labour leader, became Prime Minister of Australia.

October 6. *Biggest offensive of the war launched by Germans in the central sector of the Russian front, Moscow obviously being the ultimate objective.*

[October 6, 1941.

I SHOULD like you to convey to all those working on aircraft production in all its branches my thanks and congratulations on last month's record output. Never has the need been more important both for ourselves and our Russian ally. The pilots are ready; and I am sure you will deliver the goods.

A MESSAGE TO YOUTH

SENT TO THE INTERNATIONAL YOUTH RALLY FOR VICTORY AT THE
ROYAL ALBERT HALL, LONDON
OCTOBER 11, 1941

*October 7. President Roosevelt revealed a plan for the revision of
the United States Neutrality Act and the arming of
American merchant ships, which would then be
permitted to carry Lend-Lease materials direct to
British ports.*

*October 8. Russian-German war took a grave turn with the
evacuation of Orel (200 miles south of Moscow), a
city which commanded the communications between
the Soviet's central and southern armies.*

*October 10. Germans' threat to Moscow admitted by the Russians
to be "exceedingly grave."*

    *Lord Beaverbrook, back in London from Moscow,
revealed that British munitions were arriving in a
continuous stream in Russia on a "Lend-Lease" basis.*

[October 11, 1941.

I WAS interested to learn of this meeting of the young people of
many nations to express their determination for victory and
to make good use of the victory when it has been won. In earlier
times wars were won by the fighting spirit of a nation's young men
in the face of the enemy. The place of youth is still in the forefront
of the battle, but now the men and women working in our factories
play an equal part, and each must do his duty. You who come
from lands crushed for the moment by a vile, heartless tyranny
have your part to play. If all give of their best in the ways that
are open to them, victory will be won.

A CALL TO THE FARMERS

MESSAGE FROM THE PRIME MINISTER READ BY MR. ROBERT HUDSON, MINISTER
OF AGRICULTURE, AT A MEETING OF FARMERS AND FARM WORKERS AT
NORWICH

OCTOBER 18, 1941

October 13. *President Roosevelt announced that American supplies
were constantly leaving for Russian ports, and would
continue to do so in ever-increasing quantities.*

October 16. *Russia admitted that German troops had reached the
outer ring of the Moscow defences—a perimeter
roughly sixty miles from the capital. The Germans
claimed the capture of Odessa.*

October 17. *General Hideki Tojo, known to be strongly pro-
German, was appointed Prime Minister of Japan.*

*United States Government ordered all American
shipping in the Northern Pacific to return to port.*

[October 18, 1941.

NEVER before have farmers and farm workers carried such
a heavy responsibility as you do in this struggle. Never
before have you responded to the country's call as you have done
in the last two years. It is due in no small measure to the efforts
you have made, in spite of many difficulties, that we find ourselves
to-day in a better position on the food front than at any previous
time since the war started.

But there can be no relaxation. Far from it. The enemy's
attack at sea will be intensified. The situation demands from each
one of us still greater efforts, still greater sacrifices, than we have
yet made.

Ships that would have brought food to our shores must now be
used to meet the urgent needs of ourselves and our Russian allies
for aeroplanes and tanks. You can release more ships by growing
still more food in this country, and so hasten the day of victory.
May God speed the plough.

DEFENCE REGULATION 18B

A SPEECH TO THE HOUSE OF COMMONS
OCTOBER 21, 1941

Note.—*This speech was made in the course of a debate concerning the Home Secretary's powers of detaining persons under Defence Regulation 18b and the prevention of Mr. McGovern, M.P., from visiting Northern Ireland.*

October 19. Russians announced that British and American tanks had gone into action on the Moscow front, and Stalin declared that the city would be defended to the last.

October 20. State of siege declared in Moscow, and some Government departments removed to Kuibishev on the Volga, 550 miles away.

October 21. American anger aroused by the sinking of two more American ships in the Atlantic.

    Germans shot fifty hostages in Nantes (France) as reprisal for the killing of a German officer, and threatened fifty more hostages with death if the assassins were not found.

[*October 21, 1941.*

THERE is no part of the powers conferred on His Majesty's Government in this time of trial that I view with greater repugnance than these powers of exceptional process against the liberty of the subject without the ordinary safeguards which are inherent in British life. Those high-sounding familiar phrases like "Habeas Corpus," "petitioner's right," "charges made which are known to the law," and "trial by jury"—all these are part of what we are fighting to preserve. We all care about them and understand them, and we are determined that they shall not be trespassed upon by anything except the need of self-preservation which arises in time of war.

I recognize that this legation and the Regulations which are based upon it were passed at a moment of great danger. It is possible that if in this lull—and it is only a lull—the matter were considered, the House would be in a different temper. I must say that I should feel very proud and happy if I could come down to the House, even while the war was going on, and say, "Our position is now so good and solid, we now see the path before us so firm and clear, that even in time of war we can of our own free will give back these special powers." Unhappily that is not the case at present. The time may come, but not now. In the meanwhile, I cannot conceive how Parliament can better keep control over the use of these abnormal powers than by insisting upon their being exercised in the discretion of a Minister present in the House and accountable to the House. The Minister has been made accountable to the House. He has come down to-day and has explained in the greatest detail his use of the powers in a particular case. I should think he feels it a most objectionable thing to have this discretionary power conferred on him; but such a discretionary power there must be, and there must be a choosing between this and that. The House has given the power, and I am bound to say that the manner in which my right hon. Friend has explained the whole position has brought home to the House, first, the submissiveness of the Executive to Parliamentary institutions, and secondly, the care with which these powers are exercised.

For my part, I hope that the day may come as speedily as possible, even before the end of the war, when we may be able to relieve ourselves of these exceptional powers, or some of them. In the meanwhile, I feel that we are entitled to ask from the House a general measure of support for the Minister charged with exercising them. There can be no question of going behind the powers of the House. The powers of the House are over-riding and inalienable, and everything that is done is done on the responsibility of the House, be it right or be it wrong. The House has power to wreck the proposed action, provided, of course, it is confident that it is representing the country in the course which it is taking. Therefore, I hope the Debate when it ends may leave the impression that there has been no derogation from the authority and freedom of Parliamentary Institutions. I particularly resent the suggestion that we are adopting the methods of Fascist States. We are not. We are the servants of the House. It may be true that the House will support its servants, but if it does not the powers in their hands are without effect, and so long as that fact is established it is absolutely improper, as well as unhelpful, to place us upon the level of totalitarian Governments which have no corrective legislature, no law but their own wills, no check on the enforcement of their own particular doctrines in any way they choose.

THE SLAUGHTER OF HOSTAGES

MR. WINSTON CHURCHILL ISSUED THIS STATEMENT FOLLOWING THE SHOOTING
OF FRENCH HOSTAGES AS A REPRISAL FOR THE ASSASSINATION OF TWO
GERMAN OFFICERS
OCTOBER 25, 1941

October 22. *Spirit of revolt in France, evidenced by the assassination of two German officers, caused Petain and Darlan to issue an appeal to the French public to preserve order.*

Donetz Basin of Russia threatened by new German advances.

October 23. *Lord Beaverbrook announced that the October quota of aid to Russia had already been sent off.*

October 24. *Soviet High Command changes: Zhukov took over Moscow sector and Timoshenko the critical south, while Budenny and Voroshilov began task of organizing new armies behind the front.*

In France fifty more hostages were shot by the Germans.

Col. Knox told the United States that a clash with Japan was inevitable.

October 25. *Admiral Cunningham revealed that half the Axis reinforcements in men and supplies sent to Libya were sunk or damaged.*

[October 25, 1941.

HIS Majesty's Government associate themselves fully with the sentiments of horror and condemnation expressed by the President of the United States upon the Nazi butcheries in France. These cold-blooded executions of innocent people will only recoil upon the savages who order and execute them.

The butcheries in France are an example of what Hitler's Nazis are doing in many other countries under their yoke. The atrocities in Poland, in Yugoslavia, in Norway, in Holland, in Belgium, and above all behind the German fronts in Russia, surpass anything that has been known since the darkest and most bestial ages of mankind.

They are but a foretaste of what Hitler would inflict upon the British and American peoples if only he could get the power. Retribution for these crimes must henceforward take its place among the major purposes of the war.

THE NEW GLORY OF GREECE

A MESSAGE TO M. TSOUDEROS, PRIME MINISTER OF GREECE, ON
THE ANNIVERSARY OF THE ATTACK BY ITALY ON GREECE
OCTOBER 27, 1941

October 26. On the Russian front the Germans broke through to
within ten miles of Rostov in the south, but enveloping
moves on Moscow were still held at Kalinin and
near Orel.

October 27. President Roosevelt strongly attacked Hitler in a
speech in which he said: "Shooting has started and
America is at her battle stations." He added, "damn
the torpedoes," and said the nation would go full
speed ahead to beat Hitler.

[*October 27, 1941.*

I WISH, on this fateful anniversary of Mussolini's crime, to
express once more the gratitude of the British people to the
Hellenes for all they have done, and are doing, for the Allied cause.
To the fame already earned by the Greek people when they thrilled
the world by their Albanian victories and their undaunted resistance to Nazi might, new lustre is being added. The campaign of
resistance to the German and Italian domination which is now
being waged in Greece itself, and the warfare in which the Greek
forces of the Middle East will be engaged when their preparations
are complete, will have proved the unquenchable spirit of Greece
anew.

I wish, at the same time, to take this opportunity once more to
reaffirm to Your Excellency that your Government, now declared
to be a democratic Government under the beloved constitutional
monarch, enjoys the full confidence and support of His Majesty's
Government and the British people.

The glory of Greece shines not only in her antiquity but even
brighter in these tragic years. It is vindicated by the constancy
of her people in cruel bondage. Their martyrdom will be avenged
by the Pan-Hellenic Army of liberation. The unity of all her sons
and daughters behind their King and Government in the cause of
their Fatherland will bring its sure reward.

"THESE ARE GREAT DAYS"

A SPEECH TO THE BOYS OF HARROW SCHOOL
OCTOBER 29, 1941

October 29. The Russians announced the evacuation of Kharkov and claimed to have inflicted 120,000 casualties on the enemy.

Soviet planes raided Berlin.

[*October 29, 1941.*

ALMOST a year has passed since I came down here at your Head Master's kind invitation in order to cheer myself and cheer the hearts of a few of my friends by singing some of our own songs. The ten months that have passed have seen very terrible catastrophic events in the world—ups and downs, misfortunes— but can anyone sitting here this afternoon, this October afternoon, not feel deeply thankful for what has happened in the time that has passed and for the very great improvement in the position of our country and of our home? Why, when I was here last time we were quite alone, desperately alone, and we had been so for five or six months. We were poorly armed. We are not so poorly armed to-day; but then we were very poorly armed. We had the unmeasured menace of the enemy and their air attack still beating upon us, and you yourselves had had experience of this attack; and I expect you are beginning to feel impatient that there has been this long lull with nothing particular turning up!

But we must learn to be equally good at what is short and sharp and what is long and tough. It is generally said that the British are often better at the last. They do not expect to move from crisis to crisis; they do not always expect that each day will bring up some noble chance of war; but when they very slowly make up their minds that the thing has to be done and the job put through and finished, then, even if it takes months—if it takes years— they do it.

Another lesson I think we may take, just throwing our minds back to our meeting here ten months ago and now, is that appearances are often very deceptive, and as Kipling well says, we must

" . . . meet with Triumph and Disaster
And treat those two imposters just the same."

274

You cannot tell from appearances how things will go. Sometimes imagination makes things out far worse than they are; yet without imagination not much can be done. Those people who are imaginative see many more dangers than perhaps exist, certainly many more than will happen; but then they must also pray to be given that extra courage to carry this far-reaching imagination. But for everyone, surely, what we have gone through in this period—I am addressing myself to the School—surely from this period of ten months this is the lesson: never give in, never give in, *never, never, never, never*—in nothing, great or small, large or petty—never give in except to convictions of honour and good sense. Never yield to force; never yield to the apparently overwhelming might of the enemy. We stood all alone a year ago, and to many countries it seemed that our account was closed, we were finished. All this tradition of ours, our songs, our School history, this part of the history of this country, were gone and finished and liquidated.

Very different is the mood to-day. Britain, other nations thought, had drawn a sponge across her slate. But instead our country stood in the gap. There was no flinching and no thought of giving in; and by what seemed almost a miracle to those outside these Islands, though we ourselves never doubted it, we now find ourselves in a position where I say that we can be sure that we have only to persevere to conquer.

You sang here a verse of a School Song; you sang that extra verse written in my honour, which I was very greatly complimented by and which you have repeated to-day*; but there is one word in it I want to alter—I wanted to do so last year, but I did not venture to. It is the line—

> *"Not less we praise in darker days."*

I have obtained the Head Master's permission to alter *"darker"* to *"sterner"*:

> *"Not less we praise in sterner days."*

* The boys had previously sung the school song, "STET FORTUNA DOMUS," and this verse had been added in Mr. Churchill's honour:—

> "Not less we praise in darker days
>   The leader of our nation,
> And Churchill's name shall win acclaim
>   From each new generation.
> For you have power in danger's hour
>   Our freedom to defend, Sir!
> Though long the fight we know that right
>   Will triumph in the end, Sir!

275

Do not let us speak of darker days; let us speak rather of sterner days. These are not dark days: these are great days— the greatest days our country has ever lived; and we must all thank God that we have been allowed, each of us according to our stations, to play a part in making these days memorable in the history of our race.

"ALL WILL BE WELL"

A SPEECH AT THE GUILDHALL, HULL, DURING A TOUR OF THE
NORTH-EASTERN CITIES OF ENGLAND
NOVEMBER 7, 1941

October 31. German forces secured a foothold on the Crimean peninsula.

Soviet Government asked Britain to declare war on Finland, Rumania and Hungary.

November 1. London had its first air raid alert since July 27, though no bombs were dropped. Britain's new defences destroyed six German bombers in small scattered raids.

November 2. Germans, advancing rapidly in the Crimea, claimed the capture of the capital, Simferopol.

November 3. United States warned Finland to end their war against Russia immediately.

November 4. Vichy Government protested against the British capture of a French convoy of five ships, totalling 40,000 tons, suspected of running contraband.

November 5. Part of Soviet Russia's Black Sea Fleet reported to have left for secondary bases following heavy bombing of Sevastopol.

November 6. Stalin, in a speech on the 24th anniversary of the Russian Revolution, said Hitler could not last more than a year, and estimated German losses in the Russian campaign at 4,500,000. He hoped Britain would be able to create a second front.

President Roosevelt, in a speech warning the American people that they would have to make full sacrifice to beat Hitler, announced a £250,000,000 Lend-Lease Loan to Russia.

November 7. R.A.F. planes carried out the heaviest raid of the war on Berlin, losing 37 bombers, many through bad weather conditions.

[*November 7, 1941.*

I WANTED very much to see this city which has suffered by the malice of our assailants. I can see that it has had many of its fine buildings shattered and gutted. But I also see that it has not had the heart of its people cast down.

The resolution of the British people is unconquerable. Neither sudden nor violent shocks, nor long, cold, tiring, provoking strains and lulls can or will alter our course. No country made more strenuous efforts to avoid being drawn into this war, but I dare say we shall be found ready and anxious to prosecute it when some of those who provoked it are talking vehemently about peace. It has been rather like that in old times.

I am often asked to say how we are going to win this war. I remember being asked that last time very frequently, and not being able to give a very precise or conclusive answer. We kept on doing our best; we kept on improving. We profited by our mistakes and our experiences. We turned misfortune to good account. We were told we should run short of this or that, until the only thing we ever run short of was Huns. We did our duty. We did not ask to see too far ahead, but strode forth upon our path, guided by such lights as led us, and then one day we saw those who had forced the struggle upon the world cast down their arms in the open field and immediately proceed to beg for sympathy, mercy, and considerable financial support.

Now we have to do it all over again. Sometimes I wonder why. Having chained this fiend, this monstrous power of Prussian militarism, we saw it suddenly resuscitated in the new and more hideous guise of Nazi tyranny. We have to face once more the long struggle, the cruel sacrifices, and not be daunted or deterred by feelings of vexation. With quite a little forethought, a little care and decision, and with rather a greater measure of slow persistency, we need never have had to face this thing in our lifetime or in that of our children.

However, we are all resolved to go forward. We were equally resolved when a year and three months ago we found ourselves absolutely alone, the only champion of freedom in the whole world that remained in arms. We found ourselves with hardly any weapons left. We had rescued our Army, indeed, from Dunkirk, but it had come back stripped of all its accoutrements. Every country in the world outside this island and the Empire to which we are indissolubly attached had given us up, had made up their minds that our life was ended and our tale was told. But by unflinchingly despising the manifestations of power and the threats by which we were on all sides confronted, we have come through that dark and perilous passage, now once again masters of our own destiny.

Nor are we any longer alone. As I told the House of Commons, our own steadfast conduct and the crimes of the enemy have brought other great nations to our side. One of them is struggling with Herculean vigour and with results which are profoundly significant. The other, our kith and kin across the Atlantic Ocean, is straining every nerve to equip us with all we need to carry on the struggle regardless of cost to them or of risk to their sailors and ships. They are driving forward with supplies across the ocean and aiding us to strike down and strangle the foe who molests the passage of those supplies. Therefore we find ourselves to-day in a goodly company, and we are moving forward and we shall move forward steadily, however long the road may be.

I have never given any assurances of a speedy or easy or cheap victory. On the contrary, as you know, I have never promised anything but the hardest conditions, great disappointments, and many mistakes. But I am sure that at the end all will be well for us in our island home, all will be better for the world, and there will be that crown of honour to those who have endured and never failed which history will accord to them for having set an example to the whole human race.

"EVERYONE CAN PLAY A HERO'S PART"

A SPEECH TO THE PEOPLE OF SHEFFIELD FROM THE BALCONY
OF THE TOWN HALL
NOVEMBER 8, 1941

November 8. Colonel Knox, United States Secretary of the Navy, announced the establishment of a naval operating base in Iceland.

Hitler, in a speech at the Munich Beer Cellar, referred to Germany's ability to develop the defensive powers not only of the Reich but of all Europe.

[*November 8, 1941.*

THIS great city so intimately interwoven with our war effort has undergone this storm of fire and steel and come through with many scars, but with the conviction that however hard may be the trial, and whatever the future may bring, Sheffield will not be unequal to it.

This foul war, forced on us by human wickedness, has now gone on for more than two years. None of us can say at what moment the bugles will sound the "Cease Fire," but of this we may be sure that, however long and stern it may be, the British Nation and the British Commonwealth of Nations will come through united, undaunted, stainless, unflinching.

When we look back over the time that has passed since world peace was broken by the brutal assault upon Poland, we see the ups and downs through which we have gone. Many disappointments have occurred, very often many mistakes, but still when we look back to 15 months ago and remember that then we were alone and almost unarmed, and we now see our armed forces developing their strength with modern weapons; when we look across the wide stretches of European land and see that great warrior Stalin at the head of his valiant Russians; when we look westward across the ocean and see the Americans sending their war vessels out to rid the seas of pirate vermin, in order that they may carry to the fighting front line here, without regard to the opposition they may encounter, the weapons, munitions and food we require, it is a message of inspiration, because we are sure that before we get to the end of the road we shall all be together.

I urge you to continue your labours. The work of everyone is of vital importance. This is a struggle for life, a struggle in which every man and woman, old and young, can play a hero's part. The chance of glory and honour comes now here, now there, to each and everyone. However hard the task may be I know you will all be ready for that high moment. God bless you all.

In a speech to workers at a Sheffield Munitions Works the same day, Mr. Churchill said:—

I give you my compliments and congratulate you on the way you are getting on with the war effort. The work you are doing plays a vital part in the war. Everyone who keeps his time is doing his best to rid the world of this curse of war and Hitlerism. I am proud to come among you because I am told you have lost only 4½ hours' time during air raids, although since January there have been 120 alerts. This is the way to stand up to it as the Artillery men do with their guns, as the sailors stand on watch, as the airmen do in cutting the enemy down from the high air. You are doing your bit in the same way. Their work cannot begin until yours is finished. We have only to hold together to go safely through the dark valley, and then we will see if we can make something lasting of our victory.

A WARNING TO JAPAN

A SPEECH AT THE LORD MAYOR'S DAY LUNCHEON
AT THE MANSION HOUSE, LONDON
NOVEMBER 10, 1941

November 9. The Admiralty announced that a light cruiser and destroyer force had sunk, without loss, Italian convoys consisting of ten supply ships and two (later increased to three) destroyers.

November 10. Mr. Churchill spoke at the Lord Mayor's Day Luncheon at the Mansion House, London, and warned Japan that Britain would immediately fight on the side of the United States in the event of conflict.

[*November 10, 1941.*

ALIKE in times of peace and war the annual Civic Festival we have observed to-day has been by long custom the occasion for a speech at the Guildhall by the Prime Minister upon foreign affairs.

This year our ancient Guildhall lies in ruins, our foreign affairs are shrunken, and almost the whole of Europe is prostrate under the Nazi tyranny. The war which Hitler began by invading Poland and which now engulfs the European continent has broken into the north-east of Africa; may well involve the greater part of Asia; nay, it may soon spread to the remaining portions of the globe. Nevertheless, in the same spirit in which you, my Lord Mayor, have celebrated your assumption of office with the time-honoured pageant of Lord Mayor's Day, so I, who have the honour to be your guest, will endeavour to play, though very briefly—for in wartime speeches should be short—the traditional part assigned to those who hold my office.

The condition of Europe is terrible in the last degree. Hitler's firing parties are busy every day in a dozen countries. Norwegians, Belgians, Frenchmen, Dutch, Poles, Czechs, Serbs, Croats, Slovenes, Greeks, and above all in scale Russians, are being butchered by thousands and by tens of thousands after they have surrendered, while individual and mass executions in all the countries I have mentioned have become a part of the regular German routine. The world has been intensely stirred by the massacre of the French hostages. The whole of France, with the exception of the small clique whose public careers depend upon a German victory, has been united in horror and indignation against this slaughter of perfectly innocent people. Admiral Darlan's tributes to German generosity fall unseasonably at this moment on French ears, and his plans for loving collaboration with the conquerors and the murderers of Frenchmen are quite appreciably embarrassed. Nay, even the arch-criminal himself, the Nazi ogre Hitler, has been frightened by the volume and passion of world indignation which his spectacular atrocity has excited. It is he and not the French people who have been intimidated. He has not dared to go forward with his further programme of killing hostages.

This, as you will have little doubt, is not due to mercy, to compassion, to compunction, but to fear, and to a dawning consciousness of personal insecurity rising in a wicked heart.

I would say generally that we must regard all these victims of the Nazi executioners in so many lands, who are labelled Communists and Jews—we must regard them just as if they were brave soldiers who die for their country on the field of battle. Nay, in a way their sacrifice may be more fruitful than that of the soldier who falls with his arms in his hands. A river of blood has flowed and is flowing between the German race and the peoples of nearly all Europe. It is not the hot blood of battle, where good blows are given and returned. It is the cold blood of the execution yard and the scaffold, which leaves a stain indelible for generations and for centuries.

Here then are the foundations upon which the New Order of Europe is to be inaugurated. Here then is the house-warming festival of the *Herrenvolk*. Here then is the system of terrorism by which the Nazi criminals and their quisling accomplices seek to rule a dozen ancient famous States of Europe and if possible all the free nations of the world. In no more effective manner could they have frustrated the accomplishment of their own designs. The future and its mysteries are inscrutable. But one thing is plain. Never to those blood-stained accursed hands will the future of Europe be confided.

Since Lord Mayor's Day last year some great changes have taken place in our situation. Then we were alone, the sole champion of freedom. Then we were ill-armed and far outnumbered even in the Air. Now a large part of the United States Navy, as Colonel Knox has told us, is constantly in action against the common foe. Now the valiant resistance of the Russian nation has inflicted most frightful injuries upon the German military power, and at the present moment the German invading armies, after all their losses, lie on the barren steppes exposed to the approaching severities of the Russian winter. Now we have an Air Force which is at last at least equal in size and numbers, not to speak of quality, to the German Air Power.

Rather more than a year ago I announced to Parliament that we are getting in the Atlantic from the United tSates, owing to the destruction of the German and Italian convoys—and the Admiralty brings to-day the news of the destruction of another Italian destroyer—the passage of our own supplies in many directions through that sea, the broken morale of the Italian navy, all these show that we are still the masters there.

To-day I am able to go further. Owing to the effective help we are getting in the Atlantic from the United States, owing to the sinking of the *Bismarck*, owing to the completion of our splendid new battleships and aircraft carriers of the largest size, as well as to the cowing of the Italian navy already mentioned, I am able to go further and announce to you here at the Lord Mayor's annual celebration that we now feel ourselves strong enough to provide a powerful naval force of heavy ships, with its necessary ancillary vessels, for service if needed in the Indian and Pacific Oceans. Thus we stretch out the long arm of brotherhood and motherhood to the Australian and New Zealand peoples and to the peoples of India, whose armies and troops have already been fighting with so much distinction in the Mediterranean theatre. And this movement of our naval forces, in conjunction with the United States Main Fleet, may give a practical proof to all who have eyes to see that the forces of freedom and democracy have not by any means reached the limits of their power.

I must admit that, having voted for the Japanese alliance nearly 40 years ago, in 1902, and having always done my very best to promote good relations with the Island Empire of Japan, and always having been a sentimental well-wisher to the Japanese and an admirer of their many gifts and qualities, I should view with keen sorrow the opening of a conflict between Japan and the English-speaking world.

The United States' time-honoured interests in the Far East are well known. They are doing their utmost to find ways of preserving peace in the Pacific. We do not know whether their efforts will be successful, but should they fail I take this occasion to say, and it is my duty to say, that, should the United States become involved in war with Japan, the British declaration will follow within the hour.

Viewing the vast sombre scene as dispassionately as possible, it would seem a very hazardous adventure for the Japanese people to plunge quite needlessly into a world struggle in which they may well find themselves opposed in the Pacific by States whose populations comprise nearly three-quarters of the human race. If steel is the basic foundation of modern war, it would be rather dangerous for a power like Japan, whose steel production is only about 7 million tons a year, to provoke quite gratuitously a struggle with the United States, whose steel production is now about 90 millions; and this would take no account of the powerful contribution which the British Empire can make. I hope therefore that the peace of the Pacific will be preserved in accordance with the known wishes of Japan's wisest statesmen. But every preparation to defend British interests in the Far East, and to defend the common cause now at stake, has been and is being made.

Meanwhile, how can we watch without emotion the wonderful defence of their native soil and of their freedom and independence which has been maintained single-handed, all alone, for five long years by the Chinese people under the leadership of that great Asiatic hero and Commander, General Chiang-Kai-Shek? It would be a disaster of first magnitude to world civilization if the noble resistance to invasion and exploitation which has been made by the whole Chinese race were not to result in the liberation of their hearths and homes. That, I feel, is a sentiment which is deep in all our hearts.

To return for a moment before I sit down to the contrast between our position now and a year ago, I must remind you, I do not need to remind you here in the City, that this time last year we did not know where to turn for a dollar across the American exchange. By very severe measures we had been able to gather and spend in America about £500,000,000 sterling, but the end of our financial resources was in sight—nay, had actually been reached. All we could do at that time a year ago was to place orders in the United States without being able to see our way through, but on a tide of hope and not without important encouragement.

Then came the majestic policy of the President and Congress of the United States in passing the Lend and Lease Bill, under which in two successive enactments about £3,000,000,000 sterling were dedicated to the cause of world freedom without—mark this, for it is unique—the setting up of any account in money. Never again let us hear the taunt that money is the ruling thought or power in the hearts of the American democracy. The Lend and Lease Bill must be regarded without question as the most unsordid act in the whole of recorded history.

We for our part have not been found unworthy of the increasing aid we are receiving. We have made unparalleled financial and economic sacrifices ourselves, and now that the Government and people of the United States have declared their resolve that the aid they are giving shall reach the fighting lines, we shall be able to strike with all our might and main.

Thus we may, without exposing ourselves to any charge of complacency, without in the slightest degree relaxing the intensity of our war effort, give thanks to Almighty God for the many wonders which have been wrought in so brief a space of time, and we may derive fresh confidence from all that has happened and bend ourselves to our task with all the force that is in our souls and with every drop of blood that is in our bodies.

We are told from many quarters that we must soon expect what is called a "peace offensive" from Berlin. All the usual signs and symptoms are already manifest, as the Foreign Secretary will confirm, in neutral countries, and all these signs point in one direction. They all show that the guilty men who have let Hell loose upon the world are hoping to escape with their fleeting triumphs and ill-gotten plunders, from the closing net of doom.

We owe it to ourselves, we owe it to our Russian Ally, and to the Government and people of the United States, to make it absolutely clear that whether we are supported or alone, however long and hard the toil may be, the British nation and His Majesty's Government in intimate concert with the Governments of the great Dominions will never enter into any negotiations with Hitler or any party in Germany which represents the Nazi régime. In that resolve, we are sure that the ancient City of London will be with us to the hilt and to the end.

THE WAR SITUATION

A SPEECH TO THE HOUSE OF COMMONS IN THE DEBATE ON THE ADDRESS IN REPLY TO THE KING'S SPEECH AT OPENING OF THE NEW SESSION OF PARLIAMENT
NOVEMBER 12, 1941

November 11. *Another Italian convoy was smashed in the Mediterranean, British submarines sinking six ships and damaging four others. This attack, combined with air raids on enemy bases in North Africa, aimed at crippling Axis plans for a push against Egypt.*

November 12. *The King opened Parliament, and Mr. Churchill surveyed the war situation.*

General Huntziger, Vichy War Minister, was killed in an air crash.

[*November 12, 1941.*

I HAVE heard many Debates upon occasions like this in the forty years off and on—mostly on—during which I have been in Parliament, and I know well that it is a ceremonial occasion on which the foils have the buttons securely fastened to their tips and complimentary exchanges are made. I think there was a note of warm kindliness in both the speeches which came from the leaders representative of the two parties opposite. I am particularly grateful for the appreciation and encouragement which those Gentlemen gave to His Majesty's Government. We have had two speeches from the Mover and Seconder of the Address which every-one will feel were adequate to the occasion—very excellent speeches from a Member who has in this war already gained the Military Cross and from my hon. Friend the Member for the Brightside Division (Mr. Marshall) who in Sheffield has not been far from the fighting front.

It has been aptly remarked that Ministers, and indeed all other public men when they make speeches at the present time, have always to bear in mind three audiences, one our own fellow countrymen, secondly, our friends abroad, and thirdly, the enemy. This naturally makes the task of public speaking very difficult. At the same time under our Parliamentary and democratic system Ministers are frequently called upon to make speeches in both Houses of Parliament and in the country at war-savings meetings and the like. We have over eighty Ministers in the Government, and they cannot all be equally informed about the general course of affairs and military operations. It is not possible for me with my other duties to read all the Ministerial speeches, and of course many of our Ministers are natural orators and speak entirely extemporaneously and on the spur of the moment. In those circumstances, as anyone can see, one may easily find discrepancies arising. These discrepancies when they occur immediately attract the attention of our faithful and vigilant Press, and are paraded as examples of Ministerial discordance or at any rate lack of concert.

I hope therefore that those who feel that their war work lies especially in the direction of criticism will make allowances for these difficulties inherent in the situation. I hope they will also remember that no sensible person in wartime makes speeches because he wants to. He makes them because he has to, and to no one does this apply more than to the Prime Minister. I have repeatedly called attention to the disadvantages of my having to give too frequent reviews of the war, and I have always declined to be drawn into discussions about strategy or tactics so far as they may have relation to current or pending events. The House has shown me great indulgence in this matter, but I feel that I should be excused to-day from entering upon discussion of the war position, to which I referred in a speech I made only a month ago. Most of all shall I refrain from making any prediction about the future. It is a month ago that I remarked upon the long silence of Herr Hitler, a remark which apparently provoked him to make a speech in which he told the German people that Moscow would fall in a few days. That shows, as everyone, I am sure will agree, how much wiser he would have been to go on keeping his mouth shut.

Even I, in my modest way, run great risks of giving dissatisfaction when I speak. Some people are very hard to please. It is impossible to please everybody; whatever you say, some fault can be found. If, for instance, I were to pay—as I should like to pay —strong tribute to the splendid heroism and undaunted gallantry of our Russian Allies, I should immediately be answered, "Let us have deeds, not words." If I were to omit all reference to Russian bravery, it would, on the other hand, be said, "Not even one kindly word was spoken to cheer on these heroes." If I were to describe the help in detail which we are giving to Russia, that might be very interesting, but it would give away to the enemy secrets which are Russian as well as British. Again, if I gave an appreciation of the fighting on the Russian front, I should get hit either way. If my account were favourable, I should be accused of fostering complacency. On the other hand, if it were grave, I should be accused of spreading needless despondency and alarm, and the Russians would not thank me for underrating or disparaging their giant strength. I must mention these facts merely as illustrations of the difficulties and dangers of making too many speeches about the war at times like these, and to give a respectful explanation to the House of why, with one fleeting exception, I am not going to refer to-day to any of the changing phases of this tremendous struggle.

I am, however, able to give some information about the war at sea. The House will remember the very good reasons which were given for leaving-off publishing monthly figures of sinkings by enemy action, and how those precise periodical statements, made given for leaving-ox publishing monthly figures of sinkings by to how his varying tactics were succeeding; but there is no objection to giving exact figures for longer periods, and I take this occasion to give figures of the last four months, ending with October, without dividing them into months, and compared with the figures, already published, of the four preceding months, ending with June. They are certainly well worthy of mention. I am speaking in round numbers. In the four months ending with June, we lost just over 2,000,000 tons, or an average of 500,000 tons per month. In the last four months, ending with October, we lost less than 750,000 tons or an average of 180,000 tons per month. 180,000 contrasts very favourably with 500,000 tons. I see opposite me my right hon. Friend the Member for Carnarvon Boroughs (Mr. Lloyd George). We shared, I in a very humble position, but with full knowledge, the terrible anxieties of 1917. We saw the figures mount, but we also saw the sudden fall. However, we must not count at all that the danger is past, but the facts are more favourable than are represented by the reduction on the four-monthly period from 500,000 to 180,000, because, from the point of view of keeping alive our power to wage war at sea, and of increasing it, you have to take account not only of what is lost but of new building. You have to deduct the new building and see how the position stands. I do not intend to give exact figures about new building, but, making allowances for new building, the net loss of our Mercantile Marine, apart altogether from captures from the enemy and United States assistance, has been reduced in the last four months to a good deal less than one-fifth of what it was in the previous four months. That is an impressive fact. This has been done in spite of the fact that there were never more U-boats or more long-range aircraft working than are now. While that fact should lead us to increase our successful exertions, and should in no way favour an easy habit of mind, it does, I think, give solid and sober assurance that we shall be able to maintain our seaborne traffic until the great American shipbuilding promised for 1942 comes into service. The United States are, of course, building new merchant ships on a scale many times in excess of what we are able to do in this Island. Having regard to the manifold calls upon us, our new shipbuilding is confined to a certain proportion of our resources, but the United States are embarking on an output of ships incomparably greater than what we can produce, and far surpassing the enormous efforts they successfully made in the last war.

If we are able to get through this year, we shall certainly find ourselves in good supply of ships in 1942. If the war against the U-boats and the enemy aircraft continues to prosper as it has done—of which there can be, of course, no guarantee—the Freedom Powers will be possessed of large quantities of shipping in 1943, which will enable oversea operations to take place utterly beyond British resources at the present time. Meanwhile, the destruction of enemy shipping is proceeding with even greater violence than before. During the four months ended October, there were sunk or seriously damaged nearly 1,000,000 tons. In the Mediterranean, the enemy's losses have been particularly severe, and there is evidence that he has found it very difficult to reinforce, or even to supply, his armies on the African shores. This last convoy was a particularly valuable one, and its total destruction, together with the devastation being wrought by our submarines in the Mediterranean, is certainly very much to be rejoiced over.

There are at least 40,000 Italian women, children, and noncombatants in Abysinnia. Some time ago, guided by humanitarian instincts, we offered to let the Italian Government take these people home, if they would send under the necessary safeguards their own shipping to the ports on the Red Sea. The Italian Government accepted this proposal, and agreement was reached on all the details, but they have never been able so far to send the ships specified, because the destruction of their ships has proceeded at such a high rate and to such a serious extent. All this makes me hopeful—although, of course, I will not prophesy—that the German and Italian boasts that they would take Suez by the end of May last, will very likely remain unfulfilled at Christmas. That is much more than we had any right to expect when the Italian Government declared war upon us and the French deserted us in the Mediterranean eighteen months ago.

The fact that our shipping losses have so remarkably diminished, and diminished at the very time when Hitler boasted that his sea war would be at its height, must be taken in conjunction with our greatly increased production of food at home. I have always held the view that the British people, especially their heavy workers, must be properly fed and nourished if we are to get the full results from our war effort, and at the beginning of the year, when it looked as if we should have to choose to some extent between food and munition imports, I asked the Cabinet to approve a minimum of food imports to be maintained, if necessary, even at the expense of munition materials. There is no doubt that the dietary of our people has been severely curtailed and has become far less varied and interesting. Still, at the rate we are now going, it is sufficient for our physical health, although I am hoping that we shall be able to give a somewhat larger share of the available supplies of meat to the workers who need it most. This will be done by a rapid expansion of canteens, which will supply meals off the ration to the workers they serve at places where those workers are actually gathered.

I am glad to say that the figure which we prescribed for minimum food imports will now probably be achieved, and even a little surpassed, and that the Minister of Food has been able to make certain minor relaxations during the winter months in the severity of his restrictions. As a precaution, we have amassed stocks of bulky articles of our diet which amount to double what we had in September, 1939. We are going to make a job of this war, and those who are working on the job must have their strength fully maintained, because although much has been asked of them in the past, we are going to ask them for more as the struggle deepens. The Agricultural Ministers for England and Scotland are also to be congratulated upon the very great expansion they have made of our home food production. In the short space of two years the area under crops has been increased by no less than 45 per cent. Although the corn harvest that was gathered was not quite so good as we had hoped it would be before I left for the Atlantic meeting—and here I must say that in future I shall be as careful in abstaining from prophecy in agricultural matters as I am in military matters—nevertheless, the cereal crop was 50 per cent. greater than in 1939. We should also have very large crops of potatoes, sugar beet, fodder roots and other fodder crops this year. Despite the lack of imported feeding-stuffs, we have well maintained our head of cattle, both dairy cows and beef cattle, and I hope—I say this on the spur of the moment and shall perhaps get into trouble—that the Minister of Food will see if he can do something for the hens. All who have to do with the land, farmer and farm worker alike, have played a worthy part in this achievement. But satisfactory as are the results to date, there must be no relaxation of our efforts. Despite all difficulties, we must go on to produce still more, not only because of the ever-present menace to our importation from abroad, but because it is possible that as the war develops our military operations will make much more extensive demands on our shipping.

I mention these facts at the risk of being accused of complacency. When I spoke a month ago I mentioned the fact that our people would have better Christmas dinners this year than last year, and dinners which would be more justified by the food position. For this I incurred a rebuke from the *Daily Herald*, which wrote, with a Spartan austerity which I trust the editorial staff will practice as well as preach, that we were "making war, not wassail." It is a poor heart that never rejoices; the House may rest assured that we shall not err on the side of over-indulgence. The building-up of reserves is continuous, and I trust that we shall not be blamed for stoking-up those fires of human energy and spirit upon which our victory in this long struggle depends.

Some months ago we were anxious about the coal position for this winter, and it still gives cause for concern. I am glad to say that, thanks to the exertions of the President of the Board of Trade and of the Secretary of the Mines Department, the situation is better than appeared likely a few months ago. Our stocks of coal are now between two and three million tons larger than they were a year ago and are far better distributed, and the men, who have responded most nobly to the appeal made, are working a longer week than before. There has been great concern on the part of some of the younger miners at not being allowed to go to the Army. We have had some very hard cases of young men who wished to go and serve in the Fighting Forces, and we all understand how they feel. But they can really best help the war effort at the moment by staying where they are, although at the same time, as things develop, we must endeavour to meet the wishes of individuals as far as possible in regard to the form of service they give. I know how tremendous was the contribution which the miners made in the last war, when we had the same difficulty in holding the men at the pits. What the position will be if this country becomes the scene of actual strife, I cannot tell, but I sympathize entirely with their feelings, and if we have to ask them to make the sacrifice, it is because of the vital necessity of coal to our whole production. Against this improved situation we have to bear in mind the steadily increasing demand which is coming as our war industries expand, and it is necessary that all efforts for the production of and economy in fuel should continue. There are good grounds for the belief that we shall come through the winter all right, and that, without having deranged our Army by withdrawing thousands of coal miners from their platoons, the regular process of our coal supply will be maintained.

There is nothing that Hitler will dislike more than my recital of these prosaic but unassailable facts. There is nothing that he and his Nazi régime dread more than the proof that we are capable of fighting a prolonged war, and the proof of the failure of their efforts to starve us into submission. In the various remarks which the Deputy-Fuhrer, Herr Hess, has let fall from time to time during his sojourn in our midst, nothing has been more clear than that Hitler relied upon the starvation attack more than upon invasion to bring us to our knees. His hopes were centred upon starvation, as his boasts have made the world aware. So far as 1941 at least is concerned, those hopes have been dashed to the ground. But this only increases his need to come at us by direct invasion as soon as he can screw up his courage and make his arrangements to take the plunge. Therefore, we must have everything working forward for the improved weather of the spring, so that we are well prepared to meet any scale of attack that can be directed upon us. Although we are infinitely stronger than we were a year ago, or even six months ago, yet at the same time the enemy has had ample time for preparations, and you may be sure that if an invasion of this country is attempted by the Germans, it will be upon a plan which has been thought out in every detail with their customary ruthlessness and thoroughness.

I now come, on what I hope is a fairly solid foundation, to the criticism of the Government. The Member for South-West Bethnal Green (Sir P. Harris) spoke of criticism as being the life-blood of democracy. Certainly we are a very full-blooded democracy. In war it is very hard to bring about successes and very easy to make mistakes or to point them out after they have been made. There was a custom in ancient China that anyone who wished to criticize the Government had the right to memorialize the Emperor, and, provided he followed that up by committing suicide, very great respect was paid to his words, and no ulterior motive was assigned. That seems to me to have been, from many points of view, a wise custom, but I certainly would be the last to suggest that it should be made retrospective. Our universal resolve to keep Parliamentary institutions in full activity amid the throes of war has been proved. That is a feat of enormous difficulty, never accomplished in any such complete perfection in history. His Majesty's Government base themselves upon the House of Commons. They look to the House for aid and comfort in the incalculable perils by which we are beset. They are entitled to seek from the House from time to time the formal renewal of their confidence.

The Debate on the Address furnishes the signal outstanding Parliamentary opportunity of the year. It is the Grand Inquest of the Nation. The passing of the Address in reply to the Gracious Speech without any Amendment is the proof to the nation and to the whole world that the King's Ministers enjoy the confidence of Parliament. This is essential to any Government in times of war, because any sign of division or any suspicion of weakness disheartens our friends and encourages our foes. We shall therefore give the fullest facilities to the Debate on the Address, either upon the general Debate or upon Amendment. I should like to point out to people outside this House, and to countries abroad which do not realize the flexibility and potency of our Parliamentary institutions, nor how they work, that any Amendment, however seductive, however misleading, however tendentious, however artful, however sober, or however wide, which the wit or other qualities of man may devise, can be placed upon the Paper and can be fully debated by the arrangement of calling particular Amendments. None shall be invidiously excluded. If a Division takes place, it is a matter of confidence, which, nevertheless, enables everyone to see exactly where we stand and how far we can call upon the loyalty of the House. If such an Amendment should be moved and pressed to a Division—I say this for the information of countries abroad—those who vote against the Government will not be assaulted with rubber truncheons, or put into concentration camps, or otherwise molested in their private lives. The worst that could happen might be that they might have to offer some rather laborious explanations to their constituents. Let it not be said that Parliamentary institutions are being maintained in this country in a farcical or unreal manner. We are fighting for Parliamentary institutions. We are endeavouring to keep their full practice and freedom, even in the stress of war.

In order that there may be no misunderstanding about the basis on which this Debate takes place, I must state that the Government stand united as a corporate body, as a band of men who have bound themselves to work together in special faith and loyalty. There can be no question of any individual Ministers being singled out, by intrigue or ill-will, or because of the exceptional difficulties of their tasks, and being hounded down, in any Government over which I have the honour to preside. From time to time the force of events makes changes necessary, but none are contemplated at the present moment. Neither do I consider it necessary to remodel the system of Cabinet government under which we are now working, nor to alter in any fundamental manner the system by which the conduct of the war proceeds, nor that by which the production of munitions is regulated and maintained.

The process of self-improvement is, of course, continuous, and every man and woman throughout the land, in office or out of office, in Parliament or in the cities and municipalities of our country—everyone, great and small, should try himself by his conscience every day, to make sure he is giving his utmost effort to the common cause. Making allowance for the increase of population, we have, in the 26th month of this war, reached, and in some ways surpassed, the deployment of national effort at home which after all the slaughter was not reached until the 48th month of the last war. We cannot rest content with that, and if Parliament, by patriotic and constructive counsel, and without unduly harassing those who bear the load, can stimulate and accelerate our further advance, the House of Commons will be playing its part, unyielding, persevering, indomitable, in the overthrow of another Continental tyranny as in the olden times.

A TRIBUTE TO THE JEWS

A MESSAGE TO THE "JEWISH CHRONICLE"
ON ITS CENTENARY
NOVEMBER 14, 1941

November 13.   *The United States Neutrality Act Revision Bill was passed by 18 votes. This measure freed the vast American merchant fleet to sail direct to Allied ports in the war zone under the protection of their warships. The House of Representatives was swung in favour of the Bill at the last hour by a message from President Roosevelt declaring that the defeat of the Bill would be a victory for Hitler.*

November 14.   *The Admiralty announced the aircraft carrier Ark Royal had sunk while on tow after being torpedoed. Only one of the crew of 1,600 was lost.*

President Roosevelt ordered the withdrawal of all U.S. marines from China.

Air raid deaths in Britain during October totalled 262.

[*November 14, 1941.*

ON the occasion of the centenary of *The Jewish Chronicle*, a landmark in the history of British Jewry, I send a message of good cheer to Jewish people in this and other lands. None has suffered more cruelly than the Jew the unspeakable evils wrought on the bodies and spirits of men by Hitler and his vile régime. The Jew bore the brunt of the Nazis' first onslaught upon the citadels of freedom and human dignity. He has borne and continued to bear a burden that might have seemed to be beyond endurance. He has not allowed it to break his spirit; he has never lost the will to resist. Assuredly in the day of victory the Jew's sufferings and his part in the struggle will not be forgotten. Once again, at the appointed time, he will see vindicated those principles of righteousness which it was the glory of his fathers to proclaim to the world. Once again it will be shown that, though the mills of God grind slowly, yet they grind exceeding small.

A FLAME OF FRENCH CULTURE

A MESSAGE TO "LA FRANCE LIBRE," THE FREE FRENCH
MONTHLY MAGAZINE PUBLISHED IN LONDON, ON THE
OCCASION OF ITS FIRST ANNIVERSARY NUMBER
NOVEMBER, 1941

[November, 1941.

F RENCH literature, which all the world of culture has known
and loved for centuries, to-day in France is twisted to serve
the enemies of France, who are trying to stifle and destroy French
thought, French culture, and French freedom. On the soil of
England *La France Libre* keeps the bright flame alive for that sure
coming day when all good Frenchmen will once again be free to
think and write the truth as they see it.

A PARLIAMENTARY PRECEDENT

A TRIBUTE TO CAPT. THE RT. HON. EDWARD ALGERNON FITZROY,
SPEAKER OF THE HOUSE OF COMMONS, ON THE OCCASION
OF HIS GOLDEN WEDDING
NOVEMBER 19, 1941

November 15.   *News that Admiral Sir Roger Keyes had relinquished a secret post revealed that he had been a director of Britain's "Commandos," the special shock troops.*

November 16.   *United States warships captured a German ship, the Odenwald, which was masquerading under the American flag.*

November 17.   *United States faced its gravest labour crisis when 55,000 miners went on strike.*

       Mr. Kurusu, special Japanese envoy, and Mr. Cordell Hull began conversations in Washington.

November 18.   *Big changes in the British Army High Command were announced: General Sir Alan Brooke succeeded General Sir John Dill as Chief of the Imperial General Staff, and Major-General Nye became Vice-Chief at the age of forty-five.*

November 19.   *It was revealed that the British offensive against Libya had been launched, and that there had been a penetration of fifty miles on a 130 miles front.*

[November 19, 1941.

I RISE to commit an irregularity, and I will venture to ask the indulgence of the House. The intervention which I make is without precedent, and the reason for that intervention is also without precedent, and the fact that the reason for my intervention is without precedent is the reason why I must ask for a precedent for my intervention.

We have searched the records of Parliament back, generation after generation, century after century, at any rate until we have reached the time of Mr. Speaker Rous in 1653, before which time the occupants of the Chair held their tenure for shorter and more precarious periods; and in all this long range of Parliamentary

298

history, there has been no occasion when a Speaker of the House of Commons has celebrated his golden wedding while occupying the Chair.

This unique event demands a procedure of its own, and I would like to assure you, Sir, that you are generally beloved throughout the House of Commons, and that this affection extends to your home and your family. I would like to assure you that we have in thirteen years gained complete confidence in your impartiality, in the firmness with which you vindicate and champion the rights of the House of Commons, in the fairness with which you protect minorities and their interventions in discussion, and in the kindliness and courtesy with which you treat all Members when they have access to you.

I know I shall be expressing the feeling of the whole House—all of them, everyone—when I say that we wish to share with you in this joyous event; and we desire that our expression shall be borne upon the records of the House and shall stand as a precedent for future times, should any such extraordinary but happy occurrence arise in the cycles of the future.

I must add that it has been arranged to make a presentation to you later to-day, and that my right hon. Friend the Member for Carnarvon Boroughs (Mr. Lloyd George), the Father of the House, will bring a considerable delegation to meet you. For the convenience of Members, it would be a good thing if our Debate could end a little earlier than usual so as to enable this ceremony to take place. I thank the House for having indulged me in this manner. I trust that my action may be condoned on account of the general unanimity in the sentiments which I have expressed.

THE ATTACK IN LIBYA

A STATEMENT TO THE HOUSE OF COMMONS
NOVEMBER 20, 1941

November 20. Communique from Cairo announced that British troops, seeking to link up with Tobruk, had reached to within ten miles of the perimeter defences of the city.

[*November 20, 1941.*

THE House will, I am sure, have been interested to learn from the Cairo communiqué that an offensive against the German and Italian armies on the Libyan front has begun. This offensive has been long and elaborately prepared, and we have waited for nearly five months in order that our Army might be well equipped with all those weapons which have made their mark in this new war. There is nothing in the world quite like the war conditions prevailing in the Libyan desert, in which swift and far-ranging movements are only possible by an extraordinary use of armour, air-power and mechanization. The conditions are in many respects like those of sea war. The principal units involved keep wireless silence while preparing or making their rapid and extensive movements. The encounter, when it is achieved, is like a clash of fleets or flotillas, and, as in a sea battle, all may be settled one way or the other in the course of perhaps two hours. If, in this case, the enemy armour is destroyed or seriously defeated, and his air-power is dominated, the plight of his infantry and artillery, crowded in the coastal regions, would evidently become serious in some respects.

The object of the British and Empire offensive is not so much the occupation of this or that locality as the destruction of the army, and primarily of the armoured forces, of the enemy. For this purpose the Army of the Western Desert took up its preliminary stations on a broad front from the sea to the Giaraut oasis, and all was in readiness by nightfall on the 17th. At dawn on the 18th the general advance began. Very heavy and exceptional rains hampered the movements of our forces, which had great distances to cover. These rains, however, appear to have been far heavier in the coastal regions than in the desert, and may well prove more harmful to the enemy than to us. During the 18th, our Armies came into contact with the enemy outposts at many points, and it seems certain that the enemy was taken completely by surprise. The Desert Army is now favourably situated for a trial of strength. I do not know, up to the present, whether this trial has actually begun, or taken place, between the heavy armoured forces, but evidently it cannot be long delayed. It is far too soon to indulge in any exultation. General Auchinleck and General Cunningham, in command, under him, of the Eighth Army, have made a brilliant and successful strategic approach and obtained positions of marked advantage. All now depends upon the battle which follows. It is evident that the next few days will see developments which will include many highly interesting features. One thing is certain, that all ranks of the British and Empire troops involved are animated by a long-pent-up and ardent desire to engage the enemy, and that they will fight with the utmost resolve and devotion, feeling as they all do that this is the first time we have met the Germans at least equally well-armed and equipped, and realizing the part which a British victory in Libya would play in the whole course of the war.

MAN-POWER AND WOMAN-POWER

A SPEECH TO THE HOUSE OF COMMONS
DECEMBER 2, 1941

(Note: The Resolution moved by the Prime Minister in this speech was carried by 326 votes to 10 after an amendment had been defeated by 336 to 40.)

November 21. Great Libyan battle at its height, with determined British effort to break through to Tobruk.

November 22. In Libya, Tobruk garrison turned to the offensive in attempt to link up with advanced units of British attack from the south.

    In Russia, the Germans claimed to have entered Rostov.

November 24. Infantry battle developed in Libya alongside main tank encounter at Sidi Rezegh.

November 26. Germans tried a diversion in Libyan campaign by sending a column over the Egyptian frontier. It was heavily attacked and lost many of its tanks.

November 27. After bitter and confused fighting, advanced British forces from the south linked up with Tobruk defenders, thus ending 33 weeks' siege and barring German retreat to the west.

    Allied troops took Gondar, last Italian post in East Africa.

November 29. Russians recaptured Rostov, thus relieving danger to Caucasus.

    Admiralty announced that eight German supply ships had been sunk in the Arctic on their way to the Murmansk front.

November 30. Germans, in flight from Rostov, were pursued towards Taganrog.

December 2. General Rommel, German leader in Libya, concentrated his armoured forces, broke through the British corridor to Tobruk, and recaptured Sidi Rezegh.

[December 2, 1941.

I BEG to move:—
  "That, in the opinion of this House, for the purpose of securing the maximum national effort in the conduct of the war and in production, the obligation for National Service should be extended to include the resources of woman-power and man-power still available; and that the necessary legislation should be brought in forthwith."

We have to call upon the nation for a further degree of sacrifice and exertion. The year 1941 has seen the major problems of creating war production capacity and manufacturing equipment largely solved or on the high road to solution. The crisis of equipment is largely over, and an ever-broadening flow is now assured. The crisis of man-power and woman-power is at hand, and will dominate the year 1942. This crisis comes upon us for the following reasons: The great supply plants have largely been constructed; they are finished; they must be staffed, and they must be fully staffed. We must maintain the powerful mobile army we have created with so much pains both for Home Defence and Foreign Expedition. We must maintain our armies in the East, and be prepared for a continuance and an extension of heavy fighting there. We must provide for the expansion of the Air Force in 1942 and the far greater expansion which it will take in 1943. We must face a continuous growth of the Navy to man the great numbers of warships of all kinds coming steadily into service. We must provide modern equipment for the large armies which are being raised and trained in India.

Apart from our own needs, we must keep our engagements to send a substantial supply of tanks, aeroplanes and other war weapons or war commodities to Russia in order to help make good the loss of munition-making capacity which Russia has sustained by the German invasion. We have had also to forgo very important supplies we had expected from the United States, but which have now, with our consent, been diverted to Russia. We have also to recognize that United States production is only now getting fully under way and that the quotas we had expected will in many respects be retarded. This is only too often the case in munitions production. The House will remember how I have several times described to them in the last five or six years the time-table of munitions production. First year, nothing at all; second year, very little; third year, quite a lot; fourth year, all you want. We are at the beginning of the third year. The United States is getting through the second year. Germany started the war already well into the fourth year. If one does not prepare before a war, one has to prepare after, and be very thankful if time is given. But all this disparity of proportion will rectify itself in the passage of time. All comes even at the end of the day, and all will come out yet more even when all the days are ended.

We have been hitherto at a disadvantage in having to fight a well-armed enemy with ill-armed or half-armed troops. That phase is over, and in the future the Hun will feel in his own person the sharpness of the weapons with which he has subjugated an unprepared, disorganized Europe, and imagined he was about to subjugate the world. In the future our men will fight on equal terms in technical equipment, and a little later on they will fight on superior terms. We have to make arrangements for all this, and we have to make them in good time. A heavy burden will fall upon us in 1942. We must not be found unequal to it. We shall not be found unequal to it.

It has not been necessary, nor would it indeed have been helpful, to make the demands upon the nation which I am about to set forth until now. These demands will intimately affect the lives of many men and women. They will also affect the life of the nation in the following way. There will be a further very definite curtailment of the amenities we have hitherto been able to preserve. These demands will not affect physical health or that contentment of spirit that comes from serving great causes, but they will make further inroads upon the comfort and convenience of very large numbers and upon the character and aspect of our daily life. Much has already been done. Luxury trades have been virtually abolished by cutting off raw materials. The compulsory concentration of industry has reduced labour used in making up what is left. This is passing away rapidly. It must not be supposed that there are large reserves of idle people leading a leisurely existence who can now be called to the national ranks. The entire adult British race, with very few exceptions, gets up in the morning, works all day, and goes to bed tired out at night. In our form of society people have been accustomed to find their own jobs to a very large extent, thus saving vast Government machinery. If all the efforts of everyone were really devoted solely to making war, there would be no food or fuel, no transport or clothes. We have to recognize the fact that a very large proportion of the population, particularly women, is occupied in ministering to the needs of the more actively engaged population, and that that number has increased since the last war with the increase of the population which has to be ministered to. The process which has been continuously applied, and which is now to be applied much more vigorously, is not the calling of idle people to work, but the sharpening and shifting forward of a proportion of the effort of the workers into work which is more directly related to the war. It is a general moving-up nearer the front which will affect a large block of the people. What we have to make is a definitely harder turn of the screw. I promised eighteen months ago "blood, tears, toil and sweat." There has not yet been, thank God, so much blood as was expected. There have not been so many tears. But here we have another instalment of toil and sweat, of inconvenience and self-denial, which I am sure will be accepted with cheerful and proud alacrity by all parties and all classes in the British nation.

The severity of what is required must not be underrated. The population of Great Britain to-day is about 46,750,000. Of this, 33,250,000—16,000,000 men and 17,250,000 women—are between 14 and 65 years of age. Making allowance for the increase of population which I have just referred to, we have already reached, in the 27th month of this war, the same employment of women in industry, the Services and the Forces as in the 48th month of the last war. The munition industries in Great Britain have increased in the first two years of this war more rapidly than in four years of the last war. We have a million more men in munitions industries at this moment than we had at the end of the last war. What we have now to do is something more than that. I am not at all disguising the seriousness of the proposals which I submit to the House of Commons. On the other hand, it must also be remembered that the changes in our life which will take place, although severe, will not be violent or abrupt. They will be gradual, and gradually increasing in intensity. I propose to give to-day only the broad outlines and the principal features of the changes which we now propose. My right hon. Friend the Minister of Labour and National Service, who has devoted an immense amount of time to the proposals which are now put forward, and has been assisted in his task by very strong Cabinet Committees and by repeated conferences on every aspect, will, in winding up the Debate on the next Sitting Day, expound the policy in more detail and also reply to any points which may be raised to-day. I am not attempting in my speech to state with precision the legal form of the new obligations. There are many verbal refinements, for example, as between Forces and Services, which would be necessary in a Bill or a Defence Regulation. My words are intended to convey the general aspect and prospect to the House. Still, I imagine that what I shall say is pretty nearly related to the actual facts. But I cannot cover every detail without preventing the House from seeing the picture as a whole.

I deal first with men. There will be three important changes affecting males. Hitherto reservation from military service has been by occupational blocks. It is now proposed to change over gradually from this system of block reservation to a system of individual deferment. The method of block reservation under the Schedule of Reserved Occupations was a sufficiently good and flexible instrument so long as there was not an acute shortage of man-power. It avoided the waste of ardent men with highly specialized attainments which so disastrously characterized the opening years of the last war. There has been a very careful and steady husbanding of those who possessed specialized attainments of every kind, either in knowledge or in skill. The system of block reservation has already been modified by introducing protected work, which provides a rough test of the importance to the war effort of the work upon which the persons in particular shops were engaged; that is to say, a factory could be given protection, which meant that it was so directly connected with the war effort that its personnel would not be called up until a somewhat later age than in the non-protected factory. This refinement upon the system of block reservation by trades is already in force. The situation now demands that there should be a further refinement, so that men should no longer be reserved by virtue of their occupation, but that the sole test should be the importance to the war effort of the work upon which they are engaged. For instance, a carpenter may be doing work of direct importance to an aeroplane or to a ship, but he may also be making a piece of furniture. It is clear that at the point which we have now reached there must be a discrimination. The test will always be the relation to the war effort.

How is this transition to be accomplished? We propose to raise the age of reservation by one-year steps at monthly intervals, commencing on 1st January, 1942. That is to say, every month the reserved age will rise by one year, thus bringing a new quota into the area of those more searching, individual, detailed examinations. In this process individual deferment will be granted only to men engaged on work of national importance. Services such as the Merchant Navy and Civil Defence will, of course, be excluded from this scheme. Special arrangements will also be made for certain industries where particular problems arise, for instance, the mining and agricultural industries, and the building industry

306

with its special system of allocation, although I must say that we look to a very considerable reduction in the building industry as the great works and plants come gradually to completion.

To cope with all these new complications, the existing defer-ment machinery of the Ministry of Labour will be developed by a further decentralization of 45 districts and the setting-up of 45 District Boards. In order that these District Board may, with full knowledge, be able to give decisions, the object held in view will be twofold; first, to transfer men from less essential work to work of greater importance in the war effort, and secondly to obtain men to keep up the Armed Forces. Men in the munitions and other vital war industries and services who become de-reserved under the new scheme and in respect of whom deferment is not granted will, in general, be recognized as available for transfer to work of higher priority in those same industries, and a redistribu-tion of labour within the munitions and other essential industries will be secured. This will, of course, affect only a fraction, but a very important fraction. Men in other industries, not war indus-tries, not granted deferment, will be called up to the Forces. I am trying to keep the munitions industries clear of the new re-quirements of the Armed Forces, as far as possible. Those not granted deferment will of course retain their individual rights under the National Service Act concerning conscientious objection, post-ponement of calling-up on account of exceptional hardship, and other mitigations. They will have the full protection and rights which are enjoyed by those called up by the National Service Act.

The second great change affecting men is the raising of the age for compulsory military service from 41 to 51. Men called up over the age of 41 will not be posted for the more active duties with the Forces. They will be used either for static or sedentary duties to liberate younger men. It is not intended to call upon anybody to do tasks for which he is physically unfitted, but there are a great many tasks in the modern armed forces which can be discharged by men whom one would not expect to march with the troops. Very large numbers have volunteered already. The new-comers over 41 will all set free fighting men already in the Services for active mobile jobs. In other cases men between 41 and 51 will be directed into non-military tasks more closely concerned with the war effort than those which they are now discharging.

In raising the age of legal obligation from 41 to 51, we bring under review nearly 2,750,000 more men, the vast majority of whom are already in useful employment, but a portion of whom will now where necessary be moved forward into more direct forms of war effort. We may later have to advance another decade; in the last war, we went to 57. It is not necessary, however, to do this at the present time, because mercifully the slaughter has so far been much less. Of course, as you mount the age groups the effective field even for indirect war purposes diminishes very rapidly, and it is more than ever desirable in these advanced groups to leave persons belonging to them in those useful occupations, which they have so often naturally found for themselves. At the point we have reached in mobilizing the national war effort, the avoidance of needless friction and disturbance becomes an increasingly important matter. Although you may say that by shifting A and B from this job to that, you will get some improvement in the more direct war effort, unless it is a very marked improvement, the friction may rob you on the one hand of what you gain on the other. We must endeavour to administer the whole of this process with very great care and discrimination in the public interest, and with the sole object of bringing the utmost volume of war effort out of this vast and varied community.

The third change is in the direction of youth. It is proposed to lower the age of military service to 18½, thus bringing in an addition of 70,000 recruits to the armed forces during the year 1942. I must explain that the wastage from the Army, apart from battle casualties, is very considerable. It has been greatly reduced now that instead of moving men out of the Army when they are not fit as marching troops, they are moved into those same sedentary occupations that I have been mentioning. But the wastage is still very considerable, and has to be made good; and the first half of the 1923 class—I said it would bring in 70,000 recruits in the year 1942—will be registered on Saturday, 13th December, and their calling-up will commence in January, 1942. The second half of the 1923 class will be registered early in the New Year. Assurances were given to Parliament that no one brought into the Army under the National Service Act would be sent abroad younger than 20. This did not apply, I may point out, and has not in practice applied, either to the Navy or to the Air Force or to the many volunteers who have joined the Army, and there is no reason why it should apply to the Army above the age of 19. In case particular units have to be sent abroad at short notice, one does not want to pull perfectly fit young men of 19 and upwards out of their sections and platoons, and they themselves would be very much offended if they were to be so treated and if they had to see all their comrades going away while they were left, as if they were unfit, on the shore. It is not thought that any large use is likely to be made of this power in the near future, but none the less we ask the House to release us from this restrictive pledge.

I must now speak about the Home Guard. It is our great prop and stand-by against invasion, and particularly that form of invasion by air-borne troops carried in gliders or crashable aircraft. To-day we have nearly 1,700,000 men, the bulk of them well-armed, spread about the whole country. I say that the bulk of them are well-armed. Although we have a good many million rifles in this country, we have not got rifles for all. We have several million men who will fight to the death if this country is invaded, but for whom we have not been able to manufacture the necessary number of rifles, although our rifles are now numbered by a good many millions. Therefore we supplement them with machine-guns, tommy-guns, pistols, grenades and bombs, and, when other things fail, we do not hesitate to place in the citizen's hands a pike or a mace, pending further developments. After all, a man thus armed may easily acquire a rifle for himself. At any rate that is what they are doing in Russia in defending their country. Although they have vast supplies of rifles, they are fighting with everything, and that is what we shall certainly do, if we are assailed in our Island.

The Home Guard is therefore, as I say, the great prop and stand-by against invasion. Because of its being spread out all over the country, it is particularly adapted to meet an air-borne descent. In the summer of last year we were an unarmed people, except for the few regular troops we had. Now, wherever he comes down, the parachutist comes down into a hornet's nest, as he will find. The Home Guard was formed and founded in the passionate emotion of the summer of 1940. It has become a most powerful trained uniformed body, which plays a vital part in our national defence. We must make sure that this great bulwark of our safety does not deteriorate during the inevitably prolonged and indefinite waiting period through which we have to pass or may have to pass. Power must now be taken by Statute to direct men into the Home Guard in areas where it is necessary, and to require them to attend the drills and musters indispensable to the maintenance of efficiency. Liability for service in the Home Guard will be defined by Regulation. We do not propose to exercise this power until that Regulation has been subject to a special discussion in the House of Commons, apart altogether from the discussions of this Bill. I do not want to delay the passage of the Bill when it comes on next week by a too-detailed argument on that point. We will have a separate day for it at a later period.

There is another great change which applies to both boys and girls. It is proposed to register both boys and girls between the ages of 16 and 18. This will be done by Defence Regulations. We must be particularly careful that our boys do not run loose during this time of stress. Their education, their well-being, their discipline, and the service they can render must all be carefully supervised. All boys and girls in these age groups will be registered and subsequently interviewed under arrangements made by the Youth Committees of the education authorities, who will thus be able to establish and maintain direct contact with all of them. We have to think of the citizens of the future as well as of the business of carrying on the defence of the country. Those who are not already members of some organization or doing useful work of some kind, will be encouraged to join one or other of the organizations through which they can obtain the training required to fit them for National Service. There are fine opportunities for helping in the war open to strong, lively boys of 16 to 18. They can serve in the various Youth organizations, such as the Cadets and the Junior Training Corps, the Air Training Corps, the Sea Cadets, and in voluntary organizations on the civil side. Boys of 17 may already join the Home Guard, and we hope to be able to use some of the 16 year class—like the "powder monkeys" in Nelson's day —in areas where the Home Guard will be entrusted with anti-aircraft and coast defence duties. However, in all these fields the well-being and training of the boys will be the prime consideration.

We do not propose at the present time to extend compulsion to join the Services to any married women, not even childless married women. They may of course volunteer, but they will not be compelled. As regards married women and industry, we have already the power to direct married women into industry. This power will continue to be used with discretion. The wife of a man serving in the Forces or the Merchant Navy will not be called upon to work away from her home area; nor will women with household responsibilities be moved from their home area. But there are some married women without children or other household responsibilities whom we may have to call upon to go to another area where their industrial services are needed. Women are already playing a great part in this war, but they must play a still greater part. The technical apparatus of modern warfare gives extraordinary opportunities to women. These opportunities must be fully used, and here again the movement must be towards the harder forms of service and nearer to the fighting line. All women over eighteen are already liable to be directed by the Ministry of Labour and National Service into industry, but we have not the power at present, according to our reading of the law, to require

310

women to serve in the uniformed Forces of the Crown or in Civil Defence. We propose to ask Parliament to confer that power upon us. We seek it and take it, subject of course to the rule that all affected will have exactly the same rights and safeguards as men subject to compulsory military service. The new power will be applied in the first instance, and probably for some time to come, only to unmarried women between the ages of 20 and 30. The power is general, but the new powers will be applied only to the age group between 20 and 30. The number in this class is 1,620,000. Of course the vast majority of them are already usefully employed, and only perhaps a quarter or one-third will be affected and will be required to exchange their present employment for one more effective in the war effort. Those so required will have the option to choose, first, the Auxiliary Forces, secondly, Civil Defence, and, thirdly, such industrial work as may be specified by the Ministry of Labour as requiring workers. This work comprises primarily filling factories and also a certain number of factories in places where it is difficult to obtain the necessary woman labour by the ordinary processes; also certain other bottlenecks and industries where there is a need for exceptionally speedy reinforcement. Those women who choose to join the Auxiliary Forces will not be free to decide which force they join. The Wrens and the Waafs, to use terms which have passed into the commonplace of our daily speech, both have waiting lists, and although the increasing requirements of the W.A.A.F. may at a later date outstrip their waiting lists, it is to the A.T.S. that this special movement of young women must be directed.

Why is it that we have to make this demand on women for the Army? Here I will make a digression. Two vultures hang over us, and will hang over us until the end of the war. We do not fear them, but we must be constantly prepared against them. The first is Invasion, which may never come, but which will only be held off by our having large, well-trained, mobile forces and many other preparations in a constant high state of readiness, which has to go on month after month at the same pitch. Moreover, if we are to use the striking forces overseas at any period in the war, we must be sure that those that remain at home are of sufficient strength, because upon this Island the whole fortune and fate of the world depend. Here is a case where the saying, "Better to be sure than sorry" deserves a larger measure of respect than it usually does in war. We do not want the horrors which are perpetrated by the Germans wherever they go in so many countries to be thrust upon us here, to the utter ruin not only of ourselves but of the world cause. It is absolutely necessary that not only the armies in the East should be maintained and reinforced continually, but that we should constantly stand in this Island with a very powerful and perfectly-equipped Army ready to leap at the throat of any invader who might obtain a lodgement from the sea or the air. Anyone can see that to maintain this readiness over a long and indefinite period is a great burden and strain as well as a first charge upon our military effort, and, in order to do our full duty in the war, we must always be trying to discharge that task with the highest economy of man-power, drawing as little from munitions as necessary and keeping as few people as possible in sedentary or static situations if they are capable of acting with the mobile forces. That is the process we are applying—exactly the same process in the military forces as in industry—a move-on to a more active form of employment.

What is the other vulture for whom we must be ready It is our old acquaintance the Air Raider, whom we already know so well. We have had a very easy time for the last six months, because the enemy has been occupied in Russia, but at any time Hitler may recognize his defeat by the Russian armies and endeavour to cover his disaster in the East by wreaking his baffled fury upon us. We are all ready for him and will receive him when he comes, by day or night, with far greater forces and every modern improvement. But we have always to be ready. Great quantities of anti-aircraft equipment are now coming out of the factories. Behind them are the rangefinders and predictors and a host of elaborate appliances of a highly delicate and highly secret character which it is not necessary to specify. Besides these there are the searchlights and balloons, to which many new adaptations and complications are attached. We cannot afford to keep so many scores of thousands of trained soldiers, many of whom are fit for mobile field forces, standing about at these static defences. We must reduce the number in order to keep the field armies up to strength and to prevent our having to draw upon the munition factories for the maintenance of the field armies. This great Service called A.D.G.B., Air Defence of Great Britain, must yield a substantial proportion of its man-power to the field troops and mobile anti-aircraft artillery. Just at the time when it is receiving larger numbers of guns for which it has waited long, it has not only to manage to use these guns and bring them into service, but it has also to yield up a large proportion of the man-power it has. I must say that it has adapted itself to the task with great skill and ingenuity. It happens that all these new appliances, which so vastly increase the power of anti-aircraft artillery, require no great physical strength to handle. They are appliances which trained women can handle just as well as men, and every woman who serves in the Air Defence not only renders a high service herself, but releases a man—actually four-fifths of a man—for the active troops.

Over 170,000 women are needed for the A.T.S., and of these over 100,000 are required for the Air Defence forces. The mixed batteries which have been already formed have been a great success. They have been several times in action. There are more women than men in these establishments, which are as healthy, happy and honourable a community as anyone has ever seen.

We are asking the House to give us compulsory powers to call up single women. We propose to apply these powers to women between 20 and 30. We do not propose, when once they have joined the A.T.S., to compel them to serve in the lethal or combatant branches. Women will have the right to volunteer, but no women in the A.T.S. will be compelled to go to the batteries. It is a matter of quality of temperament, of feeling capable of doing this form of duty, which every woman must judge for herself, and not one in which compulsion should be used. I want to make it clear that a woman may be compelled to join the A.T.S., but only volunteers from within the A.T.S. will be allowed to serve with the guns. I have no doubt we shall get the response which is required.

As I stated earlier, we do no propose to extend compulsion to join the Services or Forces to any married woman at the present time. Nevertheless, it is in this great field of married women or women doing necessary household work, comprising about 11,000,000 persons, that we see our largest reserves for industry and home defence for the future. The part-time employment of women in industry has already been developed, but on nothing like the scale which must be reached in the months which lie before us. This is a matter to which employers would be wise to give their immediate attention. They should consider whether and to what extent they can adapt their businesses, particularly smaller businesses and industries, to a part-time system. An immense variety of arrangements are possible to enable women to divide up domestic tasks and then be free to work close at hand in the factory or the field. The treatment of this problem must be flexible. In some cases women will arrange to "Box and Cox." In others a group of five or more may arrange for each to cook a day in turn, or again the development of creches and public nurseries or combined nurseries may free, or partially free, mothers of families from domestic duties. Whenever practicable, work will be brought as near to the homes as possible. Some further spreading of components may be possible, which I need not refer to in detail. The whole of this process needs to be developed with the greatest energy and contrivance, and Government Departments here and in the provinces must take a share. I am very anxious that the smooth running of the great Departments, upon which so much of our life and war effort depends, should not be upset by pulling people out of the routine to which they have become accustomed. Nevertheless, a substantial contribution will have to be made from the young unmarried women in the 20 to 30 group by the public Departments.

Such are the new burdens which the hard course of our fortunes compels us to invite the nation to assume. Nothing less than these will suffice at the present time, and even more may be required by the ordeals of the future. We shall welcome Parliamentary discussion and the focusing of public opinion upon the details of a measure so intimately affecting the homes of our country. We desire to fit the knapsack with its extra load upon the national shoulders in the least galling and most effective manner. The aid of the House is required in this process, but that the load must be picked up now, and carried on henceforward to the end, embodies, we are sure, the resolve of the British people.

WAR WITH JAPAN

A SPEECH DELIVERED FIRST TO THE HOUSE OF COMMONS
AND THEN BROADCAST
DECEMBER 8, 1941

December 3. Libya armies paused to re-fit for the next stage of the battle.

In Russia, the main German army in the south retreated towards Mariupol.

December 4. Russians recaptured Taganrog and also beat off German attacks in the Moscow sector.

December 5. Britain declared war on Finland, Rumania and Hungary, the Axis partners.

December 6. President Roosevelt sent a personal note to the Emperor of Japan on the Far Eastern crisis. Reports were received of heavy Japanese troop concentrations in Indo-China.

December 7. Japan declared war on Great Britain and the United States. Japanese planes bombed the U.S. naval base at Pearl Harbour, Hawaii, sank a battleship and a destroyer, and wrecked many planes on the ground. Casualties in this raid totalled about 3000. Japanese troops invaded Thailand, made landings in Malaya and the Philippines, and seized the Shanghai International Settlement.

December 8. Great Britain and the United States declared war on Japan. Mr. Churchill spoke to a hurriedly summoned House of Commons, and afterwards repeated his speech in a broadcast to the world. The House of Commons unanimously endorsed the Cabinet's action in declaring war. President Roosevelt delivered a personal message to Congress calling for a declaration of war in consequence of the "unprovoked and dastardly attack" made by the Japanese. The Senate approved the declaration of war by 82 votes to none, and the House of Representatives by 388 votes to one.

[December 8, 1941.

A S soon as I heard, last night, that Japan had attacked the United States, I felt it necessary that Parliament should be immediately summoned. It is indispensable to our system of government that Parliament should play its full part in all the important acts of State and at all the crucial moments of the war; and I am glad to see that so many Members have been able to be in their places, despite the shortness of the notice. With the full approval of the nation, and of the Empire, I pledged the word of Great Britain, about a month ago, that should the United States be involved in war with Japan, a British declaration of war would follow within the hour. I therefore spoke to President Roosevelt on the Atlantic telephone last night, with a view to arranging the timing of our respective declarations. The President told me that he would this morning send a Message to Congress, which, of course, as is well known, can alone make a declaration of war on behalf of the United States, and I then assured him that we would follow immediately.

However, it soon appeared that British territory in Malaya had also been the object of Japanese attack, and later on it was announced from Tokyo that the Japanese High Command—a curious form; not the Imperial Japanese Government—had declared that a state of war existed with Great Britain and the United States. That being so, there was no need to wait for the declaration by Congress. American time is very nearly six hours behind ours. The Cabinet, therefore, which met at 12.30 to-day, authorized an immediate declaration of war upon Japan. Instructions were sent to His Majesty's Ambassador at Tokyo, and a communication was dispatched to the Japanese Chargé d'Affaires at 1 o'clock to-day to this effect:

Foreign Office, December 8th.

Sir,

On the evening of December 7th His Majesty's Government in the United Kingdom learned that Japanese forces, without previous warning, either in the form of a declaration of war or of an ultimatum with a conditional declaration of war, had attempted a landing on the coast of Malaya and bombed Singapore and Hong Kong.

In view of these wanton acts of unprovoked aggression, committed in flagrant violation of International Law, and particularly of Article 1 of the Third Hague Convention, relative to the opening of hostilities, to which both Japan and the United Kingdom

316

are parties, His Majesty's Ambassador at Tokyo has been instructed to inform the Imperial Japanese Government, in the name of His Majesty's Government in the United Kingdom, that a state of war exists between the two countries.

I have the honour to be, with high consideration,

Sir,

Your obedient servant,

Winston S. Churchill,

Meanwhile hostilities had already begun. The Japanese began a landing in British territory in Northern Malaya at about 6 o'clock —1 a.m. local time—yesterday, and they were immediately engaged by our Forces, which were in readiness. The Home Office measures against Japanese nationals were set in motion at 10.45 last night. The House will see, therefore, that no time has been lost, and that we are actually ahead of our engagements.

The Royal Netherlands Government at once marked their solidarity with Great Britain and the United States at 3 o'clock in the morning.

The Netherlands Minister informed the Foreign Office that his Government were telling the Japanese Government that, in view of the hostile acts perpetrated by Japanese forces against two Powers with whom the Netherlands maintained particularly close relations, they considered that, as a consequence, a state of war now existed between the Kingdom of the Netherlands and Japan.

I do not yet know what part Siam, or Thailand, will be called upon to play in this fresh war, but a report has reached us that the Japanese have landed troops at Singora, which is in Siamese territory, on the frontier of Malaya, not far from the landing they made on the British side of the frontier.

Meanwhile, just before Japan had gone to war, I had sent the Siamese Prime Minister the following message. It was sent off on Sunday, early in the morning:

"There is a possibility of imminent Japanese invasion of your country. If you are attacked, defend yourself. The preservation of the full independence and sovereignty of Thailand is a British interest, and we shall regard an attack on you as an attack on ourselves."

It is worth while looking for a moment at the manner in which the Japanese have begun their assault upon the English-speaking world. Every circumstance of calculated and characteristic Japanese treachery was employed against the United States. The Japanese envoys, Nomura and Kurusu, were ordered to prolong

317

their mission in the United States, in order to keep the conversations going while a surprise attack was being prepared, to be made before a declaration of war could be delivered. The President's appeal to the Emperor, which I have no doubt many Members will have read—it has been published largely in the papers here—reminding him of their ancient friendship and of the importance of preserving the peace of the Pacific, has received only this base and brutal reply. No one can doubt that every effort to bring about a peaceful solution had been made by the Government of the United States, and that immense patience and composure had been shown in face of the growing Japanese menace.

Now that the issue is joined in the most direct manner, it only remains for the two great democracies to face their task with whatever strength God may give them. We must hold ourselves very fortunate, and I think we may rate our affairs not wholly ill-guided, that we were not attacked alone by Japan in our period of weakness after Dunkirk, or at any time in 1940, before the United States had fully realized the dangers which threatened the whole world and had made much advance in its military preparation. So precarious and narrow was the margin upon which we then lived that we did not dare to express the sympathy which we have all along felt for the heroic people of China. We were even forced for a short time, in the summer of 1940, to agree to closing the Burma Road. But later on, at the beginning of this year, as soon as we could regather our strength, we reversed that policy, and the House will remember that both I and the Foreign Secretary have felt able to make increasingly outspoken declarations of friendship for the Chinese people and their great leader, General Chiang-Kai-Shek.

We have always been friends. Last night I cabled to the Generalissimo assuring him that henceforward we would face the common foe together. Although the imperative demands of the war in Europe and in Africa have strained our resources, vast and growing though they are, the House and the Empire will notice that some of the finest ships in the Royal Navy have reached their stations in the Far East at a very convenient moment. Every preparation in our power has been made, and I do not doubt that we shall give a good account of ourselves. The closest accord has been established with the powerful American forces, both naval and air, and also with the strong, efficient forces belonging to the Royal Netherlands Government in the Netherlands East Indies. We shall all do our best. When we think of the insane ambition and insatiable appetite which have caused this vast and melancholy extension of the war, we can only feel that Hitler's madness has infected the Japanese mind, and that the root of the evil and its branch must be extirpated together.

It is of the highest importance that there should be no under-rating of the gravity of the new dangers we have to meet, either here or in the United States. The enemy has attacked with an audacity which may spring from recklessness, but which may also spring from a conviction of strength. The ordeal to which the English-speaking world and our heroic Russian Allies are being exposed will certainly be hard, especially at the outset, and will probably be long, yet when we look around us over the sombre panorama of the world, we have no reason to doubt the justice of our cause or that our strength and will-power will be sufficient to sustain it. We have at least four-fifths of the population of the globe upon our side.

We are responsible for their safety and for their future. In the past we have had a light which flickered, in the present we have a light which flames, and in the future there will be a light which shines over all the land and sea.

Mr. Churchill repeated this speech on the radio the same evening, and added this appeal to munition workers:

It is particularly necessary that all munition workers and those engaged in war industries should make a further effort proportionate to the magnitude of our perils and the magnitude of our cause. Particularly does this apply to tanks and, above all, to aircraft. Aircraft will be more than ever necessary now that the war has spread over so many wide spaces of the earth. I appeal to all those in the factories to do their utmost to make sure that we make an extra contribution to the general resources of the great alliance of free peoples that has been hammered and forged into strength amidst the fire of war.

THE LOSS OF H.M.S. *PRINCE OF WALES* AND *REPULSE*

A STATEMENT TO THE HOUSE OF COMMONS
DECEMBER 10, 1941

December 9. President Roosevelt announced that the United States had suffered a serious setback in Hawaii. He ordered all Germans and Italians in America to be classed as enemy aliens.

Russians announced recapture of Tikhvin, southeast of Leningrad.

December 10. Japanese planes sank H.M.S. Prince of Wales and H.M.S. Repulse off Malaya, and their troops occupied Kota Bharu airport. Landings were also made in the Philippines.

December 10, 1941.

I HAVE bad news for the House which I think I should pass on to them at the earliest moment. A report has been received from Singapore that H.M.S. *Prince of Wales* and H.M.S. *Repulse* have been sunk while carrying out operations against the Japanese in their attack on Malaya. No details are yet available except those contained in the Japanese official communiqué, which claims that both ships were sunk by air attack.

I may add that at the next sitting of the House I shall take occasion to make a short statement on the general war situation, which has from many points of view, both favourable and adverse, undergone important changes in the last few days.

WAR SITUATION

A SPEECH TO THE HOUSE OF COMMONS
DECEMBER 11, 1941

December 11. Germany and Italy declared war on the United States of America, who immediately accepted the challenge.

December 11, 1941.

A GREAT many things of far-reaching and fundamental importance have happened in the last few weeks. Most of them have happened in the last few days, and I think it opportune to give the House the best account I can of where we stand and how we are.

I will begin with the Battle of Libya. A lot of people in easy positions have been very much down upon the Military Spokesman in Cairo. They accuse him of having taken unduly favourable views of our position at different times. I am not going to apologize for the Military Spokesman at Cairo. I have read every day the statements he has made, and I have also read all the reports which come continually from the front. I think the Military Spokesman in Cairo has been pretty well justified in what he has said, having regard to how things stood, or seemed to stand, at each moment when he said it. Of course, it is quite a difficult thing to have a Military Spokesman at all. It would be much more convenient to the military Commander to remain quite silent. But then it is said, "Are we to know nothing of what is going on? Is it to be kept to a small secret circle? Is nothing to be told to the public, is nothing to be told to the Empire, is nothing to be told to the Army?" Remember, there is a very great army in the Middle East. Only a small part of it is able to fight in this Battle of Libya, but all are watching with very great interest what occurs. I do not think that you could go on the basis of fighting for three weeks or a month with no information being given by our side except in very guarded communiqués, and the only stories being told coming out from the enemy, who are not always entirely truthful in their accounts. Therefore, I am in favour of the Military Spokesman in Cairo, and I think he has discharged an extremely difficult task wisely and well. Also, if anybody based their hopes on what he said, that man would find to-day that he has not been misled. There might be ups and downs, there might be disappointments, there would certainly be the ebb and flow of battle, but, in the main, news founded upon the daily output of the Military Spokesman would be found to be thoroughly in accordance with where we are at the present time.

It must be remembered that although here at Westminster, and in Fleet Street, it has been sought to establish the rule that nothing must be said about the war and its prospects which is not thoroughly discouraging, and although I must admit that the British public seem to like their food cooked that way, the Military Spokesman, addressing a large Army, might do more harm than good if he always put things at their worst and never allowed buoyancy, hope, confidence and resolve to infect his declarations. There ought to be a fair recognition of the difficulties of a task of that kind. This defence also applies to the admirable official communiqués which have been issued by General Auchinleck's headquarters, which have given a very informing and effective picture of the confused struggle which has been proceeding.

The Libyan offensive did not take the course which its authors expected, though it will reach the end at which they aimed. Very few set-piece battles that have to be prepared over a long period of time work out in the way they are planned and imagined beforehand. The unexpected intervenes at every stage. The will-power of the enemy impinges itself upon the prescribed or hoped-for course of events. Victory is traditionally elusive. Accidents happen. Mistakes are made. Sometimes right things turn out wrong, and quite often wrong things turn out right. War is very difficult, especially to those who are taking part in it or conducting it. Still, when all is said and done, on 18th November General Auchinleck set out to destroy the entire armed forces of the Germans and Italians in Cyrenaica, and now, on 11th December, I am bound to say that it seems very probable he will do so. The picture that was made by the Commanders beforehand was of a much more rapid battle that has actually taken place. They had the idea which I expressed to the House, that the whole German armoured forces would be encountered by our armour in a mass at the outset, and that the battle would be decided one way or the other in a few hours. This might have been the best chance for the enemy. However, the sudden surprise and success of our advance prevented any such main trial of strength between the armoured forces. Almost at the first bound we reached right up to Sidi Rezegh, dividing the enemy's armoured forces and throwing them into confusion. In consequence of this, a very large number of fierce detached actions took place over an immense space of desert country, and the battle, though equally intense, became both dispersed and protracted. It became a wide-spread and confused battle of extremely high-class combatants, mounted upon mechanized transport and fighting in barren lands with the utmost vigour and determination. The commander of the 21st German Armoured Division, General von Ravenstein, whom we captured, expressed himself very well when he said, "This warfare is a paradise to the tactician, but a nightmare to the quartermaster."

Although we have large armies standing in the Middle East, we have never been able to apply in our desert advance infantry forces which were numerically equal to those which the enemy had gradually accumulated on the coast. We have always been fighting with smaller numbers pushed out into the desert than he has been able to gather there, over a course of months, in his coastal garrisons. For us, the foundation of everything was supply and mechanized transport, and this was provided on what hitherto had been considered a fantastic scale. Also, we had to rely upon our superiority in armour and in the air. But most of all in this struggle everything depended for us upon an absolutely unrelenting spirit of the offensive, not only in the generals but in the troops and in every man. That has been forthcoming; it is still forthcoming. All the troops have fought all the time in every circumstance of fatigue and hardship with one sincere, insatiable desire, to engage the enemy and destroy him if possible, tank for tank, man to man, and hand to hand. And this is what has carried us on. But behind all this process working out at so many different points and in so many separate combats has been the persisting will-power of the Commander-in-Chief, General Auchinleck. Without that will-power we might very easily have subsided to the defensive and lost precious initiative, to which, here in this Libyan theatre, we have for the first time felt ourselves strong enough to make a claim.

The first main crisis of the battle was reached between 24th and 26th November. On the 24th General Auchinleck proceeded to the battle headquarters, and on the 26th he decided to relieve General Cunningham and to appoint Major-General Ritchie, a comparatively junior officer, to the command of the 8th Army in his stead. This action was immediately endorsed by the Minister of State and by myself. General Cunningham has rendered brilliant service in Abyssinia and is also responsible for the planning and organization of the present offensive in Libya, which began, as I

323

have explained, with surprise and with success and which has now definitely turned the corner. He has since been reported by the medical authorities to be suffering from serious overstrain and has been granted sick leave. Since 26th November, therefore, the 8th Army has been commanded, with great vigour and skill, by General Ritchie, but during nearly the whole time General Auchinleck himself has been at the battle headquarters. Although the battle is not yet finished, I have no hesitation in saying that for good or ill it is General Auchinleck's battle. Watching these affairs, as it is my duty to do, from day to day, and often from hour to hour, and seeing the seamy side of the reports as they come in, I have felt my confidence in General Auchinleck grow continually, and although everything is hazardous in war, I believe we have found in him, as we have also found in General Wavell, a military figure of the first order.

The newspapers have given full and excellent accounts of the strangely interspersed fighting in which the British Armoured Corps, the New Zealand Division, the South African Divisions, an Indian Division, the British 70th Division and the rest of the Tobruk garrison, including the Poles, all played an equally valiant and active part.

At the beginning of the offensive I told the House that we should for the first time be fighting the Germans on equal terms in modern weapons. This was quite true. Naturally there have been some unpleasant surprises, and also some awkward things have happened, as might be expected beforehand. Those who fight the Germans fight a stubborn and resourceful foe, a foe in every way worthy of the doom prepared for him. Some of the German tanks carried, as we knew, a six-pounder gun which, though it of course carries many fewer shots, is sometimes more effective than the gun with which our tanks are mainly armed. Our losses in tanks were a good deal heavier than we expected, and it may be that at the outset, before it was disorganized, the enemy's recovery process for damaged vehicles worked better than ours. I am not so sure of it, but it may be so. It is very good at that. However, we had a good superiority in numbers of armoured vehicles, and in the long rough and tumble we gradually obtained mastery so far as the first phase of the battle is concerned.

Our Air Force was undoubtedly superior throughout in numbers and quality to the enemy, and although the Germans have drawn in the most extravagant manner upon reinforcements from many quarters, including the Russian front, that superiority has been more than maintained. The greatest satisfaction is expressed by the troops and by the Military Authorities with the way in which they have been helped and protected by the action of the Royal Air Force. None of the complaints in the previous enterprises have reached us here upon that score. Like other people concerned, I had hoped for a quick decision, but it may well be that this wearing-down battle will be found in the end to have inflicted a deeper injury upon the enemy than if it had all been settled by manœuvre and in a few days. In no other way could a second front have been brought into action under conditions more costly to the enemy and more favourable to ourselves than by this Libyan attack. This will be realized when it is remembered that about a half, and sometimes more than a half, of everything, men, munitions and fuel, which the enemy sends to Africa is sunk before it gets there, by our submarines, cruisers and destroyers, and by the activities of our Air Force, acting both from Libya and from Malta. In this way, the prolongation of the battle may not be without its compensations to us. From the point of view of drawing weight from the vast Russian front, the continuance of the fighting in its severity is not to be regarded as an evil.

The first stage of the battle is now over. The enemy has been driven out of all the positions which barred our westward advance, positions which he had most laboriously fortified. Everything has been swept away except certain pockets at Bardia and Halfaya, which are hopelessly cut off, and will be mopped up, or starved out, in due course. It may be definitely said that Tobruk has been relieved—or, as I prefer to state it, has been disengaged. The enemy, still strong but severely mauled and largely stripped of his armour, is retreating to a defensive line to the west of the Tobruk forts, and the clearance of the approaches to Tobruk; and the establishment of our air power thus far forward to the west in new airfields, enables the great supply depots of Tobruk, which have been carefully built up, to furnish support for the second phase of our offensive, with great economy in our lines of communication. Substantial reinforcements and fresh troops are available close at hand. Many of the units which were most heavily engaged have been relieved and their places taken by others, although we have to keep the numbers down strictly to the level which our vast transportation facilities permit. The enemy, who has fought with the utmost stubbornness and enterprise, has paid the price of his valour, and it may well be that the second phase will gather more easily the fruits of the first than has been our experience in the fighting which has taken place so far. As the House knows, I make it a rule never to prophesy, or to promise, or to guarantee future results, but I will go so far on this occasion as to say that all danger of the Army of the Nile not being able to celebrate Christmas and the New Year in Cairo has been decisively removed.

Before I leave the purely British aspect of the war, I must report to the House the progress of the Battle of the Atlantic. When I last spoke on the subject, I said that in the four months ending with October, making allowance for new building but not for sea captures or United States assistance, the net loss of our Mercantile Marine had been reduced to a good deal less than one-fifth of what it was in the four months ending in June—a tremendous saving. As these were the very months when Hitler had boasted that his strangulation of our seaborne supplies would be at its height, we were entitled to rest with some solid assurance upon that fact. The House was right to treat the fact as of great importance, because these matters of sea power and sea transport involve our lives. The month of November has now gone by, and, without revealing actual figures, I am glad to say that it fully maintained the great recovery of the previous four months. In the first ten days of this month, we have also found that the progress and position have been well maintained. These are the foundations upon which we live and carry forward our cause.

Now I turn to Russia. Six weeks or a month ago people were wondering whether Moscow would be taken, or Leningrad in the north, or how soon the Germans would overrun the Caucasus and seize the oilfields of Baku. We had to consider what we could do to prepare ourselves on the long line from the Caspian Sea to the Mediterranean. Since then a striking change has become evident. The enormous power of the Russian Armies, and the glorious steadfastness and energy with which they have resisted the frightful onslaught made upon them, have now been made plain. On the top of this has come the Russian winter; and on top of that, the Russian Air Force. Hitler forced his armies into this barren and devastated land. He has everywhere been brought to a standstill. On a large portion of the front he is in retreat. The sufferings of his troops are indescribable. Their losses have been immense. The cold snow, the piercing wind which blows across the icy spaces, the ruined towns and villages, the long lines of communication, assailed by dauntless guerrilla warriors, the stubborn unyielding resistance with which the Russian soldiers and the Russian people have defended every street, every house, every yard of their country —all these factors have inflicted upon the German armies and the German nation a bloody prop, almost unequalled in the history of war. But this is not the end of the winter: it is the beginning.

The Russians have now regained definite superiority in the air over large parts of the front. They have the great cities in which to live. Their soldiers are habituated to the severity of their native climate. They are inspired by the feeling of advance after long retreat and of vengeance after monstrous injury.

In Hitler's launching of the Nazi campaign upon Russia we can already see, after less than six months of fighting, that he made one of the outstanding blunders of history, and the results so far realized constitute an event of cardinal importance in the final decision of the war. Nevertheless, we must remember the great munitions capacities which have been lost to Russia by the German invasion, and our pledges to the Russians for heavy monthly quotas of tanks, aeroplanes and vital raw materials. Although, as we can all see, our position has changed in various important ways, not all in a favourable direction, we must faithfully and punctually fulfil the very serious undertakings we have made to Russia.

A week ago the three great spheres, Libya, the Atlantic and Russia, would almost have covered the scene of war with which we were concerned. Since then it has taken an enormous and very grave expansion. The Japanese Government, or ruling elements in Japan, have made a cold-blooded, calculated, violent, treacherous attack upon the United States and ourselves. The United States have declared war upon their assailants, and we and the Royal Netherlands Government have done the same. A large part of the Western hemisphere, State after State, Parliament after Parliament, is following the United States. It is a great tribute to the respect for international law and for the independence of less powerful countries which the United States has shown for many years, particularly under the Presidency of Mr. Roosevelt, that so many other States in Central and South America and in the West Indies, powerful, wealthy, populous communities, are in the process of throwing in their lot with the great Republic of North America.

It will not stop here. It seems to me quite certain that Japan, when she struck her treacherous and dastardly blow at the United States, counted on the active support of the German Nazis and of the Italian Fascists. It is, therefore, very likely that the United States will be faced with the open hostility of Germany, Italy and Japan. We are in all this too. Our foes are bound by the consequences of their ambitions and of their crimes to seek implacably the destruction of the English-speaking world and all it stands for, which is the supreme barrier against their designs. If this should be their resolve, if they should declare themselves determined to compass the destruction of the English-speaking world, I know that I speak for the United States as well as for the British Empire when I say that we would all rather perish than be conquered. And on this basis, putting it at its worst, there are quite a lot of us to be killed. The Chinese Generalissimo, Chiang-Kai-Shek, has sent me a message announcing his decision to declare war against Japan and also against Japan's partners in guilt, Germany and Italy. He has further assured me that the whole of the resources of China are at the disposal of Great Britain and the United States. China's cause is henceforth our cause. The country which has faced the Japanese assault for over four years with undaunted courage is indeed a worthy Ally, and it is as Allies that from now on we shall go forward together to victory, not only over Japan alone, but over the Axis and all its works.

The Japanese onslaught has brought upon the United States and Great Britain very serious injuries to our naval power. In my whole experience I do not remember any naval blow so heavy or so painful as the sinking of the *Prince of Wales* and the *Repulse* on Monday last. These two vast, powerful ships constituted an essential feature in our plans for meeting the new Japanese danger as it loomed against us in the last few months. These ships had reached the right point at the right moment, and were in every respect suited to the task assigned to them. In moving to attack the Japanese transports and landing-craft which were disembarking the invaders of Siam and Malaya at the Kra Isthmus or thereabouts, Admiral Phillips was undertaking a thoroughly sound, well-considered offensive operation, not indeed free from risk, but not different in principle from many similar operations we have repeatedly carried out in the North Sea and in the Mediterranean. Both ships were sunk in repeated air attacks by bombers and by torpedo-aircraft. These attacks were delivered with skill and determination. There were two high-level attacks, both of which scored hits, and three waves of torpedo-aircraft of nine in each wave which struck each of our ships with several torpedoes. There is no reason to suppose that any new weapons or explosives were employed, or any bombs or torpedoes of exceptional size. The continued waves of attack achieved their purpose, and both ships capsized and sank, having destroyed seven of the attacking aircraft.

The escorting destroyers came immediately to the rescue, and have now arrived at Singapore crowded with survivors. There is reason to believe that the loss of life has been less heavy than was at first feared. But I regret that Admiral Sir Tom Phillips is among those reported missing. He was well known to us at Whitehall, and his long service at the Admiralty in a central position as

Vice-Chief of the Navy Staff made him many friends, who mourn his loss. Personally, I regarded him as one of the ablest brains in the naval Service, and I feel honoured to have established personal friendship with him. On his way out I was most anxious that he should see General Smuts, and so was he, and a long interview was arranged between that great statesman and a Naval Officer whose long service at or near the summit of the Admiralty had made him acquainted with every aspect of the war. It is a very heavy loss that we have suffered. I hope that in a short time it will be possible to inform the relatives of the many who have safely arrived at Singapore from both these great ships. Still, the loss of life has been most melancholy.

Naturally, I should not be prepared to discuss the resulting situation in the Far East and in the Pacific or the measures which must be taken to restore it. It may well be that we shall have to suffer considerable punishment, but we shall defend ourselves everywhere with the utmost vigour in close co-operation with the United States and the Netherlands. The naval power of Great Britain and the United States was very greatly superior—and is still largely superior—to the combined forces of the three Axis Powers. But no one must underrate the gravity of the loss which has been inflicted in Malaya and Hawaii, or the power of the new antagonist who has fallen upon us, or the length of time it will take to create, marshal and mount the great force in the Far East which will be necessary to achieve absolute victory.

We have a very hard period to go through, and a new surge of impulse will be required, and will be forthcoming, from everybody. We must, as I have said, faithfully keep our engagements to Russia in supplies, and at the same time we must expect, at any rate for the next few months, that the volume of American supplies reaching Britain and the degree of help given by the United States Navy will be reduced. The gap must be filled, and only our own efforts will fill it. I cannot doubt, however, now that the 130,000,000 people in the United States have bound themselves to this war, that once they have settled down to it and have bent themselves to it—as they will—as their main purpose in life, then the flow of munitions and aid of every kind will vastly exceed anything that could have been expected on the peacetime basis that has ruled up to the present. Not only the British Empire now but the United States are fighting for life; Russia is fighting for life, and China is fighting for life. Behind these four great combatant communities are ranged all the spirit and hopes of all the conquered countries in Europe, prostrate under the cruel domination of the foe. I said the other day that four-fifths of the human race were on our side. It may well be an under-statement. Just these gangs and cliques of wicked men and their military or party organizations have been able to bring these hideous evils upon mankind. It would indeed bring shame upon our generation if we did not teach them a lesson which will not be forgotten in the records of a thousand years.

THE WHITE HOUSE CHRISTMAS TREE

A SPEECH BROADCAST TO THE WORLD FROM THE WHITE HOUSE, WASHINGTON,
AT THE 20TH ANNUAL OBSERVATION OF THE LIGHTING OF THE COMMUNITY
CHRISTMAS TREE
DECEMBER 24, 1941

December 12. *Russians claimed that in a week's fighting 400 towns and villages had been recaptured and 30,000 Germans killed.*

December 13. *Japanese occupied United States naval base at Guam.*

December 15. *Officially announced that in the Japanese attack on Pearl Harbour, the United States battleship Arizona and five other warships were sunk, and that the battleship Oklahoma capsized.*

December 16. *Russians recaptured Kalinin and claimed they had smashed six enemy divisions.*

December 17. *Japanese made landings on Sarawak, bombarded Hong Kong, and increased their threat to Penang.*

December 18. *Allied forces occupied the Portuguese island of Timor to forestall Japanese action.*

German army in Libya, after three desperate counter-attacks, was routed and driven back thirty miles.

December 19. *Japanese landed in force on Hong Kong. British troops and civilians evacuated Penang.*

December 20. *Axis forces, in full flight in Libya, abandoned Derna.*

December 21. *Officially announced in Berlin that Hitler had taken over from Von Brauchitsch personal command of the army in the field.*

Japanese pressure in Malaya and the Philippines increased.

December 22. *Revealed that Mr. Churchill, with Lord Beaverbrook and chiefs of staff, was in Washington for conferences with President Roosevelt to co-ordinate the war effort against the Axis.*

December 23. *Mr. Churchill told a Press conference in Washington that the Allies should aim at an external knock-out of Germany rather than wait for an internal collapse.*

331

December 24. President Roosevelt and Mr. Churchill broadcast to the world from the White House Christmas Tree ceremony.

Imperial troops made Christmas Eve entry into Benghazi and also took Benina.

December 24, 1941.

I SPEND this anniversary and festival far from my country, far from my family, yet I cannot truthfully say that I feel far from home. Whether it be the ties of blood on my mother's side, or the friendships I have developed here over many years of active life, or the commanding sentiment of comradeship in the common cause of great peoples who speak the same language, who kneel at the same altars and, to a very large extent, pursue the same ideals, I cannot feel myself a stranger here in the centre and at the summit of the United States. I feel a sense of unity and fraternal association which, added to the kindliness of your welcome, convinces me that I have a right to sit at your fireside and share your Christmas joys.

This is a strange Christmas Eve. Almost the whole world is locked in deadly struggle, and, with the most terrible weapons which science can devise, the nations advance upon each other. Ill would it be for us this Christmastide if we were not sure that no greed for the land or wealth of any other people, no vulgar ambition, no morbid lust for material gain at the expense of others, had led us to the field. Here, in the midst of war, raging and roaring over all the lands and seas, creeping nearer to our hearts and homes, here, amid all the tumult, we have to-night the peace of the spirit in each cottage home and in every generous heart. Therefore we may cast aside for this night at least the cares and dangers which beset us, and make for the children an evening of happiness in a world of storm. Here, then, for one night only, each home throughout the English-speaking world should be a brightly-lighted island of happiness and peace.

Let the children have their night of fun and laughter. Let the gifts of Father Christmas delight their play. Let us grown-ups share to the full in their unstinted pleasures before we turn again to the stern task and the formidable years that lie before us, resolved that, by our sacrifice and daring, these same children shall not be robbed of their inheritance or denied their right to live in a free and decent world.

And so, in God's mercy, a happy Christmas to you all.

THE SPEECH TO CONGRESS

THE PRIME MINISTER'S ADDRESS TO THE SENATE AND THE HOUSE OF
REPRESENTATIVES IN THE SENATE CHAMBER AT WASHINGTON, AND
BROADCAST TO THE WORLD
DECEMBER 26, 1941

---

*December 25. British garrison in Hong Kong surrendered after
seven days' struggle.*

> *It was revealed that General Wavell had visited
> Chungking to discuss Far East strategy with General
> Chiang Kai-Shek.*

*December 26. Mr. Churchill delivered a speech to both Houses of
Congress in Washington.*

> *Action of Free French forces in taking over the
> Vichy islands of St. Pierre and Miquelon, off New-
> foundland met with strong objections in America.*

> *Lt.-Gen. Sir Henry Pownall appointed Commander-
> in-Chief in the Far East in place of Air Chief Marshal
> Sir Robert Brooke-Popham.*

[December 26, 1941.

I FEEL greatly honoured that you should have invited me to
enter the United States Senate Chamber and address the representatives of both branches of Congress. The fact that my American
forebears have for so many generations played their part in the life
of the United States, and that here I am, an Englishman, welcomed
in your midst, makes this experience one of the most moving and
thrilling in my life, which is already long and has not been entirely
uneventful.   I wish indeed that my mother, whose memory I
cherish across the vale of years, could have been here to see. By
the way, I cannot help reflecting that if my father had been
American and my mother British, instead of the other way round,
I might have got here on my own. In that case, this would not
have been the first time you would have heard my voice. In that
case I should not have needed any invitation, but if I had, it is
hardly likely it would have been unanimous. So perhaps things are
better as they are. I may confess, however, that I do not feel quite

333

like a fish out of water in a legislative assembly where English is spoken.

I am a child of the House of Commons. I was brought up in my father's house to believe in democracy. "Trust the people"— that was his message. I used to see him cheered at meetings and in the streets by crowds of working men way back in those aristocratic Victorian days when, as Disraeli said, the world was for the few, and for the very few. Therefore I have been in full harmony all my life with the tides which have flowed on both sides of the Atlantic against privilege and monopoly, and I have steered confidently towards the Gettysburg ideal of "government of the people by the people for the people." I owe my advancement entirely to the House of Commons, whose servant I am. In my country, as in yours, public men are proud to be the servants of the State and would be ashamed to be its masters. On any day, if they thought the people wanted it, the House of Commons could by a simple vote remove me from my office. But I am not worrying about it at all. As a matter of fact, I am sure they will approve very highly of my journey here, for which I obtained the King's permission in order to meet the President of the United States and to arrange with him all that mapping-out of our military plans, and for all those intimate meetings of the high officers of the armed services of both countries, which are indispensable to the successful prosecution of the war.

I should like to say first of all how much I have been impressed and encouraged by the breadth of view and sense of proportion which I have found in all quarters over here to which I have had access. Anyone who did not understand the size and solidarity of the foundations of the United States might easily have expected to find an excited, disturbed, self-centred atmosphere, with all minds fixed upon the novel, startling, and painful episodes of sudden war as they hit America. After all, the United States have been attacked and set upon by three most powerfully-armed dictator States. The greatest military power in Europe, the greatest military power in Asia, Germany and Japan, Italy, too, have all declared, and are making, war upon you, and a quarrel is opened, which can only end in their overthrow or yours. But here in Washington, in these memorable days, I have found an Olympian fortitude which, far from being based upon complacency, is only the mask of an inflexible purpose and the proof of a sure and well-grounded confidence in the final outcome. We in Britain had the same feeling in our darkest days. We, too, were sure in the end all would be well. You do not, I am certain, underrate the severity of the ordeal to which you and we have still to be subjected. The forces ranged against us are enormous. They are bitter, they are ruthless. The wicked men and their factions who have launched their peoples on the path of war and conquest know that they will be called to terrible account if they cannot beat down by force of arms the peoples they have assailed. They will stop at nothing. They have a vast accumulation of war weapons of all kinds. They have highly-trained, disciplined armies, navies, and air services. They have plans and designs which have long been tried and matured. They will stop at nothing that violence or treachery can suggest.

It is quite true that, on our side, our resources in man-power and materials are far greater than theirs. But only a portion of your resources is as yet mobilized and developed, and we both of us have much to learn in the cruel art of war. We have therefore, without doubt, a time of tribulation before us. In this time some ground will be lost which it will be hard and costly to regain. Many disappointments and unpleasant surprises await us. Many of them will afflict us before the full marshalling of our latent and total power can be accomplished. For the best part of twenty years the youth of Britain and America have been taught that war is evil, which is true, and that it would never come again, which has been proved false. For the best part of twenty years the youth of Germany, Japan and Italy have been taught that aggressive war is the noblest duty of the citizen, and that it should be begun as soon as the necessary weapons and organization had been made. We have performed the duties and tasks of peace. They have plotted and planned for war. This, naturally, has placed us in Britain and now places you in the United States at a disadvantage, which only time, courage, and strenuous, untiring exertions can correct.

We have indeed to be thankful that so much time has been granted to us. If Germany had tried to invade the British Isles after the French collapse in June, 1940, and if Japan had declared war on the British Empire and the United States at about the same date, no one could say what disasters and agonies might not have been our lot. But now at the end of December, 1941, our transformation from easy-going peace to total war efficiency has made very great progress. The broad flow of munitions in Great Britain has already begun. Immense strides have been made in the conversion of American industry to military purposes, and now that the United States are at war it is possible for orders to be given every day which a year or eighteen months hence will produce results in war power beyond anything that has yet been seen or foreseen in the dictator States. Provided that every effort is made, that nothing is kept back, that the whole man-power, brain-power, virility, valour, and civic virtue of the English-speaking world with all its galaxy of loyal, friendly, associated communities and States —provided all that is bent unremittingly to the simple and supreme task, I think it would be reasonable to hope that the end of 1942 will see us quite definitely in a better position than we are now, and that the year 1943 will enable us to assume the initiative upon an ample scale.

Some people may be startled or momentarily depressed when, like your President, I speak of a long and hard war. But our peoples would rather know the truth, sombre though it be. And after all, when we are doing the noblest work in the world, not only defending our hearths and homes but the cause of freedom in other lands, the question of whether deliverance comes in 1942, 1943, or 1944 falls into its proper place in the grand proportions of human history. Sure I am that this day—now—we are the masters of our fate; that the task which has been set us is not above our strength; that its pangs and toils are not beyond our endurance. As long as we have faith in our cause and an unconquerable will-power, salvation will not be denied us. In the words of the Psalmist, "He shall not be afraid of evil tidings; his heart is fixed, trusting in the Lord." Not all the tidings will be evil.

On the contrary, mighty strokes of war have already been dealt against the enemy; the glorious defence of their native soil by the Russian armies and people have inflicted wounds upon the Nazi tyranny and system which have bitten deep, and will fester and inflame not only in the Nazi body but in the Nazi mind. The boastful Mussolini has crumbled already. He is now but a lackey and serf, the merest utensil of his master's will. He has inflicted great suffering and wrong upon his own industrious people. He has been stripped of his African empire, Abyssinia has been liberated. Our armies in the East, which were so weak and ill-equipped at the moment of French desertion, now control all the regions from Teheran to Benghazi, and from Aleppo and Cyprus to the sources of the Nile.

For many months we devoted ourselves to preparing to take the offensive in Libya. The very considerable battle, which has been proceeding for the last six weeks in the desert, has been most fiercely fought on both sides. Owing to the difficulties of supply on the desert flanks, we were never able to bring numerically equal forces to bear upon the enemy. Therefore we had to rely upon a superiority in the numbers and quality of tanks and aircraft, British and American. Aided by these, for the first time, we have fought the enemy with equal weapons. For the first time we have made the Hun feel the sharp edge of those tools with which he had enslaved Europe. The armed forces of the enemy in Cyrenaica amounted to about 150,000, of whom about one-third were Germans. General Auchinleck set out to destroy totally that armed force. I have every reason to believe that his aim will be fully accomplished. I am glad to be able to place before you, members of the Senate and of the House of Representatives, at this moment when you are entering the war, proof that with proper weapons and proper organization we are able to beat the life out of the savage Nazi. What Hitler is suffering in Libya is only a sample and foretaste of what we must give him and his accomplices, wherever this war shall lead us, in every quarter of the globe.

There are good tidings also from blue water. The life-line of supplies which joins our two nations across the ocean, without which all might fail, is flowing steadily and freely in spite of all the enemy can do. It is a fact that the British Empire, which many thought eighteen months ago was broken and ruined, is now incomparably stronger, and is growing stronger with every month. Lastly, if you will forgive me for saying it, to me the best tidings of all is that the United States, united as never before, have drawn the sword for freedom and cast away the scabbard.

All these tremendous facts have led the subjugated peoples of Europe to lift up their heads again in hope. They have put aside for ever the shameful temptation of resigning themselves to the conqueror's will. Hope has returned to the hearts of scores of millions of men and women, and with that hope there burns the flame of anger against the brutal, corrupt invader, and still more fiercely burn the fires of hatred and contempt for the squalid quislings whom he has suborned. In a dozen famous ancient States now prostrate under the Nazi yoke, the masses of the people of all classes and creeds await the hour of liberation, when they too will be able once again to play their part and strike their blows like men. That hour will strike, and its solemn peal will proclaim that the night is past and that the dawn has come.

The onslaught upon us so long and so secretly planned by Japan has presented both our countries with grievous problems for which we could not be fully prepared. If people ask me—as they have a right to ask me in England—why is it that you have not got ample equipment of modern aircraft and Army weapons of all kinds in Malaya and in the East Indies, I can only point to the victories General Auchinleck has gained in the Libyan campaign. Had we diverted and dispersed our gradually growing resources between Libya and Malaya, we should have been found wanting in both theatres. If the United States have been found at a disadvantage at various points in the Pacific Ocean, we know well that it is to no small extent because of the aid you have been giving us in munitions for the defence of the British Isles and for the Libyan campaign, and, above all, because of your help in the battle of the Atlantic, upon which all depends, and which has in consequence been successfully and prosperously maintained. Of course it would have been much better, I freely admit, if we had had enough resources of all kinds to be at full strength at all threatened points; but considering how slowly and reluctantly we brought ourselves to large-scale preparations, and how long such preparations take, we had no right to expect to be in such a fortunate position.

The choice of how to dispose of our hitherto limited resources had to be made by Britain in time of war and by the United States in time of peace; and I believe that history will pronounce that upon the whole—and it is upon the whole that these matters must be judged—the choice made was right. Now that we are together, now that we are linked in a righteous comradeship of arms, now that our two considerable nations, each in perfect unity, have joined all their life energies in a common resolve, a new scene opens upon which a steady light will glow and brighten.

Many people have been astonished that Japan should in a single day have plunged into war against the United States and the British Empire. We all wonder why, if this dark design, with all its laborious and intricate preparations, had been so long filling their secret minds, they did not choose our moment of weakness eighteen months ago. Viewed quite dispassionately, in spite of the losses we have suffered and the further punishment we shall have to take, it certainly appears to be an irrational act. It is, of course, only prudent to assume that they have made very careful calculations and think they see their way through. Nevertheless, there may be another explanation. We know that for many years past the policy of Japan has been dominated by secret societies of subalterns and junior officers of the Army and Navy, who have enforced their will upon successive Japanese Cabinets and Parliaments by the assassination of any Japanese statesman who opposed, or who did not sufficiently further, their aggressive pilicy. It may be that these societies, dazzled and dizzy with their own schemes of aggression and the prospect of early victories, have forced their country against its better judgment into war. They have certainly embarked upon a very considerable undertaking. For after the outrages they have committed upon us at Pearl Harbour, in the Pacific Islands, in the Philippines, in Malaya, and in the Dutch East Indies, they must now know that the stakes for which they have decided to play are mortal.

338

When we consider the resources of the United States and the British Empire compared to those of Japan, when we remember those of China, which has so long and valiantly withstood invasion and when also we observe the Russian menace which hangs over Japan, it becomes still more difficult to reconcile Japanese action with prudence or even with sanity. What kind of a people do they think we are? Is it possible they do not realize that we shall never cease to persevere against them until they have been taught a lesson which they and the world will never forget?

Members of the Senate and members of the House of Representatives, I turn for one moment more from the turmoil and convulsions of the present to the broader basis of the future. Here we are together facing a group of mighty foes who seek our ruin; here we are together defending all that to free men is dear. Twice in a single generation the catastrophe of world war has fallen upon us; twice in our lifetime has the long arm of fate reached across the ocean to bring the United States into the forefront of the battle. If we had kept together after the last War, if we had taken common measures for our safety, this renewal of the curse need never have fallen upon us.

Do we not owe it to ourselves, to our children, to mankind tormented, to make sure that these catastrophes shall not engulf us for the third time? It has been proved that pestilences may break out in the Old World, which carry their destructive ravages into the New World, from which, once they are afoot, the New World cannot by any means escape. Duty and prudence alike command first that the germ-centres of hatred and revenge should be constantly and vigilantly surveyed and treated in good time, and, secondly, that an adequate organization should be set up to make sure that the pestilence can be controlled at its earliest beginnings before it spreads and rages throughout the entire earth.

Five or six years ago it would have been easy, without shedding a drop of blood, for the United States and Great Britain to have insisted on fulfilment of the disarmament clauses of the treaties which Germany signed after the Great War; that also would have been the opportunity for assuring to Germany those raw materials which we declared in the Atlantic Charter should not be denied to any nation, victor or vanquished. That chance has passed. It is gone. Prodigious hammer-strokes have been needed to bring us together again, or if you will allow me to use other language, I will say that he must indeed have a blind soul who cannot see that some great purpose and design is being worked out here below, of which we have the honour to be the faithful servants. It is not given to us to peer into the mysteries of the future. Still, I avow my hope and faith, sure and inviolate, that in the days to come the British and American peoples will for their own safety and for the good of all walk together side by side in majesty, in justice, and in peace.

"PREPARATION—LIBERATION—ASSAULT"

THE SPEECH TO THE CANADIAN SENATE AND HOUSE OF COMMONS
AT OTTAWA, BROADCAST TO THE WORLD
DECEMBER 30, 1941

December 27. Conferences between President Roosevelt, Mr. Churchill and Allied war chiefs took place at Washington.

Japan answered the American declaration that Manila was an "open town" by making two heavy air raids on the city.

A combined force of the Royal Navy, Army and Royal Air Force raided the Norwegian island of Vaagso, killed 120 Germans and took many German and "quisling" prisoners.

December 28. It was revealed that Mr. Anthony Eden, the Foreign Secretary, had been having conferences in Moscow with Premier Stalin and other Russian statesmen.

Japanese parachute troops landed in the Dutch island of Sumatra.

December 29. Mr. Churchill arrived in Ottawa from Washington and attended a meeting of the Canadian War Cabinet.

Ipoh, centre of the chief tin-mining area of Malaya, was captured by the Japanese.

December 30. Mr. Churchill addressed the members of the Canadian Senate and House of Commons, the speech being broadcast to the world.

Mr. Anthony Eden arrived back in London from his talks with Premier Stalin.

Russian troops landed in the Crimea and re-captured the town and fortress of Kerch.

[*December 30, 1941.*

I T is with feelings of pride and encouragement that I find myself here in the House of Commons of Canada, invited to address the Parliament of the senior Dominion of the Crown. I am very

341

glad to see again my old friend Mr. Mackenzie King, for fifteen years out of twenty your Prime Minister, and I thank him for the too complimentary terms in which he has referred to myself. I bring you the assurance of good will and affection from every one in the Motherland. We are most grateful for all you have done in the common cause, and we know that you are resolved to do whatever more is possible as the need arises and as opportunity serves. Canada occupies a unique position in the British Empire because of its unbreakable ties with Britain and its ever-growing friendship and intimate association with the United States. Canada is a potent magnet, drawing together those in the new world and in the old whose fortunes are now united in a deadly struggle for life and honour against the common foe. The contribution of Canada to the Imperial war effort in troops, in ships, in aircraft, in food, and in finance has been magnificent.

The Canadian Army now stationed in England has chafed not to find itself in contact with the enemy. But I am here to tell you that it has stood and still stands in the key position to strike at the invader should he land upon our shores. In a few months, when the invasion season returns, the Canadian Army may be engaged in one of the most frightful battles the world has ever seen, but on the other hand their presence may help to deter the enemy from attempting to fight such a battle on British soil. Although the long routine of training and preparation is undoubtedly trying to men who left prosperous farms and businesses, or other responsible civil work, inspired by an eager and ardent desire to fight the enemy, although this is trying to high-mettled temperaments, the value of the service rendered is unquestionable, and I am sure that the peculiar kind of self-sacrifice involved will be cheerfully or at least patiently endured.

The Canadian Government have imposed no limitation on the use of the Canadian Army, whether on the Continent of Europe or elsewhere, and I think it is extremely unlikely that this war will end without the Canadian Army coming to close quarters with the Germans, as their fathers did at Ypres, on the Somme, or on the Vimy Ridge. Already at Hong Kong, that beautiful colony which the industry and mercantile enterprise of Britain has raised from a desert isle and made the greatest port of shipping in the whole world—Hong Kong, that Colony wrested from us for a time until we reach the peace table, by the overwhelming power of the Home Forces of Japan, to which it lay in proximity—at Hong Kong. Canadian soldiers of the Royal Rifles of Canada and the Winnipeg Grenadiers, under a brave officer whose loss we mourn, have played a valuable part in gaining precious days, and have crowned with military honour the reputation of their native land.

Another major contribution made by Canada to the Imperial war effort is the wonderful and gigantic Empire training scheme for pilots for the Royal and Imperial Air Forces. This has now been as you know well in full career for nearly two years in conditions free from all interference by the enemy. The daring youth of Canada, Australia, New Zealand, and South Africa, with many thousands from the homeland, are perfecting their training under the best conditions, and we are being assisted on a large scale by the United States, many of whose training facilities have been placed at our disposal. This scheme will provide us in 1942 and 1943 with the highest class of trained pilots, observers, and air gunners in the numbers necessary to man the enormous flow of aircraft which the factories of Britain, of the Empire and of the United States are and will be producing.

I could also speak on the naval production of corvettes and above all of merchant ships which is proceeding on a scale almost equal to the building of the United Kingdom, all of which Canada has set on foot. I could speak of many other activities, of tanks, of the special forms of modern high-velocity cannon and of the great supplies of raw materials and many other elements essential to our war effort on which your labours are ceaselessly and tirelessly engaged. But I must not let my address to you become a catalogue, so I turn to less technical fields of thought.

We did not make this war, we did not seek it. We did all we could to avoid it. We did too much to avoid it. We went so far at times in trying to avoid it as to be almost destroyed by it when it broke upon us. But that dangerous corner has been turned, and with every month and every year that passes we shall confront the evil-doers with weapons as plentiful, as sharp, and as destructive as those with which they have sought to establish their hateful domination.

I should like to point out to you that we have not at any time asked for any mitigation in the fury or malice of the enemy. The peoples of the British Empire may love peace. They do not seek the lands or wealth of any country, but they are a tough and hardy lot. We have not journeyed all this way across the centuries, across the oceans, across the mountains, across the prairies, because we are made of sugar candy.

Look at the Londoners, the Cockneys; look at what they have stood up to. Grim and gay with their cry "We can take it," and their war-time mood of "What is good enough for anybody is good

343

enough for us." We have not asked that the rules of the game should be modified. We shall never descend to the German and Japanese level, but if anybody likes to play rough we can play rough too. Hitler and his Nazi gang have sown the wind; let them reap the whirlwind. Neither the length of the struggle nor any form of severity which it may assume shall make us weary or shall make us quit.

I have been all this week with the President of the United States, that great man whom destiny has marked for this climax of human fortune. We have been concerting the united pacts and resolves of more than thirty States and nations to fight on in unity together and in fidelity one to another, without any thought except the total and final extirpation of the Hitler tyranny, the Japanese frenzy, and the Mussolini flop.

There shall be no halting, or half measures, there shall be no compromise, or parley. These gangs of bandits have sought to darken the light of the world; have sought to stand between the common people of all the lands and their march forward into their inheritance. They shall themselves be cast into the pit of death and shame, and only when the earth has been cleansed and purged of their crimes and their villiany shall we turn from the task which they have forced upon us, a task which we were reluctant to undertake, but which we shall now most faithfully and punctiliously discharge. According to my sense of proportion, this is no time to speak of the hopes of the future, or the broader world which lies beyond our struggles and our victory. We have to win that world for our children. We have to win it by our sacrifices. We have not won it yet. The crisis is upon us. The power of the enemy is immense. If we were in any way to underrate the strength, the resources or the ruthless savagery of that enemy, we should jeopardize, not only our lives, for they will be offered freely, but the cause of human freedom and progress to which we have vowed ourselves and all we have. We cannot for a moment afford to relax. On the contrary we must drive ourselves forward with unrelenting zeal. In this strange, terrible world war there is a place for everyone, man and woman, old and young, hale and halt; service in a thousand forms is open. There is no room now for the dilettante, the weakling, for the shirker, or the sluggard. The mine, the factory, the dockyard, the salt sea waves, the fields to till, the home, the hospital, the chair of the scientist, the pulpit of the preacher—from the highest to the humblest tasks, all are of equal honour; all have their part to play. The enemies ranged against us, coalesced and combined against us, have asked for total war. Let us make sure they get it.

That grand old minstrel, Harry Lauder—Sir Harry Lauder, I should say, and no honour was better deserved—had a song in the last War which began, "If we all look back on the history of the past, we can just tell where we are." Let us then look back. We plunged into this war all unprepared because we had pledged our word to stand by the side of Poland, which Hitler had feloniously invaded, and in spite of a gallant resistance had soon struck down. There followed those astonishing seven months which were called on this side of the Atlantic the "phoney" war. Suddenly the explosion of pent-up German strength and preparation burst upon Norway, Denmark, Holland, and Belgium. All these absolutely blameless neutrals, to most of whom Germany up to the last moment was giving every kind of guarantee and assurance, were overrun and trampled down. The hideous massacre of Rotterdam, where 30,000 people perished, showed the ferocious barbarism in which the German Air Force revels when, as in Warsaw and later Belgrade, it is able to bomb practically undefended cities.

On top of all this came the great French catastrophe. The French Army collapsed, and the French nation was dashed into utter and, as it has so far proved, irretrievable confusion. The French Government had at their own suggestion solemnly bound themselves with us not to make a separate peace. It was their duty and it was also their interest to go to North Africa, where they would have been at the head of the French Empire. In Africa, with our aid, they would have had overwhelming sea power. They would have had the recognition of the United States, and the use of all the gold they had lodged beyond the seas. If they had done this Italy might have been driven out of the war before the end of 1940, and France would have held her place as a nation in the counsels of the Allies and at the conference table of the victors. But their generals misled them. When I warned them that Britain would fight on alone whatever they did, their generals told their Prime Minister and his divided Cabinet, "In three weeks England will have her neck wrung like a chicken." Some chicken; some neck.

What a contrast has been the behaviour of the valiant, stout-hearted Dutch, who still stand forth as a strong living partner in the struggle! Their venerated Queen and their Government are in England, their Princess and her children have found asylum and protection here in your midst. But the Dutch nation are defending their Empire with dogged courage and tenacity by land and sea and in the air. Their submarines are inflicting a heavy daily toll upon the Japanese robbers who have come across the seas to steal the wealth of the East Indies, and to ravage and exploit its fertility and its civilization. The British Empire and the United States are going to the aid of the Dutch. We are going to fight out this new war against Japan together. We have suffered together and we shall conquer together.

But the men of Bordeaux, the men of Vichy, they would do nothing like this. They lay prostrate at the foot of the conqueror. They fawned upon him. What have they got out of it? The fragment of France which was left to them is just as powerless, just as hungry as, and even more miserable, because more divided, than the occupied regions themselves. Hitler plays from day to day a cat-and-mouse game with these tormented men. One day he will charge them a little less for holding their countrymen down. Another day he will let out a few thousand broken prisoners of war from the one-and-a-half or one-and-three-quarter millions he has collected. Or again he will shoot a hundred French hostages to give them a taste of the lash. On these blows and favours the Vichy Government have been content to live from day to day. But even this will not go on indefinitely. At any moment it may suit Hitler's plans to brush them away. Their only guarantee is Hitler's good faith, which, as everyone knows, biteth like the adder and stingeth like the asp.

But some Frenchmen there were who would not bow their knees and who under General de Gaulle have continued the fight on the side of the Allies. They have been condemned to death by the men of Vichy, but their names will be held and are being held in increasing respect by nine Frenchmen out of every ten throughout the once happy, smiling land of France. But now strong forces are at hand. The tide has turned against the Hun. Britain, which the men of Bordeaux thought and then hoped would soon be finished, Britain with her Empire around her carried the weight of the war alone for a whole long year through the darkest part of the valley. She is growing stronger every day. You can see it here in Canada. Anyone who has the slightest knowledge of our affairs is aware that very soon we shall be superior in every form of equipment to those who have taken us at the disadvantage of being but half armed.

The Russian armies, under their warrior leader, Josef Stalin, are waging furious war with increasing success along the thousand-mile front of their invaded country. General Auchinleck, at the head of a British, South African, New Zealand and Indian army, is striking down and mopping up the German and Italian forces which had attempted the invasion of Egypt. Not only are they being mopped up in the desert, but great numbers of them have been drowned on the way there by British submarines and the R.A.F. in which Australian squadrons played their part.

As I speak this afternoon an important battle is being fought around Jedabia. We must not attempt to prophesy its result, but I have good confidence. All this fighting in Libya proves that when our men have equal weapons in their hands and proper support from the air they are more than a match for the Nazi hordes. In Libya, as in Russia, events of great importance and of most hopeful import have taken place. But greatest of all, the mighty Republic of the United States has entered the conflict, and entered it in a manner which shows that for her there can be no withdrawal except by death or victory.

Mr. Churchill then spoke in French as follows:—

Et partout dans la France occupée et inoccupée (car leur sort est égal), ces honnêtes gens, ce grand peuple, la nation française, se redresse. L'espoir se rallume dans les cœurs d'une race guerrière, même désarmée, berceau de la liberté révolutionnaire et terrible aux vainqueurs esclaves. Et partout, on voit le point du jour, et la lumière grandit, rougeâtre, mais claire. Nous ne perdrons jamais la confiance que la France jouera le rôle des hommes libres et qu'elle reprendra par des voies dures sa place dans la grande compagnie des nations libératrices et victorieuses.

Ici, au Canada, où la langue française est honorée et parlée, nous nous tenons prêts et armés pour aider et pour saluer cette résurrection nationale.

(Translation)

And everywhere in France, occupied and unoccupied, for their fate is identical, these honest folk, this great people, the French nation, are rising again. Hope is springing up again in the hearts of a warrior race, even though disarmed, cradle of revolutionary liberty and terrible to slavish conquerors. And everywhere dawn is breaking and light spreading, reddish yet, but clear. We shall never lose confidence that France will play the role of free men again and, by hard paths, will once again attain her place in the great company of freedom-bringing and victorious nations. Here in Canada, where the French language is honoured and spoken, we are armed and ready to help and to hail this national resurrection.

Mr. Churchill then continued in English:—

Now that the whole of the North American continent is becoming one gigantic arsenal, and armed camp; now that the immense reserve power of Russia is gradually becoming apparent; now that

347

long-suffering, unconquerable China sees help approaching; now that the outraged and subjugated nations can see daylight ahead, it is permissible to take a broad forward view of the war.

We may observe three main periods or phases of the struggle that lies before us. First there is the period of consolidation, of combination, and of final preparation. In this period, which will certainly be marked by much heavy fighting, we shall still be gathering our strength, resisting the assaults of the enemy, and acquiring the necessary overwhelming air superiority and shipping tonnage to give our armies the power to traverse, in whatever numbers may be necessary, the seas and oceans which, except in the case of Russia, separate us from our foes. It is only when the vast shipbuilding programme on which the United States has already made so much progress, and which you are powerfully aiding, comes into full flood, that we shall be able to bring the whole force of our manhood and of our modern scientific equipment to bear upon the enemy. How long this period will take depends upon the vehemence of the effort put into production in all our war industries and shipyards.

The second phase which will then open may be called the phase of liberation. During this phase we must look to the recovery of the territories which have been lost or which may yet be lost, and also we must look to the revolt of the conquered peoples from the moment that the rescuing and liberating armies and air forces appear in strength within their bounds. For this purpose it is imperative that no nation or region overrun, that no Government or State which has been conquered, should relax its moral and physical efforts and preparation for the day of deliverance. The invaders, be they German or Japanese, must everywhere be regarded as infected persons to be shunned and isolated as far as possible. Where active resistance is impossible, passive resistance must be maintained. The invaders and tyrants must be made to feel that their fleeting triumphs will have a terrible reckoning, and that they are hunted men and that their cause is doomed. Particular punishment will be reserved for the quislings and traitors who make themselves the tools of the enemy. They will be handed over to the judgment of their fellow-countrymen.

There is a third phase which must also be contemplated, namely, the assault upon the citadels and the home-lands of the guilty Powers both in Europe and in Asia. Thus I endeavour in a few words to cast some forward light upon the dark, inscrutable mysteries of the future. But in thus forecasting the course along which we should seek to advance, we must never forget that the power of the enemy, and the action of the enemy may at every stage affect our fortunes. Moreover, you will notice that I have not attempted to assign any time-limits to the various phases. These time-limits depend upon our exertions, upon our achievements, and on the hazardous and uncertain course of the war.

Nevertheless I feel it is right at this moment to make it clear that, while an ever-increasing bombing offensive against Germany will remain one of the principal methods by which we hope to bring the war to an end, it is by no means the only method which our growing strength now enables us to take into account. Evidently the most strenuous exertions must be made by all. As to the form which those exertions take, that is for each partner in the grand alliance to judge for himself in consultation with others and in harmony with the general scheme. Let us then address ourselves to our task, not in any way underrating its tremendous difficulties and perils, but in good heart and sober confidence, resolved that, whatever the cost, whatever the suffering, we shall stand by one another, true and faithful comrades, and do our duty, God helping us, to the end.